Aprenda a combatir el estrés

Colección Conocer y Aprender

Por Dra. Romin

Dra. Romin
Aprenda a combatir el estrés - 1a ed. - Buenos Aires : Dos Tintas, 2007.
96 p. ; 20x14 cm.

ISBN 978-987-610-057-1

1. Autoayuda. I. Título
CDD 151.1

ISBN 978-987-610-057-1

Balcarce 711
Ciudad Autónoma de Buenos Aires, República Argentina
info@doseditores.com

Hecho el depósito que marca la Ley 11.723

Impreso en la Argentina
Real Print SA
12 de octubre 569 - Avellaneda - Argentina

Este libro es informativo. Consulte siempre a su médico de confianza.

Índice

Introducción

Estrés es, con certeza, una de las palabras más escuchadas en los últimos años. Y posiblemente, también sea uno de los males más relacionados con las nuevas formas de vida y de comportamiento de las sociedades modernas.
La actividad diaria nos provoca una suma de tensiones físicas y mentales que puede desencadenar una situación de estrés permanente si no es combatido a tiempo.
El cuerpo humano cuenta con los sistemas y mecanismos de defensa necesarios para protegerse de las presiones cotidianas y de las situaciones de tensión momentáneas. Pero el ritmo de vida que llevamos y la permanente exposición a numerosas complicaciones, hacen que se genere una acumulación de sobreesfuerzo que el organismo, a veces, no puede sostener.
Todas esas cargas laborales, emocionales, físicas, psíquicas, amorosas o económicas -entre otras-, que se almacenan en el orga-

nismo, nos hacen perder el foco de nuestras actividades, de nuestros vínculos y de nuestros sentimientos. El cuerpo comienza a perder fuerza, el físico no nos responde, olvidamos las cosas que nos hacen sentir bien, desatendemos a nuestras parejas, dejamos de lado la cena semanal con nuestro grupo de amigas o amigos, peleamos muy a menudo, nos ofuscamos, durante el día tenemos sueño y por la noche no podemos descansar, y muchos otros síntomas que comienzan siendo imperceptibles o aislados y que, con el correr de los días, de las semanas y del aumento en las obligaciones se convierten en permanentes.

Algunos de estos estados de estrés necesitarán la visita al médico o al analista para encontrar la verdadera raíz del problema y buscar sus soluciones. Otros, iniciados por causas menores, si son controlados a tiempo pueden encauzarse mediante la aplicación de alguna terapia relajante como la meditación o el yoga.

Al mismo tiempo, como medida de prevención, existen algunos hábitos o costumbres que pueden ayudar al cuerpo a relajarse luego de la jornada laboral, o antes de iniciar el día para aumentar las defensas de nuestros sistemas ante las agresiones del estrés.

Este libro nos ayudará a entender el funcionamiento básico del estrés y nos propone aprender a controlarlo mediante la incorporación de distintos tipos de alimentos y aplicación de costumbres, técnicas y terapias para vivir mejor y en armonía con nuestro cuerpo, con nuestros prójimos y con el medio que nos rodea.

Colección Conocer y Aprender

¿Qué es el estrés?

Colección conocer y aprender

¿Qué es el estrés?

A lo largo de su evolución, el ser humano ha estado expuesto a diferentes tipos de peligros, ataques o progresos que alteraron su vida y le presentaron una situación de cambio: el desconocimiento de todo lo que lo rodeaba en sus primeros pasos; la disputa del lugar y de la comida frente a otras especies animales; la adaptación al terreno y a las distintas condiciones ambientales; las guerras y batallas ante otros grupos de hombres; las armas; la necesidad de trabajar; las pestes; las enfermedades; los conquistadores; la irrupción de las máquinas en su trabajo; los medios de comunicación; el dominio de la tecnología en la era digital; la inseguridad y las presiones laborales de las nuevas formas de vida.

Ante todos estos episodios, el hombre ha asimilado los cambios y, bien en algunas ocasiones y mal en otras, se ha enfrentado para adaptarse. Sin dudas, ante cada una de esas situaciones, el

hombre ha experimentado el estrés, un mecanismo de autodefensa de su organismo que, podríamos decir, muchas veces se pone fuera de control.
Aunque hoy es una palabra que nos resulta desagradable, el estrés nos ayudó a enfrentarnos a un medio hostil que requería una respuesta rápida y eficaz, una respuesta que entonces se volvió automática para ser más eficaz.
Esta respuesta inconsciente, desarrollada para facilitar la supervivencia en el pasado, es hoy el problema, pues ante las presiones internas sigue aflorando esa respuesta instintiva, inicial, la del hombre frente a la bestia, que hoy puede catalogarse de desmesurada.
En la actualidad, ese "estrés" se encuentra plenamente relacionado con la acumulación de tensiones físicas, mentales y emocionales que almacenamos en nuestro interior a lo largo de una jornada que aglutina problemas laborales, familiares, de pareja, económicos, etcétera.
La respuesta correcta en nuestro medio original frente a un elevado estrés era: pelear o huir, y en ambos casos las sustancias que se vertían a la sangre para prepararnos ante un esfuerzo intenso y explosivo eran consumidas.
El problema del estrés actual es que debemos soportarlo y aguantar situaciones de miedo, confusión y tensión ante situaciones en el trabajo, en la calle o con nuestra familia; pero sólo podemos sobrellevarlo y reprimir esa agresión primitiva.
Lo más grave de esta situación es que nuestro cuerpo lo paga: acumulamos la tensión en forma de contracturas, problemas digestivos, posturales, arritmias cardíacas, diabetes, colesterol, y un sinfín de efectos indeseados.
No podemos evitar ese acervo genético que nos condiciona como especie humana, pero sí podemos cambiar ese mar embra-

vecido de contracturas por una actitud apacible y calma, que baje los niveles de estrés en nuestro cuerpo, en vez de multiplicarlos.

Los agentes estresantes

Son múltiples los factores externos e internos capaces de producir un impacto en nuestro sistema defensivo. Entre las causas y motivos más comunes podríamos mencionar:

Agentes biológicos:
Enfermedades, acontecimientos ligados a procesos de daño sobre el cuerpo o enfermedad.

Agentes climáticos:
Las inclemencias de los cambios climáticos, exceso de frío o exceso de calor; las incomodidades prolongadas en este aspecto son agentes generadores de estrés.

Agentes químicos:
Uso y abuso de sustancias que alteran el normal funcionamiento del organismo, como alcohol, tabaco o drogas.

Agentes sociales:
Exceso de trabajo, conflictos o demandas familiares excesivas, situaciones conflictivas de pareja, divorcios, mudanzas, etc.

Los agentes biológicos

Además de desgastarse de manera normal con el paso de los años, el cuerpo está expuesto a decenas de ataques que afectan su funcionamiento como regímenes alimentarios o una vida sin actividad física.
La artrosis y otras patologías de carácter reumático u óseo tienden a afectarnos cuando la edad se eleva; estas causas naturales aumentarán nuestra predisposición al estrés ya que disminuyen nuestra capacidad de adaptación y exigen mayor esfuerzo al organismo para realizar cualquier tarea.
Todas las enfermedades merman nuestra capacidad de adaptación al medio y exigen una mayor inversión de energía. Esta situación nos es devuelta en forma de estrés, lo que a la vez alimenta otro tipo de enfermedades crónicas, como el colesterol o la diabetes. También el iniciar repentinamente una rutina de ejercicios de alta intensidad puede ser un elemento estresante que nos demandará un esfuerzo de adaptación importante incluso estando muy preparados para ello.

Los agentes climáticos

Las temperaturas o situaciones climáticas extremas son factores de estrés, capaces de hacer reaccionar a nuestro sistema vegetativo de manera excesiva produciendo reacciones de estrés. Además de las presiones diarias, el agente climático es uno de los que más se ha desarrollado en los últimos años y, posiblemente uno de los que más esté influyendo en la actualidad. El innegable cambio del clima que afecta a todas las regiones (períodos de sequía, abundancia de lluvias, inundaciones, desborde de ríos y lagos, caída de granizo, aumento de la temperatura promedio, modificación de las estaciones, etcétera) junto a los mismísimos cambios que genera el propio hombre (calor en los ómnibus, trenes y demás medios de transporte, frío en las oficinas, exceso en los aires acondicionados y calefactores) predisponen a la acumulación de estrés.

Los agentes químicos

La contaminación ambiental, los alergenos suspendidos en el aire y el uso indebido de sustancias como el alcohol, el café, el tabaco y las drogas, pueden afectar nuestra capacidad de adaptación al medio favoreciendo la aparición de reacciones desmedidas, que sumadas a otras son capaces de alterar el buen funcionamiento del organismo.

Los agentes sociales

Los seres humanos desde nuestro nacimiento, y a partir de la interacción con los demás, armamos una estructura de personalidad que si bien nos permite erigirnos en personas, a la vez nos atrapa en maniobras de conducta que deberíamos "desaprender" para dejar de tensionarnos continuamente. Esta estructura de personalidad nos es muy útil porque nos permite reaccionar de un modo fácil frente a situaciones cotidianas, pero, como dijimos, cristaliza formas de respuesta que aplica a gran velocidad, aunque no siempre sean las adecuadas. No hemos tenido un entrenamiento para desarrollar nuestra personalidad como un mecanismo capaz de resolver problemas con eficacia, y de adoptar la solución más adecuada ante la perspectiva que se nos presenta.

Es necesario aclarar que las personas no somos todas iguales ni reaccionamos de igual manera frente a una situación estresante o ante los síntomas del estrés.
Además, los seres humanos actuamos de acuerdo con pautas que nos enseña, y de algún modo impone, el medio cultural en el que vivimos. O sea que de ninguna manera podemos universalizar el estrés, lo que tenemos que tener siempre en cuenta son las formas culturales del grupo en el que el sujeto se encuentra y sus características psíquicas.
Cada cultura tiene un patrón de respuestas en relación con la muerte, la enfermedad, la realización personal o los vínculos, y es desde este lugar que cada persona adaptará las respuestas posibles ante la presión del entorno.
Cuantas menos opciones tengamos, tendremos más estrés, de modo que el poder abrir nuestra mente a nuevas formas de pensar y mecanismos más diversos para enfrentar las situaciones, así como el poder aprender técnicas que nos ayuden a despejar nuestra mente y a aliviar nuestros músculos nos permitirá evitar la fase del estrés crónico, que conlleva riesgos serios para nuestra salud. A lo largo de esta obra mencionaremos algunas técnicas terapéuticas y hábitos que nos podrán ayudar a combatir y alejar el estrés.

Las causas externas

Es difícil aunque no imposible que un solo factor estresante llegue a generar una respuesta excesiva de estrés. Lo más habitual es que se trate de una serie de factores que se van acumulando y que desencadenan en el síntoma patológico.

Cuando pasa el tiempo y no se ha relajado el cuerpo que ha sido expuesto a un factor estresante, la adrenalina y las hormonas vertidas en la sangre nunca bajan su caudal; el cuerpo va acumulando tensión; los músculos se convierten en "almacenadores" de la tensión; y existe una sobrecarga permanente e innecesaria que, si bien muchas veces es ignorada, o no es percibida por la persona, afecta el estado de vigilia, ya que el agotamiento que produce disminuye la energía que necesitamos para las cosas simples y cotidianas.

Los problemas de la tensión muscular terminan afectando al sistema circulatorio debido al sobreesfuerzo que está realizando continuamente el corazón para vencer la resistencia que impone la musculatura sobre las arterias y que las hace rígidas.

Y, como nuestro cuerpo es una estructura de sistemas interrelacionados entre sí: no es posible que los problemas de un sistema, como el circulatorio, no afecten, más tarde o más temprano, a todos los demás sistemas del organismo. Así sucederá en cadena con el resto de los sistemas por lo que una simple carga de estrés, si no es corregida y combatida a tiempo, puede desencadenar problemas más graves y serios.

La tensión y las dificultades que se nos presentan instalan la presión sobre nosotros; nuestros músculos responden de manera inmediata, tensionándose; el cuerpo nervioso decodifica esta sensación de peligro que expresan estos músculos y una emoción negativa invade todo el cuerpo.

Los análisis que se pueden hacer sobre el estrés son múltiples y muchas veces, de acuerdo con el especialista o con el profesional que los realiza se puede enfocar desde distintos puntos de vista. Para hacer una síntesis de estas observaciones, podríamos decir que existe un aspecto positivo y uno negativo dentro del estrés.

El estrés "negativo"

El estrés cuenta con un aspecto positivo –que veremos más adelante- y con uno completamente negativo –que es el que nos afecta y nos daña-. El estrés negativo es aquel que produce un esfuerzo excesivo o superior al que nuestro organismo se encuentra acostumbrado. Es decir, genera reacciones que aumentan los funcionamientos normales produciendo aceleración en el ritmo cardíaco, tensión muscular, hiperactividad y otras que ya describimos o que mencionaremos luego. Podemos decir que el organismo, por lo general, puede superar el estrés positivo y que, pierde el equilibrio de alguna forma cuando padece una situación de estrés negativo.

El estrés "positivo"

Nos referimos en esto a aquella visión que manifestamos al comienzo, sobre la reacción positiva que provocaba el estrés, que llevaba al hombre a reaccionar de manera equilibrada para la lucha o la huída que le permitía defenderse sin desequilibrar el funcionamiento orgánico. En este estado el cuerpo es capaz de enfrentarse a las situaciones repentinas e incluso obtiene sensaciones placenteras. Este buen funcionamiento de nuestro sistema de alerta nos permite experimentar el mundo como un lugar para explorar y disfrutar.

El estrés "positivo" es asimismo un estado de conciencia, en el cual pensamiento, emoción y sensación parecen organizarse para proporcionar un efecto general de alegría, satisfacción y energía vital.

Las técnicas de relajación, con su costado revitalizador y reorientador de las energías, tienden a aproximarnos a un estado de estrés "positivo", de energía puesta en el asombro, la creatividad y el disfrute.

Y como cuando hablamos de estrés, del "positivo" y del "negativo" estamos hablando de energía, se trata claramente de limpiar, revitalizar, iluminar la energía positiva que nos sirve para disfrutar de las cosas placenteras y agradables, como nuestros vínculos afectivos, nuestro exploración sobre el mundo y la cantidad inagotable de estímulos que encontramos en él, y, por qué no, nuestro vínculo con el trabajo, para que deje de ser algo que se nos aparece como opresivo y lo podamos ver como una oportunidad para ejercer nuestro talento, nuestra creatividad y nuestra energía.

Por supuesto, la meditación nos ayudará; esta dosis de energía positiva, esta capacidad de ser nuevos y renovarnos se restará de la energía que hemos estado acumulando erróneamente en sitios nocivos.

En vez de desgastar nuestra energía, de hacer funcionar nuestros sistemas endocrino, circulatorio y digestivo en contra de nosotros, todo esto será reorientado en nuestro beneficio, para nuestra salud y para nuestro placer.

Tipos de estrés

Colección conocer y aprender

Tipos de estrés

Teniendo en cuenta su forma de inicio, su duración, los daños que produce en el organismo y la manera de erradicarlo, existen dos tipos de estrés:

- el estrés agudo
- el estrés crónico

Estrés agudo

Llamamos estrés agudo a aquel que se presenta en un momento de tensión extrema, como puede ser: la enfermedad de un familiar al que tenemos que cuidar; junto a las vacaciones de nuestro socio comercial al que debemos reemplazar y aumentar

nuestras responsabilidades en el trabajo; sumado a que nos hemos peleado con nuestra pareja y que nuestro hijo no ha alcanzado a aprobar la evaluación final.
Esa carga de ansiedad producirá en la persona la sensación de que "yo no puedo con todo esto sobre mis espaldas"...
En un caso como este, al que seguramente ya nos hemos enfrentado de una u otra manera salvando las diferencias o los problemas, se pueden producir reacciones de dos tipos:

- tomar más fuerzas para luchar.
- buscar una escapatoria.

Si optamos por el primer camino, podemos superar la crisis (aquí podríamos pensar que no era tan grave) o generar una expectativa mayor y no poder cumplir con todos esos desafíos. En este caso sentiremos una desazón aún más grande, pues entenderemos el estado de estrés en el cual estamos inmersos y, al mismo tiempo, lo aumentaremos por la angustia de no haber concretado lo que nos habíamos propuesto.

Si el camino elegido fue la escapatoria, es probable que no incrementemos el nivel de estrés, pero seguramente dejaremos cuentas pendientes por allí y, más tarde o más temprano volverán a la carga sobre nuestro cuerpo y el estrés será más perjudicial.

Estrés crónico

Existen situaciones en las cuales un cuadro de estrés agudo comienza a hacerse permanente y la persona se acostumbra a convivir con el estrés, dando paso a un estado que reviste mayor gravedad y que se llama estrés crónico. Es decir, cuando las tensiones, las presiones y las angustias comienzan a convertirse en perpetuas y forman parte de nuestra forma de vida.
Cuando una persona ha caído en una permanente situación estresante, además de perjudicar gravemente su vida, provoca una disminución continua de sus defensas y de sus sistema nervioso, generando al mismo tiempo, una gran debilidad ante cada agresión de agentes biológicos, químicos, sociales o climáticos, es decir, exponiendo el cuerpo a ser más propenso al estrés.
Ese estado crónico de estrés, se manifiesta en un principio como un estrés agudo, empeora, se agudiza en todos los órdenes y, posteriormente, da inicio a otro tipo de molestias, en este caso, físicas: dolores estomacales, gastrointestinales, de cabeza; calambres en las piernas, puntadas en el pecho o la espalda, vómitos, temblores, fuertes sacudidas antes de dormir, etcétera.
Todos esos síntomas, son manifestaciones corporales de que estamos expuestos a una situación de estrés crónico.

¿Cómo darnos cuenta?

El conocimiento que cada uno posee de su cuerpo hace que podamos percibir los síntomas corporales y mentales que sufrimos ante una situación estresante. Ansiedad, nervios, malestar estomacal o alteraciones en el sueño son problemas que podemos distinguir por nuestros propios medios. Pero a su vez, hay alteraciones en el semblante, en el comportamiento o en la forma de actuar que los demás observan en nosotros. Es común que una persona afectada por algún tipo de estrés reciba comentarios como "te veo cansado"; "estás nerviosa"; "tenés la cara pálida"... Todas esas situaciones son señales inequívocas de que un estado de estrés nos está afectando.

La relación entre el estrés y cada individuo es muy variable y puede ser completamente diferente en dos personas. Sin embargo, hay una escala de acontecimientos perturbadores y estresantes que afectan a todos por igual, pues son situaciones inesperadas, tristes, insalvables, de peligro o de muy difícil solución. Otros, como casarse, son felices, pero llevan a un profundo estado de tensión. En esa escala de complicaciones podemos encontrar por orden de importancia:

- Fallecimiento del cónyuge.
- Divorcio definitivo.
- Menopausia (antes, durante y después de ese proceso).
- Separación y alejamiento de la pareja.
- Ingreso a prisión.
- Fallecimiento de un familiar cercano.

• Conocimiento de una enfermedad grave o de una lesión que llevará mucho tiempo rehabilitar.

• Contraer matrimonio.

• Despido laboral.

• Reconciliación con la pareja

• Jubilación, paso a retiro o alejamiento de un lugar donde se ha trabajo por muchos años.

• Enfermedades de los familiares más queridos.

• Embarazo.

• Disfunciones sexuales.

• Nacimiento de un hijo.

• Traslado laboral, cambio de funciones o modificaciones en el salario.

• Fallecimiento de un amigo.

• Períodos de fuertes discusiones de pareja.

• Obtención de un crédito.

• Independización de los hijos.

• Deudas con el banco.

• Discusiones con el jefe.

• Cambios laborales de la pareja.

• Mudanza.

• Modificación brusca del horario laboral.

• Descanso insuficiente.

• Cambio de institución educativa.

• Traslados de amigos a otros países.

• Comienzo o finalización de estudios, cursos, reuniones sociales, etcétera.

• Vacaciones.

• Llegada de nuevos vecinos.

Colección Conocer y Aprender

Síntomas y consecuencias del estrés

Síntomas y consecuencias del estrés

Como ya hemos visto hasta aquí, el estrés es una respuesta de nuestro cuerpo a una agresión interior o exterior de distintos orígenes: laborales, familiares, amorosos, económicos, etcétera. Es decir, el estrés es una respuesta a un peligro que, si no se elimina, se combate o se suprime a tiempo puede llevar a una alteración física.

Esas agresiones pueden afectar a cada persona de distintas maneras. Ante una complicación, el cuerpo acude a su sistema de defensa y se ponen en juego una serie de mecanismos corporales que preparan al físico y a la mente para sobrellevar el problema. Existen decenas de manifestaciones de nuestro organismo. Entre las más comunes están:

- latidos del corazón más fuertes
- picazón en la piel
- temblores
- falta de apetito
- tensión en los músculos
- sudor abundante
- sed
- sequedad bucal
- trastornos hormonales
- presión alta

Cuando la situación estresante es de corta duración (un examen, la entrega de un informe, un viaje, una reunión, etcétera) un rato de relajación o algún ejercicio descontracturante servirá para superar el malestar. En cambio, cuando la alteración se mantiene por un tiempo más extenso, el estrés se va acumulando y se manifiesta en agotamiento físico, cansancio, nerviosismo y otros síntomas que pueden variar según la persona aprovechando sus propias debilidades. Es decir, aquellos con tendencia a malestares estomacales podrán sufrir gastroenteritis; quienes estén predispuestos a dolores en la cabeza pueden sufrir una jaqueca, etcétera.

Etapas del estrés

Básicamente, la respuesta del cuerpo humano ante el estrés de manifiesta en tres etapas bien definidas:

Primera etapa:
Es el momento en el cual el cuerpo detecta un peligro, una agresión, una amenaza y se dispone a entrar en acción. La misma puede ser ignorar el ataque o activar los mecanismos para contrarrestarlo. En ese caso, son liberadas hormonas por las glándulas endocrinas que trasladan la adrenalina a lo largo del organismo. Esto se manifiesta con transpiración, dilatación en las pupilas y un ritmo respiratorio más acelerado.

Segunda etapa:
Una vez que el cuerpo ha detectado una alarma, activó sus defensas para protegerse y superó el momento, se procede a la restauración de todos los sistemas y a la regularización de sus funciones normales.

Tercera etapa:
Se pasa a esta etapa cuando la situación estresante reviste tal importancia que el organismo no puede erradicarla mediante su sistema de defensa. Es probable que si ese estado se normaliza en pocas horas o días, el cuerpo pueda recuperarse, sin embargo, cuando el problema se extiende en el tiempo el individuo comienza a recorrer un camino que necesitará la visita al médico para realizar un diagnóstico y encontrar las causas para combatirlas.

Sin embargo, si el estrés continúa, el cuerpo permanece alerta y no puede reparar los daños. Si continúa la resistencia se inicia la tercera etapa, agotamiento, cuya consecuencia puede ser una alteración producida por el estrés.

La exposición prolongada al estrés agota las reservas de energía del cuerpo y puede llevar en situaciones muy extremas incluso a la muerte. Pero aún sin llegar a extremos tales, cuando se mantienen elevados niveles de estrés, durante un período de tiempo considerable, empezamos a asumir formas de conductas inadecuadas.

Y lo que naturaleza ideó para protegernos de las agresiones del medio ambiente y prepararnos contra situaciones potencialmente peligrosas, se transforma en sí mismo en un peligro, y comienza a atacarnos.

Una de las situaciones que nos genera esta hipertrofia del estado de alerta es la ansiedad; comienza sin ser patológico al principio, pero se termina transformando en crónico, debido a la suma de tensiones y sobrecargas musculares por la hiperactivación del sistema simpático – adrenérgico. Esto hace que el cuerpo se vaya sensibilizando cada vez más a estímulos menores, que terminan desencadenando una respuesta excesiva. Por ejemplo, cuando saltamos del miedo y nuestro corazón se acelera por varios minutos sólo porque alguien habló de pronto detrás nuestro.

Colección Conocer y Aprender

Hábitos y terapias
para combatir el estrés

Colección conocer y aprender

Hábitos y terapias para combatir el estrés

Actividades para combatir el estrés

Además de todo lo que hemos ido mencionando en los capítulos anteriores, el tratamiento del estrés puede verse beneficiado con la práctica de distintas rutinas y terapias para relajar la mente, el cuerpo y las tensiones.
Entre esos hábitos o terapias favorables para el bienestar del organismo podemos encontrar:

- Tai Chi
- Relajación
- Masajes
- Acupuntura

- Shiatsu
- Meditación
- Yoga
- Reflexología
- Correcto descanso

Algunos de ellos recurren a técnicas similares de respiración, movimientos físicos, relajación, descanso; o a combinaciones de varias de ellas. Si bien en las siguientes páginas vamos a comentar las cualidades de las principales de ellas y de que manera pueden contrarrestar el estrés, lo primero que debe hacerse es recurrir a un profesional o a nuestro médico de cabecera para que evalúe el nivel de estrés que nos afecta y cual debería ser el mejor tratamiento para combatirlo pues en los casos avanzados de estrés crónico, además de estudios y análisis, será necesaria la intervención de un analista para reordenar nuestra estabilidad emocional y psíquica.

Hábitos favorables para combatir el estrés

Un correcto descanso

Uno de esos principales hábitos que se pueden llevar a cabo a diario para alejar el estrés cotidiano de nuestra vida es el ordenamiento del sueño. Tanto el sueño propiamente dicho como un pequeño intervalo en el trajín del día para tomarse un buen descanso, otorga al cuerpo mayor salud, lozanía al rostro y tranquilidad al espíritu. Además de ser un verdadero placer, dormir es una necesidad vital para todas las personas. El sueño es realmente favorable tanto para curar o disminuir estados de estrés o ansiedad, como para regenerar la piel o mantener en buen estado el sistema nervioso.

Cuando una persona duerme poco y descansa mal, no sólo le resta vitalidad al cuerpo, sino que también le ocasiona a la piel un color más grisáceo, algunas espinillas y arrugas. El hecho de dormir, ofrece al organismo la posibilidad de renovar las sustancias vitales que sirven para su funcionamiento, a la vez que se desechan aquellas sustancias que el cuerpo ha producido durante el día, y ya no precisa.

Si nuestro cuerpo no descansa lo necesario, no cuenta con la posibilidad de este intercambio en el que se almacenan sustancias vitales en las células, y nuestro cuerpo se encontraría siem-

pre cansado y en constante tensión, más vulnerable a la presencia del estrés.
Estas son algunas claves para descansar bien durante la noche, disminuyendo los niveles de estrés:

- Ventilar con frecuencia la habitación en la que se duerme.
- No dormir con una temperatura mayor a los 18ºC.
- Utilizar almohadas no demasiado gruesas.
- Intentar acostarse siempre a la misma hora.
- A medida que se acerca la noche, ir reduciendo la actividad en forma gradual.
- Tomar cenas livianas, debido a que una comida abundante interfiere en el descanso.
- Intentar acostarse con posturas adecuadas, que ayuden a una buena circulación sanguínea.
- Utilizar para dormir, vestimenta cómoda y de tejidos naturales; al igual que las sábanas que deben ser de algodón.

En muchos casos, debido a problemas surgidos durante el día, a preocupaciones de las que no nos podemos desprender o a que nuestro cuerpo presenta un estado de excitación, se apodera de nosotros el insomnio, impidiendo que disfrutemos de un buen descanso.
Para combatir este fenómeno, nada mejor que algún tratamiento natural. Si utilizamos sedantes o barbitúricos, lo que lograremos es un sueño similar a la anestesia, pero no un real descanso, además de estar consumiendo pastillas perjudiciales para la salud.

Si la acumulación de estrés nos lleva a la demora en la conciliación del sueño, estos son algunos consejos para poner en práctica:

• Tomar un vaso de leche caliente, antes de irse a dormir.
• Durante la tarde y noche, no ingerir ninguna sustancia estimulante, como puede ser el café.
• Beber una infusión sedante de hierbas naturales como tilo, melisa o lavanda.
• Sumergir los pies en agua caliente, y luego protegerlos con medias para mantenerlos con una buena temperatura, dentro de la cama.

Relajación

La eficacia de los procedimientos de la relajación (incluyendo la relajación muscular progresiva, la meditación, la hipnosis y el entrenamiento autógeno) están demostrados en el tratamiento de muchos problemas. Nos referimos a los relacionados con la salud mental y física, la tensión, el insomnio, la hipertensión, los dolores de cabeza por tensión, el asma bronquial y, especialmente, el estrés.
Los métodos de relajación se utilizan también como tratamiento coadyuvante en muchas condiciones, por ejemplo: la ansiedad de hablar en público, las fobias, la ansiedad intensa, el síndrome de colon irritable, el dolor crónico y las disfunciones sexuales. No queremos decir que la relajación sea una terapéutica para estos problemas, pero sí que es un buen complemento a las terapias médicas y psicológicas. Además nos da una herramienta que mejora nuestra calidad de vida.
Como se ve, dentro del término relajación se incluyen una técnica y varias formas de hacer o de influir sobre la tensión y la ansiedad.

Condiciones para relajarse

La relajación no presenta grados importantes de dificultad, pero debemos tener en cuenta que necesitamos concentración y comodidad, e ir avanzando paso a paso, tanto en los ejercicios de respiración como en los de relajación propiamente dichos. Además se necesita un compromiso personal para empezar a bajar las tensiones que pueden generarse desde nuestro entorno y la situación en que nos disponemos a iniciar nuestra relajación.

El lugar

La elección del lugar queda, por supuesto, limitada a las posibilidades de cada persona. Es claro que si disponemos de jardín amplio, sin ruidos molestos de la calle que nos distraigan, una colchoneta bajo un árbol, oyendo el trinar de los pájaros, sería lo ideal (con las condiciones climáticas necesarias). Pero como muchas veces no disponemos para elegir, lo que podemos hacer es adecuar algún espacio de nuestra casa, para comenzar con los ejercicios. Los requisitos son simples:

- Ambiente templado (recordemos que tanto el frío como el calor son agentes estresantes).
- Una luz tenue. Podemos iluminar con velas, usando de paso alguna vela aromática, con una fragancia que posea cualidades relajantes.
- Una colchoneta firme, o una manta doblada que nos resulte cómoda para apoyar la espalda.
- Por supuesto, prever y evitar las interrupciones.

Para los ejercicios de entrenamiento en relajación hay tres tipos de posiciones posibles:

• Acostados sobre una colchoneta o un diván con los brazos y las piernas ligeramente en ángulo y apartados del cuerpo.

• Sentados en un sillón cómodo y con apoya brazos; en este caso es conveniente que utilicemos apoyos para la nuca y los pies.

• Sentados en un taburete o una banqueta sin respaldo; en esta modalidad se usa una posición descrita por Schultz (el especialista inventor de la técnica de relajación progresiva que lleva su nombre y que describiremos más adelante) y que llama "la posición del cochero": se caracteriza por el hecho de descansar la persona, sentada, el peso de la mitad superior de su cuerpo sobre la región dorso lumbar relajada, en posición de dorso del gato.

Esta actitud corporal pasiva la encontramos en muchos profesiones que exigen permanecer sentado durante muchas horas, sin apoyo para el dorso.
De todos modos, la posición que recomendamos, sobre todo al comienzo, es la de estar acostados boca arriba, ya que de esta manera podemos relajar con mayor facilidad la musculatura voluntaria.
Los ojos deben estar cerrados, o entrecerrados sin forzar los párpados para disminuir el nivel de estimulación que proviene de lo externo, pero evitando, por lo menos hasta la conclusión del ejercicio, el quedarnos dormidos.
Si persistimos en este proyecto de aprendizaje y autoconocimiento que nos proponen las técnicas de relajación, con el paso del tiempo podremos relajarnos sentados, de pie, con los ojos

abiertos, y por lo general en situaciones que por ahora nos parecen imposibles.

Preparando el cuerpo para la relajación

Este pequeño ejercicio ayuda a la toma de conciencia del propio cuerpo.

• En primer lugar concentraremos nuestra atención en el mundo exterior, diciéndonos frases como: "Soy consciente de que está pasando un auto bajo mi ventana, de que está lloviendo, de que mi ropa es azul...". La idea es tomar una especie de nota de nosotros mismos y del entorno donde nos disponemos a relajarnos.

• Una vez que hemos tomado conciencia de lo que nos rodea, dirigiremos la atención a nuestro propio cuerpo y sus sensaciones físicas: "Soy consciente de que hace frío, de que tengo hambre, de mi tensión en el cuello, del cosquilleo en la planta del pie...".

• Ahora pasaremos alternativamente de un tipo a otro de conciencia: "Soy consciente de que me duele la cabeza, de que hay excesiva luz, de que la habitación es amplia, etc.". Es decir, pasando de percepciones internas a percepciones externas.

Con la práctica de este ejercicio podremos darnos cuenta de la diferencia entre el mundo externo y el interior y, cosa a veces no tan sencilla, para ser plenamente conscientes de esto y poder pasar a ejercicios más exigentes, como los que expondremos más adelante.

Algunas otras sugerencias

Es recomendable iniciar la práctica de los ejercicios de relajación no habiendo comido demasiado, ni con sensación de hambre. Auque hagamos los ejercicios acostados, debemos recordar que estamos aprendiendo y ejercitando una técnica de salud, no lo estamos haciendo para dormir sino para permitir que nuestros músculos, al inicio, se relajen más fácilmente.

Comienza la relajación

Esta serie de pasos previos constituyen en sí mismos ejercicios relajantes, aunque su objetivo es tomar conciencia de que hay unas cualidades por desarrollar para obtener una relajación más intensa, más profunda y eficaz.
Es decir, entramos en una etapa grado uno de relajación.
Todos son variables del desarrollo de la capacidad de atención, que necesitaremos para llevar a cabo los ejercicios de relajación.
Es recomendable empezar siempre siguiendo un camino ascendente en cuanto a la sutileza de las percepciones, es decir, ir de lo más simple a lo más complejo
Este tipo de ejercicios pueden hacerse estando sentados sin cerrar los ojos, tratando de mantener el espíritu calmo, procurando disfrutar de ello, teniendo en claro que si por alguna razón no nos resultasen gratos, debemos optar de inmediato por otros.
El tiempo mínimo de concentración y atención que buscamos para el desarrollo de todas las fases es de unos 5 minutos iniciales, que pueden transformarse, si esto nos hace sentir bien, en 20 minutos o media hora.

Podemos empezar por una o dos fases, e ir, con el tiempo, sumando las otras hasta completarlas, dedicando la cantidad de tiempo que deseemos.

Primera fase

- Nos encontramos sentados.
- Imaginamos que frente a nosotros hay una serie de objetos cuya forma no podemos determinar muy claramente.
- Pero hay algo de sus cualidades materiales que se destaca.
- Algunos objetos son de madera, otros de metal, otros vivos, como plantas y otros minerales, como una piedra.
- Elijo esta última y simplemente mi atención se posa en ella, sin hacer nada ni comprometer ninguna clase de emoción o voluntad.
- Simplemente observo, no juzgo, no deseo, no rechazo ni acepto. Mi función es la de ser un mero observador que quiere aprehender todos los detalles del cuerpo que está delante de mí, su forma, su color, tamaño, etc.
- Cuando hemos conseguido completar esta fase, sin que pensamientos extraños se interpongan, terminamos y pasamos, si queremos, a la fase siguiente.

Segunda fase

- Ahora elegiré un objeto inmóvil pero vivo, como una planta.
- Presto atención a cada detalle de color, forma, sombras, altura, volumen.
- Tomo conciencia de las partes y del todo, lenta y atentamente.
- Comienzo a percibir en este objeto cualidades que faltaban en la piedra, aquí hay algo más.
- Tomo conciencia plena de la observación y me mantengo en ella, no tomo ni rechazo nada, observo sin juzgar.

• Obtenido esto finalizo el ejercicio.

Tercera fase

• Observo con atención una flor, sólo una.

• Toda mi atención está puesta en ella, soy casi un cuerpo con una conexión única abierta al mundo y es esa flor que he visualizado.

• Contemplo su color, sus bordes, su forma, cada detalle, sin tomar ni rechazar nada.

• Cuando consigo esto doy por terminada esta fase del ejercicio.

Cuarta fase

• Ahora cierro los ojos y presto atención a mi respiración.

• Toda mi atención se encuentra en el proceso de respirar y en sus sensaciones.

• Intento que esta atención no modifique en nada la naturalidad del ingreso de oxígeno en mi cuerpo y del bienestar que éste me produce, simplemente observo como inhalo y exhalo.

• Soy un observador que observa su propia respiración como observaría la llama de una vela, sin identificarse con ella, sin juzgar.

• Cuando completo esta etapa finalizo el ejercicio.

Quinta fase

• Observo mi respirar pausado atentamente, como en la cuarta fase, durante unos instantes.

• Cuando percibo que la respiración produce un cierto estado de calma en mi interior dirijo mi atención hacia uno de mis brazos.

• Como venimos ejercitándonos, la atención permanece en la observación del brazo, sin interponer deseos, ni emociones, ni pensamientos, simplemente permanezco sintiendo mi brazo.

• Mi atención permanece en el brazo como lo hizo con la flor, observo y siento.
• Cuando el tiempo establecido llega, finalizo el ejercicio tomando conciencia de mis sensaciones en ese instante.

Sexta fase
• Comenzamos como en el ejercicio cinco.
• Ahora vamos incluyendo progresivamente la sensación del otro brazo, la respiración de nuevo, la percepción de la pierna derecha, la respiración, la pierna izquierda, la respiración.
• Luego tomaremos conciencia de la percepción de ambos brazos y la respiración, de ambas piernas y la respiración, de brazos y piernas juntos y la respiración, sin ninguna clase de apuro, lentamente...
• Si aparece como emoción predominante la calma, vuelvo a asumir mi rol de observador y le presto la misma atención distante que vengo ejercitando en las fases anteriores.
• No debe tener para mí más importancia la observación de un sentimiento que irrumpe desde mí que la importancia que tenía el contorno o las tonalidades de la flor.
• Me importa sólo la observación, observo sin juzgar, sin identificarme con la emoción de calma, de paz, de tranquilidad.
• Procuro no detenerme en la percepción de la emoción, mi atención recorre mi cuerpo, puedo sentirlo pero no permanezco en la degustación de la emoción de calma, simplemente es algo que está ahí, que es una cualidad, otra característica observable.
• Recorro mentalmente mi cuerpo y siento la sensación orgánica de mi peso, la tensión o la distensión muscular, el hormigueo, o el calor, o la relajación de los músculos.
• Cuando siento que he cumplido con esta fase, puedo dar por finalizado el ejercicio.

Séptima fase

• Empiezo como en la fase cinco, integrando mentalmente las sensaciones de brazos y piernas, la respiración y la percepción de la sensación de ambos brazos y piernas nuevamente, en un recorrido lento y suave, un recorrido dulce por las sensaciones de mis extremidades y mi respiración.

• Si eventualmente aparece algún pensamiento, lo observo sin identificarme con él, me doy cuenta de que los pensamientos tienden a aparecer por su cuenta sin que yo lo provoque, el pensamiento no soy yo, yo y mis pensamientos somos diferentes.

• Observo mi pensamiento, como haría con una vela o una flor, tomo conciencia de estos pensamientos que aparecen y desaparecen como nubes en un cielo azul, cobro conciencia de que si los observo desaparecen, pero si intento eliminarlos cobran fuerza e impiden que siga con el ejercicio.

• Sigo observando mis pensamientos pero no me identifico con ellos, no busco interpretación ni juzgo, observo con toda mi atención y cuando cumplo con esta fase finalizo el ejercicio.

Si hemos realizado correctamente toda esta serie de fases (no pretendamos hacerlas todas en un solo día, se trata de un aprendizaje), notaremos que ya podemos empezar a percibir una suerte de calma mental, y que ésta de por sí bajará también las tensiones de nuestro cuerpo y ayudará a disminuir nuestro estrés y a mejorar la respuesta de nuestro organismo ante el mismo.

Pero, más allá de esto, una vez que hemos podido automatizar esta serie de pasos que si bien son sencillos requieren de una mente dispuesta y de relativa práctica, podremos decir que ya estamos preparados para pasar a hacer ejercicios más profundos de relajación.

Meditación

¿Qué es?

La meditación tiene una larga tradición, y en general, a pesar de tener distintos tipos o variantes, no es más que una forma o un camino según el cual siguiendo una práctica determinada se consiguen algunos objetivos. Es, para los especialistas, "un sendero que la persona abre para sí misma mientras trata de llegar más allá de las limitaciones de la mente".
Por lo tanto, si bien es una práctica que se alcanza realizando determinados ejercicios que involucran el cuerpo (postura corporal, respiración, relajación), busca una actitud mental y un logro espiritual.
Por lo tanto, practicar la meditación nos conecta con estas dimensiones humanas:

- Lo corporal.
- Lo espiritual.
- Lo mental.
- En algunos casos, lo filosófico o religioso.

Estas primeras definiciones como vemos son algo amplias, pero son sencillas y, de alguna manera, tan amplias como alcances puede tener el practicar meditación.
Puede, para diferentes personas o grupos, tener la meditación distintos sentidos, aunque los objetivos a pesar de las variaciones se parecen. Lograr:

- Calmar el estrés, la ansiedad, los pensamientos negativos.
- Mayor control del cuerpo y de la mente.
- Armonía.
- Paz interior.
- Sentimientos positivos.
- Sentirse mejor y lograr bienestar personal.
- Alcanzar comunicación con el mundo interno.
- Alcanzar una dimensión espiritual que está dentro de nosotros.
- Más específicamente y con la práctica, borrar los pensamientos, poner la mente en blanco y dejar actuar otros niveles de nuestra interioridad.

Como vemos la meditación tiene algunos sencillos objetivos básicos, aunque externamente tiene muchas variantes y una amplia difusión de sus prácticas. También, a pesar de tener diferentes técnicas, éstas conservan algunos puntos comunes que son básicos. Las técnicas más comunes de meditación incluyen:

- Contar las propias respiraciones.
- Cantar un mantra.
- Bailar o escuchar música.

Una de las características principales de la meditación es que se trata de una práctica que no es compleja, en el sentido de que no requiere de dispositivos externos especiales, artefactos, cosas materiales o conocimientos elevados o esotéricos. Sí requiere de una especial disposición interna y actitud externa, que si bien no son fáciles de lograr, tampoco quedan fuera del alcance de ninguna persona.
Hay diferentes técnicas y formas de meditación, y cada persona puede seguir la que más adecuada le resulte. La meditación es,

en definitiva, un ejercicio personal. Básicamente, la meditación exige actitudes mínimas para comenzar su práctica, tales como:

• Elegir una postura y sostenerla para hacer la práctica de meditación.
• Efectuar respiraciones algo más profundas y completas de lo habitual y tomar conciencia clara de sí mismo en los niveles físico y emocional.
• Constatar que nos encontremos en un estado de tranquilidad, sin ansiedades excesivas ni tensiones físicas o psíquicas.
• Focalizarse en el nivel de la mente y darse cuenta de que estamos observando nuestra propia mente, sin estar pendientes de ningún objeto o pensamiento en particular (borrar los pensamientos conscientes).
• Dedicar un tiempo a sentir cómo se produce en nosotros mismos el automatismo natural de la respiración (esto ya lo veremos en detalle en el próximo capítulo). Tomar conciencia de nosotros mismos a través de focalizarnos sintiendo nuestra propia respiración.
• Sentir el silencio (también profundizaremos en esto, que es fundamental, en un capítulo posterior); en las zonas principales donde se debe sentir este silencio son: alrededor de la cabeza, dentro de la cabeza y dentro del pecho.

Un punto muy importante para empezar a conocer qué es la meditación es saber que no hay en ella un objetivo consciente: no se busca nada en particular. No debe haber confusión ni apoyo en ideas anteriores, conocidas, o en objetivos prefijados. Se trata de intentar buscar esa realidad interior a través de la intuición.

Esa tranquilidad, suavidad y gradualidad son necesarias para hacer la práctica y para salir de la práctica, ya que esto último hay que hacerlo de manera gradual, suavemente y sin brusquedades. Cuando se consigue un grado de meditación y de silencio, sobre todo cuando sucede por primera vez, se la recuerda como la experiencia más satisfactoria que se ha tenido en este sentido.

Otro punto importante para tener en cuenta en los rudimentos de esta práctica, es que existen distintos tipos de meditación, que mantienen puntos en común pero que no deben confundirse. Y reiteramos que cada persona puede dedicarse al tipo de práctica de meditación que más le siente.

Los diferentes tipos, son: meditación trascendental, meditación espiritual, meditación de transmisión, las técnicas de meditación clásicas, la meditación ligada al budismo y la meditación en triángulos.

Las cuestiones ligadas a la meditación y a los beneficios personales que genera, no sólo son "espirituales". También, hay varias consecuencias a nivel psicológico y físico que justifican su práctica.

Las técnicas más comunes van desde contar las propias respiraciones hasta por ejemplo, cantar un mantra o bailar. Se trata de lo más básico, y todos nosotros podemos iniciarnos eligiendo alguna que nos resulte sencilla.

Podríamos dividir esos ejercicios o esas prácticas iniciales en dos ejercicios básicos.

Un ejercicio de meditación podría incluir estos pasos:

- Elegir una postura.
- Efectuar respiraciones algo más profundas y completas que lo

habitual y tomar conciencia clara de sí mismo en los niveles físico y emocional.

• Constatar que nos encontremos en un estado de tranquilidad, cordialidad y amor suave, sin ira ni estrés.

• Pasar luego al nivel de la mente y darse cuenta de que estamos mirando u observando la mente, que está aquí presente tranquila, serena, despierta, pero sin estar pendientes de ningún objeto o pensamiento en particular.

• Dedicar un tiempo a sentir cómo se produce en nosotros mismos el automatismo natural de la respiración. Tomar clara conciencia de nosotros mismos, de que estamos presentes y sintiendo nuestra propia respiración. Esto hay que intentarlo hasta que notemos una verdadera paz, y cómo nuestra conciencia se va ahondando y profundizando.

• Se debe mantener esa conciencia de sí mismo, sin mirar nada, sintiendo el silencio.

• Las zonas principales donde se debe sentir este silencio son: alrededor de la cabeza, dentro de la cabeza y dentro del pecho.

• No hay un objetivo consciente; no se busca nada en particular. Se trata simplemente de que estemos "presentes", sin confundirnos con nada, sin apoyarnos en nada. En todo caso, hay que intentar buscar esa realidad que podemos intuir como única. No se debe perder la conciencia, y hay que mantenerla muy despierta.

• Para salir de la práctica hay que hacerlo de manera gradual, suavemente y sin brusquedades.

Cuando se consigue un grado de meditación y de silencio, sobre todo cuando sucede por primera vez, se la recuerda como la experiencia más satisfactoria que se ha tenido jamás. Y el eco de esa experiencia se mantiene, aunque luego se disuelve hasta casi perderse, por la dispersión habitual con que vivimos lo exterior. Pero, a base de hacer este trabajo con regularidad, todos los días, se va consiguiendo mantener ese punto de conciencia profunda y de paz a lo largo de todo el día, mientras haya actividad. Una vez que hayamos adoptado el hábito de la meditación, la misma nos ayudará a eliminar el estrés producido en cada jornada impidiendo que una acumulación del mismo produzca males mayores.

Música y cine

Muchas personas tienen dificultades para relajarse, concentrarse y dejar de pensar en las situaciones que producen el estrés. Pero aquellos que no logran salir de sus complicaciones diarias, pueden dar un paso inicial para lograr la relajación. Esto se puede conseguir ubicándose en un lugar adecuado, sentado cómodamente y disfrutando de una película preferida, con un actor o actriz que les resulte agradable o de una temática que los distraiga. Otra opción, y quizás más valedera, es atenuar las luces, encender una vela aromática y colocar en el equipo de audio un disco de nuestro músico preferido o con una melodía suave y serena.
Luego de haber visto una película, o de haber escuchado un disco compacto, será el momento de iniciar una relajación o meditación más profunda.

Terapias para combatir el estrés

Masajes

El acelerado ritmo de vida actual hace que sean muy pocas las personas que logran detenerse, dejar de acumular estrés, escuchar los sonidos de su propio cuerpo y conectarse con algo que no sean sus obligaciones. Ese "algo" para reencontrarnos con nosotros mismos pueden ser los masajes que son la solución al estrés cotidiano, al cansancio o a las molestias físicas.
Adoptar una sesión de masajes como hábito es el primer paso para equilibrar el cuerpo, el alma y la mente. Es decir, colabora con el bienestar físico y con la serenidad de la mente.
La elección del ambiente para una sesión de masajes incluye muchas cosas, entre ellas: un masajista o una masajista; la luz y la música del lugar; la rigidez de la cama o camilla sobre la cual nos acostaremos, o las distintas técnicas.
En este punto juegan los gustos personales y las condiciones más propicias para que cada persona encuentre el clima distendido y apropiado para el masaje.
Entre las distintas técnicas de masajes podemos mencionar al circulatorio, al shiatsu, la reflexología (que describiremos más adelante), el holístico, etcétera. Cada una de esas técnicas están destinadas a tratar diferentes dolencias o enfermedades; sin em-

bargo, para combatir el estrés, podemos recurrir a cualquiera de ellos, pues su objetivo principal es reducir las contracturas, los calambres y las molestias que manifiesta el cuerpo como consecuencia de las actuales condiciones de vida.

Yoga

¿Qué es el Yoga?

El yoga es uno de los seis sistemas ortodoxos de la filosofía india. Según estos principios filosóficos trascendentales, todo está penetrado por el Espíritu Supremo Universal (Paramatma o Dios) del que nuestro espíritu es parte. Por eso el nombre yoga de esta disciplina, ya que estudia y enseña los métodos por los cuales el jivatma (espíritu humano) puede unirse o hallarse en comunión con el Paramatma asegurándose así la propia liberación (motsa).
Es, como decíamos, una de las seis antiguas filosofías de la India, uno de los seis darshanas (literalmente: enfoques). Un cuerpo de conocimientos, representando el método más antiguo de desarrollo físico y espiritual.
Actualmente se ha definido el yoga como la ciencia clásica de la India que concierne a la unión entre el individuo, cuya existencia es finita, y lo Divino, que es infinito.
Los medios adecuados para obtener esta comunión trascendental se establecen en ocho grados, o niveles, considerados etapas para llegar al conocimiento del alma:

• Yama (son los mandamientos de la moral universal).
• Niyama (autopurificación por la disciplina).
• Asana (refiere a las posturas corporales).
• Pranayama (control rítmico de la respiración).
• Pratyahana (recogimiento y emancipación del espíritu de la dominación de los sentidos y objetos externos)
• Dharana (concentración).
• Dhyana (meditación).
• Samadhi (estado de superconsciencia alcanzado mediante una profunda meditación en la que el aspirante individual "Sadhaka" se convierte en uno con el objeto de su meditación, o sea, con Paramatma o Espiritu Universal).

Como aquí estamos sólo describiendo las bondades del yoga en el tratamiento del estrés, para poder, de alguna manera, simplificar la esencia de los preceptos descritos más arriba, los resumiremos en 5 principios fundamentales: el ejercicio adecuado, la respiración adecuada, las relajación adecuada, la alimentación adecuada y la meditación adecuada.

Ejercicio adecuado (Asanas)

Nuestro cuerpo físico está diseñado para moverse y ejercitarse, como el cuerpo de todos los seres del universo. Si nuestro estilo de vida es sedentario y priva a los músculos y las articulaciones de su movimiento natural, estipulado por la naturaleza, nos transformaremos en un blanco fácil para las enfermedades. Y si nos excedemos con ejercicios violentos para los que no estamos preparados, con una visión del cuerpo humano de sólo lo físico, los desgarros y lesiones aparecerán.

El ejercicio adecuado debe ser agradable para el practicante a la vez que beneficioso para el cuerpo, mente y vida espiritual. El yoga ve al cuerpo como un vehículo para el alma en su viaje hacia la perfección, los ejercicios físicos del yoga no están diseñados sólo para desarrollar el cuerpo; sino que fundamentalmente ayudan a la concentración y la paz interior, que se traduce en salud y bienestar.
Los ejercicios físicos del yoga se llaman Asanas, un término que significa postura. El Asana (o postura) debe mantenerse por cierto tiempo.
Aunque existen muchas Asanas, se resumen en 12 posturas básicas: Postura sobre la cabeza (Sirshasana); postura sobre los hombros (Sarvangasana); postura del arado (Halasana); postura del pez (Matsyasana); postura de la pinza (Paschimothanasana); postura de la cobra (Bhujangasana); postura del saltamontes (Shalabhasana); postura del arco (Dhanurasana); postura de la torsión (Ardha Matsyendrasana); postura del cuervo (Kakasana); postura de la pinza vertical (Pada Hasthasana) y postura del triángulo (Trikonasana). La más conocida, la postura del loto, se emplea para la meditación.

Respiración adecuada (Pranayama)

Una de las enseñanzas del yoga es la optimización del uso de toda nuestra capacidad pulmonar, con la consiguiente oxigenación sanguínea y de todo nuestro cuerpo. La respiración adecuada debe ser profunda, lenta y rítmica. Esto aumenta la vitalidad y la claridad mental. La mayoría de las personas usamos solamente una fracción de nuestra capacidad pulmonar. Respiramos de modo superficial, apenas expandiendo la caja torácica. Esto nos encorva, nos genera tensión en el cuello y la parte alta de la espalda. Esto se resuelve con una buena y completa respiración yóquica.

Hay tres tipos distintos de respiración.

• La respiración clavicular: es la más superficial y la peor. Durante la inhalación los hombros y la clavícula son elevados mientras que el abdomen es contraído. Se realiza un esfuerzo máximo, pero una mínima cantidad de aire es obtenida.
• La respiración torácica: es realizada con los músculos intercostales expandiendo el tórax, y constituye el segundo tipo de respiración incompleta.
• La respiración abdominal profunda: es la mejor, por cuanto lleva aire a la parte más baja y más amplia de los pulmones. La respiración es lenta y profunda, efectuándose por tanto un uso adecuado del diafragma.

De todos modos, ninguno de estos tipos es completo. Una respiración yóguica completa combina los tres, comenzando con una respiración profunda y continuando la inhalación a través de las zonas intercostal y clavicular.

Relajación adecuada (Savasana)

Por medio de una relajación adecuada de todos los músculos el practicante de yoga es capaz de rejuvenecer completamente su sistema nervioso y alcanzar una profunda sensación de paz. Cuando el cuerpo y la mente trabajan constantemente de modo excesivo, la persona se agota, transita por caminos errados y confusos, pierde energía y disminuye su eficacia natural. La vida social moderna, la comida, el trabajo, e incluso las actividades del tiempo libre, que deberían ser para descansar y aflojarse, hacen que la relajación resulte difícil. Muchos, hasta olvidaron que el descanso y la relajación, son modos naturales de reponer las energías. El común de la gente gasta mucha energía física y mental incluso al tratar de descansar, debido a la tensión. Gran cantidad de vigor corporal se consume inútilmente. Es decir, estamos completamente expuestos a la aparición del estrés. Recordemos que, en el curso de un día, nuestro cuerpo elabora todas las sustancias y energías necesarias para el día siguiente. Pero, sucede con frecuencia, que todas estas energías pueden ser consumidas en pocos minutos, por malhumor, cólera, ofensas, o irritación intensa. El proceso de irrupción y represión de emociones violentas, crece con frecuencia hasta convertirse en una conducta habitual. El resultado es desastroso, no sólo para la mente, sino también para el cuerpo. Nos conduce a un círculo vicioso del cual es más difícil cada vez salir.

Durante la relajación completa, no se consume prácticamente energía o "Prana", aunque se conserva un poco para mantener el cuerpo en condición normal, mientras que la porción restante se almacena y acumula. Para poder lograr una relajación perfecta, los yoguis utilizan tres tipos de relación: física, mental y espiritual.

Dieta adecuada

Los alimentos que consumimos no sólo nos proporcionan nutrientes, sino que afectan nuestra vida de manera global. Para una máxima eficiencia cuerpo-mente y una completa concien-

cia espiritual, el yoga propone una dieta lacto-vegetariana. Esta es una parte integral del estilo de vida yóguico.
La dieta yóguica es vegetariana, consistiendo en alimentos puros, simples y naturales los cuales se digieren en forma sencilla y promueven la salud. Las comidas simples ayudan a la digestión y asimilación de los nutrientes.
Los requerimientos nutricionales se dividen en cinco categorías: proteínas, carbohidratos, minerales, grasas y vitaminas. Uno debe tener un cierto conocimiento sobre dietética para poder balancear la dieta. Comer alimentos recién cosechados, frescos, provenientes de la naturaleza, que crecen en tierras fértiles (preferentemente orgánicos, libres de químicos y pesticidas), nos ayudan a tener un mejor aporte de estas necesidades nutricionales. El procesar, refinar y cocinar en exceso, destruye la mayor parte del valor de los alimentos.
Para el yoga, el sol es la fuente de energía para toda la vida en nuestro planeta, nutre las plantas (el vértice de la cadena alimenticia) las cuales luego son ingeridas por animales (vegetarianos), los cuales son comidos por otros animales (carnívoros). Los vegetales, al nutrirse directamente del sol, tienen las mayores propiedades para promover la vida. El valor alimenticio de la carne como fuente nutritiva se conoce como "de segunda mano", y es inferior en la naturaleza. Todos los alimentos naturales (frutas, vegetales, semillas, frutos secos y granos) tienen, en distintas proporciones, estos nutrientes esenciales. Como fuente de proteína son fácilmente asimilables por el organismo. Sin embargo, los alimentos de "segunda mano" son más difíciles para digerir y son de menor valor para el metabolismo del cuerpo. Una máxima de la filosofía del yoga expresa: "Come para vivir, no vivas para comer". Lo mejor es si entendemos que el propósito de comer es suministrar a nuestro organismo fuerza vital o

Prana, la energía vital para la vida. Por lo tanto el mejor plan nutricional para un estudiante de yoga es la dieta simple con alimentos naturales y frescos.

Meditación (Dhyana)

El yoga puede ayudarte a tener una visión positiva, entusiasta y alegre de las cosas. La mente podrá ser traída a un perfecto estado de control por medio de la práctica regular de la meditación. Cuando la mente está en calma, sin pensamientos ni deseos, puedes ver el "Ser", a esto se le llama "yoga". Podemos controlar la agitación mental de dos formas: concentrando la mente ya sea externa o internamente. Internamente, nos enfocamos en el "Ser" o la conciencia del "Yo soy". Externamente nos enfocamos en cualquier otra cosa que no sea "el Ser" o "Yo soy". Cuando nos tomamos un tiempo para concentrarnos en algo que estamos haciendo, en algo que requiere nuestra concentración, los demás pensamientos se aquietan.
La meditación no es algo que un yogui tenga que enseñarnos, ya que todos poseemos la habilidad para silenciar los pensamientos. La única diferencia entre esto y meditación (en forma positiva), es que aprendemos a concentrar la mente externamente, en objetos. Toda la felicidad que se logra a través de la mente es temporaria y efímera, está limitada por la naturaleza. Para alcanzar un estado de felicidad duradera y paz absoluta, primero debemos conocer como calmar la mente, concentrarnos e ir más allá de la mente. Llevando la concentración mental hacia el interior, hacia el ser, podemos profundizar la experiencia de la concentración perfecta. Este es el estado de meditación.

Hay ciertos puntos a tener en cuenta relacionados con las técnicas y estados de la meditación. Pero si bien hay distintas técnicas, la meditación yóguica debería tener en cuenta estos puntos:

- La regularidad en el tiempo, lugar y práctica es muy importante.
- Las horas más efectivas son al amanecer y al atardecer.
- Trata de poseer un cuarto adecuado y separado de otras actividades para la meditación.
- Selecciona tu orientación, (especialmente hacia el norte o hacia el este para poder tomar ventaja de las vibraciones magnéticas favorables).
- Comienza con cinco minutos de respiración abdominal profunda para llevar oxígeno al cerebro. Luego enlentece el ritmo hasta hacerlo imperceptible.
- Mantén la respiración rítmica.

La meditación es el tónico nervioso y mental más poderoso. La energía divina fluye libremente en la persona durante la meditación, ejerce una influencia benigna en la mente, los nervios, los órganos sensoriales y el cuerpo. Abre la puerta a un conocimiento intuitivo y reinos de dicha eterna. La mente se vuelve calma y firme impidiendo que se desarrollen las condiciones para la aparición del estrés.

¿Qué es?

El Tai Chi es una de las prácticas físicas provenientes de oriente, relacionada con la filosofía china, que las modernas sociedades occidentales descubrieron (y adoptaron) en el siglo que pasó. Su práctica trae aparejada mejoras en la salud, mayor capacidad de resistencia, fortaleza física y disminución del estrés. Es decir, es una actividad absolutamente relacionada entre salud física y mental.
El Tai Chi es un arte marcial de origen chino que se basa en el desarrollo de la energía interior mediante la práctica de movimientos suaves y predeterminados. Es una práctica intensa y completa, que resulta beneficiosa a cualquier edad.
El trabajo del Tai Chi ejercita conjuntamente al cuerpo, la mente y el espíritu, lo que lo convierte en el arte de la acción. Es por medio de la acción y del movimiento como se consigue a través del Tai Chi la fuerza y la relajación.
La práctica del Tai Chi desarrolla una energía interior que progresivamente se hace más sutil y refinada a la vez que aumenta la capacidad de estar activo con atención, flexibilidad y calma, con firmeza pero sin tensión. La armonización que provocan los movimientos del Tai Chi aumenta con la práctica, lo que hace que cada individuo que se dedica a la disciplina con constancia y concentración desarrolle por sí mismo el arte de la acción, arte que se manifiesta no solamente en el ejercicio específico sino también en la vida cotidiana, que comenzará a mejorar (a nivel no solamente físico sino también emocional, disminuyendo los factores estresantes) con el inicio de las sesiones de Tai Chi.

El Tai Chi sirve, entonces, para ser más equilibrado, más ágil, más fuerte, más veloz. La diferencia con las gimnasias occidentales (que prestan atención sólo a los aspectos físicos) se basa en que lo que busca el Tai Chi no es convertir a su practicante en una persona más fuerte, ágil o veloz solamente en el aspecto físico sino también en el aspecto mental: practicar Tai Chi nos volverá más veloces mentalmente, más seguros en nuestros razonamientos, más equilibrados en nuestros juicios.

En la práctica de este arte oriental se realizan movimientos circulares, lentos y suaves siempre coordinados con la respiración. Esta es fundamental para adquirir el dominio de los movimientos que constituyen el Tai Chi.

La respiración ayuda a la relajación y, con la relajación del cuerpo y de la mente, se consigue la armonía espiritual necesaria para desarrollar la práctica del Tai Chi. Con la tarea conjunta de cuerpo, mente y espíritu se proporcionará un masaje interno a los distintos órganos del cuerpo movilizando los músculos, tendones y articulaciones y, sobre todo, facilitando una buena oxigenación en los pulmones.

La conjunción entre práctica física y filosofía es total en la disciplina del Tai Chi: la forma misma de los movimientos del Tai Chi se relaciona con la forma del ying y el yang que tan popular se volvió en nuestras ciudades en los últimos decenios. Con la práctica del Tai Chi lograremos la fortaleza de la suavidad, el equilibrio y el encuentro de opuestos que son la base de la concepción china del ying y el yang.

En una sesión de Tai Chi se realizan ejercicios de calentamiento y estiramiento suaves que dotan al practicante de flexibilidad en forma gradual. Se realizan también ejercicios de respiración que incrementan la oxigenación y nos enseñan a respirar de forma completa.

Los movimientos de Tai Chi refuerzan los tendones, las articulaciones y la estructura ósea; realiza un trabajo constante en los músculos de la espalda y de la columna vertebral; alivia los hombros y el cuello, y aleja las contracturas, los mareos y las jaquecas, todos síntomas relacionados con el estrés cotidiano. Además, como valor agregado, el Tai Chi previene enfermedades, aumenta la resistencia del cuerpo, previene la osteoporosis, combate las dolencias en la espalda, ayuda a abrirse a quien sufre introversión y centra al extrovertido.

¿Cómo se practica el Tai Chi?

La práctica del Tai Chi es sumamente beneficiosa y, a la vez, placentera. No provoca el tipo de agitamiento físico característico de las gimnasias occidentales sino que, al contrario de éstas, se basa en movimientos continuos y relajados que no fuerzan los músculos del practicante sino que los hacen más ágiles y flexibles. Una sesión de Tai Chi se convierte así en un momento relajante y placentero.
Casi todos los ejercicios se realizan de pie e intervienen en su ejecución manos, dedos, brazos, piernas, espalda y cabeza. Vista desde afuera, la práctica del Tai Chi se asemeja entonces a un baile suave y lento, siempre buscando el equilibrio, siempre relajado y bello. Además de relajar y alejar el estrés, sirve para endurecer ciertos músculos y mantenerse en perfecta forma física. Una sesión de Tai Chi para principiantes consta de unos ejercicios de apertura de articulaciones y estiramiento de músculos y tendones para centrar la atención y la respiración. Lo que se practica es lo que se llama secuencia (en chino, kuen), lo que se busca es el aprendizaje de posiciones y movimientos de la se-

cuencia. Consiste en ejercicios de estiramiento, de relajación y de respiración, sentados o estirados.
La secuencia es, como dijimos, el centro de la práctica. Es una serie prefijada de posiciones y movimientos en los que se sintetizan las enseñanzas que se deben adquirir.
Como en la pintura, el piano o cualquier arte (y el Tai Chi, como vimos, es un arte marcial) al principio es necesario adquirir técnicas simples a través de repeticiones. Será, por lo tanto, iniciar la tarea con ganas y dedicación.
La guía del maestro o instructor será de completa ayuda, pero nunca suficiente. El alumno deberá practicar en su casa (si es posible todos los días, en todo caso con constancia y seriedad) para lograr, a través de la repetición del movimiento, la flexibilidad necesaria. Los efectos sobre el estado de ánimo y el tono general serán inmediatos.

¿Cualquiera puede practicar Tai Chi?

La respuesta a esta pregunta es definitiva: sí, totalmente. Cualquiera puede practicar Tai Chi, no existen contraindicaciones. A diferencia de las gimnasias o deportes occidentales (en muchos casos contraindicados por la violencia de sus movimientos o por la agitación que provocan), el Tai Chi puede ser practicado por cualquier persona, cualquiera sea su estado físico. Y para todos será beneficioso.
Este arte marcial chino provee de múltiples beneficios a sus practicantes. Para muchos el inicio en la práctica de la disciplina será el momento de comenzar a descubrir su cuerpo y las posibilidades del movimiento. Se aprenderá a respirar de manera completa, se ejercitarán la memoria y la concentración. Se aprende-

rá a valorar el silencio, a estar atentos a nuestro cuerpo, a sus mínimas reacciones. Se desarrollará el sentido del equilibrio.
Durante una sesión de Tai Chi se aprenderá, también, a estar más cómodamente de pie. Esta disciplina nos procurará mayor flexibilidad mental, nos ayudará a ser más creativos. Nos ayudará a ejercitar la vista y entrenar la visión periférica, nos facilitará el descanso nocturno, aumentará nuestro buen humor. Si podemos practicar la disciplina al aire libre los resultados serán más positivos aún.
Todos estos beneficios que provoca la práctica del Tai Chi son los que nos llevan a afirmar que cualquiera puede practicar Tai Chi. Durante el embarazo, por ejemplo, la futura madre demanda una mayor cantidad de oxígeno y la práctica del Tai Chi ayuda a oxigenar tanto el organismo de la futura madre como el del bebé. También ayuda a lograr la relajación y concentración necesarias para afrontar sin miedo el momento de la dilatación en el parto.
También pueden practicar el Tai Chi los niños (desde los cinco años sería la edad recomendada, pero en realidad desde el momento en que logra estar parado el niño puede comenzar a practicar la disciplina) así como los adultos y ancianos de cualquier edad. Esto es posible porque el Tai Chi no requiere de una resistencia física especial y no cansa, tan sólo hacen falta para su práctica la paciencia y el tesón.
En ocasiones a las personas demasiado nerviosas o ansiosas les cuesta iniciarse en la práctica del Tai Chi, porque la disciplina requiere, como dijimos, de concentración y constancia. Pero una vez superada la barrera inicial incluso aquellas personas demasiado ansiosas descubrirán que la práctica del Tai Chi ayuda a liberar tensiones y ansiedades. Estas personas agradecerán especialmente la relajación que obtienen en su mente y la flexibi-

lidad que adquiere su musculatura acostumbrada a estar en constante tensión.

¿Qué necesitamos para practicar Tai Chi?

Parte del éxito de la disciplina del Tai Chi, como dijimos, se basa en el hecho de que este puede comenzar a practicarse a cualquier edad, y en que cualquiera pueda practicarlo. Pero no es solo esta razón la que explica el éxito de la disciplina. Otra poderosa razón es que, para practicar el Tai Chi, no se precisa de ningún accesorio, nos bastamos nosotros solos y un espacio no demasiado grande.

La ropa que utilizaremos deberá ser cómoda, y los ejercicios podrán ser desarrollados en cualquier lugar. Lo ideal, claro, sería realizarlos en medio de la naturaleza, pero esto no es excluyente.

Podremos, además, practicar el Tai Chi en grupo o en soledad. La práctica en grupo favorece el sentimiento de unidad entre los practicantes; la práctica individual puede usarse como meditación en movimiento y nos ayudará a encontrar en nosotros aquello que tenemos en común con nuestro entorno; podrá entonces decirse que la práctica del Tai Chi, al ayudarnos a entender que entre la naturaleza y la especie humana no hay una línea divisoria sino que una y otra son inseparables, nos vuelve entorno.

La Forma, el conjunto de movimientos encadenados que se realizan de manera lenta, uniforme y sin interrupción y que es la base del Tai Chi, puede ejecutarse con las manos vacías o también con armas. Existe también un conjunto de ejercicios que se realizan por parejas, denominados Tui Shous.

Si no tenemos mucho espacio para desarrollar toda la Forma podemos escoger un movimiento y ejercitarlo sin movernos del sitio, en posición estática. A medida que aumentamos la práctica, podemos exigirnos más en las posiciones de los movimientos y así escoger si queremos más meditación, con más lentitud en el desarrollo, o más ejercicio físico, extremando las posiciones, dentro, por supuesto, de los principios fundamentales del Tai Chi.

¿Cómo cumple el Tai Chi con su función terapéutica?

El Tai Chi, como dijimos, ejerce su función terapéutica a través de los movimientos que propone. La respiración abdominal, por ejemplo, tiene un gran valor en el campo terapéutico. En la práctica de la disciplina el abdomen está flexible y el pecho relajado, convirtiendo la respiración en profunda, lenta, uniforme y suave, aportando así un mayor equilibrio en el funcionamiento del sistema respiratorio y siendo uno de los pilares para alejar los estados de estrés por el esfuerzo cotidiano.
El Tai Chi favorece la digestión. Sus movimientos activan el funcionamiento intestinal y la respiración abdominal relaja el estómago, por lo que la práctica de la disciplina se convierte en particularmente recomendable para las personas de edad.
El Tai Chi ayuda a mejorar la psicomotricidad. Durante la práctica debe de existir una estrecha relación entre la flexibilidad y la estabilidad, la respiración, la continuidad y la fluidez del movimiento. La perfecta armonía entre todos estos factores hacen resaltar los beneficios del Tai Chi sobre la tonicidad muscular y la motricidad.

Todos los movimientos son realizados de forma unificada, sin rupturas. Los movimientos parten de la cintura en donde está situado el centro de gravedad del cuerpo. La cintura, en el Tai Chi, podríamos decir, es el amo y el cuerpo el criado. La forma circular de los movimientos, la experiencia de la energía y su dirección, interior y exterior, constituyen la base del principio de globalidad y unidad que rige la concepción de la disciplina.
El ejercicio del Tai Chi ayuda progresivamente a sentir la unión entre relajación y estabilidad en el movimiento. En la práctica se aprende a guardar la energía que no es débil ni rígida. Así el abatimiento, la crispación y la discontinuidad del gesto ceden poco a poco a una armonía de gestos y posturas. Este aspecto está relacionado con una regulación de la respiración que se hace más profunda, lenta y regular.
El Tai Chi contribuye también a un mejor empleo y a un control más consciente de la energía. Descubrir con la atención la relación entre la dirección del movimiento, la flexibilidad y la respiración abdominal es el medio para alcanzar este equilibrio tónico.
En el tratamiento de las personas disminuidas en el plano motor, el aporte del Tai Chi puede ser muy beneficioso. Dos aspectos importantes aparecen relacionados con este tema: por un lado la globalidad del movimiento y las posturas ayudan a la persona a sentir una parte del cuerpo en relación con su cuerpo entero, por otra parte la práctica despierta una sensibilidad que contribuye a integrar la parte corporal disminuida. En el caso de lesiones perdurables y difíciles de sanar, los ejercicios del Tai Chi pueden desarrollar una percepción más unificada del cuerpo y a la vez contribuir a una mejoría.
La inhibición del cuerpo puede expresar la pena, la angustia, la desconfianza consigo mismo, entre otras cosas. La práctica del

Tai Chi puede contribuir a remediar y favorecer una armonización y una liberación progresiva del movimiento, de la respiración y de la atención. La práctica lleva a sentir la fluidez de los gestos, lleva al practicante a sentir aquello que lo une con la tierra, ayuda a descubrir la suavidad en la actividad -y esto influye sobre la mente y nos permite percibir cómo nos volvemos, poco a poco, menos rígidos y más flexibles- como dijimos, no solo a nivel físico sino también a nivel mental y espiritual. La conciencia de uno mismo en la acción y una mayor y mejor percepción del espacio ayudan a desarrollar a la vez una diferenciación y una unificación entre uno mismo y el exterior, entre el dentro y el afuera, entre lo interior y lo exterior.
La atención en la respiración permite que poco a poco las imágenes y los pensamientos se expresen sin que uno sea invadido por esa actividad interior. La práctica ayuda a percibir el movimiento de la energía interior, a sentir y a contener la ola de la actividad mental y emocional sin huir y sin luchar. La fluidez en el movimiento se refleja en la fluidez de los pensamientos y sensaciones, que comienzan a pasar por nuestro cuerpo como un río que siempre es el mismo pero siempre es diferente.
La práctica del Tai Chi desarrolla la capacidad de percibir las imágenes y los sentimientos inconscientes, que se corresponde también al principio de atención y de no luchar que es la base del Tai Chi. La práctica de la disciplina conlleva así un beneficio terapéutico cuando uno lo practica con constancia.
Tradicionalmente se ha dicho que el Tai Chi favorece la longevidad. La práctica del movimiento y la circulación de la energía y la acumulación del aliento en el abdomen producen un efecto regenerador. El aliento interior es la fuerza vital.
Por esto, cuando se dice que el Tai Chi es beneficioso para la longevidad, significa no solamente que la práctica contribuye a

un mejoramiento y a una regeneración celular de todas las partes de nuestro cuerpo, sino también que el aliento interno unificado proporciona una salud vigorosa.

La práctica del Tai Chi también desarrolla progresivamente un equilibrio interior entre el cuerpo y la mente. Las energías dispersadas en el cuerpo provocan las enfermedades cuando las mismas circulan de una forma desordenada y caótica. El Tai Chi ayuda a sentir, a unificar y a guiar estas energías; la medicina tradicional china atribuye las enfermedades a un desequilibrio entre el ying y el yang, para remediarlo es necesario disminuir el exceso de uno y evitar la insuficiencia del otro. La armonía de la práctica aparece aquí en su dimensión psicosomática.

Favoreciendo el equilibrio y la unificación interna, el Tai Chi permite transformar la alternancia de tensión y depresión que nos propone la vida en las sociedades occidentales modernas. Reencontrar la fuente de unidad no lleva al practicante a refugiarse en la práctica del Tai Chi: muy por el contrario, todo el equilibrio que logramos con el Tai Chi se trasladará a nuestra vida cotidiana y a nuestras relaciones; esto nos permitirá actuar con seguridad y confianza en todos los ámbitos de nuestra vida.

Este arte del movimiento cumple una función terapéutica muy eficaz para prevenir las enfermedades, conservando y vigorizando la salud, y puede ayudar a numerosas personas a descubrir que existe una unidad entre cuerpo y espíritu que nunca sospecharon. Así como la medicina occidental divide a las enfermedades del cuerpo de las de la mente (unas son tratadas por médicos y otras por psicólogos), el Tai Chi entiende que cuerpo y mente conforman un todo indivisible. La práctica del Tai Chi mejora, entonces, cuerpo y mente a través de la fluidez del movimiento. Todo esto puede ser esencial para cuidar nuestro cuerpo y erradicar el estrés de nuestra vida.

¿Cómo aprender el arte del Tai Chi?

El que se inicia en la práctica del Tai Chi, por el propio desconocimiento de la disciplina, pocas veces puede saber, en un primer momento, si el maestro elegido es lo suficientemente bueno o capaz. En todo caso, será bueno averiguar bastante antes de elegir un maestro. Mucha gente se equivoca y elige al maestro sólo por la cercanía con el hogar propio o porque los horarios que maneja le resultan cómodos, pero no parece esta la opción adecuada: a veces será más beneficioso resignar un poco de comodidad para acceder a las clases de aquel maestro con el que nos hayamos sentido más cómodos o confiados.
En cuanto al aprendizaje sin instructor sólo es posible tras conocer los principios básicos de las posiciones y el movimiento. Sin este conocimiento es fácil cometer errores.

El Tai Chi y la salud

Desde el punto de vista terapéutico, el Tai Chi es un arte excelente que ayuda a conservar la salud y a detener las enfermedades. Como se puede leer en el libro de medicina clásica china de Huang Ti: "Aquellos que están constantemente enfermos, fatigados ó afiebrados, deben ser tratados con ejercicios físicos livianos". Esto es lo que hace el Tai Chi, nos propone movimientos suaves pero sumamente poderosos.
La energía que fluye por nuestro cuerpo y nos mantiene vivos parte de lo que los orientales denominan Tan Tien (un punto que se sitúa a tres dedos del ombligo) lugar donde se encuentra el centro vital que permite realizar cualquier movimiento sin el empleo de la fuerza y sin provocar tensión de ningún tipo, lo

que contribuye a que con el tiempo los gestos cotidianos se realicen de forma natural, sin posibilidad de dolor por una mala postura o el giro brusco de alguna articulación.
Uno de los postulados que manejan los maestros del Tai Chi es que cuanto más tiempo se puede retener el aliento, mayor será el volumen de aire inspirado. Este incremento representa un aumento del poder del Chi (energía).
El método para concentrar el Chi es una característica que identifica al Tai Chi y es lo que la diferencia de otros tipos de ejercicios. Al eliminar el estrés, permite controlar todas las patologías que el mismo provoca.
Esto demuestra la importancia del Tai Chi que, a diferencia de otras gimnasias o deportes clásicos, cumple con las siguientes funciones terapéuticas:

• Reunifica toda la energía que habitualmente está dispersa y se malgasta. El primer efecto que sentirá el practicante del Tai Chi será una sensación de bienestar en todo el cuerpo, los músculos trabajarán sin rigidez produciendo una verdadera descontracción muscular que hará desaparecer poco a poco las tensiones nerviosas, favoreciendo el buen funcionamiento de las glándulas internas.

• Aumenta y procura una respiración profunda y abdominal, que produce un efecto benéfico sobre los órganos internos. La rotación continua de las caderas y la cintura, aporta gran elasticidad a los músculos abdominales que, al contraerse, efectúan un verdadero masaje sobre el hígado, bazo e intestinos; este masaje provoca un mejoramiento de los procesos nutritivos y digestivos, previniendo la aparición de úlceras.

• Tonifica el corazón y regulariza su ritmo, mejorando la circulación de la sangre, previniendo la presión arterial alta así como las enfermedades cardíacas, la tuberculosis pulmonar, el reumatismo articular, la anemia, la obesidad y otras dolencias en especial las crónicas.

• Previene los dolores lumbares. El Tai Chi está indicado para prevenir y hacer desaparecer tanto dolores lumbares como cualquier otra patología de columna vertebral, elemento primordial del cuerpo que se refuerza y flexibiliza con la práctica constante del Tai Chi.

• Otorga un carácter estable y apacible, dando una serena energía para enfrentar los problemas cotidianos. Este aspecto es fundamentalmente notable, en especial para el público occidental, que no comprende cómo una actividad física puede redundar en beneficios psicológicos. Esto es posible, como dijimos, porque el Tai Chi no entiende al cuerpo y a la mente como entidades separadas sino como parte de un mismo individuo en el que todas las partes están interrelacionadas.

• Moviliza las articulaciones y grupos musculares sin dañarlos. Los movimientos que propone el Tai Chi movilizan articulaciones y músculos sin forzarlos. Esto es lo que permite que todos puedan practicar el Tai Chi.

• Concentra al máximo la atención con el consiguiente beneficio del sistema central.

La capacidad de concentración que nos brinda el Tai Chi se relaciona con la meditación que el Tai Chi nos propone. Es un tipo de meditación que suele ser incomprendida en occidente. En occidente se vincula a la idea de meditación con la de reflexión o pensamiento. En oriente la idea de meditación significa todo lo contrario. Meditar, para un oriental, significa liberarse de los pensamientos, poner la mente en blanco. Y esto, que suena tan fácil pero que resulta tan difícil de lograr en la vida cotidiana, se logra justamente a través del movimiento. La concentración en la secuencia de movimientos que nos propone la disciplina logra que la mente se despeje de todo tipo de preocupaciones o pensamientos. Mientras dura la sesión de Tai Chi, la secuencia lo es todo, porque el practicante se convierte en la encarnación de la secuencia, esto hace que el practicante se acerque a la perfección, porque la secuencia es perfecta.

Una gimnasia terapéutica

Todo lo dicho hasta aquí, suponemos, podría convencer hasta al más escéptico sobre las bondades de la disciplina. Pero esto no es todo. Hay más.

El estado actual de la investigación médica indica que el Tai Chi es un excelente ejercicio para tratar a las personas mayores de edad. La práctica del Tai Chi mejora el equilibrio, reduce la posibilidad de sufrir caídas e incrementa la fuerza en las piernas. Rebaja las hormonas del estrés, mejora las funciones respiratoria, cardiovascular e inmunitaria, y promueve el bienestar emocional.

Para la medicina tradicional china, como mencionamos anteriormente, la enfermedad se produce cuando existen bloqueos en la libre circulación de la energía por los meridianos del cuerpo.

Al igual que la acupuntura, el Tai Chi, con sus movimientos suaves y armónicos contribuye a flexibilizar las articulaciones, disolver los bloqueos crónicos y restaurar el libre flujo energético.
En la actualidad, oriente busca mejorar los resultados obtenidos con sus técnicas tradicionales, combinando su medicina con la clásica medicina occidental. En tanto, en occidente, los centros de salud holísticos incorporaron no sólo el Tai Chi, sino todas las propuestas de la medicina tradicional china, como una forma de ofrecer a las personas todos los métodos existentes para su curación.
En resumen, el Tai Chi constituye una gimnasia sana y terapéutica que conserva la salud y ayuda a la curación de distintas enfermedades y a combatir el estrés. Para obtener estos beneficios, es de destacar lo que enseñan los maestros: en la práctica del Tai Chi debemos tener disciplina, perseverancia y paciencia.

Reflexología

¿Qué es?

La reflexología es una técnica oriental milenaria, que ayuda a equilibrar el nivel energético corporal, estimulando el propio mecanismo de autocuración del cuerpo. Este método ayuda a activar los poderes curativos de nuestro organismo. Es una forma moderna y a la vez muy antigua de mejorar la calidad de vida.
Es básicamente una técnica benéfica, basada en la estimulación

y manejo de puntos específicos (llamados puntos reflejos). Dichos puntos están distribuidos en sitios claves del cuerpo humano: manos, pies, ojos, etc.
La reflexología trabaja estimulando estos puntos específicos en manos y pies, principalmente, como una forma de terapia, para aliviar dolor u otro síntoma en los diferentes órganos del cuerpo. Es una experiencia relajante, segura, saludable, no es invasora y estimula al organismo en los procesos de curación. En concreto la reflexología es una forma muy sencilla y práctica de poder restablecer la salud de las personas y disminuir la influencia del estrés en nuestra vida.
La reflexología tiene su base en el conocimiento de la localización de una serie de zonas que se manipulan para, mediante una reacción refleja, restaurar las corrientes energéticas linfáticas y sanguíneas, y liberar mediante el masaje, una serie de impulsos eléctricos que activan y vitalizan el tono de los órganos sobre los que tienen influencia.
Las personas que practican la reflexología, se han concentrado principalmente en los pies, a pesar de que trabajar los reflejos a lo largo de todo el cuerpo también puede resultar favorable.
La reflexología no utiliza ningún tipo de medicación, simplemente se trata de dar un masaje específico en la zona correspondiente del cuerpo. De esta forma, provoca que la energía del cuerpo fluya por determinados canales, conectando cada órgano y cada glándula con su punto final o punto de presión en los pies, las manos u otra parte del cuerpo.
En la reflexología, los masajes actúan como disparadores de un efecto tranquilizante, que aumenta el flujo sanguíneo y permite obtener un beneficio global para el cuerpo.
El objetivo de la reflexología es obtener una respuesta saludable de los órganos, sistemas o estructuras, mediante la adecuada es-

timulación aplicada a sus correspondientes zonas micro reflejas; logrando con ello establecer el balance natural de la energía y funcionalidad armónica de todo el organismo.
La reflexología reduce la tensión, activa la circulación sanguínea y linfática y restablece el funcionamiento orgánico y hormonal. Se utiliza en infinidad de casos y resulta especialmente efectiva aliviando el estrés y la tensión; en dolores (de espalda, cabeza y dientes), en tratamientos de desórdenes digestivos, resfriados y gripes, asma, artritis, entre otras.
La acción del masaje de reflexología produce un efecto tranquilizante, que aumenta el flujo sanguíneo y permite obtener un beneficio global para el cuerpo.
A modo de síntesis, nombramos algunos de los beneficios que se obtienen por medio de la reflexología:

- Reduce el estrés, produciendo una relajación profunda. Alivia los síntomas producidos por el mismo, ayuda a controlarlo, reduce la ansiedad y permite que el organismo recobre el equilibrio perdido.

- Mejora la circulación sanguínea, facilitando el transporte de oxígeno y nutrientes a las células.

- Ayuda en la limpieza de toxinas e impurezas, contribuyendo a eliminarlas. De esta forma, se evita que pasen a las células.

- Ayuda al equilibrio de los distintos sistemas del organismo. Todos los elementos de nuestro cuerpo contribuyen de forma sinérgica para su buen funcionamiento.

- Elimina bloqueos existentes, revitalizando la energía.

• Estimula el sistema inmunológico, previniendo así la aparición de enfermedades y recaídas.

• Mejora la calidad de vida en procesos crónicos y terminales.

Acupuntura

¿Qué es la acupuntura?

La acupuntura es una técnica fundamental dentro del sistema médico chino. Mediante la inserción de agujas en precisos puntos anatómicos del cuerpo, favorece el equilibrio del sistema energético-vital, aliviando ciertos síntomas asociados con muchas enfermedades. Se cree que los puntos anatómicos (puntos de la acupuntura) tienen ciertas propiedades eléctricas, las cuales afectan a los neurotransmisores químicos del cuerpo.
Dichos puntos se encuentran situados en una serie de canales o meridianos: existen doce meridianos básicos, correspondientes a los cinco órganos y cinco vísceras fundamentales, a través de los cuales se distribuye la energía vital (o Chi) por todo el cuerpo.
Cada uno de estos puntos se punza para lograr un resultado determinado. La punción puede tener tres fines:

• Volver al equilibrio el flujo vital desequilibrado.
• Estimular el flujo vital.
• Sedar el flujo vital.

Los puntos más importantes, aquellos que regulan el fondo energético, se hallan situados de codos a dedos (en los antebrazos) y de rodillas a pies (en la pierna).

Para la medicina tradicional china tanto los órganos (que son de naturaleza ying) como las entrañas o vísceras (de condición yang), tienen funciones asociadas mucho más amplias que las otorgadas en occidente. Funciones que van desde su estructura más fisiológica a la más profunda o emocional; a modo de ejemplo: el corazón, órgano ying, regula el flujo y el ritmo sanguíneo, la sangre y los vasos. Pero, además, controla el pensamiento, el habla, la memoria, la calidad del sueño y la alegría y se refleja en la lengua, por lo que, en ocasiones, para tratar a un paciente cardíaco es necesario trabajar sobre la lengua del mismo. Esto permite, claro, dejar de lado las costosas operaciones que nos propone la medicina occidental, que utiliza mayormente técnicas invasivas.

La acupuntura es una de las prácticas médicas más antiguas del mundo, originada en China hace más de cuatro mil quinientos años. De acuerdo con las teorías de la medicina tradicional china, el cuerpo humano tiene más de dos mil puntos de acupuntura conectados por medio de vías o meridianos. Estas vías crean un flujo de energía (Chi) a través del cuerpo que es el responsable de la salud general. La interrupción en el flujo de la energía puede causar enfermedades. La acupuntura puede corregir estos desequilibrios cuando se aplican las agujas en puntos precisos, mejorando el flujo de Chi.

Las teorías de la acupuntura han sido corroboradas en extensas investigaciones de laboratorio y se han vuelto, entonces, muy conocidas y aceptadas. Además, en estudios controlados se ha demostrado la efectividad de la acupuntura para tratar ciertas dolencias.

Son, hoy, cientos de miles los acupuntores certificados en occidente. No todos los acupuntores son médicos pero sí lo son una tercera parte de los mismos, profesionales que han integrado la acupuntura a su práctica médica.

La acupuntura generalmente se realiza con agujas metálicas, sólidas y delgadas como del tamaño de un cabello. La gran mayoría de los pacientes siente un dolor mínimo en el momento de inserción de la aguja -otros, ni siquiera eso- incluso muchos pacientes expresan que, al final de la sesión de acupuntura, se sienten relajados y fuertes.
Además de las agujas, la acupuntura utiliza otras formas de estimulación. Entre ellas podemos mencionar las siguientes:

- Calor
- Presión (acupresión)
- Fricción
- Succión
- Impulsos de energía electromagnética

¿Para qué sirve?

La acupuntura es una terapia global, es decir, una terapia que sirve para tratar diversos tipos de enfermedades y dolencias. La acupuntura se utiliza generalmente para aliviar dolores, pero sus aplicaciones terapéuticas se han ampliado gradualmente. En la actualidad, la acupuntura se utiliza ampliamente en el tratamiento de adicciones, en tratamientos contra el exceso de peso y también para acelerar la recuperación del paciente después de una cirugía.

Pero la lista de dolencias que pueden ser tratadas con la acupuntura es muy amplia y, más importante, crece a medida que la investigación continúa.

Mencionaremos, en la siguiente lista, algunas de las enfermedades y dolencias que hoy son tratadas por medio de la acupuntura: falta de hambre, hemorroides, insomnio, asma, lesiones musculares, depresión, dolores de muela, espalda, cabeza, garganta u oído; náuseas, artritis, resfríos, sinusitis y, en el caso que nos interesa, todos los tipos de estrés, sus síntomas y consecuencias.

Como la meta de la acupuntura es ayudar al organismo en su proceso de autosanación, es de gran ayuda para mantener y mejorar la salud, ya que los acupuntores pueden detectar y ajustar los pequeños desbalanceos de energía antes de que lleguen a generar una enfermedad seria.

¿Cómo es el tratamiento?

Para evaluar las necesidades del paciente, el acupuntor inicia la sesión con un extenso cuestionario al paciente. Éste será amplio, mucho más extenso que el que realizan habitualmente los médicos occidentales. El acupuntor preguntará por las horas de sueño, por la alimentación habitual e, incluso, hasta por los ingresos económicos del paciente (en el "Nei King" se justifica esta curiosidad explicando que si el paciente es rico y su comida abundante es difícil que su energía defensiva pueda estar debilitada).

Después procederá al examen físico del paciente, tomándole el pulso, mirándole la lengua y haciéndole diversas preguntas acerca de su estado de salud, alimentación y estilo de vida. El acupuntor necesitará saber si debe tratar con una persona sedentaria o con alguien que realiza ejercicio físico, si su paciente se alimenta de manera correcta o si lo hace de manera desordenada. El examen físico incluirá el estudio del pulso radial, en el que el médico distingue hasta doce diferentes tipos de pulsación: seis en cada muñeca, que se dividen en superficiales, profundas y medias.

Cada uno de ellas proporciona indicaciones precisas sobre el estado de cada órgano. Tras este examen, el acupuntor hace tenderse al paciente y, de acuerdo con los datos del pulso, busca en los meridianos correspondientes los puntos de mayor resistencia, que es donde sitúa las agujas. En este momento se inicia el tratamiento propiamente dicho.

Mientras éste dure, el acupuntor insertará agujas en la piel del paciente. Las agujas penetrarán solamente unos milímetros en las áreas de piel delgada y más profundamente en zonas donde la piel es más gruesa.

El número de agujas que se utilizan, su tamaño, su forma y la profundidad a la que se clavan depende del efecto que quiera conseguirse. La rotación que el acupuntor les da en el momento de su inserción puede hacer que el efecto sea sedante o bien que aumente la energía del punto.

Una alimentación
anti-estrés

Colección conocer y aprender

Una alimentación anti-estrés

Como ya hemos visto, el estrés nos afecta en el plano físico, mental y espiritual. Y lo físico está completamente vinculado con la calidad de nuestra alimentación. En este caso, en la relación estrés-alimentación, podemos decir que se trata de un camino de ida y vuelta: el estrés afecta la alimentación y, la mala alimentación que llevamos a cabo diariamente puede desarrollar el terreno para que el estrés nos invada.

Más allá de los síntomas que ya hemos detallado, una mala alimentación sumada a las condiciones laborales, familiares o personales propensas al estrés, pueden provocar una reducción en nuestra calidad de vida. Entre los errores más comunes podemos citar:

• Ingerir alimentos de digestión larga.
• Comer fuera de horarios.
• No desayunar para llegar temprano al trabajo o llevar a los niños a la escuela, sin entender que la primera comida del día es la más importante.
• No respetar los requerimientos diarios de hidratos de carbono, grasas, proteínas, vitaminas y minerales.
• Realizar una sola comida fuerte al día, y generalmente a la noche, cuando lo esencial es cenar muy liviano.

Todo eso se manifiesta en:

• Comportamientos irascibles frente a familiares, amigos o compañeros de trabajo.
• Un descanso incompleto pues el cuerpo tarda en digerir los alimentos.
• Aparición de enfermedades estomacales o gastrointestinales.
• Menor deseos de realizar otras actividades, perdiendo el tiempo de ocio y pensando solo en las complicaciones que nos afectan a diario.

Conociendo los errores que cometemos al alimentarnos y las consecuencias que tienen sobre el estrés, podemos emprender un programa para eliminar de nuestra dieta la mayor carga de tensiones, presiones y malestares que se generan por una ingesta inadecuada de alimentos.

Algunas de las costumbres saludables que podríamos adoptar son:

• Relajarse antes de comer.
• No buscar escapar de las presiones cotidianas sentándonos a comer.
• Si ha llegado la hora de la comida y no tenemos hambre, es preferible no comer por costumbre.
• No comer nunca hasta saciar el apetito, sino que debemos ingerir sólo una porción normal para disminuir la ansiedad.
• No irse a la cama hasta que hayan pasado al menos dos horas de la cena, para hacer la digestión despiertos y no durante el sueño.

Obviamente que un estado de estrés necesitará el chequeo y la revisión de un médico junto a un tratamiento. No podremos superarlo solamente con un cambio en la dieta, pero, indudablemente, podremos aliviar las cargas que producen una digestión larga y pesada si dejamos de lado los alimentos contraindicados.

La idea es modificar la manera de alimentarnos, incorporar a la dieta aquellos productos beneficiosos para los distintos órganos del cuerpo y acostumbrarnos a un nuevo régimen que, en un tiempo medio, traerá muchos beneficios al organismo, como la reducción del estrés.

Más allá de aconsejar sobre determinados alimentos que son saludables, aquí se trata de tomar conciencia, poner un poco nuestro propio sentido común y eliminar aquellas sustancias que todos sabemos que nos afectan, dificultan nuestra digestión

o aumentan la acumulación de grasas: frituras, aceites, excesos de carne roja o de caza, chocolates, dulces, etcétera. El primer paso para alimentarnos sanamente, es darnos cuenta de aquellas cosas que nos afectan y dejarlas de lado.
Una vez que hayamos comprendido esa situación, habremos dado un paso fundamental que nos ayudará en el segundo escalón de este camino: añadir a nuestras comidas los productos ricos en vitaminas, minerales, antioxidantes o proteínas de origen natural, sin la necesidad de recurrir a esos complejos químicos alimentarios que se comercializan en el mercado y que, en la mayoría de los casos, son más perjudiciales de lo que pensamos.

Como todo esto quizás no parece tan relacionado con el estrés, es necesario señalar que los alimentos ricos en minerales y vitaminas son los nutrientes esenciales del sistema nervioso, por tal razón, si ese sistema se encuentra fuerte la posibilidad de que se desarrolle el estrés se encontrará más lejana.

Entre los recursos naturales que debemos incorporar, no deberían faltar los siguientes minerales, vitaminas y alimentos:

Alimentos ricos en magnesio:
- alejan la depresión.
- son tranquilizantes y no producen irritabilidad.
- debe combinarse con calcio para maximizar su rendimiento.

Alimentos ricos en calcio y fósforo:
- son fundamentales pues el estrés disminuye las reservas de ambos minerales.
- favorecen la fortaleza mental y la estabilidad nerviosa.

• aceleran la recuperación corporal en los casos de estrés agudo.
• necesitan la presencia de vitamina C y D.

Alimentos ricos en hierro:
• colabora en el transporte del oxígeno a los diferentes órganos, especialmente a los pulmones.
• son "protectores" naturales contra el estrés.
• producen mayores beneficios cuando se combinan con el cobre.

Alimentos ricos en vitamina A:
• cuidan las células nerviosas e impiden el desgaste del sistema nervioso.
• protegen las membranas mucosas.
• evitan las infecciones.

Alimentos ricos en vitamina B:
• son los principales protectores del sistema nervioso y, especialmente las de los grupos B12 y B15, son imprescindibles en los cuadros de estrés agudo.
• regeneran el nivel de glóbulos rojos.
• están íntimamente relacionados con la acumulación de energía y fuerza.

Alimentos ricos en vitamina C:
• recomponen las células afectadas por estrés.
• ayudan en los procesos auto-curativos del cuerpo en la mayoría de los órdenes.

Alimentos ricos en vitamina D:
• ayudan en la absorción del fósforo y del calcio.

Alimentos ricos en vitamina E:

• colaboran en la oxigenación del sistema nervioso y de los músculos; facilitando el trabajo del corazón.

• son unos de los más recomendados en estados agudos de estrés pues previenen todas las enfermedades cardíacas.

• impiden la formación de coágulos sanguíneos provocados por fuertes presiones o ataques de nervios.

Todos estos minerales y vitaminas deben ser ingeridos de manera natural, a través de los distintos alimentos que los contienen. En todos los casos una visita al nutricionista será fundamental para elaborar una dieta que reúna todos estos nutrientes. Dentro de lo posible, y salvo por prescripción médica, deben evitarse los complementos dietarios para reemplazarlos. A continuación enumeramos algunos alimentos que podrían incluirse en una dieta anti-estrés:

Naranja y otros cítricos:

• aporta la cuota diaria necesario de vitamina C.

• refuerza las defensas.

Banana:

• incluye varias vitaminas, entre ellas, la A, la B y la C.

• contiene los minerales básicos (magnesio, potasio, calcio, hierro y cobre).

• calma el apetito y se digiere muy fácilmente.

Brócoli:

• posee vitamina C.

• como todas las verduras, cuanta menor cocción reciban, serán más nutritivas.

Nueces:

• son una fuente de energía y proteínas que pueden consumirse junto a otros alimentos.
• son altamente vigorizantes para los estados de estrés.

Pasas de uva:

• poseen magnesio, hierro, calcio, potasio, fósforo y cobre.
• cuentan con un alto nivel de vitaminas B1 y B6.

Almendras:

• es un alimento muy completo.
• posee la mayoría de los nutrientes necesarios para el sistema nervioso.
• contiene minerales y es una alta fuente de proteínas.

Espinaca:

• es una verdura rica en vitamina A.
• al igual que todas las verduras de hojas verdes, cuenta con distintos minerales (hierro, cobre, magnesio, calcio, etcétera) y todas las vitaminas del grupo B.

Leche:

• es una de las principales fuentes de calcio y uno de los alimentos esenciales.
• aporta potasio, fósforo y varias vitaminas, como la B12.

Cereales:

• la mayoría de ellos son curativos.
• poseen varias vitaminas, entre ellas, la B y la E y numerosos minerales.
• son beneficiosos para el sistema nervioso y curativos del estrés.

Alimentos nocivos

Muchos productos y alimentos son consumidos por ser sabrosos "me fascinan los chocolates", o por tener distintas cualidades "el café me mantiene despierto"; sin embargo, detrás de ellos se esconden muchos de los males que afectan a nuestra alimentación, dañan el sistema nervioso central, aceleran el ritmo cardíaco, aumentan los niveles de colesterol, producen males estomacales, perjudican la digestión, alteran el normal descanso y, finalmente, agudizan los estados de estrés. Además pueden ser adictivos.

Entre estos elementos perjudiciales podemos mencionar:

• cafeína, que se encuentra presente en el café, en el té, en los chocolates y en la mayoría de las bebidas gaseosas

• azúcar, presente en muchos alimentos y muy dañina cuando se la consume en exceso (se puede reemplazar por la miel). Impide la absorción de vitamina B.

• sal, neutraliza la asimilación de calcio en el organismo.

American Missionaries, Korean Protestants, and the Changing Shape of World Christianity, 1884–1965

This book examines the partnerships and power struggles between American missionaries and Korean Protestant leaders in both nations from the late nineteenth century to the aftermath of the Korean War. Yoo analyzes American and Korean sources, including a plethora of unpublished archival materials, to uncover the complicated histories of cooperation and contestation behind the evolving relationships between Americans and Koreans at the same time the majority of the world Christian population shifted from the Global North to the Global South. American and Korean Protestants cultivated deep bonds with one another, but they also clashed over essential matters of ecclesial authority, cultural difference, geopolitics, and women's leadership. This multifaceted approach—incorporating the perspectives of missionaries, migrants, ministers, diplomats, and interracial couples—casts new light on American and Korean Christianities and captures American and Korean Protestants mutually engaged in a global movement that helped give birth to new Christian traditions in Korea, created new transnational religious and humanitarian partnerships such as the World Vision organization, and transformed world Christian traditions ranging from Methodism to Presbyterianism.

William Yoo is Assistant Professor of American Religious and Cultural History at Columbia Theological Seminary.

Perspectives on Modern America

American Missionaries, Korean Protestants, and the Changing Shape of World Christianity, 1884–1965

William Yoo

NEW YORK AND LONDON

First published 2017
by Routledge
605 Third Avenue, New York, NY 10017

and by Routledge
2 Park Square, Milton Park, Abingdon, Oxon OX14 4RN

First issued in paperback 2022

Routledge is an imprint of the Taylor & Francis Group, an informa business

Publisher's Note
The publisher has gone to great lengths to ensure the quality of this reprint but points out that some imperfections in the original copies may be apparent.

Library of Congress Cataloging-in-Publication Data
Names: Yoo, William, author.
Title: American missionaries, Korean Protestants, and the changing shape of world Christianity, 1884–1965 / by William Yoo.
Description: New York : Routledge, 2016. | Series: Perspectives on modern America ; 1 | Includes bibliographical references and index.
Identifiers: LCCN 2016028398 (print) | LCCN 2016029579 (ebook) | ISBN 9781138696020 (alk. paper) | ISBN 9781315525570
Subjects: LCSH: Protestant churches—Korea—History—20th century. | Missions, American—United States—Influence. | Christianity—20th century. | Christianity—21st century.
Classification: LCC BR1328 .Y67 2016 (print) | LCC BR1328 (ebook) | DDC 266/.023730519—dc23
LC record available at https://lccn.loc.gov/2016028398

ISBN 13: 978-1-138-69602-0 (hbk)
ISBN 13: 978-1-03-240240-6 (pbk)
ISBN 13: 978-1-315-52557-0 (ebk)

DOI: 10.4324/9781315525570

Typeset in Sabon
by Apex CoVantage, LLC

To Sarah, Maddy, and Caleb

Contents

Figures

Introduction

In 1925, a group of sixty American missionaries and Korean church leaders met in the city of Seoul for a conference with John R. Mott. As chairman of the International Missionary Council, Mott was visiting the country to learn more about the progress of the Korean Church. During the meeting, Mott asked the group to talk about their challenges. His question prompted varying responses from the participants. They discussed the economic depression, growing Korean interest in socialism, and the threat of theological modernism.[1] But one veteran Korean pastor, Han Seok-jin, expressed the view that the greatest danger to indigenous Christian growth was the missionary. Instead of transferring their work to Korean leaders, the missionaries ruled over the churches and schools with a "sense of superiority" that ran contrary to the "true spirit of the gospel."[2] He then turned to his dearest missionary friend, Samuel Austin Moffett, who was sitting nearby, and said, "Reverend Moffett, even you, if you do not leave soon, your presence will do more harm than good."[3]

Samuel Austin Moffett had no intention of leaving. Despite their close relationship—Han was one of Moffett's first students—the two pastors simply disagreed about the demands of Korean Protestants for a greater measure of control over their churches, schools, and hospitals. Moffett still had plans for the mission station in Pyongyang that he had founded three decades ago. Until he retired in 1934, he directed operations on a 120-acre Presbyterian campus with a modern hospital, a college, a seminary, industrial shops, several Korean churches and schools, a separate foreign school for missionary children, and numerous Western-style houses for missionaries to live comfortably.[4] He had no interest in suddenly, or even slowly, turning this vast investment of time and energy (and money) over to the Koreans who, as Moffett saw it, benefited immensely from the efficient organization that knowledgeable American missionaries were able to provide. To have followed Han Seok-jin's advice would have been to accept a reversal in the authority and control of the Korean Church that Moffett could barely even imagine.

This book examines the encounter between American and Korean Protestants in both Korea and the United States from the late nineteenth century to the aftermath of the Korean War. The discord between Moffett and Han was one example of the complicated patterns that marked relations between American missionaries and Korean Protestants. Although Americans and Koreans cultivated deep bonds with one another, they did not always share the same religious perspectives. When missionaries first arrived to Korea in 1884, Koreans viewed them suspiciously and branded Christianity a foreign religion. But as Koreans began converting to Christianity, they adapted the religion to their own context and formed their own beliefs and practices both in concert with and apart from missionary activities.

The Development of Protestantism in Korea and the United States

American missionaries and Korean Protestants together shaped the development of Protestantism in Korea and the United States. The two parties participated in a complex cross-cultural process of religious transmission charged with constant negotiations, oppositions, tangled reciprocities, and unexpected reversals. This thesis has three interconnected strands. The first strand is that American missionaries contributed to the making of Korean Protestantism. They established the first Protestant churches, the first modern hospitals, and the first Western schools in Korea. Missionaries instructed many Korean converts, including a majority of the early Korean church leaders, on matters of religion, politics, and culture. The second strand is that Korean Protestants across Korea and the United States remade Christianity in their own image by combining their cultural and colonial experience with Western elements that the missionaries initially imported to Korea. Koreans engaged in this cross-cultural process of religious transmission on their own terms. They accepted some features of the missionaries' Christianity; they rejected other features; they altered many features to fit their context. The third strand is that Korean ministers and migrants ultimately reversed American religious expectations and increasingly saw it as their mission to revitalize and reform Christianity in the United States.

These three interconnected strands of American and Korean participation took place within the American foreign mission in Korea and Korean immigration to the United States, which are best seen as interconnected and overlapping narratives of a larger world Christian story. In his 1968 presidential address to the American Historical Association, John King Fairbank found the overseas missionary to be the "invisible man of American history."[5] But by 2003, Daniel H. Bays and Grant Wacker posited that Fairbank's claim was no longer true because of the escalating number of studies on American foreign missions.[6] Scholars treating the American Protestant foreign missionary enterprise in East Asia alone have advanced our knowledge of how American women and men interacted with diverse cultures, different religions, and indigenous Christians abroad.[7] Because immigration has been a major source of Christian diversity in the United States, it has likewise received significant scholarly attention, and recent investigations on Christian immigrants from Africa, Asia, and Latin America demonstrate how world Christian movements have transformed American Christianity.[8] Yet instead of treating foreign mission and immigration as two disparate topics, I integrate the histories of the American foreign mission in Korea and Korean immigration to the United States in order to move beyond unidirectional paradigms of "foreign mission" and "immigration" that trace American Christian influence "abroad" or the impact of world Christian movements "at home" as isolated episodes. In looking at the multidirectional currents that flowed between American and Korean Protestants in the United States and Korea, the book captures American and Korean Protestants—missionaries, migrants, ministers, diplomats, and interracial couples—mutually engaged in a global movement that helped give birth to new Christian traditions in Korea and involved numerous American evangelical and mainline Protestant groups.

The American Protestant mission to Korea underwent reversals in different forms. The mission experienced a reversal of expectation when Americans discovered that Korean converts reinterpreted their religious teachings in surprising and sometimes disappointing ways. A different form of reversal—what one might call a reversal of position—came when, from the perspective of many of the missionaries, Koreans like Han Seok-jin insisted too soon on controlling the churches, hospitals, and schools that the missionaries had helped to build. As Korean Protestantism exploded from approximately 380,000 adherents in 1940 to over 9,000,000 in 1997, the bond between American and Korean Protestants across many denominations, from Presbyterian to Pentecostal, grew stronger. But as Korean Protestant leaders across Korea and the United States increasingly assumed authority to lead their institutions, they eventually felt authorized to teach Americans about church growth. And some Americans were eager to learn from successful Korean pastors. Although this last form of reversal—a real reversal of authority—did not become fully visible until the 1980s, the story that I tell delineates the preconditions for it.

American Missionaries, Korean Protestants, and the Changing Shape of World Christianity

The growth of Korean Protestantism is part of larger demographic shifts in the world Christian population. At the beginning of the twentieth century, 80 percent of the world's Christian population lived in Europe and North America. By the end of the century, 60 percent of the world's Christians were found in Africa, Asia, and Latin America.[9] In 1974, African theologian John S. Mbiti challenged Western Christians to acknowledge the axis of Christianity had tilted southward. Because "the centers of the Church's universality" were moving away from Geneva, London, New York, and Rome toward "Kinshasa, Buenos Aires, Addis Abada, and Manila," Mbiti called for more equal relations between Western and non-Western Christians.[10] Without "true theological reciprocity and mutuality" between the two parties, Mbiti argued it was impossible for Christians in the Global North and the Global South to form effective and lasting cross-cultural partnerships.[11]

In 2002, Justo L. Gonzalez observed that "this new map of Christianity" and the religion's increasingly polycentric nature required new studies of the past that no longer made "it appear that North Atlantic Christianity was the goal of church history."[12] The terms "world Christianity" and "global Christianity" first appeared in U.S. literature in 1929 and in 1943 respectively, but more thorough and sustained thinking about the ramifications of the demographic changes in the world Christian population emerged in the 1980s through the scholarship of David Barrett, Kwame Bediako, David Bosch, Samuel Escobar, Philip Jenkins, Peter Phan, Dana Robert, Lamin Sanneh, Andrew Walls, and others.[13] In 2003, Sanneh notably presented contrasting definitions of "world Christianity" and "global Christianity," arguing that the former encompasses "the movement of Christianity as it takes form and shape in societies that were not Christian" whereas the latter involves "the faithful replication of Christian forms and patterns developed in Europe."[14] Throughout my book I use the term "world Christianity" but also recognize that Christian expressions in the Global South and the Global North are connected to one another—through phenomena such as foreign mission, immigration, and the adaptable nature of the religion as it takes root in diverse cultures—in ways that make Sanneh's distinctions harder to distinguish in practice.[15]

The changing shape of world Christianity has also stimulated new evaluations of the Western mission legacy that challenge older myths about missionaries and indigenous converts. The monolithic portrait of missionaries as either evangelical heroes or imperial villains has given way to more intricate understandings of how missionaries functioned in foreign lands.[16] And indigenous Christians no longer reside in the shadows or margins of history, as scholars recognize their often decisive participation in religious transmission and reception.[17] The attention to indigenous Christians recognizes their agency and creativity in remaking the religion with their own ecclesial structures, rituals, and theologies. But the tangled relationships between American missionaries and Korean Protestants demonstrate that the two parties brought different aspirations, fears, ambitions, and frustrations to these transnational religious endeavors.[18] Ultimately, the Koreans would "win out" and control their own churches, as indigenous Christians always have, but minimizing American involvement obscures our historical understanding as much as ignoring Korean initiatives.

Missiologists seek to emphasize "the indigenous discovery of Christianity rather than the Christian discovery of indigenous societies" by turning away from Western missionaries and focusing instead upon how Christians in other societies transformed the religion.[19] But early Korean Protestantism had local and global components that worked both in tandem and against one other. This tension is inherent in Christianity as a universal religion practiced in particular social settings, and Korean churches at home and abroad were local expressions of faith marked by their own cultural distinctiveness. Yet they also maintained connections to the Western churches and felt their continuing influence. American missionaries held superior material resources that gave them power and stature in Korea, and Korean Protestants also respected them for their piety. This stature enabled the missionaries to believe that they knew how the Koreans ought to organize their denominations and practice their worship. As late as 1988, one Korean American Presbyterian pastor in Los Angeles explained that his church's worship service excluded every remnant of Korean culture other than language "because the missionaries told us to throw away our own culture . . . so we adopted the American style."[20] His comment did not reflect any Korean consensus, certainly not in 1988 and probably not in 1938, but it is a reminder that missionaries left an imprint, whether positive or negative, on the Korean Church.

American missionaries held an ambivalent view of Korea. On the one hand, their accounts resembled reports by American diplomats, visitors, and journalists: Korea was underdeveloped, impoverished, and caught in an intricate web of geopolitical struggle in East Asia, with Japan, China, and Russia all seeking hegemony over the peninsular nation until Japan formally annexed Korea as its colony in 1910. However, as the missionaries enjoyed unparalleled success in evangelizing the Koreans, they also depicted Korea as an indigenous laboratory to create a purified Christianity that would serve as a religious antidote to theological liberalism and secularism. By the early twentieth century, Americans treasured Korea as one of their most promising foreign mission fields. In 1923, the Presbyterian Church in the U.S.A. devoted more missionaries and more money to Korea than any other foreign nation.[21] Methodist recruitment materials boasted that the "lure of Korea" was the promise of teaching pious Koreans who obeyed the Christian Scriptures and prayed fervently.[22] But although Americans now saw Koreans not as primitive heathens but rather as fellow believers, they could not entirely escape prevailing racial ideologies. Koreans remained a "people of color," inferior to whites. If non-Christian, they were uncivilized and uncouth; if Christian, they were admirable people of indefatigable spirit. Yet too often Americans also saw them as simpleminded children who required protection from secular and liberal influences.

But from its beginnings, Korean Protestantism was not a facsimile of American missionary forms. The early missionaries saw themselves primarily as heralds of the gospel, but the Koreans saw the missionaries as conduits of Western knowledge, and they wanted to learn American political and economic ideas from them, not simply religion. They attended mission schools in hopes of acquiring both religious and technological knowledge with which they would both expand their churches and elevate their economy. The early missionaries insisted on the most rigorous political neutrality to preserve the spiritual purity of the Korean Church, but Koreans integrated biblical teaching and resistance to Japanese imperialism in ways that strengthened their Christian and anti-colonial resolve. Korean Christians at home and abroad threw themselves into the independence movement. Although Christians comprised little more than 1 percent of the population in 1919, sixteen of the thirty-three signers of the Declaration of Independence and 17 percent of the arrested protesters during the March First uprisings were Christian. Of the 471 women arrested, more than 65 percent were Christian.[23]

Although mission records can be "frustratingly silent" about the thoughts and desires of indigenous Christians, historians have crafted innovative strategies to analyze these one-sided accounts.[24] Derek Chang treats missionary documents as "points of departure" for understanding how converts received and resisted the cultural, religious, and racial discourses.[25] Arun Jones seeks "revelatory cracks" in missionary literature by investigating a wider array of primary historical data, such as private letters and colonial government documents, to catch glimpses of indigenous thought and activity.[26] In addition to using these interpretive tactics, I also analyze Korean sources—books, diaries, essays, letters, and sermons—to present a more complete view of the relationships between Americans and Koreans.[27] Historians have observed that what most Americans know about Korea has been told from the point of view of the U.S. military, or a Christian missionary. Soldiers and missionaries often depicted Korea as an Eastern nation of "prostitutes, beggars, and orphans, many of them mixed race children, never speaking but always spoken for and about, souls being saved by the civilizing missions of neocolonialism and evangelism."[28] By incorporating the voices of Korean Protestants, I demonstrate how they determined their own course by creatively adapting the religion, retaining their own cultural traditions at the same time that they gladly learned from the American forms of Christian traditions.

A Transnational Focus

Every chapter reflects the transnational currents that flowed through the highly diverse relationships between Americans and Koreans. Thomas Tweed defines religions as "confluences of organic-cultural flows that intensify joy and confront suffering by drawing on human and suprahuman forces to make homes and cross boundaries."[29] The book devotes attention to American missionaries and Korean Protestants across both nations to illustrate how the two parties often found in religion a means to cross boundaries in unfamiliar lands. But the religious ambitions of both parties sometimes seemed to sink beneath the cultural flows between the two nations. The first chapter examines how American missionaries brought their religion and culture to Korea. They endeavored to learn the Koreans' language and understand their culture so that they could convince the Koreans that Jesus was a universal savior. But they also separated themselves from Koreans in their well-built American-style houses, which revealed the vast economic discrepancies between the two groups. Even the wealthiest Koreans marveled at the missionary residences.

Beginning in the late nineteenth century, a number of influential Korean Protestant leaders traveled to the United States as foreign students or political exiles. The second chapter analyzes the transnational journey of Yun Ch'iho, an early Korean convert to Methodism in 1887 who studied in the United States from 1888 to 1893 before emerging as a prominent spokesperson for the Korean Church at events like the World Missionary Conference in 1910.[30] Yun's experiences demonstrate how some Korean Protestants encountered a form of racial discrimination in the United States that propelled them into disenchantment with the broken promises of a missionary religion that reduced Koreans to inferior human beings on account of their yellow skin. Korean Protestants like Yun appreciated the support they received from American missionaries, but they also deplored the limits of American Protestant support for their national interests and criticized Americans for obscuring the harsh realities of daily Korean life under Japanese rule in order to promote their religious mission. One Korean observed that missionaries on furlough dressed in Korean clothes in order to raise funds "for Koreans," but they never actually consulted with Koreans to discern what they really wanted and needed.[31]

The third chapter looks at another Korean Protestant leader, Syngman Rhee, and his transnational journey across Korea and the United States. Rhee's fractured relationships with the missionaries and his opposition to their motivations illumine how American and Korean Protestants participated in different sets of transnational networks for religious interaction and exchange. American missionaries lived and worked in Korea, but they remained in close contact with Protestants in the United States through what Ian R. Tyrrell has identified as "multilateral webs" of formal and informal connections with domestic churches, mission boards, friends, and family.[32] Missionaries became cultural brokers providing new information about Korean conditions to Americans, but they also exhibited how their religious successes could advance Protestant causes at home. One scholar of Korean Christianity has highlighted Presbyterian foreign mission board secretary Arthur Judson Brown's identification in 1919 of the "typical missionary" in Korea as "a man of the Puritan type" to emphasize the rigorous religious and ethical standards missionaries imposed upon early Korean converts.[33] But the missionaries' greatest ambition encompassed more than eradicating the sins of dancing, smoking, and gambling in the Korean Church. They most resembled the Puritan pioneers of colonial North America in their vision to create a new religious society in a far-flung land that would serve as a visible and imitable design of Christian witness and practice. Just as the Puritan colonists endeavored to reform European Christianity through their settlements in the "wilderness" of the "new world," missionaries in Korea similarly desired to craft their own "city upon a hill" for American

Protestantism at home and abroad.[34] They increasingly promoted within their transnational network the idea that Korea was "the Palestine of the Far East."[35] In the biblical era, God's message emerged from Palestine, a weak nation surrounded by larger ones. In the twentieth century, Korea, small and feeble, would model an ideal form of Protestantism—with the missionaries as the watchful shepherds—as divine instruction to the world Christian community.

Rhee's religious and political activism provides a clear example of the ways in which Korean Protestants also established transnational connections to communicate with one another and mobilize support for the Korean independence movement. In the age of Japanese imperialism, Koreans in the United States inhabited multiple worlds. They were colonized subjects in their home country and racialized Asians in the prejudiced society of their host country. Koreans across Asia and North America produced numerous channels to exchange letters, raise funds, and update one another on the latest developments from both the homeland and diasporic communities. Historians have recognized how migration to the United States created "an avenue of exile for Koreans to keep alive the vision of a free Korea."[36] But Korean Protestant students in American colleges and seminaries also utilized these educational habitats to learn more about world Christian relations from the Western perspective. As they acquired knowledge of American Christian forms, some transnational Koreans gained access to global Christian networks that simultaneously enhanced their abilities to articulate their religious and geopolitical positions to an international audience and exacerbated their frustrations with Western indifference to a cause they saw as grounded in Christian principles.

The fourth chapter turns its attention to American and Korean Protestant women to illustrate how cross-cultural conflicts strained even the closest partnerships between Americans and Koreans. American and Korean women worked together to improve female education and public health in Korea, but the two groups also disagreed about how Korean women should live each day. Female missionaries trained their Korean students to remain in the home as virtuous wives and mothers, but Korean women wanted to break free from patriarchal forms of Confucianism and evangelical Christianity and rise up as leaders in the church and society.

The fifth chapter investigates the tumultuous time period from 1945 to 1965. Though liberated from Japanese imperial rule, Korea was divided into two nations and soon entangled in a war setting North Korean and Chinese military forces against South Korean and American soldiers. After the Korean War, American and Korean Protestants worked together to relieve suffering and overcome hatreds throughout the world. But these transnational alliances ran up against the same tensions that marked the inception of the Protestant mission. Earlier generations of missionaries failed to mold the Koreans in their own image, but Americans persisted in trying to direct the Korean Church according to their Western prescriptions.

This transnational approach takes seriously the contention that "Korean Christianity is wider than Korea" and also comprises "diaspora and mission movements."[37] The transnational networks that Korean religious leaders abroad constructed—some like Syngman Rhee lived in the United States for decades as political exiles whereas others like Helen Kim and Kyung-Chik Han resided only for a few years as foreign students at American colleges and seminaries—are treated in this study as a critical component, alongside the activities of Korean pastors and theologians at home, such as Gil Seon-ju and Choi Byeung-hyeun, in the making of Korean Protestantism.

American and Korean Protestants maintained their own transnational networks, but a third type of network developed as the two groups began communicating with one another across Asia and North America through letters and periodicals. Korean Protestants conveyed measured critiques of the missionaries in *The Korea Mission Field* and *Korean Student Bulletin*. Missionaries published *The Korea Mission Field* in Korea, but it was a transnational magazine distributed to American Protestants in the United States and other foreign nations in order to provide reports and bolster support for their work.[38] Korean students in the United States created the *Korean Student Bulletin* in 1922 with two distinct readerships in mind: "To serve all the Korean students in this country in a way to bring them into close contact with the Christian influence" and "to deepen and widen the interest of American Christians in Korea and her people."[39] Issues were sent to Korean and American subscribers in both countries, including many missionaries working in Korea.[40] In 1927, *The Korea Mission Field* devoted a monthly issue to Korean authors, who seized the opportunity to articulate their opposition to the missionaries' paternalism, overemphasis on evangelism, and reluctance to designate Korean leaders.[41] Before then, Yun Ch'iho translated an essay written by Yi Kwang-su, a Korean intellectual and non-Christian, which condemned the missionaries for treating Koreans like primitive savages by insisting they adhere to a simplistic form of biblical interpretation that had more in common with the forms of Christianity "that prevail[ed] in Africa and China" than in Japan or the United States.[42] Although Yun was no proponent of liberal theology, he thought that missionaries should stop viewing Koreans as spiritual toddlers unable to deal with sophisticated ideas. In the *Korean Student Bulletin*, L. George Paik voiced another grievance when he argued that Horace H. Underwood's book on the history of modern education in Korea read as if American initiatives should be the sole object of the reader's attention. Underwood was not only biased in his history; he was simply inaccurate.[43]

The two groups differed, they argued, they fought. But Korean Protestants remain an enigma if we try to pretend that the missionaries were nothing but interlopers devoid of any influence on the Korean Church. Recognizing the agency of Americans does not require any discounting of Korean agency. Some Korean Protestant leaders regarded the missionaries with ambivalence—they were simultaneously allies and rivals. Americans introduced many Koreans to wider global Christian networks, but they also sometimes blocked Koreans from achieving their religious aims. Resistance to the missionaries was more subtle, more hidden and soft-spoken, than the overt hostility that Korean Protestants exhibited toward Japanese imperialists or Communists. There were occasions when Koreans confronted the missionaries, like the Mott Conference in 1925, but the discontent surfaced more often in private diaries and letters.

Some of the missionaries recognized what they were doing, repented, and tried to change. They assimilated to Korean ways and pursued more equal relations with Koreans. Annie Baird recounted that one of the most rewarding moments in her life was when a Korean friend told her that she was "just like a loving-hearted old Korean woman": "Years of expatriation, and effort to project myself into the language, customs and feeling of another people, were richly repaid by that sentence."[44] In 1915, the cancer-stricken missionary defied her doctor's orders in the United States to set sail for Korea so she could be buried there. When Baird arrived in Pyongyang several months later, she wrote letters to her family to tell them she had made it back home to where she belonged.[45] After she died, one of her Korean students mourned her loss as if he had lost one of his own parents. In his eulogy, he praised Baird's love for Korea: "In life or in death the thought of her soul was ever directed toward this people, and ever will be. She lived for us. She died for us. Oh, woe is me! In the land of eternal blessing she will peacefully rest."[46]

Scholars have amply documented the American Protestant mission in Korea, the expansion of Korean Protestantism at home and abroad, and Korean-American foreign relations.[47] We still know too little, however, about the evolving interplay between American and Korean Protestants from their first encounters to the end of the Korean War. Sharing the same religion, the two groups crossed national and racial boundaries to develop deep friendships and new transnational partnerships. But the religious loyalties that bound them together often divided them. To look anew at the relationships between American and Korean Protestants—examining when their perspectives overlapped and when they clashed—is to see how the transmission of Christian faith could both confound and connect, how complicated "agency" could be, and how the mission produced a series of reversals, often unintended, that ultimately turned the modern American missionary dream upside down.

Notes

1. Alfred W. Wasson, *Church Growth in Korea* (Concord, NH: Rumford Press, 1934), 125–126.
2. Ch'ae, P'il-Gŭn, *Han Sŏk-chin Moksa wa kŭ sidae: Han'guk Kidokkyo kaech'ŏksa* [Pioneer of Korean Christianity: The Reverend Han Seok-jin and his Times] (Seoul, Korea: Korean Christianity Association, 1950), 230.
3. Ch'ae, 231. See also Sung-Deuk Oak, *Sources of Korean Christianity* (Seoul, Korea: Institute for Korean Church History, 2004), 446–447.

4. "A Bird's Eye View of the Presbyterian Mission Station at Pyeng Yang," *The Korea Mission Field* (March 1932), no page number, and Donald N. Clark, *Living Dangerously in Korea: The Western Experience, 1900–1950* (Norwalk, CT: EastBridge, 2003), 123–125.
5. J.K. Fairbank, "Assignment for the '70s," *American Historical Review* (February 1969), 877, as cited in Daniel H. Bays and Grant Wacker, "Introduction: The Many Faces of the Missionary Enterprise at Home," in *The Foreign Missionary Enterprise at Home: Explorations in North American Cultural History*, edited by Daniel H. Bays and Grant Wacker (Tuscaloosa and London: The University of Alabama Press, 2003), 1.
6. Bays and Wacker, 1.
7. Several examples are Wayne Flynt and Gerald A. Berkley, *Taking Christianity to China: Alabama Missionaries in the Middle Kingdom, 1850–1950* (Tuscaloosa and London: The University of Alabama Press, 1997), Hamish Ion, *American Missionaries, Christian Oyatoi, and Japan, 1859–73* (Vancouver and Toronto: UBC Press, 2009), Lawrence D. Kessler, *The Jiangyin Mission Station: An American Missionary Community in China, 1895–1951* (Chapel Hill and London: The University of North Carolina Press, 1996), Gordon D. Laman, *Pioneers to Partners: The Reformed Church in American and Christian Mission with the Japanese* (Grand Rapids, MI: Wm. B. Eerdmans, 2012), Karen K. Seat, *"Providence Has Freed Our Hands": Women's Missions and the Encounter with Japan* (Syracuse, NY: Syracuse University Press, 2008), and Lian Xi, *The Conversion of Missionaries: Liberalism in American Protestant Missions in China, 1907–1932* (University Park, PA: The Pennsylvania State University Press, 1997).
8. Several examples are Mark R. Gornik, *Word Made Global: Stories of African Christianity in New York City* (Grand Rapids and Cambridge: Wm. B. Eerdmans, 2011), Jehu J. Hanciles, *Beyond Christendom: Globalization, African Migration, and the Transformation of the West* (Maryknoll, NY: Orbis, 2008), Ho-Youn Kwon, Kwang Chung Kim, and R. Stephen Warner (eds.), *Korean Americans and Their Religions: Pilgrims and Missionaries from a Different Shore* (University Park, PA: The Pennsylvania State University Press, 2001), Juan Francisco Martínez, *Los Protestantes: An Introduction to Latino Protestantism in the United States* (Santa Barbara, CA: Praeger, 2011), Hjamil A. Martínez-Vázquez, *Made in the Margins: Latino/a Constructions of U.S. Religious History* (Waco, TX: Baylor University Press, 2013), Daniel Ramírez, *Migrating Faith: Pentecostalism in the United States and Mexico in the Twentieth Century* (Chapel Hill: The University of North Carolina Press, 2015), and Catherine A. Brekus and W. Clark Gilpin (eds.), *American Christianities: A History of Dominance and Diversity* (Chapel Hill: The University of North Carolina Press, 2011).
9. Peter Vethanayagamony, "Mission from the Rest to the West," in *Mission after Christendom: Emergent Themes in Contemporary Mission*, edited by Ogbu U. Kalu, Peter Vethanayamony, and Edmund Kee-Fook Chia (Louisville, KY: Westminster John Knox Press, 2010), 59. See also Todd M. Johnson and Cindy M. Wu, *Our Global Families: Christians Embracing Common Identity in a Changing World* (Grand Rapids, MI: Baker Academic, 2015), 7–9.
10. John S. Mbiti, "Theological Impotence and the Universality of the Church," in *Mission Trends No. 3: Third World Theologies*, edited by Gerald H. Anderson and Thomas F. Stransky (New York: Paulist Press, 1976), 9. Mbiti's essay originally appeared in *Lutheran World* 21:3(1974).
11. Mbiti, 17.
12. Justo L. Gonzalez, *The Changing Shape of Church History* (St. Louis, MO: Chalice Press, 2002), 15.

13. Robert Wuthnow, *Boundless Faith: The Global Outreach of American Churches* (Berkeley and Los Angeles, CA: University of California Press, 2009), 34.
14. Lamin Sanneh, *Whose Religion Is Christianity? The Gospel Beyond the West* (Grand Rapids: Wm. B. Eerdmans, 2003), 22.
15. In his revised and expanded edition of *The Next Christendom: The Coming of Global Christianity*, Philip Jenkins appreciates the implications of Sanneh's definitions but contends that different forms of Christianity "often mutate and merge into each other" and therefore continues to use "global Christianity" in a "broad and nonjudgmental sense." Sebastian Kim and Kirsteen Kim also find Sanneh creates an "impossible distinction because 'global Christianity' often gives rise to 'world Christianity' as local churches become independent of foreign control." Nami Kim likewise sees heterogeneous forms of Christianity in the Global South that cannot be strictly divided into indigenous and foreign categories. Dyron B. Daughrity uses both terms interchangeably but also acknowledges the debate over identifying this new subfield as either global Christianity or world Christianity requires "sensitivity" because of the history and reach of Western colonialism in the Global South. See Philip Jenkins, *The Next Christendom: The Coming of Global Christianity, Revised and Expanded Edition* (Oxford and New York: Oxford University Press, 2007), xiii, Sebastian Kim and Kirsteen Kim, *Christianity as a World Religion* (London and New York: Continuum, 2008), 13, Nami Kim, "A Mission to the 'Graveyard of Empires'? Neocolonialism and the Contemporary Evangelical Missions of the Global South," *Mission Studies* 27(2010), 8–11, and Dyron B. Daughrity, *To Whom Does Christianity Belong? Critical Issues in World Christianity* (Minneapolis, MN: Fortress Press, 2015), 12.
16. For example, scholars have focused on the roles of missionaries as linguistic translators, transnational moral reformers, unwitting colonial co-conspirators, beneficent cultural imperialists, and transmitters of global modernity. See Lamin Sanneh, *Translating the Message: The Missionary Impact on Culture, 2nd ed.* (Maryknoll, NY: Orbis, 2009), Ian R. Tyrrell, *Reforming the World: The Creation of America's Moral Empire* (Princeton and Oxford: Princeton University Press, 2010), John L. Comaroff and Jean Comaroff, *Of Revelation and Revolution, Volume 1, Christianity, Colonialism, and Consciousness in South Africa* (Chicago: University of Chicago Press, 1991), Carol C. Chin, "Beneficent Imperialists: American Women Missionaries in China at the Turn of the Twentieth Century," *Diplomatic History* 27 (June 2003), 327–352, and Ryan Dunch, "Beyond Cultural Imperialism: Cultural Theory, Christian Missions, and Global Modernity," *History and Theory* 41 (October 2002), 301–325.
17. See Andrew Walls, *The Cross-Cultural Process in Christian History* (Maryknoll, NY: Orbis, 2002), Peter C. Phan (ed.), *Christianities in Asia* (Maiden, MA: Wiley-Blackwell, 2011), Mark Noll and Carolyn Nystrom, *Clouds of Witnesses: Christian Voices from Africa and Asia* (Downers Grove, IL: IVP Books, 2011), Ondina E. Gonzalez and Justo L. Gonzalez, *Christianity in Latin America: A History* (Cambridge and New York: Cambridge University Press, 2008), and Ogbu U. Kalu, *African Christianity: An African Story* (Trenton, NJ: Africa World Press, 2007), and *African Pentecostalism: An Introduction* (Oxford and New York: Oxford University Press, 2008).
18. I intentionally use the term "transnational" rather than "international" to explain the relationships between Americans and Koreans based on Ian Tyrrell's definitions of "transnational" and "international." Tyrrell delineates how "international" refers to the formal, political interactions of nation-state institutions whereas "transnational" includes the broader field of non-governmental social, cultural, and economic activities, which includes the movement of peoples, goods, and ideas across national boundaries. See Ian R. Tyrrell, *Reforming the World: The Creation of America's Moral Empire*, 6–7.

19. Lamin Sanneh, *Whose Religion Is Christianity? The Gospel Beyond the West*, 13.
20. Ira Rifkin, "Korean Immigrants Flock to Growing Congregations," *Los Angeles Times*, December 15, 1988.
21. The Presbyterian Church in the U.S.A. had 151 missionaries in Korea. Only one other country had more than 100; thirteen nations had over 50 and the remaining eleven nations had less than 50 missionaries. The denomination also spent $271,982.48 in Korea. They spent over $200,000 in only three other nations. See G.S. McCune, "Fifty Years of Promotion by the Home Board and Home Church," in *The Fiftieth Anniversary Celebration of the Korean Mission of the Presbyterian Church in the U.S.A., June 30–July 3, 1934* (Seoul, Korea: 1934), 35.
22. See Jennie Fowler-Willing and Mrs. George Heber Jones, *The Lure of Korea* (Boston: Methodist Episcopal Church Woman's Foreign Missionary Society Publishing Office, 1910).
23. Douglas Jacobsen, *Global Gospel: An Introduction to Christianity on Five Continents* (Grand Rapids, MI: Baker Academic, 2015), 176, and Timothy S. Lee, *Born Again: Evangelicalism in Korea* (Honolulu: University of Hawaii Press, 2010), 43.
24. Derek Chang, *Citizens of a Christian Nation: Evangelical Missions and the Problem of Race in the Nineteenth Century* (Philadelphia: The University of Pennsylvania Press, 2010), 11.
25. Ibid., 12.
26. Arun W. Jones, *Christian Missions in the American Empire: Episcopalians in Northern Luzon, the Philippines, 1902–1946* (Frankfurt: Peter Lang, 2003), 20–22.
27. In this endeavor, I am indebted to the work of Korean Studies scholars over the last several years. They have published a bevy of historical documents from various American missionaries and Korean religious and political leaders to grant researchers in the West access to a diverse range of previously hard-to-find materials. For example, the Institute for Modern Korean Studies at Yonsei University published a ten-volume set of Syngman Rhee's private correspondence in 2009. In 2008, the Korea Institute for Advanced Theological Studies began publishing the Korean Christian Classics Series with volumes on the writings of early Korean Protestant pastors and theologians such as Choi Byeoung-hyeun and Gil Seon-ju. In 2010, Pai Chai University Press in South Korea published a two-volume set of Henry Gerhard Appenzeller and Henry Dodge Appenzeller's sermons, prayers, and memoirs. See *The Syngman Rhee English Correspondence, Volumes 1–10*, edited with an introduction by Young Ick Lew in collaboration with Yeong Sub Oh, Steve G. Jenks, and Andrew D. Calhoun (Seoul, Korea: Institute for Modern Korean Studies, Yonsei University, 2009), Gil Seon-Ju, *Mansaseongchwi (The Attainment of All Things): Korean Christian Classics Series, Volume 1* (Seoul, Korea: KIATS Press, 2008), Choe Byeong-Heon, *Seongsan Myeong Gyeong (The Clear Mirror of Sacred Mountain): Korean Christian Classics Series, Volume 4* (Seoul, Korea: KIATS Press, 2010), and *The Appenzellers: How They Preached and Guided Korea into Modernization, Volumes 1–2* (Daejeon, Korea: Pai Chai University Press, 2010).
28. Elaine H. Kim, "Myth, Memory, and Desire: Homeland and History in Contemporary Korean American Writing and Visual Art," in *Holding Their Own: Perspectives on the Multi-Ethnic Literatures of the United States*, edited by Dorothea Fischer-Hornung and Heike Raphael-Hernandez (Tubingen: Stauffenburg-Verlag, 2000), 80.
29. Thomas A. Tweed, *Crossing and Dwelling: A Theory of Religion* (Cambridge: Harvard University Press, 2006), 54.
30. Eun Soo Kim, "The Edinburgh Conference and the Korean Church," translated by Gi Jung Song, in *Korean Church, God's Mission, Global Christianity*, edited

by Wonsuk Ma and Kyo Seong Ahn (Eugene, OR: Wipf & Stock, 2015), 7–11, and Brian Stanley, *The World Missionary Conference, Edinburgh 1910* (Grand Rapids and Cambridge: Wm. B. Eerdmans, 2009), 120.

31. "Declaration of Yusin Hoi, by Sa Ilhwan," in Korea General Collection, Missionary Research Library Collection, Burke Theological Library, Columbia University, New York, NY.
32. Tyrrell, 36.
33. Dae Young Ryu, "The Origins and Characteristics of Evangelical Protestantism in Korea at the Turn of the Twentieth Century," *Church History* 77:2 (June 2008), 377, and Arthur Judson Brown, *The Mastery of the Far East: The Story of Korea's Transformation and Japan's Rise to Supremacy* (New York: C. Scribner's Sons, 1919), 540.
34. See Perry Miller, *Errand into the Wilderness* (New York: Harper & Row, 1956), 12–13, and William R. Hutchison, *Errand to the World: American Protestant Thought and Foreign Missions* (Chicago and London: The University of Chicago Press, 1987), 5–6.
35. "Korea, the Palestine of the Far East," *The Korea Methodist* (September 1905), 151.
36. David K. Yoo, *Contentious Spirits: Religion in Korean American History, 1903–1945* (Stanford, CA: Stanford University Press, 2010), 8. See also Sucheng Chan, *Asian Americans: An Interpretive History* (New York: Twayne, 1991), Bong Youn Choy, *Koreans in America* (Chicago: Nelson-Hall, 1979), and Ronald Takaki, *Strangers from a Different Shore: A History of Asian Americans, Updated and Revised Edition* (Boston and New York: Little, Brown and Company, 1998).
37. Sebastian C.H. Kim and Kirsteen Kim, *A History of Korean Christianity* (New York: Cambridge University Press, 2015), 5.
38. In 1911, *The Korea Mission Field* circulated 16,310 copies throughout the world, averaging nearly 1,360 monthly subscriptions. See *The Annual Report of the Korean Religious Book and Tract Society, 1911–1919* (Seoul, Korea: The Society, 1917–1919).
39. "This Bulletin Is," *Korean Student Bulletin* 1:1 (December 1922), 1.
40. See *Korean Student Bulletin* 8:4 (December 1930) for a list of Korean and American contributors to their annual campaign.
41. See *The Korea Mission Field* (February 1927), 23–41.
42. Yi Kwang Su, "Defects of the Korean Church Today," *The Korea Mission Field* (December 1918), 255–256.
43. L. George Paik, "Book Review: Modern Education in Korea," *Korean Student Bulletin* 4:4 (October 1926), 7–8. In 1927, Paik completed his PhD at Yale University and returned to Korea to join Underwood as a faculty member at a Korean Christian college.
44. Annie L.A. Baird, *Inside Views of Mission Life* (Philadelphia: Westminster Press, 1913), 129.
45. S.S. Estey, "In Memoriam: Mrs. Anna Adams Baird, June 25, 1916," in Annie Laurie Baird Papers, RG172, Presbyterian Historical Society, Philadelphia, PA.
46. Kim Tai Yun, "A Korean Appreciation for Mrs. W.M. Baird," in Annie Laurie Baird Papers, RG172, Presbyterian Historical Society, Philadelphia, PA.
47. See Gregg Brazinsky, *Nation Building in South Korea: Koreans, Americans, and the Making of a Democracy* (Chapel Hill: University of North Carolina Press, 2007), Robert E. Buswell Jr. and Timothy S. Lee (eds.), *Christianity in Korea* (Honolulu: University of Hawaii Press, 2006), Hyaeweol Choi, *Gender and Mission Encounters in Korea: New Women, Old Way* (Berkeley: University of California Press, 2009), Donald N. Clark, *Living Dangerously in Korea: The Western Experience, 1900–1950* (Norwalk, CT: EastBridge, 2003), Bruce Cumings, *Korea's Place in the Sun: A Modern History* (New York: W.W. Norton,

1997) and *The Korean War: A History* (New York: Modern Library, 2010), Rebecca Y. Kim, *The Spirit Moves West: Korean Missionaries in America* (Oxford and New York: Oxford University Press, 2015), Sebastian C.H. Kim and Kirsteen Kim, *A History of Korean Christianity* (New York: Cambridge University Press, 2015), Timothy S. Lee, *Born Again: Evangelicalism in Korea* (Honolulu: University of Hawaii Press, 2010), Sung-Deuk Oak, *The Making of Korean Christianity: Protestant Encounters with Korean Religions, 1876–1915* (Waco: Baylor University Press, 2013), Albert L. Park, *Building a Heaven on Earth: Religion, Activism, and Protest in Japanese-Occupied Korea* (Honolulu: University of Hawaii Press, 2015), Kil-sop Song, *American Protestant Missionary Perceptions of the Korean Independence Movement in 1919 and its Effects upon the Churches of Korea*, ThD diss., Boston University, 1976, Elizabeth Underwood, *Challenged Identities: North American Missionaries in Korea, 1884–1934* (Seoul, Korea: Royal Asiatic Society, Korea Branch, 2003), David K. Yoo, *Contentious Spirits: Religion in Korean American History, 1910–1945* (Stanford: Stanford University Press, 2010), and Theodore Jun Yoo, *The Politics of Gender in Colonial Korea: Education, Labor, and Health, 1910–1945* (Berkeley: University of California Press, 2008).

Bibliography

Archives and Manuscript Collections

Missionary Research Library Collection. New York, NY: Burke Theological Library, Columbia University.

Presbyterian Historical Society. Philadelphia, PA.

Books and Journal Articles

The Appenzellers: How They Preached and Guided Korea into Modernization, Volumes 1–2. Daejeon, Korea: Pai Chai University Press, 2010.

The Annual Report of the Korean Religious Book and Tract Society, 1911–1919. Seoul, Korea: The Society, 1917–1919.

Baird, Annie L.A. *Inside Views of Mission Life*. Philadelphia: Westminster Press, 1913.

Bays, Daniel H. and Grant Wacker, eds. *The Foreign Missionary Enterprise at Home: Explorations in North American Cultural History*. Tuscaloosa and London: The University of Alabama Press, 2003.

Brazinsky, Gregg. *Nation Building in South Korea: Koreans, Americans, and the Making of a Democracy*. Chapel Hill: University of North Carolina Press, 2007.

Brekus, Catherine A. and W. Clark Gilpin, eds. *American Christianities: A History of Dominance and Diversity*. Chapel Hill: The University of North Carolina Press, 2011.

Brown, Arthur J. *The Mastery of the Far East: The Story of Korea's Transformation and Japan's Rise to Supremacy*. New York: C. Scribner's Sons, 1919.

Buswell Jr., Robert E. and Timothy S. Lee, eds. *Christianity in Korea*. Honolulu: University of Hawaii Press, 2006.

Ch'ae, P'il-Gŭn. *Han Sŏk-chin Moksa wa kŭ sidae: Han'guk Kidokkyo kaech'ŏksa* [Pioneer of Korean Christianity: The Reverend Han Seok-jin and his Times]. Seoul, Korea: Korean Christianity Association, 1950.

Chan, Sucheng. *Asian Americans: An Interpretive History*. New York: Twayne, 1991.

Chang, Derek. *Citizens of a Christian Nation: Evangelical Missions and the Problem of Race in the Nineteenth Century*. Philadelphia: The University of Pennsylvania Press, 2010.

Chin, Carol C. "Beneficent Imperialists: American Women Missionaries in China at the Turn of the Twentieth Century." *Diplomatic History* 27:3 (June 2003): 327–352.

Choe, Byeong-Heon. *Seongsan Myeong Gyeong (The Clear Mirror of Sacred Mountain): Korean Christian Classics Series, Volume 4*. Seoul, Korea: KIATS Press, 2008.

Choi, Hyaeweol. *Gender and Mission Encounters in Korea: New Women, Old Ways*. Berkeley: University of California Press, 2009.

Choy, Bong Youn. *Koreans in America*. Chicago: Nelson-Hall, 1979.

Clark, Donald N. *Living Dangerously in Korea: The Western Experience, 1900–1950*. Norwalk, CT: EastBridge, 2003.

Comaroff, John L. and Jean Comaroff. *Of Revelation and Revolution, Volume 1: Christianity, Colonialism, and Consciousness in South Africa*. Chicago: University of Chicago Press, 1991.

Cumings, Bruce. *Korea's Place in the Sun: A Modern History*. New York: W.W. Norton, 1997.

Cumings, Bruce. *The Korean War: A History*. New York: Modern Library, 2010.

Daughrity, Dyron B. *To Whom Does Christianity Belong? Critical Issues in World Christianity*. Minneapolis, MN: Fortress Press, 2015.

Dunch, Ryan. "Beyond Cultural Imperialism: Cultural Theory, Christian Missions, and Global Modernity." *History and Theory* 41:3 (October 2002): 301–325.

Flynt, Wayne and Gerald A. Berkley. *Taking Christianity to China: Alabama Missionaries in the Middle Kingdom, 1850–1950*. Tuscaloosa and London: The University of Alabama Press, 1997.

Fowler-Willing, Jennie and Mrs. George Heber Jones. *The Lure of Korea*. Boston: Methodist Episcopal Church Woman's Foreign Missionary Society Publishing Office, 1910.

Gil, Seon-Ju. *Mansaseongchwi (The Attainment of All Things): Korean Christian Classics Series, Volume 1* (Seoul, Korea: KIATS Press, 2008).

Gonzalez, Justo L. *The Changing Shape of Church History*. St. Louis, MO: Chalice Press, 2002.

Gonzalez, Ondina E. and Justo L. Gonzalez. *Christianity in Latin America: A History*. Cambridge and New York: Cambridge University Press, 2008.

Gornik, Mark R. *Word Made Global: Stories of African Christianity in New York City*. Grand Rapids and Cambridge: Wm. B. Eerdmans, 2011.

Hanciles, Jehu J. *Beyond Christendom: Globalization, African Migration, and the Transformation of the West*. Maryknoll, NY: Orbis, 2008.

Hutchison, William R. *Errand to the World: American Protestant Thought and Foreign Missions*. Chicago and London: The University of Chicago Press, 1987.

Ion, Hamish. *American Missionaries, Christian Oyatoi, and Japan, 1859–73*. Vancouver and Toronto: UBC Press, 2009.

Jacobsen, Douglas. *Global Gospel: An Introduction to Christianity on Five Continents*. Grand Rapids, MI: Baker Academic, 2015.

Jenkins, Philip. *The Next Christendom: The Coming of Global Christianity, Revised and Expanded Edition.* Oxford and New York: Oxford University Press, 2007.

Johnson, Todd M. and Cindy M. Wu. *Our Global Families: Christians Embracing Common Identity in a Changing World.* Grand Rapids, MI: Baker Academic, 2015.

Jones, Arun W. *Christian Missions in the American Empire: Episcopalians in Northern Luzon, the Philippines, 1902–1946.* Frankfurt and New York: Peter Lang, 2003.

Kalu, Ogbu U. *African Christianity: An African Story.* Trenton, NJ: Africa World Press, 2007.

Kalu, Ogbu U. *African Pentecostalism: An Introduction.* Oxford and New York: Oxford University Press, 2008.

Kessler, Lawrence D. *The Jiangyin Mission Station: An American Missionary Community in China, 1895–1951.* Chapel Hill and London: The University of North Carolina Press, 1996.

Kim, Elaine H. "Myth, Memory, and Desire: Homeland and History in Contemporary Korean American Writing and Visual Art." In *Holding Their Own: Perspectives on the Multi-Ethnic Literatures of the United States*, edited by Dorothea Fischer-Hornung and Heike Raphael-Hernandez. Tubingen: Stauffenburg-Verlag, 2000.

Kim, Eun Soo. "The Edinburgh Conference and the Korean Church." Translated by Gi Jung Song. In *Korean Church, God's Mission, Global Christianity*, edited by Wonsuk Ma and Kyo Seong Ahn. Eugene, OR: Wipf & Stock, 2015.

Kim, Nami. "A Mission to the 'Graveyard of Empires'? Neocolonialism and the Contemporary Evangelical Missions of the Global South." *Mission Studies* 27(2010): 3–23.

Kim, Rebecca Y. *The Spirit Moves West: Korean Missionaries in America.* Oxford and New York: Oxford University Press, 2015.

Kim, Sebastian and Kirsteen Kim. *Christianity as a World Religion.* London and New York: Continuum, 2008.

Kim, Sebastian C.H. and Kirsteen Kim. *A History of Korean Christianity.* New York: Cambridge University Press, 2015.

Kwon, Ho-Youn, Kwang Chung Kim, and R. Stephen Warner, eds. *Korean Americans and Their Religions: Pilgrims and Missionaries from a Different Shore.* University Park, PA: The Pennsylvania State University Press, 2001.

Laman, Gordon D. *Pioneers to Partners: The Reformed Church in American and Christian Mission with the Japanese.* Grand Rapids, MI: Wm. B. Eerdmans, 2012.

Lee, Timothy S. *Born Again: Evangelicalism in Korea.* Honolulu: University of Hawaii Press, 2010.

Lew, Young Ick, Yeong Sub Oh, Steve G. Jenks, and Andrew D. Calhoun, eds. *The Syngman Rhee English Correspondence, Volumes 1–10.* Seoul, Korea: Institute for Modern Korean Studies, Yonsei University, 2009.

Lian, Xi. *The Conversion of Missionaries: Liberalism in American Protestant Missions in China, 1907–1932.* University Park, PA: The Pennsylvania State University Press, 1997.

Martínez, Juan Francisco. *Los Protestantes: An Introduction to Latino Protestantism in the United States.* Santa Barbara, CA: Praeger, 2011.

Martínez-Vázquez, Hjamil A. *Made in the Margins: Latino/a Constructions of U.S. Religious History*. Waco, TX: Baylor University Press, 2013.

Mbiti, John S. "Theological Impotence and the Universality of the Church." In *Mission Trends No. 3: Third World Theologies*, edited by Gerald H. Anderson and Thomas F. Stransky. New York: Paulist Press, 1976.

McCune, G. S. "Fifty Years of Promotion by the Home Board and Home Church." In *The Fiftieth Anniversary Celebration of the Korean Mission of the Presbyterian Church in the U.S.A., June 30–July 3, 1934*. Seoul, Korea, 1934.

Miller, Perry. *Errand into the Wilderness*. New York: Harper & Row, 1956.

Noll, Mark A. and Carolyn Nystrom. *Clouds of Witnesses: Christian Voices from Africa and Asia*. Downers Grove, IL: IVP Books, 2011.

Oak, Sung-Deuk. *The Making of Korean Christianity: Protestant Encounters with Korean Religions, 1876–1915*. Waco, TX: Baylor University Press, 2013.

Oak, Sung-Deuk. *Sources of Korean Christianity*. Seoul, Korea: Institute for Korean Church History, 2004.

Park, Albert L. *Building a Heaven on Earth: Religion, Activism, and Protest in Japanese-Occupied Korea*. Honolulu: University of Hawaii Press, 2015.

Phan, Peter C., ed. *Christianities in Asia*. Maiden, MA: Wiley-Blackwell, 2011.

Ramírez, Daniel. *Migrating Faith: Pentecostalism in the United States and Mexico in the Twentieth Century*. Chapel Hill: The University of North Carolina Press, 2015.

Ryu, Dae Young. "The Origins and Characteristics of Evangelical Protestantism in Korea at the Turn of the Twentieth Century." *Church History* 77:2 (June 2008): 371–398.

Sanneh, Lamin. *Translating the Message: The Missionary Impact on Culture, 2nd ed.* Maryknoll, NY: Orbis Books, 2009.

Sanneh, Lamin. *Whose Religion Is Christianity? The Gospel Beyond the West*. Grand Rapids, MI: Wm. B. Eerdmans, 2003.

Seat, Karen K. *"Providence Has Freed Our Hands": Women's Missions and the Encounter with Japan*. Syracuse, NY: Syracuse University Press, 2008.

Song, Kil-sop. *American Protestant Missionary Perceptions of the Korean Independence Movement in 1919 and Its Effects upon the Churches of Korea*. PhD diss., Boston University, 1976.

Stanley, Brian. *The World Missionary Conference, Edinburgh 1910*. Grand Rapids and Cambridge: Wm. B. Eerdmans, 2009.

Takaki, Ronald. *Strangers from a Different Shore: A History of Asian Americans, Updated and Revised Edition*. Boston and New York: Little, Brown and Company, 1998.

Tweed, Thomas A. *Crossing and Dwelling: A Theory of Religion*. Cambridge: Harvard University Press, 2006.

Tyrrell, Ian R. *Reforming the World: The Creation of America's Moral Empire*. Princeton: Princeton University Press, 2010.

Underwood, Elizabeth. *Challenged Identities: North American Missionaries in Korea, 1884–1934*. Seoul, Korea: Royal Asiatic Society-Korea Branch, 2003.

Vethanayamony, Peter. "Mission from the Rest to the West." In *Mission after Christendom: Emergent Themes in Contemporary Mission*, edited by Ogbu U. Kalu, Peter Vethanayamony, and Edmund Kee-Fook Chia. Louisville, KY: Westminster John Knox Press, 2010.

Walls, Andrew F. *The Cross-Cultural Process in Christian History: Studies in the Transmission and Appropriation of Faith*. Maryknoll, NY: Orbis Books, 2002.
Wasson, Alfred W. *Church Growth in Korea*. New York: International Missionary Council, 1934.
Wuthnow, Robert. *Boundless Faith: The Global Outreach of American Churches*. Berkeley and Los Angeles: University of California Press, 2009.
Yoo, David K. *Contentious Spirits: Religion in Korean American History, 1910–1945*. Stanford, CA: Stanford University Press, 2010.
Yoo, Theodore Jun. *The Politics of Gender in Colonial Korea: Education, Labor, and Health, 1910–1945*. Berkeley: University of California Press, 2008.

Newspapers and Periodicals

The Korea Methodist
The Korea Mission Field
Korean Student Bulletin
Los Angeles Times

1 The Discovery of an Ideal Mission Field

Introduction

On April 5, 1885, Horace Grant Underwood, Henry Gerhard Appenzeller, and Ella Dodge Appenzeller arrived in Incheon, an open port city on the western coast of Korea. The three Americans were among the earliest missionaries to set foot in the peninsular nation. Underwood was the second Presbyterian and the Appenzellers the first Methodists. Incheon was the site of a pivotal battle in the Korean War. On this cold and rainy April evening in 1885, the three Americans landed with little fanfare. Three miles from the port, they boarded a sampan (a small boat propelled by oars) to get ashore. As they stepped upon the bare rocks of the Korean shore, a horde of men rushed to their sampan to earn some money by carrying their luggage. Despite their uncertainties about Korea, the missionaries were eager to begin their work. For centuries, Korea largely remained secluded from the rest of the world. Western merchants and missionaries had entered other Asian countries from the sixteenth century, but Korea maintained an isolationist policy until signing its first foreign treaty with Japan in 1876 and Western powers in the 1880s. Thus, Korea was called "the hermit nation" and "the forbidden land."[1] As Henry Appenzeller breathed the cool night air and gazed upon Incheon, he believed that he had "landed upon terra firma as yet untouched and unimproved by the hand of man."[2]

American Protestant missionaries imagined Korea as a religious *tabula rasa* for their making. They saw Korea's weak geopolitical position and recent opening to foreigners as a unique opportunity for them to introduce their religion to a vulnerable indigenous population looking for new systems of meaning. Unlike other Asians, Koreans did not adhere to one or two dominant non-Christian religious traditions. To the missionaries, the Korean religious landscape represented a blank canvas for them to inscribe their religious visions upon. Appenzeller noted the date of his arrival: "We came here on Easter," he wrote. "May He who on that day burst asunder under the bands of death break the bands that bind this people, and bring them to the light and liberty of God's children."[3]

In *Modern Social Imaginaries*, Charles Taylor traces the development of a new moral order in Western modernity by highlighting three social forms: the market economy, the public sphere, and self-governance. According to Taylor, each of these three social forms embodies a distinctive Western social imaginary centered on the fundamental notion of mutual benefit for equal participants. Taylor defines "social imaginary" as "the ways people imagine their social existence, how they fit together with others, how things go on between them and their fellows, the expectations that are normally met, and the deeper normative notions and images that underlie these expectations."[4] As missionaries learned the Korean language, built new homes, evangelized to Koreans, and established modern schools and hospitals, they constructed a cross-cultural social imaginary that delineated their social existence in Korea, how they fit together with one another and Koreans, their religious expectations, and the normative notions and images that undergirded these expectations.

In contrast to the language of social theory, which Taylor observes is usually the possession of a small minority and sometimes limited to disengaged intellectual analysis of social reality, he proposes that the term *imaginary* captures the way ordinary people imagine their social surroundings and embodies a collective understanding that makes "common practices" and a "widely shared sense of legitimacy" possible in any given society.[5] As an example, Taylor demonstrates how the modern practice of voting, in which all citizens decide on their governing officials by each choosing individually from among the same alternatives, reflects the Western social imaginary.[6] In Korea, American missionaries found themselves in an entirely different culture, with its own religions, traditions, and ways of life. They themselves came from diverse geographical backgrounds and religious denominations. Methodists, Presbyterians, and non-denominational Protestant men and women from cities and rural areas across North America migrated to Korea, a nation roughly the size of the U.S. state of Kansas. The American Protestant social imaginary in Korea entailed fierce contestation as missionaries argued over "common practices" such as evangelism, lodging, and teaching. During their first twenty years in Korea, missionaries agreed upon a normative image of Korea as a religious *tabula rasa*, ripe for Protestant inscription, but they disagreed about how to accomplish their task.

American Missionaries and the Korean Religious *Tabula Rasa*

The earliest missionaries were not drawn to Korea for its political or cultural prestige in Western eyes. Before 1876, Western nations had very little contact with Korea and it is likely fewer than one hundred Westerners had even visited the country.[7] On June 21, 1880, in one of its first substantive articles on Korea, the *New York Times* reported that "the only forbidden land on the surface of the globe is the kingdom of Corea."[8] Curious readers of the *Times* learned that day how Korean people wished to be free of foreign influences and visitors, desiring to remain "shut up from the rest of the population of the globe as hermetically as if it were one of the subdivisions of the moon's surface." Debunking any notion that Korea was a long-lost lavish paradise or a "land flowing with milk and honey, teeming with riches of all kinds, and filled with gorgeous palaces and cloud-capped towers, the like of which we have not seen since the days of Kublai Khan and his Oriental splendor," the *Times* reported that Koreans were in fact "primitive in dress, manners, and mode of life" and living in impoverished houses "utterly destitute of any attempt at luxury."[9] In 1885, George William Knox, a Presbyterian missionary in Japan who had lobbied his denomination to send missionaries to Korea, conceded that Korea was not nearly as attractive a mission field as Japan, because Korea was "not a great empire with a great history," but a rather "weak people" in comparison to her stronger neighbors, Japan and China.[10]

On October 1, 1884, Horace Newton Allen, the first American Protestant missionary in Korea, wrote about his impressions of the country. Having spent two weeks there, Allen found the nation's scenery to be pleasant, with luscious mountains, deep valleys, and rich fields of rice and barley, but he saw the Koreans as "exceedingly lazy and dirty," commenting how the middle and upper classes spent their days "strutting leisurely around in their white (outside) robes and tall open-work hats."[11] The only attractive building he saw belonged to the Japanese Consulate. The Korean workers hired by foreigners, such as the Japanese, Chinese, and a few Europeans, did not complete their tasks and instead got drunk on rice liquor and foreign alcohol, which found its "way into the country in great quantities, notwithstanding the customs duty of 20 per cent."[12] Allen noted that the Korean government did not welcome foreign missionaries but he was permitted to remain as physician to the American legation, which was established in 1883, one year after the United States became the first Western power to conclude a treaty with Korea. The Korean-American Treaty of 1882 acknowledged that Korea was a fully sovereign kingdom and that therefore the United States was bound to treat Korea as an independent country.[13]

Although the Korean-American Treaty of 1882 included the "most favored nation clause," which fixed rates of tariff and permitted American citizens the right to trade freely, it did not mention religious toleration or secure the rights of missionaries. In 1883, Frederick T. Frelinghuysen, the U.S. Secretary of State, wrote to Lucius H. Foote, the American Minister in Korea, about the absence of any mention of religion in the treaty. Frelinghuysen contended that "the general propaganda of foreign faiths is not deemed a proper subject for inclusion in any treaty," but he urged Foote to counsel the Koreans toward an open policy toward missionaries because "the toleration of faiths is the true policy of all enlightened powers."[14] In 1885, the Korean government allowed American missionaries to enter into their nation but prohibited direct proselytism. Thus, Allen, Appenzeller, Underwood, and other missionaries engaged chiefly in medical and educational work during their first several years.

Although Korea was not as civilized as her Asian neighbors, missionaries determined that Korean people were not physically or mentally inferior to either the Japanese or the Chinese. In 1885, a Presbyterian writer reported that Koreans were "a fine stalwart and robust class of men" with physique "infinitely superior to that of either the Chinese or the Japanese."[15] The Japanese, he added, looked like "a nation of pigmies" in comparison.[16] In 1889, a Methodist magazine, *The Gospel in All Lands*, confirmed the fine physical stature of Koreans, describing them as tall and well-built. Koreans also possessed intelligence, but the lower classes neither displayed the rational clarity of the Japanese nor the business acuity of the Chinese. The report did not attribute these mental deficiencies to the innate Korean mind, but instead deplored Korea's protracted isolation from the modern world, which left the nation in a stagnant civilization.[17] Despite their uncivilized environs and the unsophisticated thinking of the lower classes, missionaries concluded, Koreans were not only able-bodied but also mentally competent to comprehend Christian doctrines.

Although missionaries decried Korea's squalor and unsanitary living conditions, they thought the nation's primitiveness was charming. It was like they had traveled back in time to an enchanted land fixed in an ancient age. In Seoul, they were captivated by the sights of white-robed men traveling on donkeys and fully cloaked women carrying jars of water from the public well to their rice-straw huts. "It is therefore not so strange that the Bible student finds much in Korea to remind him of the manner of life that prevailed in the land of Bible story," wrote one Presbyterian missionary in 1889, "even though thousands of miles and thousands of years have come between."[18] Yet, missionaries also recognized that Korea was changing as outside forces from China, England, France, Japan, Russia, and the United States sent diplomats, merchants, missionaries, and speculators to introduce new economies, new trade agreements, new philosophies, and new religions. And as the missionaries witnessed Korea awakening from her ancient slumber, they wanted their influence to rank foremost among the many foreigners.

In comparing Korea and her Asian neighbors, missionaries determined that the Korean religious landscape was wholly unlike that in Japan and China. Because of deeply entrenched traditional Asian religious systems in Japan and China, such as Shinto-Buddhism in Japan and Confucianism in China, missionaries in these countries experienced strong indigenous resistance to their religious message. But missionaries in Korea rejoiced at the absence of a single dominating and unifying national religion. In 1885, one Presbyterian declared that the lack of a national Korean religion made evangelization possible: "It is remarkable providence that Christianity should be entering Korea, as it entered the old Roman world, just at the time when all the ancient faiths are in a state of decay."[19] The Korean government had suppressed Buddhism from the seventeenth century to the end of the nineteenth. High-ranking Confucian scholars viewed Buddhism as a rival religion that would diminish Confucian influence. In 1659, the government forbade any novice from taking monastic orders. The following year, it destroyed two Buddhist academies. In 1749, an edict reinforced a ban on Buddhist clerics from entering Seoul.[20] Korean Buddhists were prevalent in the countryside and mountain villages, but missionaries gladly reported that Buddhism was "enfeebled and plainly doomed" within the ruling class as "the reigning dynasty long since decreed its disestablishment."[21] As Koreans experienced the upheaval of opening their nation to foreigners, missionaries rejoiced that Koreans appeared to be searching for new religions.

In 1885, the Presbyterian Board of Publication published William Elliot Griffis's *Corea, Without and Within*, in which the author reprinted and annotated the journal of Hendrick Hamel, a Dutch bookkeeper for the Dutch East India Company who was accidentally shipwrecked in Korea en route to Nagasaki, Japan in 1653. Hamel had recorded the absence of a national religion. "As for religion, the Coreans have scarce any," Hamel observed.[22] They paid little respect to idols and disregarded Buddhist monks. Koreans only believed in the basic religious notion that "he who lives well shall be rewarded, and he who lives ill shall be punished."[23] Griffis confirmed Hamel's observations by noting the steep decline of Korean Buddhism in the nineteenth century: "The mind of the Corean peasant resembles a peat-bog in its mixture of decay. The faiths which influence him once had each a distinctive life and form. Their frame and substance now gone, he propitiates all gods and professes all superstitions."[24] In 1888, Griffis added in *The Gospel in All Lands* that "the Koreans offer the spectacle of a nation without a religion and waiting for one."[25] In 1889, the Presbyterian foreign mission secretaries described the potential: "Since Buddhism was put under bans, sevenfold superstitions have entered to fill in the void, yet they are not religions. Wanted, a religion for Korea. What shall it be?"[26] In 1890, a Methodist writer for the *Heathen Children's Friend* told its young readers: "I cannot find that the Koreans have much religion of any kind. They have idols, and temples, but are not devout worshipers like the Chinese."[27] The missionaries believed that Korea's geopolitical fragility created an open mission field, noting that Korean religions constituted "no such barrier to Christianity as the subtle and plausible philosophy of India, or the proud and fiery fanaticism of Moslem lands."[28]

As missionaries witnessed popular Korean religious rituals, such as ancestor, nature, and spirit worship, they determined that Koreans were not religious but superstitious. Whereas Buddhism, Confucianism, Hinduism, and Islam were rival religions to Christianity, popular Korean superstitions were deemed less threatening. The religious obstacles to the Protestant mission amounted to "innumerable superstitions," "half fetichism," "half spiritualism," and "a medley of goblins and genii," all of which would diminish after Koreans encountered "the science of a schoolboy, to say nothing of the whole apparatus of Western learning and the revelations of Christianity."[29] In 1891, Methodist missionary George Heber Jones wrote that "'the Superstitions' comprise a vast number of gods, demons, demi-gods, [and] the legacy of centuries of nature worship."[30] He detailed a ritual in which Koreans gathered beneath a tree to sacrifice rice and choice food on a pile of stones to a local deity; the deity ate the spiritual essence of the food while the physical substance remained. Jones observed that "while the deity feasts on the essence or spiritual element of the food, lighted paper is kept burning beneath the branches and prayer offered for the desired blessing."[31] Jones noted that this dualism in Korean thought displayed a "well-defined distinction between the gross, material subjects thus sanctified and a supposed inner spiritual presence which the Korean claims is the object of worship."[32] Yet Jones maintained that Korea was without a national religion. Despite the ubiquity of popular Korean religions, Jones claimed the "the Korean's soul has remained untouched by the exercises in which he engages." Christian conversion would result in "his first taste of religion."[33]

Jones described Korea as heathen. Without defining the term, he simply assumed that Koreans were "heathens" because they were non-Christians. But the lack of a national religion made Korea's heathenism less severe in comparison to other nations. Jones quoted another well-traveled missionary, who told him that "heathenism in India is vile, in China defiant, in Japan desperate, in Korea indifferent, in Africa triumphant."[34] Yet, in the very next paragraph Jones decried the heathen conditions of Korean social and domestic life. Heathenism in Korea was "indifferent" religiously, but culturally it was entrenched in Korean habits, customs, laws, and traditions. Koreans were heathens not simply because of their non-Christian beliefs, but because they were uncivilized and uncouth foreigners.

During his first year in Korea, Henry Appenzeller wrestled with the meaning of heathen: "I suspect some of us at home think of the heathen as being a different being than ourselves . . . we think them a very queer folk and congratulate ourselves that the Lord did not use the same dust in creating them as us."[35] He denounced the racist attitudes of the American Protestants who considered Koreans as lesser human beings and classified them as "heathens" because of their physical appearance. In his private sermon notes, he asked "What is a heathen?" and answered the question exclusively in religious terms: "Nearly everything gone but the idea of a supreme being . . . Heathenism must go because of its inability to cope with sin and its failure to satisfy these natural longings."[36] Koreans were not racially inferior to Westerners, but Korea was for Appenzeller still a heathen nation.

To Evangelize or to Civilize: Mission Debates

Though granted permission to teach English, Appenzeller was eager to pursue direct evangelism; so also was Underwood. Both men did not come to Korea to work in schools and hospitals, but rather to evangelize a nation. Allen, their predecessor, had advocated a cautious approach to evangelistic work. Though the Korean government tolerated foreign missionaries, Allen wished to build trust between the two parties by adhering to the king's proscriptions of proselytism. Moreover, as a physician, Allen wanted to establish a modern hospital in partnership with the Korean government. Allen also believed that Korea was ripe for Protestant inscription, but he promoted social uplift and public health as the right tools. He rebuffed other missionaries who sought to evangelize Korean patients and worked to defeat rumors that "no person would be treated unless promising to believe in Christ."[37] But Underwood began to preach to Koreans, distribute Bible pamphlets, and plan itinerating trips with Appenzeller. Disagreement over civilizing and evangelizing approaches was not unique to the Korean mission field. Missionaries debated over the two strategies throughout the nineteenth century. After inspecting overseas mission work in 1854 and 1855, Rufus Anderson, senior secretary of the American Board of Commissioners for Foreign Missions (ABCFM), shut down English-language mission schools in various countries, such as India and Sri Lanka, because they detracted from evangelistic work. Incensed ABCFM missionaries operating these schools protested Anderson's decision.[38] In Korea, Allen and Underwood came into conflict over the two approaches. Each threatened to resign from the Presbyterian mission because of the other. Underwood thought Allen was too concerned about his hospital and his profile as a medical doctor. In a letter to the Presbyterian foreign mission board dated September 17, 1886, Underwood charged that Allen entertained foreign visitors at his Korean home with alcohol, cigarettes, and card-playing.[39] Allen thought Underwood was turning a blind eye to the real needs of the Korean people. As missionaries in Korea, Allen believed they were bearing Christian witness by providing educational and medical facilities. He also compared the many hours he spent in hospital administration and patient care to the other missionaries' more lax schedules, which seemed to supply ample time for language training, religious study, and leisure. On October 10, 1886, Allen wrote in his diary: "I am of opinion that mission work is a farce. I am kept busy by various outside duties . . . Underwood has as much leisure. So have Methodists. I think it is a nutty soft thing."[40] The strife reflected both religious differences and personal animosities.

George C. Foulk, the highest-ranking American diplomat in Korea in 1885, agreed with Allen. Prior to his appointment as charge d'affairs of the American legation, Foulk graduated from the United States Naval Academy, served as a naval officer in East Asia, and learned to speak Chinese, Japanese, and Korean. His language abilities and his knowledge of East Asian cultures impressed his colleagues and superiors. Foulk was a Protestant, but he was tolerant of other religions and disagreed with missionary strategies that marked Asian religions as false and evil. A month before arriving in Korea, Foulk was in India and he observed foreign missionaries in that country, noting how their work was "not now so much toward making downright converts out of the patrons of an idolatrous religion," but was "first to elevate the people in a body by education and by introducing ideas of the comforts enjoyed by people of Christian countries."[41] Foulk did believe that Protestantism represented the highest form of moral enlightenment and wished for missionaries to introduce their religion through Western education and medicine. After providing modern civilization, they could convert the Koreans to Christianity in due time.[42]

But as soon as missionaries arrived in 1885, Foulk complained about their presence. In private letters to his family, Foulk criticized them for coming to Korea with little understanding of the culture and no language skills. He expressed disappointment in their missionary work and did not hesitate to call them "the greenest, most useless people" he had ever seen.[43] "Heretofore I have wrangled always against talk about them," Foulk confessed. "Now I have much to do with missionaries and I find that the amount of miserable, petty jealousy among them is very great. I help a Presbyterian, at once the Methodists get glum and object."[44] On September 15, 1885, Foulk wrote that his chief trouble in Korea was on account of the missionaries.[45] In addition to constantly bickering within and across their denominational missions, they incessantly called upon the legation for help because they did not know anything about Korean life, even entreating the diplomat to find wet nurses for their infants. They had tried to hire indigenous wet nurses themselves, as American missionaries in Japan had done, but discovered that Korean women were reluctant to work alone in foreign homes. Early missionaries like Appenzeller and Underwood would later become proficient in the Korean language and highly knowledgeable of Korean ways. They authored Korean-English dictionaries, worked on Korean translations of the Bible, and emerged as among the most reliable Western experts of Korean history and culture. But they initially struggled to understand their new surroundings. Foulk complained the missionaries were "helpless": "Every day I am besought to help: to help get servants, talk to their servants, settle quarrels, and now to get wet nurses." Foulk's parents at home supported American missions, but now their son wrote to them about the "stupendous stupidity" of the mission boards in the United States, who had sent "ignoramuses" to Korea. Foulk exclaimed: "They do no good, can speak no Oriental language, are gawky, ignorant of the world at large, and have come saddled down with babies to a land where any night the people might rise and end them and their babies!"[46] For the next two years, Foulk maintained his criticism that the missionaries were "ignorant of Oriental ways," but he praised them for their educational and medical work. He reported to his family that Allen's hospital was flourishing. He also expressed a favorable opinion of mission school teachers and described his efforts in helping the Presbyterian missionaries obtain permission from the Korean government to establish an orphan school in Seoul.[47]

During the first seven years of the Protestant mission in Korea, Foulk and subsequent American diplomats lauded the missionaries for their educational and medical gains. But the legation always wanted to halt their evangelism. Unlike the French legation, which had pressed the Korean government to remove all religious restrictions against their Catholic missionaries, the

Americans were more cautious. In the nineteenth century, before the opening of Korea in 1876, French Catholic missionaries furtively entered Korea through Chinese and Manchurian borders and hid amongst the Korean people dressed in Korean garb. These missionaries, along with Korean Catholic converts, were charged with sedition and violently persecuted by the Korean government. In 1839, the regime executed three French missionaries and other Catholics. In 1865, there were more than twenty thousand Catholics in Korea. From 1866 to 1873, approximately eight thousand of them were killed for their religious activities.[48] In 1866, France responded to the execution of nine missionaries with military force against Korea. French forces successfully invaded Kanghwa Island, but were repelled by Korean forces before reaching Seoul.[49] Thus, France was insistent on securing religious freedom for their missionaries during negotiations for the French-Korean Treaty in 1886.

Though the Catholic presence in Korea was not large, American missionaries increasingly saw Catholic movements, missionary and Korean, as potential threats to their work. Jeong Yak-jong, a Korean who converted to Catholicism in 1786 and adopted Augustine as his baptismal name, composed the first Korean Christian catechism, which detailed the "essentials of the Lord's teaching," such as God's creation of the world, soteriology, and eschatology, before the Korean government beheaded him in 1801.[50] In 1885, Underwood reluctantly hired a Korean Catholic to be his language teacher because he was the best instructor that the missionary could find.[51] In 1886, Underwood reported that French Catholic missionaries, well-versed in Korean, were actively evangelizing in Seoul and had sent fifteen to twenty Koreans to their theological seminary in Nagasaki, Japan. If he and his fellow missionaries did not act fast, Underwood feared, the Korean religious *tabula rasa* would be heavily marked by Roman Catholicism. "I fear that if the Protestants do not do their duty," asserted Underwood, "we will have a Romish instead of a heathen people to convert."[52]

On February 5, 1887, W.W. Rockhill, the charge d'affairs of the American legation after Foulk, appealed to T.F. Bayard, the U.S. Secretary of State, for guidance in relation to missionary activities. Although he supported the mission schools, hospital, and orphanage in Seoul, Rockhill disapproved of evangelistic efforts. "But while doing so much good work," expressed Rockhill, "the missionaries have had always in view the main object of their coming to Korea, the evangelization of the natives."[53] American missionaries complained about their religious restrictions in comparison to the French Catholics. Yet unlike the French Catholics, who lived among the Koreans, recognized Korean laws, and submitted to the Korean justice system, the American missionaries expected the legation to protect their rights and those of Korean Protestant converts from any potential Korean oppression. Rockhill opined to Bayard that the missionaries must not yet evangelize because influential parties within the Korean government were opposed to Christianity: "Although no persecutions of Christians have occurred of late years, still their enmity cannot be lost sight of . . . our countrymen should restrain their ardour and wait the day when religious freedom is granted the Koreans."[54]

In 1890, the Korean government eased its restrictions on religious propaganda. The next year, the U.S. State Department directed to extend the most favored nation clause to the missionaries, which gave them the right to travel freely throughout the country.[55] Despite their newfound freedoms, they did not have great initial success in evangelizing. Samuel Austin Moffett, a Presbyterian missionary who arrived in Korea in January 1890, discovered in his first months in Seoul that their mission still struggled to sustain their myriad educational, evangelistic, and medical endeavors.[56] Though Koreans appeared to be growing more receptive to their religious overtures, Moffett reported that missionaries remained fiercely divided between civilizing and evangelizing approaches. After ten months in Seoul, Moffett asked Frank Field Ellinwood, secretary of the Presbyterian Board of Foreign Missions, for permission to establish a new mission station in Pyongyang. In a recent visit to Pyongyang, he had met Koreans there who welcomed foreign missionaries. Additionally, he wished to leave the missionary community in Seoul and begin afresh in northern Korea, without the discord about strategy. Unhappy with the mission in Seoul, Moffett sought his own mission field—a new, unmarked religious *tabula rasa*—upon which to inscribe his religious vision for Korea. Unlike Allen, Moffett prioritized evangelism over education and medicine. He believed that missionaries in Seoul had erred by establishing schools and hospitals "without the preliminary years of evangelistic work which they had in China and Japan."[57] Some of Moffett's Presbyterian colleagues agreed with him; they almost refused a gift of ten thousand dollars to establish a medical school in 1900.[58]

In December 1892, a British Anglican missionary reported that Koreans in Incheon flocked to their medical doctors and dispensaries but gave little heed to their preaching.[59] In 1893, another American Presbyterian, William Martyn Baird, also had little success on two itinerating trips. From April 17 to May 20, Baird traveled approximately four hundred miles in southern Korea. In his diary, he complained of his "very few opportunities to preach" as Koreans deliberately avoided him.[60] Though Baird engaged in several religious conversations and sold Bible pamphlets, he surmised that the Koreans he had encountered were "dull of hearing" with "no vision beyond this earth."[61] One Korean Catholic warmly approached Baird and prostrated himself before the missionary, but he immediately dismissed Baird upon learning he was not a Catholic priest.[62] On his second itinerating journey in the autumn months, in which Baird traveled 200 miles from Busan to Seoul, he was disappointed because some Koreans were purchasing missionary literature to paper the walls in their homes.[63] From 1889 to 1893, the number of Korean communicants within the Presbyterian mission fluctuated between 100 and 150 annually.[64] In the United States, the Korean mission field received scant attention in comparison to Japan and China. James

Shepard Dennis delivered a series of lectures on foreign missions before the faculty and students at Princeton Theological Seminary in the spring of 1893. Dennis devoted four pages to the brief history of the Protestant mission in Korea between ten pages detailing the progress and promise within the more storied Japanese and Chinese mission fields.[65]

Experiencing Success in the Midst of Social and Political Upheaval

Between 1895 and 1905, American missionaries had greater success in Korea with increased numbers of indigenous conversions. By 1900, the two Methodist missions (Methodist Episcopal Church and Methodist Episcopal Church, South) reported 4,512 Korean members and probationers.[66] In the same year, the Presbyterian mission station in Pyongyang alone counted 10,055 Korean adherents.[67] Baird attributed Protestant growth in Pyongyang to (1) Moffett's singular focus on evangelism over educational and medical work, (2) the Holy Spirit, which had done "a thorough work of grace," and (3) the presence of Korean Protestants in Pyongyang before American missionaries had arrived there.[68] Moffett reported in 1891 that twenty to thirty Korean Protestants preceded him in Pyongyang, "many of them at work and freely talking of the gospel."[69] Because of Pyongyang's close proximity to Chinese and Manchurian borders, a number of Koreans in the city had already heard of Protestant work in those neighboring countries. The Korean Protestant cadre in Pyongyang had traveled to Manchuria and learned about Christianity from John Ross, a Scotch Presbyterian missionary stationed there. Moffett met one Korean who had assisted Ross in translating the New Testament into the Korean language.[70] In 1882, two years before the first American Protestant missionary set foot on Korean soil, Ross, with the help of three Korean converts, published and distributed his translation of the Korean New Testament.[71] During Baird's trip to Pyongyang in 1897, he wrote to his brother that "the best thing of all" was encountering Koreans "who had never seen a missionary," but self-identified as Protestants. Baird was also pleased that these Korean converts gladly received his instruction, readily submitted to his supervision, and "talked a language that could only have been taught them by the Holy Spirit."[72] Baird and his colleagues also saw the first Korean church in Sorae, a rural village on the coast of Hwanghae province, which two Korean converts from Ross's ministry in Manchuria, Suh Sang-u and Suh Sang-ryun, founded before the American missionaries had arrived, as a providential sign.[73] During his excursion to Sorae in 1888, Underwood rejoiced in encountering the church and especially in being asked to baptize seven Korean Christians, all of whom regarded the missionary as a trustworthy religious authority.[74]

Another reason for Protestant expanse in Korea from 1895 to 1905 was the social and political upheaval caused by the Sino-Japanese War (1894–1895). As Korea established foreign relations with other countries, beginning in 1876, the Korean government increased taxes in order to pay for their entry into a global economy. Korean peasants suffered the heaviest burden. Chinese and Japanese merchants also penetrated the countryside, agitating peasants "in a society neither used to outsiders nor experienced in a modern commercial economy."[75] From 1892 to 1894, peasant unrest resulted in numerous revolts around the country, which were led by a group of Koreans following the *Donghak* (Eastern Learning) religious movement. In 1860, Choi Je-u fused traditional Korean folk religions with Confucian, Buddhist, and Taoist teachings to create *Donghak*, a new religion designed to counter Roman Catholicism (and other Western teachings) and promote a more egalitarian social order.[76] In response to these peasant uprisings, known as the Donghak Rebellion, on June 4, 1894, the anxious Korean government requested Chinese military assistance. Five days later, Japan sent its own troops to Korea in order to deter Chinese influence and exert imperial might. Japanese forces thoroughly routed Chinese troops, forcing China to recognize Korea as an independent state and cede Taiwan and the Liaodong Peninsula to Japan at the Treaty of Shimonoseki on April 17, 1895.[77] During the Sino-Japanese War, Koreans suffered at the hands of both foreign military forces. The war severely damaged cities like Incheon and Pyongyang and thousands of Koreans fled from their homes. After winning the war, Japan established geopolitical primacy in East Asia and a strong grip over the Korean government.

American missionaries grieved at the terrible price Korea had incurred during the Sino-Japanese War but also conceived that the war's devastating aftermath created an opportunity for evangelization. James Scarth Gale, a Canadian Presbyterian missionary who first came to Korea with the Y.M.C.A. in 1888 and then joined the American Presbyterian mission in 1891, deplored how the war "passed like a cyclone" over northern Korea, "leaving the country despoiled of its population, its ancestral groves and tablets."[78] But Gale observed that Japan's victory effectively eradicated China's sway in Korea, which potentially diminished any Confucian strongholds. Pyongyang was not only in physical ruins after the Sino-Japanese War, but also Gale found that the Koreans who had returned to their shattered homes no longer viewed China as supremely powerful. After centuries of paying tribute to China as "elder brother," Korea was no longer beholden to Chinese direction.[79] Gale declared that the decisive Battle of Pyongyang in mid-September 1894 was the site where "Korea's worship of China" had ended.[80] The battle also turned Koreans away from Confucianism, a religious import from China, and began a search for new religions: "Confucianism binds a man to one piece of ground, separate him from that particular place and you have separated him from his gods . . . the population that came back after the war, came back to a certain degree without their deities and shrines."[81] Robert E. Speer, secretary of the Presbyterian Board of Foreign Missions, visited Korea two years after the Sino-Japanese War and found that Protestant mission work had advanced "leaps and bounds." In

1894 the Presbyterian mission had 141 Korean communicants. "Then came the furrowing, renovating influence of the war, and now, after the most prosperous year yet known, there are 932 communicants, 2,344 catechumens, 101 meeting places, and 38 church buildings," Speer wrote in August 1897.[82] Gale and other missionaries seized upon the Sino-Japanese War as an opportune time to evangelize Koreans.[83]

American Missionaries as Migrants in Korea and the Problem of Difference

By 1900, one American diplomat estimated that 150 of the 250 Americans in Korea were missionaries.[84] In 1901, the country had 74 American Presbyterian and 45 American Methodist missionaries, who accounted for 119 of the 170 Protestant foreign missionaries in the country.[85] As they built new homes in Korea, missionaries sought to recreate their Western lifestyles as migrants in the East. As evangelists, the lure of Korea was the new receptivity to their religious message. As migrants, the same missionaries rejoiced in the relative ease by which they were able to erect Western-style homes with familiar comforts from home. They were initially repulsed by Korea and complained about filthy streets and unsanitary living conditions. Because missionaries first traveled to Japan en route to Korea, they compared the modernization of Japanese life, with its luxurious Western hotels, modern railroads, and pristine streets, to what they saw as the woebegone conditions in a primitive Korea. Upon arriving in Seoul after two months in Japan, Methodist missionary William B. Scranton was surprised to find that the capital city was not at all attractive. In a letter to his executive mission secretary on June 1, 1885, Scranton wrote that the city's rampant pollution and ignorance of the outside world were "the causes most apparent for its failure to please our Western ways." Describing the city's residents, Scranton added: "From prince to pauper, they are all dirty in their homes."[86] By and large, the missionaries liked how the primitive conditions resembled biblical times, but they did not wish to imitate the Korean way of life. To perform ministry like a first-century apostle was exhilarating, but to live in first-century conditions was repugnant.

Although the living conditions in Korea paled in comparison to Japan and China, the missionaries found the Korean people more hospitable to foreigners. After her first three weeks in Seoul, Mattie Wilcox Noble in 1892 wrote in her journal: "The foreigners here are highly respected in contrary to the custom in China where they are called the foreign devil. We are here called 'the great man' or 'the great lady.' "[87] American missionaries were only granted access into China after the country was forced to sign a series of unequal treaties with Western nations after the Opium War (1839–1842). Although the treaties included official toleration of Christianity, missionaries encountered resentment and anti-foreign hostility from many Chinese because their access was inextricably linked with the heavy hand of Western imperialism.[88] In contrast, Noble was pleased that Korean crowds made clear paths for the missionaries when they traveled on crowded city streets. In 1898, the Presbyterian women's missionary magazine, *Woman's Work for Woman*, sought to recruit additional female missionaries for Korea. In addition to sharing stories about the multitudes of Korean women in cities like Pyongyang and Wonsan eager to learn about Christianity, the magazine included excerpts from Robert E. Speer's 1897 report that highlighted the warm regard and respect.[89] Readers learned that missionaries "gained a position of supreme dignity and influence" and that female missionaries, like the men, could travel throughout the country as they pleased. Speer described a missionary's departure from Seoul for her furlough: "When Mrs. Gifford left Seoul for her furlough last year, the Christians insisted on carrying her chair for her and all her baggage . . . A great crowd, with presents accompanied her, and as her steamer sailed off they sat on a hill, with banners, singing Christian songs."[90] The following year, Annie Laurie Baird wrote from Pyongyang, stating that the city's residents were "lovable Koreans" who extended their assistance when a missionary was in need: "Sometimes people who leave the beaten tracks of travel and visit our remote little country ask us if we really can learn to love these poor, hard-featured, not overclean folks. Some of us are very ungrateful if we do not love them, for we owe them much."[91] Upon learning that one of his friends in the United States had applied to join the Presbyterian mission in Japan, a missionary explained to his family in 1901 how his placement in Korea was better than Japan. Koreans by and large respectfully welcomed the American missionaries whereas the Japanese regarded Westerners with hostility and contempt: "But ever since I have seen our neighbors the Japanese, I am profoundly thankful it was not my lot to live and work with them . . . They are among the most conceited and sensitive people of whom I have ever known. They snub foreigners on every occasion. The Chinese do too but theirs is ignorance."[92]

Because of these compliant characteristics, American missionaries found the Korean people capable servants. Presbyterian Eugene Bell arrived in 1895. Born in Kentucky in 1868, Bell graduated from Central University of Kentucky in 1891 and Louisville Theological Seminary three years later. Upon graduating, he married Lottie Charlotte Witherspoon and after being ordained in the Louisville Presbytery worked as a supply preacher in northern Kentucky. But after a year, Bell set his sights toward wider horizons. Throughout their first several years in Korea, Eugene and Lottie Bell composed weekly letters, sometimes writing two to three letters in a week, to relatives in Kentucky. Unlike official mission reports or correspondence to the mission board secretary, these letters provide a vista into the private thoughts and lived experiences of a missionary couple in Korea. In a number of their early letters they wrote about their Korean servants. During her first month in Seoul, Lottie Bell wrote to her mother: "I suppose you are anxious to know how I am getting along with my housekeeping," and then proceeded to describe the fine work of her three servants, including how they cooked, cleaned, and set the table for every meal. Bell had taught her Korean cook how to make American cuisine, such as biscuits and steak, and was delighted that the cook was able to prepare nearly anything Bell asked for without her help. Bell added that the other two servants were also learning how to perform household tasks: "My boy also is quite capable. And I do thoroughly enjoy having my table nicely set for every meal without my having any trouble, and everything daintily served." Bell happily told her mother that she had effectively recreated her genteel Kentucky lifestyle in Korea at little financial cost. She favorably compared her Korean servants to her servants at home: "I had never hoped to keep house so entirely after my own notions of how it should be done—certainly I could have never done it at home, with the servants one usually has—and to think I can get it all for $14.00 silver—three servants!"[93] In letters to his parents, Eugene Bell similarly praised one of his servants for his work ethic and willingness to please: "He is a splendid gardener and doesn't seem to have a lazy bone in his body and seems to take a delight in doing what I want and in the way I want it."[94] Bell also wrote of how he spent several difficult hours each day in a classroom learning Korean. After two months, Bell noted that he was far from ready to engage in direct evangelistic work among Koreans, but that he had acquired enough of the language to be able to command his servants.[95]

Another Presbyterian missionary couple in Korea, John Fairman and Annie Shannon Preston, arrived in Korea in 1903. They had wed earlier the same year. The son of a Presbyterian minister, John Preston was ordained in the Enoree Presbytery (in South Carolina) in 1903 after receiving degrees from Furman University (BA in 1898), Princeton University (MA in 1902), and Princeton Theological Seminary (BD in 1902). In a letter to her mother-in-law, Annie Preston also wrote favorably about her Korean servants. Like Lottie Bell, Preston praised her servants for their ability to perform household tasks exactly as she wished. "We certainly started to housekeeping under the most favorable conditions, with two well-trained servants and another teachable one," wrote Preston. As she was preparing to hire two additional Korean servants for the hot summer months, she confessed that the act of employing five servants was hardly in tune with the "missionary simplicity" reported in domestic missionary literature. But Preston contended that she was not at an "awfully extravagant daughter-in-law" who would ruin her son less than a year into their marriage, but simply following the example of other missionaries.[96] Preston, like Bell, also drew comparisons between her Korean servants and servants back home in the American South, but added a racial association between Koreans and African Americans in her observations. Though her Korean servants required constant supervision and occasional reprimand, Preston wrote, "I think, on the whole, that Korean servants must be more satisfactory than negroes, unless you find one of the 'befo de wah' [before the American Civil War] variety. The Koreans can learn to do anything very well after being told a few times, and seem to take a good deal of pains."[97] Just as white southern

Presbyterians commonly employed black servants for their housekeeping in the United States, Preston was able to recreate a commensurate lifestyle with Korean servants.

Missionaries Respond to Criticisms of Their Luxurious American Homes

Angus Hamilton, a foreign correspondent in East Asia for the *London Times*, published a book based on his travel through Korea. Hamilton accused the foreign missionaries for creating conflict and violence in Korea. The journalist believed American missionaries, with their wanton zeal for proselytism and ostentatious imperial lifestyles, threatened to foment anti-foreign and anti-Christian feelings among Koreans. Unlike Japan or China, with their long experience with European Catholic and Protestant missionaries, Korea was unique, Hamilton conceded, for the preeminence of American Protestant missionaries, who had made Korea "their peculiar field." In Seoul, Hamilton observed the ubiquity of missionaries "who prattle of Christianity in a marked American accent." But instead of devoting their days to helping Koreans within "their mission to the heathen," the missionaries invested their resources toward maintaining their homes. As they occupied the most "attractive and commodious houses in the foreign settlements," the American missionaries, Hamilton charged, exploited Korean workers by hiring multiple servants at low wages. "As a class," he added, "American missionaries have large families, who live in comparative idleness and luxury."[98]

As Hamilton's critique began circulating throughout East Asia and the United States, Presbyterian clergyman and mission secretary Arthur Judson Brown defended the missionaries in a pamphlet entitled "Truth and Falsehood about Korea Missionaries." From the onset, Brown marked his intent to debunk Hamilton, writing: "Anyone who has visited Korea or is acquainted with even the ABCs of the situation there will read with curious interest Mr. Hamilton's book, 'Korea.' The reader notes that the author criticizes pretty nearly everybody and everything."[99] Brown accepted Hamilton's right to express his opinions, no matter how tactless or tasteless, but he sought to correct Hamilton's statements on three fronts: missionary salaries, houses, and idleness. He disclosed that the annual salary of a Presbyterian missionary in Korea was approximately $600 a year, with free rent and an allowance of $100 for a child. A missionary couple received $1,200, because both spouses were given $600. Brown conceded that at first glance missionary salaries appeared high. According to the 1900 U.S. Census, the average annual salary for a male carpet mill worker was $468 (female carpet mill workers averaged $268).[100] The average salary for a Protestant minister in 1890 was $574.[101] But because Korea did not produce "the kinds of food and clothing that an American has to use," missionaries had to pay expensive freight fees for goods purchased in the United States. Additionally, Brown compared the rising salary of clergymen with each year of service in contract to the unchanging salary of foreign missionaries. "I admit that the salary of the missionary is adequate to his support," Brown wrote, "but it is designed to cover only his reasonable needs, and while ministers in this country may look forward to an increase, sometimes to large figures, the most eminent foreign missionary receives the same modest stipend to the day of his death."[102] Brown also observed that experienced missionaries like Horace Underwood, Samuel Austin Moffett, and James S. Gale had forfeited the opportunity to earn greater salaries from large churches in American cities. Missionaries and ministers averaged nearly equal annual salaries, but some clergymen in large urban churches received $3,000 in 1890.[103]

Like Hamilton, Brown had visited Korea in 1901. In his survey of missionary estates, he conceded that two or three houses were markedly luxurious because they were built by wealthy relatives of particular missionaries. One Presbyterian missionary, Horace Underwood, used financial support from his family's lucrative typewriter sales in the United States to build a magnificent modern home equipped with a steam-heater, hot and cold water, and grand fireplaces in three bedrooms, which earned him the derisive moniker "millionaire missionary" from other foreigners in Korea. In 1903, the Korean emperor, in search of a safe palace site, eyed and purchased Underwood's house.[104] But the majority of the missionary houses were modest and comparable to "the home of a country clergyman or school teacher in the United States."[105] Yet even an ordinary American house far exceeded typical Korean standards. During Mattie Wilcox Noble's visits to Korean homes throughout Pyongyang in 1897, she lamented the cramped conditions. In her journal, she wrote that a Korean home barely had sufficient space for an American double bed. "How thankful I feel that I have rooms like an American," Noble reflected. "Just one of our rooms, small though they are, would make four living rooms for four Korean families, for they seldom have but one room."[106] In 1903, Noble recalled an incident in which several Korean women followed her home to obtain a glimpse of the missionary's house. After Noble invited them in, she observed that the Korean women were "surprised and delighted," marveling that the missionary's house was "beautiful, like heaven." Then the Korean Protestant woman accompanying Noble said, "Do our people live like this? No, but the lady serves God and He allows them to live in a pretty home in a foreign country."[107] In a letter to his family in 1897, Eugene Bell sketched a picture of his new home in Korea, which included twelve rooms serving various purposes (study, pantry, dining room, kitchen, sitting room, bedroom, drug room, and bathroom) and ranging in size from 8 × 8 square feet to 24 × 18 square feet.[108] The architectural blueprints of a Methodist Episcopal Church, South missionary residence in Songdo from 1913 illustrates a multistoried home with a basement consisting of four rooms (furnace room, vegetable room, laundry room, work room), the first floor consisting of a kitchen (11 × 12 square feet), a study (also 11 × 12), a dining room (12 × 15), and a sitting room (12 × 15), a second floor consisting of a bathroom, closet, and three bedrooms (two 12 × 15 bedrooms and one 12 × 11 bedroom), and an attic.[109] Brown was not unaware of the material discrepancies between the American missionaries and the Koreans they came to serve. He did not deny that missionary houses appeared "palatial in comparison with the wretched hovels in which the natives herd like rabbits in a warren," but insisted that mission residences were constructed to sustain physical health in unfamiliar and unsanitary Korean environs. And because the typical Protestant missionary couple consisted of a "man of education and refinement" and a "woman of cultivation and good taste," they naturally fashioned for themselves an attractive home in sharp contrast to the "miserable habitations of a heathen city."[110] Instead of accusing the missionaries for lavish spending, as Hamilton had done, Brown believed that missionary houses in Korea evinced the missionaries' resourcefulness and commitment. With scarce supplies and modest income, the missionaries had cultivated a "home for life" in the Korean mission field.[111]

Finally, Brown refuted Hamilton's charge of missionary idleness by detailing the work of his mission. Seventy missionaries were in charge of 323 congregations, 79 schools, 5 hospitals, and about 35,000 communicants and adherents. Missionaries were hardly idle but rather overworked and undermanned in their efforts to found churches, schools, and hospitals, and "create in a heathen land some of the conditions of decent society."[112] According to Brown, each missionary was doing the labor of several workers in the United States, because no competent Korean assistants could aid them. Despite the missionaries' praise for Korean household servants, Brown's emphasis on the dearth of qualified indigenous workers reveals how the mission was hesitant about employing Koreans in religious activities. Thus, every missionary adopted several occupations: "Each one of them is a preacher, pastor, Sunday-school superintendent, architect, builder and bishop combined, with a diocese a hundred miles."[113] And the missionaries had to travel in harsh conditions without modern transportation. Brown had traveled with them and he knew intimately of the arduous journey "through heat and cold and dust and mud, burned by the midday sun, drenched by the sudden storms, eating unaccustomed food, sleeping on the floor in vermin-invested huts—enduring every privation incident to travel in an uncivilized land."[114] Several times each year, the male missionary left his family and went on a long itinerating journey to visit all the churches in his assigned district. Though Eugene Bell enjoyed preaching to and baptizing Koreans in remote regions, some of whom he thought possessed the most sincere and childlike faith, he also complained about his lodging. "If you could look into a little dirty Korean inn," he told his mother in 1897, "in a small room with mud floor, mud walls and paper doors and windows, you could see me as I am sitting on a Korean chair, that is the floor, writing on a box."[115] In the same year, Bell confessed to his sister that he despised leaving Seoul and was unhappy in the "wilds of southern Korea."[116] A few months later in December, Bell lamented to his mother about his temporary accommodations—a small room with a low ceiling and smoke-covered paper walls: "I am sure you never saw a negro cabin any dirtier."[117]

As male missionaries itinerated, their spouses stayed at home caring for their children. Some wives grew lonely; others were envious and longed to be out ministering to Koreans rather than ensconced at home. In many ways, the married female missionaries had more responsibilities than their husbands. In addition to housekeeping and rearing children, all without their husbands for months at a time, female missionaries like Annie Baird were also evangelists who taught Bible classes for Korean women. In a letter to a friend, Augusta McCoy, Baird described herself in 1891 as a "temporary widow" whenever her husband William itinerated. But in the same letter, she conveyed joy in her evangelizing work alongside the other Presbyterian women, recounting the conversion of a fourteen year-old Korean girl, "Chongee," whose appearance had been transformed after adopting Christianity. "Looking at her now," Baird wrote, "it is hard for me to realize that she was the miserable little bundle of rags and dirt when she came that they say she was."[118] Baird wrote that though she had adjusted nicely to life in Korea, she longed to see more conversions: "We have everything we need out here to make us comfortable and happy, except the one thing that we want most of all, and that is, more direct results of our life and labor here . . . to see this poor people illuminated with the love of Christ."[119] In her correspondence, Baird described her missionary life in three categories: as a wife, a mother, and an evangelist. She was sensitive about the negative views of other foreigners in Korea against American missionaries and their large families, numerous servants, and luxurious houses. She confessed to McCoy that she and her husband were deliberating about whether to petition the government for a land grant in order to become farmers. They could pursue more direct evangelism by living within an indigenous community and they could be self-supporting by selling their own crops. According to Baird, her denominational mission board wrote constantly about "the difficulty of raising money for missions at home" and of "the adverse criticisms of passing travelers upon the style in which missionaries live." Baird wrote that she and her husband "would like to relieve the church as much as possible of our support, and to put ourselves outside the range of such criticisms, however unjust they may be."[120] But Baird remained in the Presbyterian mission, receiving full salary, until her death in 1916.

In October 1895, Baird and Ella Dodge Appenzeller delivered addresses about the vocation of the missionary wife at the decennial anniversary of Protestant missions in Seoul. Both of them tacked the question of whether missionary wives were a help or a hindrance. Baird acknowledged that many missionary wives experienced frustration with feeling trapped at home with their children. Baird shared how missionary wives had envisioned enthralling experiences of evangelizing to Koreans alongside their husbands, "but as one little head after another bobs up around the family table, we find that our time and strength are almost entirely taken up with the ordering of our household and the care of our children."[121] But Baird encouraged the women to embrace their no less significant duties of raising children and maintaining a clean home. Additionally, she added that they had abundant opportunities within the mission compound to learn the language, attend indigenous services, and teach religious classes to female servants. Though Baird presented married female missionaries as mainly wives and mothers, she also carved out a small space for teaching the gospel.

Appenzeller was more abrasive and accusatory. She said that missionary wives depended too much on their husbands for help maintaining their homes. They must accept their roles as wife and mother by learning to be self-reliant at home, training competent servants, and nurturing healthy and godly children. To illustrate her point, she rebuked women who asked their husbands to help lay the new carpet in their homes when servants could do it: "How pleasant it is to have one's husband always at one's beck and call, but that is not what he was sent for."[122] The perpetually needy wife, beseeching her husband's assistance for every little chore at home, was a hindrance to his work. Appenzeller also reprimanded women who were leaving their children in the care of servants in order to accompany their husbands on evangelizing trips. Jane Hunter contends that the "women's missionary enterprise celebrated Christian domesticity for the benighted existence of women around the world."[123] Married female missionaries assigned priority to the domestic sphere and sought to imbue their Victorian notions of wifehood and motherhood upon indigenous women through teaching and example. Appenzeller feared that married female missionaries in Korea were abdicating their responsibilities as supportive wives and nurturing mothers in order to take on their husbands' roles. Unlike their husbands, they were in fact inadequate to evangelize in regions beyond the mission compound. The women did not even know whether the Koreans they were praying with were "exalting Buddha or Jesus."[124] She also asked her female colleagues to question their motives: "May it be part conceit to want to go out and do something which will show or read well in a report?"[125] Unlike Baird, who noted evangelistic opportunities for women in mission compounds, Appenzeller instructed wives to observe their spousal and parental duties. This was their true religious vocation in Korea.

The cultivation of comfortable homes created a paradoxical situation. On the one hand, the wives were pleased that they had recreated Western lifestyles in a remote nation. Not unlike any other migrant community, American missionaries were building new homes and raising young children in a foreign land. But they sensed that their lifestyles could detract from their mission. Unlike other immigrant communities in late nineteenth- and early twentieth-century North America, who were creating religious centers like Jewish synagogues and Roman Catholic parishes for fellow ethnic migrants, American missionaries had set out chiefly to convert Koreans and plant indigenous churches. Yet, they established physical boundaries. In 1902, one Presbyterian missionary marveled at his colleagues' houses in Wonsan, a port city in northern Korea, which were impressively built and standing beautifully on a high bluff overlooking the harbor. But he expressed some concern that these houses were "very much removed from the Koreans," not only different from but also superior to Korean residences, even those belonging to Korean gentry.[126] These economic inequalities provoked hostility and produced the phenomenon that the missionaries feared most: scores of Koreans who expressed interest in Christianity solely for material gain.

In her address, Baird tackled this paradox by noting how married female missionaries largely determined the style of living for their families. A beautiful home did not merely display a woman's prudent resourcefulness, but also reflected her religious faithfulness. Nevertheless, the very same home left her open to harsh criticism from other foreigners and Koreans. She recalled a conversation with a Western traveler visiting her home: "Something was said about the lives of the natives in the interior and he looked about our little parlor which seemed plain enough to me and said, 'Why, this is palatial, simply palatial.' "[127] A married female missionary who had recently entered into Korea also questioned Baird about their way of life: "We came out expecting to find such missionary simplicity but, oh, it was all so different from the start from what we thought it would be."[128] Instead of preaching in remote villages, the new couple attended "stylish little teas" in homes with "such nice Brussels carpets and things."[129] Baird acknowledged the disparity: "Compared with the Vanderbilts we live in a humble, not to say, mean way . . . compared with the people whom we have come to serve and to save, we live like princes and millionaires."[130] But she defended the missionaries; they were frugal, concerned about health rather than display, and likely to purchase their Brussels carpets secondhand at low prices from foreign vendors en route to Korea, which would prove cheaper than replacing several carpets over time. Tea parties meant not merely recreation but friendship and the alleviation of stress. Women's tea parties and men's tennis games strengthened bonds and reinvigorated commitments.

As a physician, Lillias Underwood cited health reasons in defense of a seemingly lavish way of life. Upon entering Seoul for the first time in 1888, Underwood noticed the stark contrast between the filthy streets and low mud houses in the city and the Presbyterian mission property. "We left behind us these dirty streets and saw around us a lovely lawn, flower beds, bushes and trees, and a pretty picturesque mission home," Underwood wrote. "It was like magic."[131] She later argued that the missionary residences were not extravagant but essential for physical and mental welfare. The sanitation system in Seoul, in which all sewage flowed out into ditches on either side of the street, rendered it impossible for missionaries to live among the Korean people without exposure to infectious diseases. Underwood referred to the death of a Canadian Presbyterian missionary, William John McKenzie, who committed suicide in 1895. McKenzie eschewed the safety of the mission compound in order to live among the Koreans.[132] But after several months of Korean-style dwelling and eating, McKenzie became physically ill,

Figure 1.1 Lillias Horton Underwood (Presbyterian Historical Society, Philadelphia, PA)

suffering from feverish spells and frequent vomiting. In the summer of 1895, McKenzie's physical condition worsened. McKenzie entered his symptoms in his last diary entry, then concluded, "Hope it is not death, for the sake of Korea and the many who will say it was my manner of living like Koreans.

神學博士
法學博士
元杜尤牧師
一八五九年生
一九一六年死
自一八八五年
至一九一六年
朝鮮에宣教
REV. HORACE GRANT UNDERWOOD, D. D., L. L. D.
1859–1916
Missionary in Korea, 1885–1916

Figure 1.2 Horace Grant Underwood (Presbyterian Historical Society, Philadelphia, PA)

It was imprudence, on part of myself, traveling under hot sun and sitting out at night till cold."[133] The next day, he asked the Korean Protestants in his town to distribute his money among the poor and to bury him beside the church if he died. As the Koreans participated in the worship service, McKenzie departed into the wilderness and shot himself in the head with his gun.[134] The missionary community in Korea was shaken by his suicide. In a letter to Henry Appenzeller, George Heber Jones wrote, "I am shocked. I am grieved. I cannot collect my thoughts at the news of Bro. McKenzie's death. Such a man . . . Such an end! Alone, sick, insane, a suicide! Oh! God, there is some mystery here."[135] Despite McKenzie's last wishes, Underwood attributed McKenzie's death precisely to his decision to live among the Koreans, which, she thought, accounted for his debilitating physical health and mental insanity. In her diagnosis, McKenzie succumbed to a solitary life that eroded his mental acuity and the physiological realities "that a body which has reached maturity, fed on plenty of nutritious food, cannot suddenly be shifted to a meager, unaccustomed and distasteful diet of foreign concoction, and retain its power to resist disease."[136] Underwood presented McKenzie's suicide as a cautionary tale for missionaries who left the hermetic cocoon of mission compounds.

Another missionary, George W. Gilmore, argued in 1892 that their superior residence was a constructive force for evangelism. He did not deny the criticism that missionary houses were comparatively lavish by Korean standards. Instead, Gilmore insisted that their property ought to be employed as an apologetic for the positive benefits of Christianity over against Buddhism and Confucianism. Gilmore proudly noted that Koreans, even those in the highest positions, had visited missionary residences and expressed awe at their material splendor. Rather than instigating Korean resentment, as other foreigners and even some missionaries supposed, Korean wonderment at missionary luxuries fostered further curiosity about Christianity. He witnessed firsthand how Korean visitors would "admire the comforts" and then "go home to ponder on the religion which takes hold of the present life of man and makes it more enjoyable."[137] Therefore, missionaries need not feel shame or apologize for living comfortably because their homes demonstrated "the advantages of a distinctively Christian civilization" in primitive Korea.[138] Gilmore found the accusation that Koreans inquired about Christianity only to receive material handouts from the missionaries to be too simplistic. The cheerful and civilized missionary community served as tangible evidence for Christian potential to transform Korean society.

An Independent Canadian Missionary Embraces the Free Korean Religious Marketplace

In 1889, Malcolm C. Fenwick, a twenty-six-year-old from the outskirts of Toronto, Canada, devoted his life to becoming a missionary to Korea. He first learned about Korea from reading a newspaper story about an American

Presbyterian missionary there who was imprisoned and faced execution by hanging for openly proselytizing. Although the Korean government prohibited proselytism, the story was untrue. Like all of the other members in his Canadian church, however, Fenwick knew little about Korea. The ignorance manifested itself when the minister in Fenwick's church instructed the Lord about the country: "You know, Lord, Corea is an island in the Pacific Ocean." Confusing Korea for Corsica, Fenwick too initially believed that Korea was an island in the Mediterranean Sea. And he knew as little about mission work as he did about East Asian geography. Fenwick had heard of David Livingstone's mission work in Africa and had seen pictures from missionaries on furlough, but possessed scant knowledge of actual mission work. He imagined an austere preacher standing before a crowd of natives with a Bible in his hand while another native held a peculiar-shaped umbrella over his head. When his friend decided to go to Korea as a missionary, Fenwick offered to accompany him and hold the umbrella while he preached.[139]

Despite knowing little about mission work and Korean culture, Fenwick was drawn to Korea for several reasons in addition to his desire to preach the gospel to unbelievers in a foreign land. Fenwick was an enterprising businessman, utilizing his experience working on the family farm and in various emerging industries along the Canadian Pacific Railway to become a manager of a wholesale hardware business with forty employees. Because Korea was a new and undeveloped mission field, Fenwick believed that his years in the northwestern Canadian frontier would prove useful in the unknown Korean wild. The newspaper stories he read about Korean laws against direct proselytism and the perils of imprisonment appealed to Fenwick's sense of adventure. Like other missionaries, Fenwick envisioned Korea as a religious *tabula rasa* and leapt at the opportunity to be a pioneer in a foreign mission field.[140] But when he arrived in Korea, Fenwick disagreed with how the Americans lived, trained, and evangelized to Koreans.

Though Fenwick was officially sent to Korea under a newly established Toronto-based mission agency in 1888, the "Corean Union Mission," he would largely be free from denominational strictures, able to work in Korea as an executive manager who made his own decisions.[141] Fenwick eventually established his own mission agency to Korea, the Corean Itinerant Mission, and sought to recruit other missionaries. Like the Methodist and Presbyterian mission organizations in Korea, Fenwick instilled a policy that prohibited employment of Korean converts as pastors, for fear they would preach false doctrine.[142] In 1897, Speer reported that Presbyterian missionaries had planted ten or more churches in their first thirteen years of mission work but did not ordain indigenous ministers and elders in the churches because the missionaries wanted the Koreans sufficiently trained to administer properly the ineffable and holy sacraments of Baptism and the Lord's Supper.[143]

Fenwick enjoyed his freedom from denominational mission boards, but he was often lonely. Methodist and Presbyterian missionaries attended English-language worship services, shared meals, and played tennis together in their mission compounds, but Fenwick did not have access to such a cohesive network of Westerners. But living outside a Western community, Fenwick could learn more about the Korean people. In his frequent association with all types of Koreans, not just Protestant converts, Fenwick felt their wariness toward Westerners acutely. Although other missionaries had ably studied Korean cultural, racial, and religious characteristics, Fenwick thought they had not sufficiently considered how Koreans perceived the Western missionary: "But it is not so much a study of the natural ability of the Oriental which is difficult; the difficult thing is to acquire a working knowledge of his process of thinking; to learn, unmistakably, his opinion of the barbarian from the West, who dares to teach a mighty yellow man."[144] Though missionaries frequently heralded the warm greetings they received from Koreans, Fenwick noted the underlying hostility that belied outward appearances. Koreans welcomed the white missionary courteously, even bowing respectfully during the encounter, but Fenwick contended that their inner attitude was one of disgust and loathing toward the foreigner: "The white man is rude; he is arrogant; he does not know how to efface himself; he smells of soap."[145] Just as Americans frequently complained about the foul stenches rising from Korean cities and villages, Fenwick noted that Koreans grumbled about the offensive odor of missionaries in equal measure.

Fenwick defined his social existence in Korea as a preacher and teacher from the civilized West, but his views evolved as he began to reflect upon and criticize Western notions of cultural dominance over the East. The Koreans were not a slow and slovenly people, as often depicted in popular and religious Western literature, but Fenwick adopted the position of "the stupid Westerner" receiving a Korean education.[146] "The Coreans taught me in many ways that we of the West do not know everything," noted Fenwick, "and the Easterner usually has a good practical reason for what he does, generally well adapted to his circumstances and always economical."[147]

In 1896, Fenwick therefore altered his mission philosophy completely. Despite his painstaking efforts, Fenwick was still struggling to convert Koreans. As he continued preaching, he realized that his listeners viewed him strictly as a foreigner teaching his strange religion. Just as Fenwick had experienced difficulty crossing cultural boundaries as a "stupid Westerner" in Korea, he felt that his Korean audiences could not look past his foreign appearance to hear his religious message. Fenwick envisioned a mighty river with the white missionary on one side and Koreans on the other. From his reading of 1 Corinthians, Fenwick believed the only way for the missionary to get across the river was through preaching. But preaching in fluent Korean, a skill that Fenwick had adroitly acquired, proved insufficient. "I shall never forget how hard I tried to cross," wrote Fenwick, as he recalled testifying "in tears" about the gospel "Sunday after Sunday, month after month" to no avail.[148] When pleading with the Koreans to convert, Fenwick perceived that his listeners did not want to do so because the message came from a crude white savage. Fenwick had inverted the missionary discourse that cast white Christians as superior to lowly, benighted Koreans: "And if this Jesus I talked so much about was likely to make them into a being as this white barbarian before them, the best thing they could do was to have nothing whatever to do with Jesus."[149] Fenwick called for a reversal. Korean converts, not white missionaries, would be the most effective preachers in Korea.

Fenwick was not the only missionary in Korea who believed in the importance of indigenous preaching. Methodist and Presbyterian missionaries identified and cultivated the most promising Korean converts in their churches to be evangelists. But Fenwick differed from the other missionaries about training methods for prospective Korean preachers. Methodist missionaries established a four-year course of study for Korean preachers with a curriculum that included memorizing multiple catechisms, studying nearly every book of the Bible, reading works from the English Puritan author John Bunyan and the German Protestant missionary Ernst Faber, and writing sermons on the atonement, baptism, and filial piety.[150] Even after Korean preachers had completing their training, Methodist missionaries provided rigorous supervision and listened to their sermons to ensure the promulgation of correct doctrine. In contrast, Fenwick's training consisted of sending out Korean converts to preach while he led them in Bible study, with no need for other religious books. In one case, Fenwick commissioned a Korean convert to preach almost immediately after witnessing the man's conversion.[151]

Fenwick's strategy of employing Korean preachers achieved mixed results. Instead of modeling his evangelistic methods, Fenwick's assistant teacher used the business skills that he had learned from the missionary to engage in emerging Korean industries. Two of Fenwick's earliest students converted to Seventh Day Adventism and accepted employment from an Adventist missionary; a different student left Fenwick to find an educator who would exclusively teach English; another student eventually dismissed Christianity altogether.[152] At the same time, Fenwick found encouragement in the work of one of his disciples, "Pastor Sen," whom Fenwick had appointed to Kongju, a district three hundred miles away from his home in Wonsan.[153] Like Fenwick, Pastor Sen did not receive formal theological training or constant missionary supervision, but he successfully established churches and trained preachers in his district. Fenwick acknowledged that Pastor Sen's students preached better than his own. To Fenwick, Pastor Sen was more than a faithful minister but also vindication of his iconoclastic methods and ultimately evidence that the Christian God "is no respecter of persons."[154] Fenwick reversed course, de-emphasizing the recruitment of additional white missionaries from North America in favor of training and sending Korean preachers throughout remote and unreached districts in the peninsular nation. In his interpretation of a well-trodden biblical passage on foreign missions in Matthew 9:35–38, with the command that prayerful Christians are to ask God, "the Lord of the harvest," to send more workers, Fenwick noted that the scriptural injunction never specified nationality. "We did not dictate what nationality they should be," explained Fenwick about how his mission selected itinerating evangelists, "and it pleased [God] to send all Coreans, whom the world has been educated to believe are poor, worthless, helpless beings."[155]

As Fenwick began employing Korean preachers, he recognized the economic benefits of his methods. In addition to evangelizing more effectively than foreign missionaries, Korean evangelists did not require nearly as much money. Because Fenwick's training for mission work was largely as an entrepreneurial businessman and not as an ordained minister, Fenwick accentuated cost-effectiveness alongside religious results. Unlike foreign missionaries, who received approximately six hundred U.S. dollars in annual salary, Fenwick's Korean preachers received sixty U.S. dollars a year. Fenwick calculated that investing in his mission's Korean workers only cost domestic contributors sixteen and a half cents a day in American currency, producing much better value than financially supporting white missionaries at a cost of up to five dollars per day.[156]

Furthermore, the travel expenses for Korean evangelists were exceedingly less than those of new foreign missionaries. Fenwick recalled sending out nine Korean evangelists from Wonsan to the distant Tumen River district more than seven hundred miles away in the far northern reaches of Korea, bordering China and Russia, giving each worker the equivalent of 5 U.S. dollars for the journey. In contrast, Fenwick estimated that "it would have cost nine white missionaries three thousand dollars to reach the [Tumen River] from New York or London." Unlike white missionaries, Fenwick wrote, Korean evangelists traveled simply with "no elaborate outfit, no Pullman car to travel in, no expensive voyaging to pay for," and they carried little more than clothing and Bibles for luggage. Fenwick also estimated that the cost of educating a white missionary to cross what he described as the "three great mountains" of the Korean mission field—learning the language, the customs, and the people—was approximately 5,000 U.S. dollars. So, Fenwick's Korean evangelists to the Tumen River district not only cost less to send but they also cost far less to train. The nine Korean evangelists had already crossed these three great mountains "without one cent of cost to the home churches." Overall, not including annual salaries, domestic supporters saved 47,940 U.S. dollars by investing in Fenwick's nine Korean evangelists rather than nine white missionaries. Refuting critics who questioned the productivity of Korean evangelists, Fenwick noted that the work of white missionaries in the Tumen River district would not necessarily reap religious success. Citing the region's harsh physical conditions and cross-cultural obstacles, Fenwick predicted that white missionaries "would have been more of a hindrance than a help, and only a few of them, at best, would have made useful servants; as some would die, others break down, and still others turn out misfits."[157] In Fenwick's financial accounting of mission work in Korea, indigenous preachers proved the superior investment.

Fenwick was invigorated by the opportunities to evangelize in previously unreached areas. Unlike the other nations in Asia, such as China, Japan, or India, foreign Protestant mission work in Korea did not begin in the 1790s or early 1800s, but only five years before Fenwick's arrival in 1889. In 1890, the Korean government eased its strict regulations on direct evangelization, which created unlimited avenues for mission work beyond existing medical centers and schools. Fenwick approached the Korean mission field as a free religious marketplace primed for exploration and development. In their work on American religious history, sociologists Roger Finke and Rodney Stark use economic concepts like the marketplace to analyze the growth and decline of different Christian denominations and to explain how "religious economies are like commercial economies in that they consist of a market made up of a set of current and potential customers and a set of firms seeking to serve that market."[158] Fenwick viewed Methodist and Presbyterian missionaries, the two largest missionary groups in Korea, as his competitors in the Korean religious marketplace.

Fenwick opposed the comity agreements between Methodist and Presbyterian missionaries to create equal territorial divisions for their work. In March 1888, Henry Appenzeller delivered an address in Seoul on comity agreements that called for Methodist and Presbyterian missions to demarcate specific regions throughout Korea for each mission's work. In large cities, each denominational mission would work parallel with one another. But only one denominational mission would be permitted in smaller areas with populations of less than 5,000 Koreans, and existing Korean Protestants in these smaller areas were to become members of the approved denominational mission. Consequently, the comity agreement would have Korean Presbyterians transfer to Methodism and vice versa. Although missionaries questioned the notion of coercing Korean Protestants to switch denominations, they ultimately decided that the benefits of comity outweighed the agency of Koreans. Appenzeller defended the proposal: "What right have I to force a man into the Methodist Church? But if in dividing the field we can so manage as to get our peculiar doctrines and forms of governments in the centers, we shall be doing permanent good."[159] Missionaries from the Methodist Episcopal Church (MEC) and Presbyterian Church in the U.S.A. met together in Korea to sign a comity agreement on February 3, 1893.[160] But Fenwick saw the comity agreement as a cartel that went against the working of the Holy Spirit in the free Korean religious market. He deeply regretted that he had once left a group of Korean Protestants in a new church out of respect for these denominational boundaries during his early years of mission work, upset that he had betrayed God's call for the sake of "heeding conventionalities."[161]

Fenwick's competitive spirit led him to slander other missionaries for exaggerating their successes in Korea and performing hasty baptisms of unconverted Koreans.[162] In response, other missionaries criticized Fenwick for impairing mission work in both North America and Korea. They charged

Fenwick with damaging the image of the Korean mission field in North America by divulging disharmonious relationships among missionaries.[163] In Korea, Fenwick was accused of sending out arrogant Korean preachers who brazenly regarded themselves more highly than converts in the missionary-led Methodist and Presbyterian churches.[164] Gale had an ambivalent view of the independent missionary. He respected Fenwick's orthodox faith, kind heart, and practical skills, but Gale deemed Fenwick reckless and feared his intemperate zeal and impatient methods threatened all Protestant mission work in Korea.[165] Nonetheless, Fenwick continued to train indigenous converts and establish mission districts. As an independent missionary, he need not submit to denominational authorities. As an entrepreneurial businessman, possessing what he viewed as managerial skills unique among all missionaries in Korea, Fenwick set out to unleash Korean preachers into the marketplace, because they were untapped resources with the potential to become the best religious communicators and most cost-effective workers.

Conclusion

In his work on Christian mission and world Christianity, Andrew Walls argues that the fundamental foreign missionary experience entails the idea of "living on terms set by other people."[166] He emphasizes how missionaries are essentially strangers in a foreign land who must adapt to another world by learning their host country's culture, language, and society. Yet in Korea, missionaries struggled to live on indigenous terms because of cultural differences and economic inequalities between their home and host countries. But the missionaries' greatest obstacle to understanding Koreans on their own terms was neither cultural nor economic. Some missionaries, like Fenwick, adapted to Korean life better than others, but all of them possessed religious ambitions that simultaneously intensified their commitment to the mission work and obstructed their vision of Korean perspectives on cultural and political changes in the country.

Jehu J. Hanciles, in his study of global Christian migrations, observes that "when people move, they carry their ideas, beliefs, and religious practices with them."[167] Despite Fenwick's many disagreements with other missionaries, his Christian aspirations were no different than theirs. He too saw Korea as an ideal mission field and regarded Korea as a religious *tabula rasa* for his making. The independent missionary resisted calls to conform to Methodist and Presbyterian designs for two reasons. Not only did Fenwick possess the same freedoms as other foreigners to capitalize on Korea's recent opening to the West, but he was also certain that his mission approach of enlisting Korean evangelists more quickly and more expansively than the Methodists or the Presbyterians would produce more indigenous Christians. In Fenwick's praise of Korean preachers, he expressed his own changing cultural and racial perceptions of Koreans. But he also pointed to the effectiveness of Koreans in order to revel in his own religious success. North American missionaries attributed Christian expansion in Korea to divine favor and indigenous initiatives, but they mostly explained how their own methods generated the religious growth.

Despite their high religious expectations, the number of Korean Protestants in 1904 was 31,905 across all denominations, which was a miniscule figure when compared to the total Korean population of 12 million.[168] But a few missionaries, such as Horace and Lillias Underwood, gained political influence with the Korean royals, and another missionary, Horace Allen, resigned from mission work to accept a diplomatic position in Korea. A number of Korean elites also converted to Protestantism and sought to reform their nation in accordance with Christian principles. Some of them came to the United States as foreign students or political exiles. They would find themselves ambivalent about the forms of Christianity that they encountered in the United States. The ambition and reach of the American Protestant foreign mission enterprise inspired these Koreans, but they also came to deplore the paternalism and racism of white American Protestants.

In 1907, a wave of revivals throughout Korea increased the numbers of converts and shaped Korean Protestant beliefs and practices. But just as North American Protestants clashed with one another in Korea, they would also find themselves at odds with Korean Protestants over common religious beliefs and practices, relationships between missionaries and converts, and the direction of the Korean Church. Korean Protestant expansion confirmed that the Americans were right to identify Korea as a promising mission field. But some of the ways that Korean Protestants at home and abroad reinterpreted the religion stunned and frustrated the missionaries.

Notes

1. William Griffis, *Corea, the Hermit Nation* (New York: Charles Scribner's Sons, 1882) and Ernst Oppert, *A Forbidden Land: Voyages to Corea* (London: Sampson, Low, Marston, Searle, and Rivington, 1880).
2. Henry G. Appenzeller, "Correspondence from Methodist Episcopal Missions: Our Mission in Korea, April 9, 1885," *The Gospel in All Lands* (July 1885), 328.
3. Ibid.
4. Charles Taylor, *Modern Social Imaginaries* (Durham and London: Duke University Press, 2004), 23.
5. Ibid.
6. Ibid., 24.
7. Young-Iob Chung, *Korea under Siege, 1876–1945: Capital Formation and Economic Transformation* (Oxford and New York: Oxford University Press, 2006), 9.
8. *New York Times*, June 21, 1880. In the late nineteenth century, the spellings of "Corea" and "Korea" were both employed in the English language.
9. Ibid.
10. "The Country and People of Corea," *The Gospel in All Lands* (January 1885), 8.
11. Horace N. Allen, "Our First Letter from Korea," *The Foreign Missionary, Containing Particular Accounts of the Work of the Board of Foreign Missions*

of the Presbyterian Church and Selected Articles and Facts from the Missionary Publications of other Protestant Societies (December 1884), 303.
12. Ibid.
13. Yur-Bok Lee, "Korean-American Diplomatic Relations, 1882–1905," in *One Hundred Years of Korean-American Relations, 1882–1982*, edited by Yur-Bok Lee and Wayne Patterson (University, AL: The University of Alabama Press, 1986), 16.
14. "Letter from Frederick T. Frelinghuysen to Lucius H. Foote, October 23, 1883," in *Korean-American Relations: Documents Pertaining to the Far Eastern Diplomacy of the United States, Volume I: The Initial Period, 1883–1886*, edited by George M. McCune and John A. Harrison (Berkeley and Los Angeles: University of California Press, 1951), 35.
15. J. R. Wolfe, "A Visit to Korea," *The Foreign Missionary* (September 1885), 162.
16. Ibid.
17. Frank Carpenter, "The Koreans at Home," *The Gospel in All Lands* (October 1889), 436.
18. Daniel L. Gifford, "Korea and Bible Times," *The Church at Home and Abroad* (November 1889), 419.
19. "The Hour for Korea," *The Foreign Missionary* (September 1885), 153.
20. James Huntley Grayson, *Korea: A Religious History* (Oxford: Oxford University Press, 1989), 172–173.
21. Ibid.
22. William Elliot Griffis, *Corea, Without and Within: Chapters on Corean History, Manners and Religion with Hendrick Hamel's Narrative of Captivity and Travels in Corea, Annotated* (Philadelphia: Presbyterian Board of Publication, 1884), 130.
23. Ibid., 131.
24. Ibid., 170.
25. William Elliot Griffis, "Korea and its Needs," *The Gospel in All Lands* (August 1888), 371.
26. "Foreign Mission Notes by the Secretaries," *The Church at Home and Abroad* (August 1889), 117.
27. "A Glimpse of Korea," *Heathen Children's Friend* (June 1890), 2.
28. "The Hour for Korea," 154.
29. Ibid., 153–154.
30. George Heber Jones, "The Religious Development of Korea," *The Gospel in All Lands* (September 1891), 415.
31. Ibid.
32. Ibid., 416.
33. Ibid., 417.
34. Ibid.
35. Henry G. Appenzeller, "July 10, 1885," as cited in Everett N. Hunt, *Protestant Pioneers in Korea* (Maryknoll, NY: Orbis Books, 1980), 90.
36. Henry G. Appenzeller, "Sermon notes, n.d.," in Henry Gerhard Appenzeller Papers, Missionary Research Library Collection, Burke Theological Library, Columbia University, New York, NY.
37. H. N. Allen, "Medical Work in Korea," *The Foreign Missionary* (July 1885), 74.
38. William R. Hutchison, *Errand to the World: American Protestant Thought and Foreign Missions*, 84–86.
39. Horace G. Underwood, "To the Board of Foreign Missions of the Presbyterian Church of America, September 17, 1886," in *Ŏndŏudŭ Moksa ŭi sŏn'gyo p'yŏnji: 1885–1916* [Rev. Underwood's Missionary Letters], edited by In-su Kim and Horace Grant Underwood (Seoul, Korea: Changnohoe Sinhak Taehakkyo Ch'ulp'anbu, 2002), 649.

40. Horace N. Allen, "Diary Entry on October 10, 1886," in *Allen Ŭisa ŭi sŏn'gyo, oegyo p'yŏnji* [Horace N. Allen, M.D.'s Missionary and Diplomatic Letters], edited by In-su Kim and Horace Newton Allen (Seoul, Korea: K'umnan Ch'ulp'ansa, 2007), 510.
41. George Clayton Foulk, *America's Man in Korea: The Private Letters of George C. Foulk, 1884–1887*, edited by Samuel Hawley (Lanham, MD: Lexington Books, 2008), 17.
42. Ibid.
43. Ibid., 123.
44. Ibid.
45. Ibid., 126.
46. Ibid., 126–127.
47. Ibid., 146, 203, and 208–210.
48. Timothy S. Lee, *Born Again: Evangelicalism in Korea*, 5.
49. Ki-baek Lee, *A New History of Korea*, translated by Edward W. Wagner with Edward J. Schulz (Cambridge and London: Harvard University Press, 1984), 264.
50. See Jeong, Yak-jong, *Jugyo Yoji (The Essentials of the Lord's Teaching): Korean Christian Classics Series, Volume 6* (Seoul, Korea: KIATS Press, 2012) and Sebastian C.H. Kim and Kirsteen Kim, *A History of Korean Christianity*, 30.
51. Horace Underwood, "Securing a Romanist as Teacher," *The Foreign Missionary* (November 1885), 272.
52. Horace Underwood, "Romanists Wide Awake," *The Foreign Missionary* (May 1886), 567.
53. W.W. Rockhill, "Letter to Secretary of State on February 5, 1887," in *Korean-American Relations: Documents Pertaining to the Far Eastern Diplomacy of the United States, Volume II: The Period of Growing Influence: 1887–1895*, edited and with an introduction by Spencer J. Palmer (Berkeley and Los Angeles: University of California Press, 1963), 205.
54. Ibid.
55. Alvey A. Adee, "Letter to Augustine Heard on May 19, 1891," in *Korean-American Relations: Documents Pertaining to the Far Eastern Diplomacy of the United States, Volume II: The Period of Growing Influence: 1887–1895*, 231.
56. Samuel A. Moffett, "Letter to Dr. Ellinwood on March 18, 1890," in *Samuel A. Moffett: First Letters from Korea, 1890–1891* (Seoul, Korea: Hyesun Press, 1975), 9.
57. Samuel A. Moffett, "Letter to Dr. Ellinwood on October 20, 1890," in *Samuel A. Moffett: First Letters from Korea, 1890–1891* (Seoul, Korea: Hyesun Press, 1975), 31.
58. Young-Iob Chung, 319.
59. C.J. Corfe, "The Bishop's Letter from Chemulpo, December 1892," *The Morning Calm* (April 1893), 45–47.
60. William M. Baird, "Diary entry on April 20, 1893," in *William M. Baird of Korea: A Profile* (Oakland: Richard H. Baird, 1968), 31.
61. Baird, "Diary entry on April 26, 1893," in *William M. Baird of Korea: A Profile*, 33.
62. Baird, "Diary entry on May 8, 1893," in *William M. Baird of Korea: A Profile*, 35.
63. Baird, "Diary entry on October 7, 1893," in *William M. Baird of Korea: A Profile*, 42.
64. Roy E. Shearer, *Wildfire: Church Growth in Korea* (Grand Rapids: Wm. B. Eerdmans Co., 1966), 47.
65. James S. Dennis, *Foreign Missions after a Century: Students' Lectures on Missions, Princeton Theological Seminary* (New York: Fleming H. Revell Co., 1893), 63–85.

66. Alfred W. Wasson, *Church Growth in Korea* (New York: International Missionary Council, 1934), 166.
67. Korea Presbyterian Mission, *Report for 1899–1900 of the Pyeng Yang Station, Presented to the Annual Meeting held at Pyeng Yang, September 1900*, no page number.
68. Baird, 64–65.
69. Moffett, "Letter to Dr. Ellinwood on March 25, 1891," in *Samuel A. Moffett: First Letters from Korea, 1890–1891*, 42.
70. Ibid.
71. L. George Paik, *The History of Protestant Missions in Korea, 1832–1910, 4th ed.* (Seoul: Yonsei University Press, 1987), 57–58, and James Huntley Grayson, "The Legacy of John Ross," in *Critical Readings on Christianity in Korea, Volume 1*, edited by Donald Baker (Leiden and Boston: Brill, 2014), 193–203.
72. Baird, 65.
73. Sebastian C.H. Kim and Kirsteen Kim, *A History of Korean Christianity*, 58–59.
74. Lillias H. Underwood, *Fifteen Years among the Top-Knots or Life in Korea, 2nd ed.* (Boston: American Tract Society, 1908), 33–34.
75. Michael J. Seth, *A Concise History of Modern Korea: From the Late Nineteenth Century to the Present* (Lanham, MD: Rowman & Littlefield Publishers, 2010), 23.
76. Ibid.
77. Seth, 24–25.
78. James Scarth Gale, *Korean Sketches* (Chicago and New York: Fleming H. Revell Co., 1898), 209.
79. In 1887, Korean Foreign Minister Kim Yun-sik told an American diplomat that his nation was a "truly independent kingdom and China is only our elder brother and because we are weak and a small country we ask China to advise and assist us." See Yur-Bok Lee, 19.
80. James Scarth Gale, *The Vanguard: A Tale of Korea* (Chicago and New York: Fleming H. Revell Co., 1904), 101.
81. Gale, *Korean Sketches*, 209.
82. Robert E. Speer, "Report on the Mission in Korea of the Presbyterian Board of Foreign Missions, 1897," edited and with an introduction by Seung-Tae Kim, *Korea Institute for Advanced Theological Studies Theological Journal* 2:2 (Fall 2006), 419.
83. Gale, *Korean Sketches*, 209–210.
84. Scott S. Burnett, "Introduction," in *Korean-American Relations: Documents Pertaining to the Far Eastern Diplomacy of the United States, Volume III: The Period of Diminishing Influence: 1896–1905*, edited by Scott S. Burnett (Honolulu: University of Hawaii Press, 1989), 11.
85. In addition to the 74 American Presbyterians and 45 American Methodists, there were 31 British Protestants, 10 Canadians, 9 Australians, and 1 American missionary from the YMCA. See "Appendix 5: Protestant Missionaries in Korea in 1901," in Sung-Deuk Oak, *The Indigenization of Christianity in Korea: North American Missionaries' Attitudes Towards Korean Religions, 1884–1910*, ThD diss., Boston University, 2002, 484.
86. William B. Scranton, "Letter to John M. Reid, June 1, 1885," in *Letters of William B. Scranton* (Korea: William Scranton Foundation, 2010), 21.
87. Mattie Wilcox Noble, "November 14, 1892," in *The Journals of Mattie Wilcox Noble, 1892–1934* (Seoul, Korea: Han'guk Kidokkyo Yŏksa Yŏn'guso, 1993), 22.
88. Lian Xi, *Redeemed by Fire: The Rise of Popular Christianity in Modern China* (New Haven and London: Yale University Press, 2010), 6–7.

89. Annie Laurie Baird, "A Korea Chapter from Pyeng Yang, Swallen, W.L., Some New Christians in Gensan Field, Korea, and How Missionaries Are Treated In Korea," *Woman's Work for Woman* (August 1898), 201, 203, and 210.
90. Ibid., 210.
91. Annie Laurie Baird, "Lovable Koreans," *Woman's Work for Woman* (August 1899), 219.
92. Eugene Bell, "Letter to His Family on February 10, 1901," in Eugene Bell and Lottie Bell Papers, RG435, Presbyterian Historical Society, Philadelphia, PA.
93. Lottie Bell, "Letter to Her Mother on April 21, 1895," in Eugene Bell and Lottie Bell Papers, RG435, Presbyterian Historical Society, Philadelphia, PA.
94. Eugene Bell, "Letter to His Mother on June 4, 1895," in Eugene Bell and Lottie Bell Papers, RG435, Presbyterian Historical Society, Philadelphia, PA.
95. Eugene Bell, "Letter to His Father on May 17, 1895 and Letter to His Mother on June 4, 1895," in Eugene Bell and Lottie Bell Papers, RG435, Presbyterian Historical Society, Philadelphia, PA.
96. Annie Shannon Preston, "Letter to Her Mother-In-Law on May 21, 1904," in John Fairman Preston Papers, RG441, Presbyterian Historical Society, Philadelphia, PA.
97. Annie Shannon Preston, "Letter to Her Mother-In-Law on January 26, 1905," in John Fairman Preston Papers, RG441, Presbyterian Historical Society, Philadelphia, PA.
98. Angus Hamilton, *Korea* (London: W. Heinemann, 1904), 266.
99. Arthur J. Brown, *Truth and Falsehood about Korea Missionaries* (New York: Board of Foreign Missions of the Presbyterian Church, 1904), 1.
100. Twelfth Census of the United States, "Special Reports: Employees and Wages," (1900), xxxi.
101. E. Brooks Holifield, *God's Ambassadors: A History of the Christian Clergy in America* (Grand Rapids and Cambridge: Wm. B. Eerdmans, 2007), 179.
102. Brown, 8–9.
103. Holifield, 179.
104. Lillias H. Underwood, *Underwood of Korea: Being an Intimate Record of the Life and Work of the Rev. H.G. Underwood, D.D., LL.D., for Thirty One Years a Missionary of the Presbyterian Board in Korea* (New York: Fleming H. Revell, 1918), 208–210, and Fred Harvey Harrington, *God, Mammon, and the Japanese: Dr. Horace N. Allen and Korean-American Relations, 1884–1905* (Madison: The University of Wisconsin Press, 1944), 96, 110–111.
105. Brown, 11.
106. Noble, "August 28, 1897," *The Journals of Mattie Wilcox Noble, 1892–1934*, 66.
107. Noble, "October 28, 1903," *The Journals of Mattie Wilcox Noble, 1892–1934*, 112.
108. Eugene Bell, "Letter to His Sister on January 2, 1897," in Eugene Bell and Lottie Bell Papers, RG435, Presbyterian Historical Society, Philadelphia, PA.
109. "Missionary Residence, Songdo, Korea, February 24, 1913, Methodist Episcopal Church, South," in General Commission on Archives and History, The United Methodist Church, Drew University, Madison, NJ.
110. Brown, 11–12.
111. Ibid., 12.
112. Ibid., 16.
113. Ibid., 17.
114. Ibid.
115. Eugene Bell, "Letter to His Mother on March 18, 1897," in Eugene Bell and Lottie Bell Papers, RG435, Presbyterian Historical Society, Philadelphia, PA.
116. Eugene Bell, "Letter to His Sister on September 5, 1897," in Eugene Bell and Lottie Bell Papers, RG435, Presbyterian Historical Society, Philadelphia, PA.

117. Eugene Bell, "Letter to His Mother on December 2, 1897," in Eugene Bell and Lottie Bell Papers, RG435, Presbyterian Historical Society, Philadelphia, PA.
118. Annie Baird, "Letter to Augusta McCoy on March 6, 1891," in Annie Laurie Adams Baird Papers, RG172, Presbyterian Historical Society, Philadelphia, PA.
119. Annie Baird, "Letter to Augusta McCoy on April 12, 1894," in Annie Laurie Adams Baird Papers, RG172, Presbyterian Historical Society, Philadelphia, PA.
120. Ibid.
121. Annie L. Baird, "The Relation of the Wives of Missionaries to Mission Work," *The Korean Repository* (November 1895), 417.
122. Ella Dodge Appenzeller, "Mrs. Appenzeller's Address," *The Korean Repository* (November 1895), 421.
123. Jane Hunter, "The Home and the World: The Missionary Message of U.S. Domesticity," in *Women's Work for Women: Missionaries and Social Change in Asia*, edited by Leslie A. Fleming (Boulder, San Francisco, and London: Westview Press, 1989), 160.
124. Appenzeller, 422.
125. Ibid.
126. Charles F. Bernheisel, in Charles F. Bernheisel Diary, October 31, 1902, Presbyterian Historical Society, Philadelphia, PA.
127. Baird, 418.
128. Ibid., 419.
129. Ibid.
130. Ibid., 418.
131. Lillias H. Underwood, *Fifteen Years among the Top-Knots or Life in Korea, 2nd ed.*, 5.
132. Elizabeth A. McCully, *A Corn of Wheat or the Life of Rev. W.J. McKenzie of Korea* (Toronto: The Westminster Co. Limited, 1903), 221.
133. Ibid.
134. Martha Huntley, *Caring, Growing, Changing: A History of the Protestant Mission in Korea* (New York: Friendship Press, 1984), 116–117.
135. George Heber Jones, "Letter to Henry G. Appenzeller, n.d.," in Henry Gerhard Appenzeller Papers, Missionary Research Library Collection, Columbia University, Burke Theological Library, New York, NY.
136. Underwood, 125.
137. George W. Gilmore, *Korea from its Capital: With a Chapter on Missions* (Philadelphia: Presbyterian Board of Publication and Sabbath-School Work, 1892), 316.
138. Ibid.
139. Malcolm C. Fenwick, *The Church of Christ in Corea* (New York: George H. Doran Co., 1911), 10–11.
140. Fenwick was the third Canadian missionary to Korea. In the 1880s and 1890s, Canadian Protestants, motivated by the fervor surrounding foreign missions in the United States and Britain, began to send out missionaries to Africa and Asia. In 1886, Canadian Congregationalist missionaries went to Angola to partner with American colleagues there. The first Canadian Anglican missionary, J. Cooper Robinson, went to Japan in 1888. In 1892, Canadian Methodists launched a mission to west China, which developed into one of the largest Protestant overseas mission outposts in the twentieth century. See John Webster Grant, *The Church in the Canadian Era: The First Century of Confederation* (Toronto: McGraw Hill Ryerson Limited, 1972), 55–56.
141. Created by several Toronto-area Christian businessmen in 1888, the Corean Union Mission's requirements for its missionaries were unlike those of other denominational mission boards. The Corean Union Mission did not require their missionary candidates to be ordained ministers or claim membership in

a particular denomination. See Heui Yeol Ahn, *The Influence of the Niagara Bible Conference and Adoniram Judson Gordon on Malcolm Fenwick and Korean Baptist Missions*, PhD diss., Southwestern Baptist Theological Seminary, 2002, 23.

142. Fenwick, 57.
143. Robert E. Speer, "Report on the Mission in Korea of the Presbyterian Board of Foreign Missions," *Korea Institute for Advanced Theological Studies Theological Journal* 2:2 (Fall 2006), 426–428.
144. Fenwick, 50.
145. Ibid.
146. Fenwick, 28.
147. Ibid., 35.
148. Ibid., 54.
149. Ibid.
150. "Course of Study for Korean Local Preachers," *Minutes of the Annual Meeting of the Korean Mission of the Methodist Episcopal Church (1896)*, 18–19.
151. Fenwick, 58–67.
152. Ibid., 68–69.
153. L. George Paik, 194–195.
154. Fenwick, 72.
155. Ibid., 110–111.
156. Ibid., 111.
157. Ibid., 107–108.
158. Roger Finke and Rodney Stark, *The Churching of America, 1776–2005: Winners and Losers in Our Religious Economy* (New Brunswick, NJ and London: Rutgers University Press, 2005), 9. Hannah W. Stewart-Gambino utilizes the lens of the "religious marketplace" and the concept of "religious consumers" to examine the reasons behind the growth and expansion of Pentecostalism in Latin American countries with predominantly Roman Catholic demographic majorities. See Hannah W. Stewart-Gambino, "'Religious Consumers' in a Changing 'Religious Marketplace,'" *Latin American Research Review* 36:1 (2001), 193–206.
159. Henry G. Appenzeller, "Mission Cooperation Address in Seoul, Korea, March 1888," in *The Appenzellers: How They Preached and Guided Korea Into Modernization, Volume 1* (Daejeon, Korea: Pai Chai University Press, 2010), 36.
160. "The Rules of Comity of Co-operation in their revised Form, Recommended by the Joint Committee at their Meeting, Feb. 3, 1893," in *The Appenzellers: How They Preached and Guided Korea into Modernization, Volume 1*, 40–41. Leading Methodist bishop R.S. Foster, wishing to maintain Methodist distinctiveness in foreign mission work, disapproved of the comity agreement and prevented it from becoming official mission policy. But missionaries in Korea essentially abided by the policies. See In Soo Kim, *History of Christianity in Korea* (Seoul, Korea: Qumran Publishing House), 168.
161. Fenwick, 46.
162. "Editorial Department—A Letter from Mr. M.C. Fenwick," *The Missionary Review of the World* (August 1894), 618–619.
163. Lillias H. Underwood, *Underwood of Korea* (New York: Fleming H. Revell Co., 1918), 127.
164. Fenwick, 67.
165. Gale, *The Vanguard: A Tale of Korea*, 213–214.
166. Andrew F. Walls, *The Cross-Cultural Process in Christian History: Studies in the Transmission and Appropriation of Faith*, 199.
167. Jehu J. Hanciles, *Beyond Christendom: Globalization, African Migration, and the Transformation of the West*, 4.
168. "Statistics of Missions in Korea," *The Missionary Review of the World* (February 1904), 161.

Bibliography

Archives and Manuscript Collections

General Commission on Archives and History. Madison, NJ: The United Methodist Church, Drew University.

Missionary Research Library Collection. New York, NY: Columbia University, Burke Theological Library.

Presbyterian Historical Society. Philadelphia, PA.

Books and Journal Articles

Ahn, Heui Yeol. *The Influence of the Niagara Bible Conference and Adoniram Judson Gordon on Malcolm Fenwick and Korean Baptist Missions*. PhD diss., Southwestern Baptist Theological Seminary, 2002.

The Appenzellers: How They Preached and Guided Korea into Modernization, Volumes 1–2. Daejeon, Korea: Pai Chai University Press, 2010.

Baird, William M. *William M. Baird of Korea: A Profile*. Oakland: Richard H. Baird, 1968.

Brown, Arthur J. *The Truth and Falsehood about Korea Missionaries*. New York: Board of Foreign Missions of the Presbyterian Church, 1904.

Burnett, Scott S. "Introduction." In *Korean-American Relations: Documents Pertaining to the Far Eastern Diplomacy of the United States, Volume III: The Period of Diminishing Influence: 1896–1905*, edited by Scott S. Burnett. Honolulu: University of Hawaii Press, 1989.

Chung, Young-Iob. *Korea under Siege, 1876–1945: Capital Formation and Economic Transformation*. Oxford and New York: Oxford University Press, 2006.

Dennis, James S. *Foreign Missions after a Century*. New York: Fleming H. Revell, 1893.

Fenwick, Malcolm C. *The Church of Christ in Corea*. New York: George H. Doran Co., 1911.

Finke, Roger and Rodney Stark. *The Churching of America, 1776–2005: Winners and Losers in Our Religious Economy*. New Brunswick, NJ and London: Rutgers University Press, 2005.

Foulk, George Clayton and Samuel B. Hawley. *America's Man in Korea: The Private Letters of George C. Foulk, 1884–1887*. Lanham, MD: Lexington Books, 2006.

Gale, James Scarth. *Korean Sketches*. Chicago and New York: Fleming H. Revell, 1898.

Gale, James Scarth. *The Vanguard: A Tale of Korea*. Chicago and New York: Fleming H. Revell, 1904.

Gilmore, George W. *Korea from its Capital: With a Chapter on Missions*. Philadelphia: Presbyterian Board of Publication and Sabbath-School Work, 1892.

Grant, John Webster. *The Church in the Canadian Era: The First Century of Confederation*. Toronto: McGraw Hill Ryerson Limited, 1972.

Grayson, James Huntley. *Korea: A Religious History*. New York: Oxford University Press, 1989.

Grayson, James Huntley. "The Legacy of John Ross." In *Critical Readings on Christianity in Korea, Volume 1*, edited by Donald Baker. Leiden and Boston: Brill, 2014.

Griffis, William Elliott. *Corea, the Hermit Nation*. New York: C. Scribner's Sons, 1882.

Griffis, William Elliott. *Corea: Without and Within: Chapters on Corean History, Manners and Religion with Hendrick Hamel's Narrative of Captivity and Travels in Corea, Annotated*. Philadelphia: Presbyterian Board of Publication, 1885.

Hamilton, Angus. *Korea*. London: W. Heinemann, 1904.

Hanciles, Jehu J. *Beyond Christendom: Globalization, African Migration, and the Transformation of the West*. Maryknoll, NY: Orbis, 2008.

Harrington, Fred Harvey. *God, Mammon, and the Japanese: Dr. Horace N. Allen and Korean-American Relations, 1884–1905*. Madison: The University of Wisconsin Press, 1944.

Holifield, E. Brooks. *God's Ambassadors: A History of the Christian Clergy in America*. Grand Rapids and Cambridge: Wm. B. Eerdmans, 2007.

Hunt, Everett N. *Protestant Pioneers in Korea*. Maryknoll, NY: Orbis Books, 1980.

Hunter, Jane. "The Home and the World: The Missionary Message of U.S. Domesticity." In *Women's Work for Women: Missionaries and Social Change in Asia*, edited by Leslie A. Fleming. Boulder, San Francisco, and London: Westview Press, 1989.

Huntley, Martha. *Caring, Growing, Changing: A History of the Protestant Mission in Korea*. New York: Friendship Press, 1984.

Hutchison, William R. *Errand to the World: American Protestant Thought and Foreign Missions*. Chicago and London: The University of Chicago Press, 1987.

Jeong, Yak-jong. *Jugyo Yoji (The Essentials of the Lord's Teaching): Korean Christian Classics Series, Volume 6*. Seoul, Korea: KIATS Press, 2012.

Kim, In Soo. *History of Christianity in Korea*. Seoul, Korea: Qumran Publishing House, 2011.

Kim, In-su and Horace Newton Allen. *Allen Ŭisa ŭi sŏn'gyo, oegyo p'yŏnji* [Horace N. Allen, M.D.'s Missionary and Diplomatic Letters]. Seoul, Korea: K'umnan Ch'ulp'ansa, 2007.

Kim, In-su and Horace Grant Underwood. *Ŏndŏudŭ Moksa ŭi sŏn'gyo p'yŏnji: 1885–1916* [Rev. Underwood's Missionary Letters]. Seoul, Korea: Changnohoe Sinhak Taehakkyo Ch'ulp'anbu, 2002.

Kim, Sebastian C.H. and Kirsteen Kim. *A History of Korean Christianity*. New York: Cambridge University Press, 2015.

Korea Presbyterian Mission. *Report for 1899–1900 of the Pyeng Yang Station, Presented to the Annual Meeting held at Pyeng Yang, September 1900.*

Lee, Ki-baek. *A New History of Korea*. Translated by Edward Wagner with Edward J. Schulz. Cambridge and London: Harvard University Press, 1984.

Lee, Timothy S. *Born Again: Evangelicalism in Korea*. Honolulu: University of Hawaii Press, 2010.

Lee, Yur-Bok. "Korean-American Diplomatic Relations, 1882–1905." In *One Hundred Years of Korean-American Relations, 1882–1982*, edited by Yur-Bok Lee and Wayne Patterson. University, AL: The University of Alabama Press, 1986.

Lian, Xi. *Redeemed by Fire: The Rise of Popular Christianity in Modern China*. New Haven and London: Yale University Press, 2010.

McCully, Elizabeth A. *A Corn of Wheat or the Life of Rev. W.J. McKenzie*. Toronto: The Westminster Co. Limited, 1903.

McCune, George M. and John A. Harrison, eds. *Korean-American Relations: Documents Pertaining to the Far Eastern Diplomacy of the United States, Volume I: The Initial Period: 1883–1886*. Berkeley and Los Angeles: University of California Press, 1951.

Moffett, Samuel Austin. *Samuel A. Moffett: First Letters from Korea, 1890–1891*. Seoul, Korea: Hyesun Press, 1975.

Noble, Mattie Wilcox. *The Journals of Mattie Wilcox Noble, 1892–1934*. Seoul, Korea: Han'guk Kidokkyo Yŏksa Yŏn'guso, 1993.

Oak, Sung-Deuk. *The Indigenization of Christianity in Korea: North American Missionaries' Attitudes Towards Korean Religions, 1884–1910.* PhD diss., Boston University, 2002.
Oppert, Ernst. *A Forbidden Land: Voyages to Corea.* London: Sampson, Low, Marston, Searle, and Rivington, 1880.
Paik, George L. *History of Protestant Mission in Korea, 1832–1910, 4th ed.* Seoul, Korea: Yonsei University Press, 1987.
Palmer, Spencer J., ed. *Korean-American Relations: Documents Pertaining to the Far Eastern Diplomacy of the United States, Volume II: The Period of Growing Influence: 1887–1895.* Berkeley and Los Angeles: University of California Press, 1963.
Scranton, William B. *Letters of William B. Scranton.* Korea: William Scranton Foundation, 2010.
Seth, Michael J. *A Concise History of Modern Korea: From the Late Nineteenth Century to the Present.* Lanham, MD: Rowman & Littlefield Publishers, 2010.
Shearer, Roy E. *Wildfire: Church Growth in Korea.* Grand Rapids, MI: Wm. B. Eerdmans Co., 1966.
Speer, Robert E. and Seung-Tak Kim. "Report on the Mission in Korea of the Presbyterian Board of Foreign Missions, 1897." *Korea Institute for Advanced Theological Studies Theological Journal* 2:2 (Fall 2006): 411–468.
Stewart-Gambino, Hannah W. "'Religious Consumers' in a Changing 'Religious Marketplace.'" *Latin American Research Review* 36:1 (2001): 193–206.
Taylor, Charles. *Modern Social Imaginaries.* Durham: Duke University Press, 2004.
Underwood, Lillias H. *Fifteen Years among the Top-Knots, 2nd ed.* Boston: American Tract Society, 1908.
Underwood, Lillias H. *Underwood of Korea: Being an Intimate Record of the Life and Work of the Rev. H.G. Underwood, D.D., LL.D., for Thirty One Years a Missionary of the Presbyterian Board in Korea.* New York: Fleming H. Revell, 1918.
United States. *Twelfth Census of the United States, 1900.*
Walls, Andrew F. *The Cross-Cultural Process in Christian History: Studies in the Transmission and Appropriation of Faith.* Maryknoll, NY: Orbis Books, 2002.
Wasson, Alfred W. *Church Growth in Korea.* New York: International Missionary Council, 1934.

Newspapers and Periodicals

The Church at Home and Abroad
The Foreign Missionary, containing particular accounts of the work of the Board of Foreign Missions of the Presbyterian Church and selected articles and facts from the missionary publications of other Protestant societies
The Gospel in All Lands
Heathen Children's Friend
The Korean Repository
Minutes of the Annual Meeting of the Korean Mission of the Methodist Episcopal Church
The Missionary Review of the World
The Morning Calm
New York Times
Woman's Work for Woman

2 Yun Ch'iho and the Making of a Korean Protestant in Dixie

Introduction

On December 3, 1888, a twenty-three-year-old Korean exile, Yun Ch'iho, wrote a letter from Nashville, Tennessee, reporting his experiences as a foreign student in the Theological Department at Vanderbilt University. The letter was addressed to his professor, Young John Allen, at Anglo-Chinese College in Shanghai, China, where Yun had studied from 1885 to 1888. As a scion of the prestigious and powerful Haep'yong clan, Yun was a member of the Korean aristocracy and enjoyed all of the privileges of the royal Court, which included wealth, education, and the opportunity to work closely with Lucius Foote, the first American Minister of Korea. Yun's father was a military officer who was commissioned to Japan in 1880 to learn Japanese military techniques in order to train Korean troops. The following year, the Korean government sent Yun to Japan to study the country's modern reforms under Meiji rule. In 1883, Yun was recalled to Korea in order to serve as Foote's interpreter. From their government positions, both Yun and his father advocated civil and military reform in Korea, which placed their family directly in the maelstrom of fiery political clashes between conservatives, who wished to maintain traditional ways, and progressives, who called for modernizing changes. In addition to intra-national strife, Yun's family was also involved in international affairs, as China, England, France, Japan, Russia, and the United States signed treaties with Korea during the 1870s and 1880s.[1]

When Yun was wrongly implicated in the abortive Korean reform coup d'état of 1884, he fled to Japan. Once in Japan, Yun initially wished to go to the United States, in order to breathe what he called "the pure, healthful and civilized air of the New World," but he was dissuaded by high living expenses in America and instead decided to go to Shanghai.[2] Upon his arrival in Shanghai, he approached the American legation with a letter of endorsement from Foote. The consul general in Shanghai, Julius Stahl, paved the way for the Korean exile to enroll at Anglo-Chinese College.[3] Allen, a missionary with the Methodist Episcopal Church, South (MECS) and founder of Anglo-Chinese College, served not only as Yun's academic professor but also as a religious mentor. While a student, Yun converted to

Christianity, received baptism, and became the first Korean member of the MECS.[4] By the fall of 1888, Yun had completed his study, which included courses in chemistry, physics, zoology, physiology, botany, history, literature, English, and Chinese.[5] Sensing Yun's academic and ministerial potential, Allen encouraged him to study theology at Vanderbilt, promising to make all the necessary arrangements. Upon graduating from Vanderbilt in 1891, Yun went to Allen's alma mater, Emory College, in Oxford, Georgia, for further study in topics beyond theology.[6]

Judging from his encounters with American diplomats and missionaries in Asia and his reading of American literature, Yun believed that America was a promised land representing the peak of modern civilization and Christian influence.[7] After spending three days in San Francisco, he boarded a transcontinental train to Nashville and had his first experience of racial discrimination. Hotels in Kansas City refused him lodging and forced him to sleep at the railroad station.[8] He encountered the racial realities of nineteenth-century America. The white hotel managers in Kansas City did not receive Yun as a government official or a mission school graduate but saw him as an anonymous Korean, to be treated as other persons of color. Yun learned what it meant to be thrust into a foreign world. As he better understood the social scripts embedded in American culture, Yun received an education in racial inequality, white privilege, and sexual boundaries. Poised between the cultural traditions of his homeland and his American education, Yun used this interstitial space to observe other resistance histories, political approaches, racial ideologies, and Western theologies as he developed his own Protestant beliefs.[9] He supported the American Protestant mission to Korea, but he also came to oppose the missionaries' paternalism and strict emphasis on evangelism. After studying abroad, Yun was convinced that Koreans needed to apply Christian moral teachings to enact educational and social reforms that would remake their nation into a modern civilization.

Encountering Racial Boundaries in Dixie

Although he was more warmly received at Vanderbilt and Emory than in Kansas City, Yun continued to struggle with racism as a foreign student in the American South. During his years at Vanderbilt and Emory, Yun determined to write his lifelong diary in English (previous entries were in Korean and Chinese) in order to improve his knowledge of the language.[10] As a Korean Protestant, Yun experienced "double-consciousness" in America as both religious partner and racial other. He was invited to preach in white Protestant churches across Tennessee and Georgia, but he also felt ostracized as a Korean in an American Protestant culture that demarcated racial boundaries between whites and non-whites. Like the African Americans who lived, according to W.E.B. DuBois, with a "double-consciousness," both African and American—which entailed a "sense of always looking at one's self through the eyes of others, of measuring one's soul by the tape of a world that looks on in amused contempt and pity"—Yun collided with the color line.[11] Like American Jews, who struggled with ambivalence and anxiety in relation to their identities in the United States, Yun had to find a place in a culture intensely conscious of race and ethnicity. Yun wrestled with his racial identity at several different levels. As a Korean, Yun did not fit the American black-white dichotomy because he was neither black nor white. But unlike acculturated American Jews, who could define themselves as whites, Yun included in his diary no recognition whatsoever of "insider" status in the racialized American South.[12]

When Yun began his studies at Anglo-Chinese College in 1885, he had no interest in Christianity. Rather, the Korean sought to acquire a Western education from his American teachers. But as he progressed in his academic work, Yun began reading the Bible alongside his other schoolbooks. In 1887, Yun converted to Christianity and submitted his declaration of faith to one of his professors in Shanghai. Young John Allen kept Yun's conversion narrative, dated March 23, 1887, entitled "Synopsis of What I Was and What I Am," and signed by Yun. He began his conversion narrative by noting that he had not heard of God before he came to Shanghai, because "(1) I was born in a heathen land, (2) I was brought up in heathen society, and (3) I was taught in heathen literature."[13] For three reasons, Yun "continued in sin" even after being informed of Christianity: "(1) sensual gratification, (2) I reasoned that human life being short, one must be allowed to enjoy as much pleasure as he is able, and (3) I thought that a whole man does not need a physician."[14] But for three reasons, he found himself walking in a different path: "(1) I became conscious of my wickedness and of the necessity of preparing [a] purer soul for the future, (2) Confucian proverbs cannot satisfy the demands of the soul, and (3) I attempted to shake off many evil practices and in some measure succeeded in doing away with some of the leading sins which I love like honey."[15] Yun credited religious lectures from professors and his reading of the Bible as helpful guides.

At the time of Yun's conversion in March 1887, he was one of the first Koreans to become a Protestant and the first Korean convert of the Methodist Episcopal Church, South. The first Presbyterian baptism in Seoul took place in July 1886, and the first full-fledged Korean Protestant church was established in 1887. Even when Yun returned to Korea in 1895, the country had probably no more than several hundred Protestants, almost all from the lower classes. "It has been chiefly among the poorest classes that we have done our work, often even among outcasts," reported Henry G. Appenzeller in 1886.[16] Koreans seemed interested only in the study of English, because they saw "a little knowledge of the new tongue . . . as a stepping stone to something higher."[17] Yun's conversion narrative demonstrates a rational progression to the Christian faith, not a burst of emotion. As an exiled nobleman, Yun required neither medical services nor education in the English language—two of the most common reasons Koreans sought out missionaries in the early years of the Protestant mission.[18] He was already fluent in four languages (Chinese, Japanese, Korean, and English). Yun feared a precipitous decline in his social status due to his conversion, writing that the obstacles to his conversion were "the fear of persecution and mockery" and "the liability of making adversaries of former friends." Yet Yun desired to be baptized, and he ended his narrative with a profession of belief: "I believe that God is love, Christ is the Saviour," and "if the prophecies concerning this physical world have been so almost literally fulfilled then [those] concerning [the] future world must be as true."[19]

American missionaries defended immigrant rights and articulated relatively egalitarian racial ideologies to combat the scientific racism common in public debate. They defined difference as religious, not racial. The boundaries between "Christian" and "heathen," though connoting superiority and inferiority, could be transcended through religious conversion, which demonstrated that Asian immigrants could enjoy social assimilation into American life.[20] In his conversion narrative, Yun observed his "heathen" past. After converting to Christianity, he ostensibly crossed the religious boundaries from "heathen" to "Christian." But during his years in the United States, Yun despaired that whites often called him a "heathen," demonstrating that they defined difference in both religious and racial categories. On February 6, 1890, his theology professor at Vanderbilt, Wilber Fisk Tillet, published Yun's Systematic Theology examination in a local newspaper with his own commentary. Tillet wrote that such fine theological work answered the question, "Is a heathen worth educating?" In his diary, Yun displayed ambivalent feelings. He welcomed praise for his work, but he felt deeply insulted by Tillet's comments about the value of educating foreign converts. He saw Tillet's remarks as condescending to all foreign Christians, and he felt that his professor had marked him as a converted heathen rather than a fellow student on equal footing with white students.[21]

Yun's reaction to Tillet's comments reflected his larger ambivalence toward American Protestantism. For American Protestant missionaries in Korea, the lure of Korea was the opportunity to evangelize in a nation bereft of dominant indigenous religious traditions with little resistance from local populations. For Yun, the promise of America was the prospect of witnessing American civilization firsthand and cultivating relationships with American Protestants. As a Korean Protestant, Yun believed that he would be able to promote closer transnational relations between the two nations. A group of Korean officials traveled to America with Horace Allen in December 1887 to represent Korean interests and meet President Grover Cleveland. But Allen observed that these Koreans, dressed in their native garb, engendered amusement rather than respect from the Americans they encountered. Unaccustomed to Western life, the Koreans made a poor impression with their smoking habits and unfamiliarity with modern technology like the elevators in their hotels.[22] Unlike this earlier assembly of Koreans in America, Yun had more frequent contact with Westerners in Asia and was well-schooled in American culture. He not only wore Western dress to match American appearances, but he was also a Protestant who could connect with the religious ethos in the United States.

But Yun soon discovered at Vanderbilt that racial identity trumped religious confession in American life. Within his first year of study in Nashville, Yun learned the veracity of DuBois's assertion that in America "the problem of the Twentieth Century is the problem of the color line."[23] In December 1889, Yun wrote in his diary how "prejudice against the colored race is very strong in the South" and that "a Southerner does not believe in educating this inferior race," wishing to discourage any aspiration to social equality. He also heard a theology student say that he "would sooner mill down his church than to admit a colored member to its congregation." Yun questioned whether white racism toward blacks was compatible with the virtues of American Protestantism.[24] Five days later, after reading articles on Korea in missionary reports at the Vanderbilt library, Yun was dismayed that the missionaries had nothing bright to say about his homeland. Yun describes the picture of Korea in the late nineteenth-century American Protestant imagination: "The government bad, people poor, housed wretched, streets filthy . . . Another [missionary] says he would rather be hanged than to be a minister to Corea."[25]

One month later, Yun complained of being friendless on account of his race. Another foreign student told Yun to avoid female students because "they don't treat foreigners like men."[26] At the end of the semester, a white student told Yun that he might have to eat with the Chinese laundrymen in the outskirts of the city because the mess hall would be closed for the summer. The white student referred to the Chinese laundrymen as Yun's "town bretheren." Although he kept silent, Yun felt shame and indignation for this "undisguised insult."[27] As a Korean, Yun lamented the poor white southern opinion of Chinese immigrants and yearned to prove that he was not a "beastly Chinaman."[28] Postbellum white southern planters viewed Chinese immigrants as potential replacements for African slaves. Though these planters distinguished between the paid labor of Chinese "coolies" and the African slave trade, they regarded the Chinese as colored laborers, inferior to whites. But unlike African Americans, the Chinese were incapable of obtaining citizenship.[29] In his advocacy of Chinese immigrants, Frederick Douglass asserted that white southerners sought "laborers who will work for nothing" and "they hope [the Chinese] will work for next to nothing."[30] When Yun traveled away from the confines of Vanderbilt and Emory, people shouted racial epithets—"Chinaman" and "Chinamen eat rats"—as he strolled through southern towns and cities. In 1892, after nearly four years in America, Yun bemoaned: "I hate being called a Chinaman from the core of my heart. Not that I am better than the Chinese, but that the sense in which the word 'Chinaman' is used here is simply abominable."[31]

Yun displayed his growing disenchantment with America because of the gap between America's egalitarian ideals and racist practices. He gathered that the promise of inalienable rights in America was restricted by racial boundaries that privileged whites above persons of color. Despite his conversion to Methodism, Yun perceived that he remained a "heathen" in many white American eyes and acknowledged his Korean race precluded him from equal standing in America.

An Ambivalent Journey As Religious Partner and Racial Other

Although he felt ostracized as a racial other in the United States, Yun was a religious partner with white American Protestants in raising money for foreign missions. He often received invitations to preach in white Protestant churches throughout Tennessee and Georgia, often in tandem with white ministers and missionaries. Yun recited the content of his speeches in his diary. Unlike earlier observers like Alexis de Tocqueville, who spent ten months traveling in antebellum America and emphasized America's voluntary religious associations, Yun understood more deeply the revivalism that often restricted itself to individualistic salvation and ignored flaws like racial oppression, ethnic hatred, and systematic discrimination against foreigners.

In an address Yun delivered to a missionary society in 1890 at Humphrey Street Methodist Church in Davidson County, Tennessee, he implored his audience to enlist in the cause of world missions, employing biblical examples alongside his own conversion narrative. Although he despised the word "heathen," he used the term in his public addresses, declaring that his own experience "refutes the argument that the heathen need no Gospel because he has a religion as old and as good as Christianity."[32] As the American Protestant foreign missionary enterprise expanded, Americans abroad not only reported the increasing numbers of foreign converts but also provided Americans at home with new information about world religions. And some Protestants at home discovered important religious truths embedded in other religions.[33] Yun, however, spoke the language of conservative Protestantism; no religion was "as good as Christianity."

Thomas Wentworth Higginson, a Unitarian minister from New England, wanted to treat all faiths on equal terms.[34] The Hindu Swami Saradananda traveled across America in the 1890s teaching that "all religions are true, they have the same goal."[35] The Japanese Buddhist D.T. Suzuki taught about the vitality of Asian religious traditions. But Yun encouraged Americans to help make the whole world Christian: one billion heathens "should no more frighten 134 million Protestants than 120 million Roman and Greek pagans discouraged 1 apostle—St. Paul."[36]

He did, however, begin subtly to resist American patronizing of foreigners. Yun spoke briefly in 1891 during the Inter-Seminary Missionary Alliance in Nashville after addresses by missionaries in Japan, Korea, and China. The Presbyterian Horace Underwood spoke on Korea. So did Yun. W.D.

Reynolds, a student delegate from Union Theological Seminary in Virginia who initially wanted to join the China mission, remarked that the crowd felt deeply impressed by the words of both men.[37] The addresses from Yun and Underwood so moved Reynolds that he decided to go to Korea instead of China.[38] But Yun privately disagreed with H.P. Beach, a missionary to China, who said that he was disgusted by the dirty Koreans he had encountered during his short stay in the country. Yun wrote that Beach's comments on Koreans were misinformed because Beach had likely only seen lower-class Korean workers in the docks. He felt angry that Beach had created an embarrassing scene: "Necessary or unnecessary, just or unjust this remark instantly focalized all eyes on my involuntarily crimsoned face. O, the exquisite torture my whole soul then experienced!"[39]

The day after the Inter-Seminary Missionary Alliance, Yun was invited to address a voluntary Methodist society, the McKendree Epworth League in Nashville. Following the main speakers, Underwood and Robert E. Speer, Yun shared remarks about his homeland and seized the opportunity to challenge condescending statements about Korea. He refuted an earlier statement about "12 *perishing* millions in Corea" who desperately hunger and thirst for Christianity by emphasizing "that Corea has 12 *living* millions." Koreans did not simply comprise a mass of hopeless degenerates, but should be characterized as "living" because they possessed the requisite mental and spiritual faculties to become genuine Christians. Yun added that he disliked the phrase "Come over and help us," which was derived from Paul's Macedonian call in the Book of Acts and frequently employed by American Protestant missionaries to depict foreign nations like Korea as hapless and helpless. Instead, Yun appealed to the universal love of Jesus Christ as the "common Savior" for all nations:

> I don't believe in a missionary of human persuasion. I don't therefore ask or persuade anybody. If however, you are convinced that Corea is embraced in our common Savior's order . . . if you realize the fact that your light will shine brighter in Corea because of the heathen darkness; that your work which may be a brick in the temple of God here will be a cornerstone of the Church of Christ in Corea; if you prefer the most useful and Christlike life to the enjoyment of comforts for a season; if the Spirit of God tells you to go there because of the great need and few laborers—if those are appeals, if those are calls, let them appeal to you and let them call you to the field.[40]

In Yun's concluding remarks, he noted that his heart and prayers were with those who heeded the call to Korea and that he desired to join them "in the common cause of winning Corea for our Lord." In a dramatic altar call after Yun's speech, Speer asked the audience to volunteer for overseas mission work. Two persons stood to become missionaries to Korea; two others volunteered for Japan, three for China, and two for Chile.[41]

During his five-year sojourn in America, Yun changed religiously. His religious persuasions evolved from rational assent to experiential piety. In chapel services at Vanderbilt, open-air revival meetings in Nashville, and the writing of sermons for his preaching classes, Yun began to stir with strong religious affections. In September 1890, Yun wrote that he felt "a personal love to Christ" for the first time and exclaimed that the experience was sweet. Two months later, Yun was preparing a sermon on Revelation 3:20, in which the angel of the church of Laodicea beckons individuals to repent and enter into union with Christ. Yun observed that he had a powerful experience of God's love in his soul: "My soul, all this day, has really enjoyed religion. True religion is simply this—to have God in our hearts."[42] He wrote a prayer to God: "Give me this experience of thy love of thy presence always and I am satisfied. My soul which had for the few days past been tossed about on the gloomy sea of doubts . . . found today rest and conscious joy never-before-known."[43] Yun's religious journey was radically transformed by his experiences of divine grace in 1890.

But Yun's greatest religious struggles resulted from race relations. As a Korean Protestant, Yun's double-consciousness colored his travails as a religious partner and racial other. He relished his theological studies and earned high marks in his classes: marks of 92, 95, and 90 in Systematic Theology and 100, 93, 94, and 95 in Homiletics during his first year at Vanderbilt.[44] Tillet remarked that Yun possessed the keenest mind of any student who sat in his classes over forty years of teaching.[45] But he was disappointed that his white classmates did not treat him as an equal and lamented that he made almost no genuine friendships in America. After he returned to Asia, Yun exchanged letters with professors and missionaries he had met in America, but none with his fellow students.[46]

Yun's experience in America differed from experiences of most Asian immigrants in the late nineteenth century. Unlike most Chinese and Japanese immigrants, who endured harsh labor conditions in their menial jobs as railroad workers, cooks, or laundrymen, Yun matriculated as a foreign student at academic institutions. But Yun's experience was also unique because he was the only Korean to reside in the American South from 1888 to 1893. The first Korean immigrant community did not arrive in the current United States until January 13, 1903, when 102 Korean immigrants arrived by ship to the port of Honolulu with the intention of working on sugar plantations in Hawaii.[47] Yun was profoundly and utterly alone.

As more of Yun's classmates were getting engaged and married, he grew forlorn and longed for female companionship. In Korea, Yun was fourteen years of age when he married a young Korean woman in 1877. But his wife died in 1886, when Yun was in Shanghai.[48] On a cold and rainy spring day at Vanderbilt in March 1891, Yun wrote that his loneliness made him feel "so weak that moving up and down the stairs [is] a great and trying task."

His heart panted for a "kind and sympathizing lady friend" to whom he could confide his hopes, fears, sorrows, and joys.[49] Several months later at Emory, a phrenologist came to campus and examined the heads of several students. Yun was told that his head indicated that he was a thoughtful, ambitious, and stubborn man who might consider a career in either law or literature. The phrenologist also predicted that Yun would "marry a woman of slender form, auburn hair, blue eyes and of fair complexion." Though Yun admired the striking beauty of several white women he met in Tennessee and Georgia—and wished to marry one—he dismissed the phrenologist's forecast and wrote that his chances to marry a woman befitting the phrenologist's description were no more likely than the odds of his "becoming a Vanderbilt."[50] Yun suffered through a stint of depression after a conversation with his professor's wife, Sarah Antoinette Candler, in which she teased and mocked him for cherishing a picture of a young white woman, which he had received from the woman during his brief stay in Griffin, Georgia. As Yun was telling the story of how he had befriended a lovely southern belle named "Lucy," Candler cut him short and said, "You didn't stay long enough, as if, had you stayed long, you could have gotten one." Candler's words wounded him deeply and hauntingly echoed in his soul: "Even if you stayed long, who would have you for a sweetheart—you are a Corean!"[51]

From the first large-scale appearance of Chinese immigrants to America in the 1850s and through the rise of Japanese immigration in the early twentieth century, the white American public expressed fear and abhorrence toward Asian immigrants.[52] Though a few capitalists and missionaries welcomed Asian immigrants as inexpensive laborers or potential converts, anti-Asian activists largely succeeded in propagating a fear of "yellow peril" and an "Asiatic invasion" that would take jobs from Americans and endanger American civilization. Moreover, anti-Asian activists became preoccupied with the sexual relations of Asian men and white women. "No matter how enraged or emotional West Coast anti-Asian activists became over the issue of 'Oriental' immigration in general, they became even more enraged with the subject of interracial sex—the idea of 'mongrelization' and 'dirty Orientals' lewdly fondling 'white' women."[53]

In November 1892, his professor, Warren A. Candler, asked Yun if he would marry before leaving the United States. After Yun had replied, "No sir," Candler responded by asking "Why not?" and Yun answered, "Because nobody would have me."[54] In his diary, Yun wrote that his decision was not determined by his own volition but rather because "no American girl of social standing, of education and of beauty would condescend to marry me."[55] In 1893, Yun developed a romantic relationship with a white Protestant woman, "Tommie," in Georgia. He wrote of being enamored with her as they enjoyed long walks, intimate conversations, and holding hands. In spite of his affection for the young woman, he dismissed the relationship as a "hopeless passion" because of the "impassable gulf from our racial differences."[56] Despite his credentials as an exceptional student who had earned high grades, a talented polyglot fluent in several languages, and an ardent Methodist who preached in white American churches, the notion of interracial marriage raised a racial boundary that Yun believed he could not cross.

In the absence of a Korean church, Yun visited several black churches in Tennessee and Georgia. After worshipping at one black Baptist church, he was astounded by the preaching of Dr. Joseph Charles Price. Yun felt Price earned his moniker as a "Black Demosthenes," who provided Yun with "a living argument against the opinion that the Negro, unless mixed, has no mental powers."[57] After visiting another black Baptist church, Yun gave special attention to what DuBois characterized as "the preacher, the music, and the frenzy" of black religion.[58] Yun was surprised that the preaching contained "no text, no logic, no rhetoric, no grammar," recording that the sermon was "a string of inarticulate sound and articulate nonsense seasoned with Scripture quotations or allusions." But he was impressed by the music, describing the songs as "melancholy and mournful" and "well suited to touch and arouse the emotion of [an] emotional people smarting under wrong, contempt, and prejudice." The tune even reminded him of the harvest songs from the southern villages in Korea. And Yun observed that the congregation was more physically active in comparison to the white churches he had attended, emphasizing the dancing, fainting, embracing, shrieking, and kissing that took place during the worship service.[59]

Yun also recorded his encounters with African Americans outside of churches. After a black cobbler fixed his shoes, Yun noted that he did not hear a word of profanity during the hour he spent at the shop with "many negroes of lower grade."[60] During his third year in the American South, Yun first shook hands with a black woman and observed that she had handsome features, but he maintained that white women were more beautiful.[61] He noted that Sarah Candler told him that she did not know how to pull off her shoes or socks as a young girl because African American servants did it for her.[62] After visiting a black college, he found the students there were quieter and less confident than his white classmates.[63] He was fascinated by Harriet Beecher Stowe's *Uncle Tom's Cabin*, believing the book illumined the problem of racial relations between blacks and whites, but he could not find a copy of Stowe's oeuvre in the South. He asked nearly every white pastor he met if they owned the book, but none did.[64] In 1891, Yun attended a children's prayer meeting at a local white Methodist church in Nashville with one of his university professors. Yun thought his professor gave an insightful and instructive talk, which was followed by an invitation for those children who wanted to accept Jesus Christ to kneel down. Yun wrote of how "the beautiful sight of pretty little boys and girls kneeling touched my emotion, roused my prayers, [and] moved my tears." But he then added: "Here I like to ask myself whether I would have been so moved by the sight if the boys and girls were Negro children. I don't think I would."[65] Yun's experiences in white-dominated churches and schools shaped his own opinion of blacks as a lesser race to whites and Asians. Yun despised white racism toward

Asian immigrants, but he concluded that the Asian race was superior to the African one.

Geopolitical Awareness and the Limits of American Missionary Perspectives

Yun not only struggled with his racial identity as a Korean in America, but he also wrestled with the fragile geopolitical position of his country. As a government official in Korea, Yun feared foreign intrusion into his country and believed that embracing modernization was the only way to ensure national independence and avoid colonization. Like many Korean progressives, he marveled at Japanese reforms in the nineteenth century. Before coming to America, Yun read Western newspapers, primarily from Britain and the United States, because he believed they provided the most complete information about daily events throughout the world. When Western papers were unavailable, Yun sought out Japanese ones, which contained many translations from foreign periodicals. In a letter from Shanghai in 1885, Yun wrote that Japan was the "best civilized nation" in Asia.[66] After visiting Japan in 1883, Yun was jarred by the contrasts between Korea and Japan.

Yun's transnational experiences revealed to him the even greater gap between Korea and the West.[67] Yun's knowledge of Western perspectives on East Asia grew beyond American newspapers as he witnessed anti-Asian racism toward Japanese and Chinese immigrants firsthand. Yun saw that the Japanese in the United States, despite coming from the "best civilized nation" in Asia, were regarded as inferior to whites. If Americans had such little regard for Japan, the most modernized nation in East Asia, and China, the largest nation in the region, Yun was aghast at Korea's feeble standing in world politics, creating what he called "the consciousness of my national disgrace and shame."[68] Although Yun was persuaded that Protestantism was the superior world religion, he was dismayed that Koreans were inferior to the West in every regard, including public health, fair governance, and modern technology. In a letter to Allen in 1891, Yun surmised that there were five alternatives for Korea as the nation became further entangled in the age of imperialism in East Asia: (1) peaceful self-reformation, (2) internal revolution, (3) continuance in the present condition, (4) Chinese yoke, and (5) English or Russian rule. Of the five options, Yun believed that foreign imperial rule over Korea was probable and preferred English or Russian rule over the Chinese, because these nations would more likely introduce modern reforms to Korea.[69]

In Yun's conversion narrative from China, he noted that "Confucian proverbs cannot satisfy the demands of the soul."[70] After his studies in the United States, Yun elaborated on why he believed Christianity, and not Confucianism, was the religion of hope and liberation for Korea. Because of its emphasis on filial piety, Yun found in Confucianism a philosophy centered on self-interest that constricted moral boundaries in the ways it demanded obedience to family above all else. Though Yun acknowledged that Confucian maxims brilliantly represented the traditions of ancient Asian civilization, he deemed Confucianism as powerless in the modern age of nation-state formation because its foundation was no higher than filial piety, which promoted absolute submission to kings and perfunctory subservience to tradition.[71] For Yun, this Confucian emphasis on filial piety lacked the requisite moral vision needed to empower, unite, and uplift all citizens in Korean society. Rather, he believed that the Protestant principles of civic morality and communal solidarity would be stronger foundations for Korea's transformation into a modern nation-state.

Early Korean Protestant pastors in Korea also found that Christianity prescribed a superior and more complete ethic on social relations over Confucianism. Beginning in 1900, Choi Byeung-hyeun, an influential Korean Methodist who was ordained in 1902 and succeeded Henry Appenzeller as pastor of Chungdong Methodist Church in Seoul one year later, wrote theological treatises that presented interreligious dialogue with imagined representatives of Buddhism, Confucianism, Taoism, and Christianity. Choi found Confucian teachings on filial piety to be ambiguous and confusing. For example, the instruction that a son must not alter from the ways of his father for three years after his death did not specifically account for differences between virtuous and wicked fathers. Choi contended Christianity offered perspicacious and more useful principles on "the ethics of benevolence, righteousness, civility, and wisdom" as well as "the substance and application of religious principles."[72] Choi drew a sharp contrast between Eastern Confucianism and Western Christianity. He attributed China's geopolitical weakness at the hands of encroaching Western powers to their adherence to Confucianism whereas wise and enlightened Christians governed over Western nations like England and the United States.[73] Gil Seon-ju, one of the first Korean Presbyterian ministers and pastor of Jangdaehyeon Church in Pyongyang, preached that the Christian ethics of obeying God and honoring parents—revealed in the Ten Commandments and New Testament teachings—encapsulated the true aims of filial piety more fully than Confucian rites like wearing mourning clothes for three years after the death of a parent.[74]

Yun likewise pinned his hopes for Korea on Christianity because of its moral emphasis on individual responsibility for the mutual benefit of the entire community. Yun was attracted to the Protestant vision of stewardship because it entailed a social emphasis on civic morality, which emphasized the responsibility of individual citizens to create a moral and upright society.[75] Believing that Confucian notions of filial piety had corrupted and enslaved Korea for several hundred years, Yun saw that the urgent need in his homeland was to "teach morality" and "cultivate patriotism" through Christianity: "There is no foundation other than Christianity that will help the education of our country and restore the people's spirit."[76] On a Sunday in November 1892, Yun recorded in his diary a prayer that he had offered up to God during a worship service in Oxford, Georgia. In contrast to Confucianism, Christianity taught him the ethics of equality, freedom, stewardship, and a unified moral community:

> As I knelt to pray this morning in the church the following thought presented itself: Here I am. I am enjoying the blessings that millions of my countrymen know nothing of. I am in the light of pure religion; intellectual freedom; political liberty. They are groping in the darkness of superstition; ignorance; political slavery. Heaven grant me the way to spread my measure of light among them! God forbid that I should use the moral and intellectual advantages I have received for my selfish ends and not for the good of my fellow men in darkness![77]

But Yun's racialized experiences in the United States and his reflections on international relations tempered his embrace of Christianity. He read books on Western history and politics, such as Thomas Macaulay's *History of England* and Thomas Carlyle's essays, and grew dismayed by the sheer volume of violent acts and vicious crimes that civilized nations committed against their own people and other countries. Yun displayed a critical eye toward contemporary nineteenth-century England, identifying "the opium trade with China, the unjust treatment of Indians and the Chinese, the slave and rum trade with the Africans, the conquest of India, [and] the partition of Poland" as wicked deeds in sharp contrast to the country's imperial declarations as a conduit of philanthropy, morality, and religion throughout the world. Precisely because Western nations had been both enlightened and Christianized, he believed they deserved severe censure for their injustices. He also confessed that "these international sins have lately disturbed my faith in a merciful God."[78]

As Yun considered all the world religions, he professed that Christianity was superior to all others. But he also had religious doubts because of the regnant racial ideologies of the late nineteenth century, particularly social Darwinism. In 1892, he wrote that the greatest obstacle to his faith was the prevailing notion of "the inferiority of one race to another," as Western intellectuals applied Darwin's biological concepts to racial groups.[79] In the nineteenth century, the concept of evolution shaped scientific arguments for ranking racial groups. Ernst Haeckel, a leading German zoologist, argued that "ontogeny recapitulates phylogeny" to explain how human development from infancy to adulthood entailed passing through a series of stages representing adult ancestral forms.[80] This theory of recapitulation detailed how modern white children, as members of a superior racial group, bore traits of primitive adult ancestors from inferior racial groups. A number of American school boards prescribed Henry Wadsworth Longfellow's *The Song of Hiawatha*, a poem featuring Native American folkloric traditions, to primary-school children because the poem's themes would resonate with pupils passing through the savage stage of their ancestral past.[81] In 1895, the English sociologist Herbert Spencer summed up his notion of social Darwinism: "The intellectual traits of the uncivilized . . . are traits recurring in the children of the civilized."[82] In 1900, Protestant minister Josiah Strong contended that American imperial rule over the Philippines should not be motivated by geopolitical ambition or commercial interest. Rather, Strong stressed America's moral obligation to train and uplift the primitive Filipinos, a weaker race incapable of self-government.[83]

Yun wondered why God did not "give equal chance to all the races, Caucasians no superior to Mongolians and Africans no worse than either in physical and mental powers." As he sought to reconcile the cruel realities of social Darwinism with Protestant doctrines detailing God's omnipotence and love, he found himself trapped in a paradox as he searched for theological reasons to explain the creation of superior and inferior races. If social Darwinism betrayed God's intention, Yun questioned God's omnipotence. But if social Darwinism was indeed part of God's plan, Yun doubted God's perfect love. Yun was most disturbed by the thought that Korea might not be among the fittest. Ultimately, Yun resolved to acknowledge his finitude and not indulge in thoughts about God's design and social Darwinism, which were so paralyzing to his faith, and to instead commit himself to making Korea a strong nation: "All we poor mortals can do is to do our best in our respective spheres and the leave the Why's and What-will-be's to God."[84]

Yun's double-consciousness appeared also in his ambivalence toward the American Protestant foreign missionary enterprise. As a religious partner, he clearly supported it in his public remarks in America. But Yun also detested the racism of some of the American missionaries he had met. Just as Yun believed Western nations, with their longer history of Christian influence, deserved more censure than non-Western nations for committing international injustices, Yun denounced missionary racism as more appalling than general racist attitudes in American public life. Because American missionaries accepted a higher calling to be human ambassadors of divine grace and universal justice, Yun contended that they must not propagate racist attitudes that demeaned the people they sought to convert. In 1893, Yun was disgusted with a missionary to China who preached on the themes of humility and lowliness by calling upon white Protestants to willfully descend from their high standing in order to uplift the downtrodden likes of Africans and Asians. Though Yun did not publicly refute the missionary, he protested by refusing to partake in the Lord's Supper after the sermon: "What he said about the people here not even thinking of Chinamen and Japs as their equals kept me from the Lord's table. For if the people are too proud to regard us as equals, then I am too proud to claim that equality by taking the Supper with them."[85]

An Ambiguous Position and an Uncertain Future

After nearly five years in America, Yun's own racism surfaced in this incident, as he criticized the missionary for classifying Asians on the same level as African Americans, which he thought was "very unfair and unjust."[86] Yun also disliked how some missionaries debated how best to train indigenous ministers by discussing the promise and peril of giving them a Western education. Yun was told that some missionaries did not advocate educating indigenous converts in the United States because their faith would be shaken with exposure to liberal theologies, secular learning, and nominal American Christians. Although Yun faced these very challenges at Vanderbilt and Emory, he disliked missionary descriptions of indigenous adult believers as if they were no better or wiser than susceptible children.[87]

Despite his critique of missionary racism, Yun determined that American missionaries did more good than harm and considered becoming a missionary to Korea himself. But unlike American Protestant missionaries in Korea, who debated between evangelizing and civilizing approaches, Yun did not separate the two methods. Some American missionaries placed priority on modern hospitals and schools over evangelism in order to gain the trust of the Korean government and to create the foundation of a modern society that would pave the way for future conversions. Others wished to focus primarily on evangelism because they did not want Koreans to convert for material benefits like modern medicine and foreign education. From his Korean viewpoint, Yun believed that the missionaries had little reason to become entangled in such acrimony over the two approaches. He contended that Koreans needed churches, schools, and hospitals simultaneously, and he thought that the debates distracted Christians from their work and sapped the religion of its potency. In his reflection on Edward Gibbon's history of the theological controversies that tore apart the early church, Yun believed that Christians in early centuries allowed disagreements over intricate doctrines like monophysitism to hamper their witness to the wider Greco-Roman world. Yun was wary of disputes that overtook the living moral force of Christianity.[88]

Yet Yun internally debated about whether to become a minister or educator if permitted to return to Korea. In numerous letters to Allen, Yun wrote of his desire to establish a system of Christian education in Korea to prepare younger generations for new patterns of modern life. He also privately disparaged the notion of becoming a minister in his homeland because his abilities were too high and social standing too elite for the vocation:

> How shall I work? Shall I be contented with 5 or 7 dollars per month in a small mission, thinking that I have done a great work when I shall have preached 2 or 3 sermons in a week and baptized one or two infants in a year? This is, no doubt, very contemptible. But, should Providence put me into this kind of work and I be faithful to my duties in the sight of God and of men, then the meanest sphere of life and labor shall be made great.[89]

Yun was convinced that Protestant advance in Korea would promote equality among all social classes, but his antipathy toward becoming a lowly minister

Figure 2.1 Yun Ch'iho at Emory College, 1893 (Early Emory College Photographs, Emory University Archives, Oxford College Library, Emory University)

revealed his reluctance to abdicate his own high position in Korean society. In 1893, Yun happily reported to Allen that he had raised two hundred dollars for his Christian school in Korea by taking up collections throughout churches in Tennessee, Georgia, and North Carolina.[90] But the Korean nobleman privately confessed that he loathed having to ask for money. In addition to feeling humiliated, Yun believed his fundraising pleas further lowered his social status among white American Protestants.[91]

The subtle differences between what Yun wrote in letters to Allen and in his private records reveal the complexities surrounding his situation as a Korean Protestant thrown into a new social existence in America. In Korea, Yun garnered respect as an influential government official who worked as the translator for the American legation. Yet in the United States he understood that he was little more than a strange foreign convert on display to illustrate white Protestant accomplishments in world missions. Yun sensed that white Protestants came to hear him speak primarily because they wished to see what a peculiar Korean looked and sounded like. In a letter to Allen, Yun wrote about his speaking opportunities: "I know they want to hear me more from curiosity than perhaps any other cause, but so far as I am concerned, I am willing to avail myself of every opportunity to increase, if possible, missionary interest in the people here."[92] After his talks, Yun answered demeaning questions about his homeland, such as whether Koreans knew how light and darkness were generated.[93] Yun criticized American Protestant culture, which he viewed as racist, but he used his position to raise financial support for his future endeavors.

Henry H. Em argues that Yun's "questioning, feeling, self-conscious self" in his diary became fully formed only after his switch from Korean to English in 1889 because "vernacular Korean in the late 1880s, as a written language did not have the kind of literary conventions that English developed after the eighteenth century" for Yun to write about his own subjectivity from external and internalized viewpoints.[94] In the absence of true friends in the United States, Yun sought refuge in his diary writing. Diary writing had long been an American religious practice, especially among women but also among clergy and pious laymen. As they wrote in their diaries, women like Sarah Osborn in eighteenth-century New England engaged in "a form of prayer" and "a deeply meaningful discipline" that brought them "into union with the Divine."[95] Likewise, Yun turned inward to diary writing as a religious practice in order to express his private thoughts and make sense of his life in America. On January 8, 1892, Yun changed his writing style, resolving to compose his diary in letter form to real or fictitious correspondents.[96] Over the following weeks, Yun addressed his professors and their spouses in his diary, expressing opinions he dare not reveal publicly, such as scathing critiques of white privilege and missionary paternalism.[97] He also composed prayers to God and wrote to his future-self about his ambitions, plans, and pains. As a Methodist, Yun held to Wesleyan notions of free grace and divine love for all humankind. In his diary, he expressed joy on account of his religious conversion and yearned for Protestant expansion in Korea. He also disclosed feelings of pride and embarrassment because of his Korean identity: "I wish I belonged to a nationality which I may think of without shuddering with disgust and blushing with shame. Poor Corea! Beautiful Corea!"[98]

In December 1892, Yun met Allen and his family in Atlanta during their furlough. Upon meeting Allen's son, Edgar P. Allen, for the first time, Yun noted that they were approximately the same age but shared little else in common. Unlike Yun, Allen's son belonged to "a nationality that entitles him to the very best treatment wherever he may go in the civilized world." Comparing himself to Allen's son, Yun wrote: "He is honored. I am despised. He is comparatively rich. I am poor. He is self-confident. I am shrinking. I wonder what kind of history time and changes will write for each of us—starting, as we do, under so different circumstances."[99] Yun's American education and exposure to Protestantism influenced his own notions of divine providence, human stewardship, and religious reforms for Korea.[100] But Yun also experienced the broken promises of American Protestantism, which allowed him to be a religious partner but defined him as the racial other. In America, Yun both experienced the affective power of American revivalism and suffered the emotional pain engendered by American racism. He was invited to preach at local churches, but he also experienced life as a racial "inferior," ostracized as a stranger and objectified as a "Chinaman." As he prepared to depart North America for Asia in 1893, he possessed new visions for how Protestantism could transform Korea, but he also anticipated how Western racial attitudes could hamper Korea's development into a modern nation-state.

In 1885, the recently exiled Korean described the United States in glowing terms as a kind and generous nation and longed to breathe the civilized air of the West. In the same year, Josiah Strong published a book entitled *Our Country, Its Possible Future and Its Present Crisis*, in which he championed Anglo-Saxon Protestants in the United States as the greatest representatives of Christian civilization. Combining racial and religious virtues, American Protestants, in Strong's view, were divinely commissioned to lead the modern world into a brighter and more prosperous future.[101] Eight years later, Strong confirmed his view by asserting that the United States was at the center of Anglo-Saxon power and Protestant influence: "Surely, to be a Christian and an Anglo-Saxon and an American in this generation is to stand on the very mountain-top of privilege."[102] Yun, after earning two academic degrees over five years at Vanderbilt and Emory, lambasted American Protestants like Strong who proclaimed that they were "the last effort of the Almighty" and presumed that America stood at the peak of civilization for generations to come.[103] Yun retorted back in 1893: "Who knows but that one of those days the nations whom the American condescends to call barbarians and savages will put the cap on the world's civilization?"[104]

Navigating Racial and Religious Boundaries from Chicago to Shanghai

After graduating from Emory in 1893, Yun worked as a teacher at Anglo-Chinese College in Shanghai before returning to Korea in 1895. As Yun traveled by rail from Georgia to Vancouver in order to board a ship to China, he stopped in Chicago to attend the World's Fair and World's Parliament of Religions in September 1893. With representatives from a myriad of religious traditions, the two-week Parliament marked a significant religious encounter between the East and the West. Followers of Brahma, Buddha, Confucius, and Mohammed from Asia and the Middle East shared the stage with American Christians and Jews in "the most elaborate display of religious cosmopolitanism yet seen on the continent."[105] Asian speakers, such as the Chinese Confucian scholar Pung Kwang Yu, the Indian Hindu philosopher Manilia Dvivendi, and the Sinhalese Buddhist teacher Anagarika Dharmapala, challenged Western notions of Judeo-Christian triumphalism with charismatic and persuasive presentations of the intellectual and spiritual vitality of their religions and cultures. Elegantly dressed in traditional garb, the Asian scholars dazzled thousands of participants with their ability "to effectively communicate with the American public by connecting the relatively unknown mythological universes of the East to more familiar Western ideas."[106]

White speakers also propagated the ideals of religious tolerance and mutual understanding between East and West. American philosopher Paul Carus called for a "Broad Christianity" to replace the exclusive and narrow tenets of so-called orthodox Christianity.[107] But as Yun watched events unfold at the Parliament, he disagreed with its cosmopolitan ethos and religious themes. After two days in attendance, Yun wrote that he grew tired of hearing terms like "liberal-mindedness," "broadness," "universal faith," "fraternity," "brotherhood of men," and "fatherhood of God," words employed as shallow mantras with little meaning. Instead of substantive dialogue covering the differences between world religions, Yun believed the Parliament only superficially addressed religious content and that Eastern and Western participants masked their genuine beliefs in order to support a thinly conceived pluralism. The Korean Protestant preferred to be "narrow and earnest" rather than "broad and indifferent."[108]

Two years after the Parliament, George S. Goodspeed, professor of comparative religion and ancient history at the University of Chicago, touted its importance as a consequential meeting invoking an ongoing spirit of many faiths joined together in common purpose: "When the Parliament was past, it really only then began to live . . . In fact, the farther we are removed from the Parliament, the more extraordinary and significant its character becomes."[109] But many American Protestants were displeased by the Parliament for propagating a message that betrayed the central tenets of their religion. Arthur Tappan Pierson lashed out against the Parliament and one of its founders, fellow Presbyterian clergyman John Henry Barrows, for promoting the impression that Christianity "may not be the only Divine religion."[110] Famed evangelist Billy Sunday announced that the Parliament was one of the most scurrilous events in American history.[111] Yun also thought the Parliament was a failed experiment on two levels. On one level, Yun confirmed Pierson's fears as he reported that scores of white American Protestants, especially women, were enchanted by the Asian speakers and their "beautiful teachings" on Buddhism, Confucianism, Hinduism, and other Asian religions. He determined that "the presentations which different religions have made will no doubt shake the faith of many Christians."[112] On another level, Yun believed the Parliament's hope to usher the world into an era of religious pluralism was false prophecy. "The war between Christianity and other creeds has just begun," Yun wrote from Chicago. "In spite of all the sentimental talks I have heard in the past few days about universal faith . . . the war between Christianity and other creeds will go on."[113] As Yun reflected on his conversion from Confucianism to Christianity and what he regarded as the impassable differences between Confucian ethics of filial piety and Christian moral teachings emphasizing communal solidarity, he predicted that increased knowledge of world religions would create more intense clashes between Eastern religions and Christianity.

Yun also commented on Hirai Kinzo's address, which garnered acclaim from many participants and local newspapers. The *Chicago Daily Tribune* reported that Hirai electrified the audience with his "fiery eloquence" and "forceful presentation of the truth as he believed it."[114] A Japanese Buddhist layman, Hirai accused Western Christians of racist practices in America and abroad that contradicted their biblical teachings. He surmised that Western Christians treated the Japanese unequally because of their status as "idolaters and heathen," but then countered: "Admitting for the sake of argument that we are idolaters and heathen, is it Christian morality to trample upon the rights and advantages of a non-Christian nation, coloring all their natural happiness with the dark stain of injustice?"[115] Hirai's paper was considered so inflammatory that Barrows attempted to prevent him from delivering it before the assembly.[116] Yun had a mixed reaction. He agreed with Hirai's appraisal of American Protestant racism but also criticized the Japanese Buddhist's proposed "Synthetic Religion" based on an "a priori belief in an unknown entity."[117] Yun opposed Hirai's denial of an infinite Creator and Sustainer of all life, writing how Hirai's belief that "the creator of conditioned and finite beings could not be infinite and unconditioned" was as foolish as saying "the maker of unintelligent dolls can't be intelligent."[118]

Hirai also contended that morality was more important than distinctive religious identities. "Whether Buddhism is called Christianity or Christianity is named Buddhism, whether we are called Confucianists or Shintoists, we are not particular," declared Hirai, "but we are very particular about the truth taught and its consistent application."[119] Although Yun was attracted to Christianity because of its moral teachings, he disavowed Hirai's emphasis on morality at the expense of religious dogma as hollow relativism. After hearing a Protestant minister declare the universal harmony of all world religions, Yun accused the minister of preaching nonsense: "If bigotry can see but one phase of truth, extreme broadness can't see anything save the surface of the whole."[120] Despite Yun's disagreements with Hirai and the Parliament's religious message, he noted that one good effect of the Parliament was that the American public could see that Asians like Hirai were intelligent persons who could reason, think, and write as well as Westerners. Yun's aspirations for the Parliament's long-term effects were for racial and not religious unity. After hearing articulate addresses from a number of Asian speakers representing several different countries, Americans might begin to treat all Asians more respectfully.

Life on the Margins of an American Missionary Community in Shanghai

Although Yun disputed the notion that Anglo-Saxon American Protestants would forever maintain their high position, he sometimes wished to be one. He was especially attracted to white American women. After returning to Shanghai, the twenty-nine-year-old Korean desperately yearned for female companionship. In 1894, Yun confessed to being overcome by his emotional and sexual longings and wrote that the only remedy was a "pretty, sensible, pious, and loving wife."[121] Allen arranged for Yun to wed a young Chinese Protestant woman, Mo Sien-tsung, a student at McTyeire Home and School for Girls, established by MECS missionaries in Shanghai. But Mo's parents were reluctant to give their consent because of Yun's foreign race and his refusal to participate in a traditional Chinese wedding ceremony with Chinese dress. Yun rejected Chinese Confucian traditional rites on racial and religious grounds. As a Korean, Yun asserted pride in his own national identity and resisted Chinese garb, which would symbolize his acquiescence to Chinese rule. As a Protestant, he opposed Chinese rites as pagan ceremonies that went against his religious principles.[122]

For two months, Yun engaged in debates with Mo's parents about wearing Chinese dress at the wedding ceremony. Laura Askew Haygood, founder of McTyeire Home and School for Girls and sibling of MECS bishop Atticus Green Haygood, mediated the sartorial deliberations. In a letter to a friend back home, Haygood wrote: "I am arranging for another wedding before I go away—that of Mr. Yun, the young Korean who studied at Emory College for a time, and one of our best girls, a lovely young Chinese woman, Mo Sien-tsung, a pupil-teacher in McTyeire School."[123] Haywood described Yun and Mo as "earnest Christians" who would make a "happy pairing" but also complained about the tiresome negotiations between Yun and Mo's parents.[124] Three days prior to Haygood's letter, Yun relented to Mo's parents' demands, after Haygood had scolded him: "I am sorry that you ever wanted to marry a Chinese wife, not that you and she have not all the elements to make a happy match, but that the complications are too troublesome. Mrs. Mo will not yield on this point and if you persist on your position, you had better break the engagement."[125] As Yun weighed his marital options, he felt he had no choice but to marry Mo without any Korean women in Shanghai. Although single American female missionaries were present, Yun believed that no white American woman would consider marrying him on account of his race. During the two-month-long deliberation between Yun, Haygood, and Mo's parents, Yun despaired over what he called his "heartsick, or rather lovesick" condition and his own ambiguous identity as an American-educated Korean Protestant exile in Shanghai: "If I were a heathen, I might find sinful pleasure in the society of loose women. If I were an American or European, I might find a purer consolation in the refined company of Western girls."[126] But Yun defined himself as "being neither the one nor the other," and just as he was in America, Yun was a stranger who lived on the margins in Shanghai.[127] Although he was a teacher at Anglo-Chinese College, he worshipped with American missionaries, and he conversed regularly with Allen and Haygood, Yun did not feel welcomed as an equal in the American missionary community.

After reconciling all the issues between Yun and Mo's parents, Yun married Mo on March 21, 1894 at McTyeire Home and School. Yun and Mo had exchanged letters with one another during their two-month engagement, but shared very little time with one another until the day of the wedding ceremony. Despite all Yun's misgivings, he was delighted to marry Mo and trusted God had answered his prayers for a faithful wife. The wedding in Shanghai was a transnational affair with American and Chinese guests, a Chinese bride, and a Korean groom (in Chinese dress), but Yun's description of the proceedings demonstrates how MECS missionaries orchestrated their marriage:

> My "Darling," dressed in pink looked lovely indeed, and deserved all the praises she got. After refreshments the visitors went away one by one. Just before the carriage came for us, Miss Hughes told me in Miss Haygood's parlor with a deal of emotion, "Mr. Yun, you must be good to my dear girl. I love her just as my sister. And now I love you as my brother." About 8, the carriage came. Miss Haygood led Sientsung to her study where I was; and for the first time the bride and I looked full at each other's face. As the dear creature stood by Miss Haygood with one of her pretty hands in Miss Laura's, her sweet and childlike smile and confidence were in harmony with the almost parental love and pride with which the good missionary looked up on her pupil . . . As Sientsung and I came out from the study side by side Miss Haygood, out of her great heart, said "God bless you both!" Just outside of the door of the hall, the ladies of the Mission and the girls of the school stationed themselves on both sides and showered rice on us. When we got into [the] carriage,

> all I could do was to hold her willing hands, pressing them with mine as warmly as newly married love could. On our arrival at home, we found Prof. and Mrs. Bonnell waiting for us. The Rubico[n] is crossed.[128]

At every step of their wedding, from the ceremony to the marital bed, American missionaries counseled and directed Yun and Mo. But here Yun neither detected nor deplored any hint of the paternalism he so detested in American missionaries. On the contrary, Yun was grateful for how missionaries arranged and supported his marriage to Mo. A month after their wedding, Yun praised Haygood for providing him an affectionate, refined, and pious wife who was "as free from the superstitions of her people as a girl brought up in an American family."[129]

Contesting the Attitudes and Perspectives of American Missionaries

As Yun readjusted to life in Shanghai, he identified several faults within the American missionary operation in Asia. In America, Yun criticized how missionaries presented foreigners in their speech and writing. In China, Yun more closely observed how the missionaries lived, and he debunked their notions of using domesticity as a means of religious witness. As in Korea, American missionaries in China established Western-style homes in Shanghai and hired indigenous servants. They believed that they were creating a tangible example of a faithful Christian home to both Christian and non-Christian families in Asia. Despite their good intentions, American women missionaries imposed imperialistic Western values in their transmission of the "Christian home" to indigenous women abroad.[130] In Korea, missionaries debated the proper role of wives on the mission field. As they erected Western-style houses and employed Korean servants for low wages, they wrestled with the material inequalities between their ways of life. Yun was not offended by the economic disparity between Western and indigenous homes. The Korean nobleman, who had traveled to Japan and the United States, appreciated refined Western lifestyles and did not fault missionaries for seeking to recreate their Western modes of living in Asia. But Yun was incredulous over the way missionaries employed the "Christian home" as an evangelizing and teaching strategy: "But the story that a missionary family is valuable as setting [a] good example to the non-Christian families is a pretty little fable—pretty indeed but only a fable."[131] He thought the notion of domesticity as religious witness was patently false because of how the missionaries had intentionally separated themselves in compounds apart from indigenous populations. Because missionaries had created these physical boundaries, Yun believed there was no way for indigenous persons to learn from or even see missionary homes.[132]

He also noted that the few locals who entered into missionary homes were servants, many of whom were mistreated by their missionary employers.

Yun found that the missionary home did not enhance but rather had more potential to impair Christian influence in Asia. And he felt that the missionaries knew these realities all too well and therefore only offered the idea of the "Christian home" as an evangelizing tool to validate their social existence abroad. Yun did not charge the missionaries with conceit for how they lived in Asia, but he accused them of deceit for hiding behind religion to justify their riches.

In Shanghai, Yun also contested missionary views on religion. Missionaries to China and Korea believed that Christianity stood superior to Asian religions like Buddhism, Confucianism, and Hinduism on intellectual and theological grounds. In 1893, G.T. Candlin examined world religions in *The Chinese Recorder*, a Presbyterian missionary magazine published in Shanghai, and concluded that Christianity alone "furnishes spiritual objects which can give full development and perfect expression to the spiritual nature of all mankind."[133] But Candlin conceded that foreign nations practicing other religions were better off than if they had no religion whatsoever: "India may be as bad as you please under the reign of Brahmanism; China, Thibet, and Corea as degraded as you choose under that of Buddhism and Confucianism; Arabia and Turkey as cruel and hurtful as you can imagine under Mohammedism . . . all would have been worse without these."[134] In the United States, Yun likewise delivered religious addresses to rally support for foreign missions by trumpeting the superior doctrines of Christianity over other world religions. But as Yun conversed with Asian Buddhist and Confucian scholars in Shanghai, he began to believe that the power of Christianity resulted from its practical morality, not its rational theology. As he debated one Asian Buddhist scholar on creation, transmigration, and the treatment of animals, Yun refuted each of the Buddhist's points by advancing his Christian beliefs, recording the religious contest in his diary. He identified his counterpart with the initials "C.O.Y.," and himself as "T.H.Y.":

C.O.Y.: "If you say that God created all things how can you reconcile His goodness with the cruel butchery of animals for your food? If you don't believe in the existent [soul of] an animal, how can you count for the love of life and dread of death an ox or a bird manifests?"

T.H.Y.: "Let me state clearly my belief. I believe that God created the Universe as well as my soul; that everything in this world is for the use of man—[and] of me; that animals have no souls and were made for our benefit. Now call this wrong or right belief as you please. But don't you know it is no sin to me who [eats] animal food believing it was made for me while it is cruelty and sin for you to eat beef or fish, knowing, as you say you do, that an animal has a soul?"[135]

But unlike Candlin, Yun did not appeal to Christian doctrine as the perfect expression of spiritual truths. Instead, his main argument for Christianity rested upon its moral teachings and practical results. He tied Buddhism to current social conditions in China and Korea, charging the Buddhist scholar with practicing a religion that "enables some few intelligent and acute thinkers like you to indulge in the luxuries of speculation while tens of millions of common people live and die in moral and spiritual degradation."[136] Ultimately, Yun defended Christianity because its teachings emphasized individual moral responsibility for the larger community. "A subtle Buddhist or Confucianist or Taoist is easily a match, nay more than a match for any average Christian," observed Yun, "but Christianity put in life is a power before which nothing can stand."[137] As he continued to discuss religious matters with Asian scholars, Yun postulated that the practical results of Christianity, such as mission schools that educated children from the lower classes, were the best evidence to support Christianity in comparison to other world religions.

Although Yun supported American mission work in Korea, he disagreed with how missionaries to Korea characterized the Korean religious landscape as bare and empty, as if it were a *tabula rasa* ripe for Protestant inscription. Missionaries witnessed traditional Korean religious rituals but categorized them in the lesser category of "superstition" rather than religion. They indicated that Koreans had no national religion and were generally indifferent to religion.[138] Yun thought these depictions of Korean religious thought were too simplistic. Indeed, Koreans, like non-Christians in other nations, needed to abandon their traditional religious practices in favor of Christianity. But Yun contended that the fact that Koreans zealously turned to idols, chants, and charms uncovered an active—not apathetic—national religious consciousness.[139] In 1929, L. George Paik also refuted missionary conceptions of Korean religious indifference. Paik argued that missionaries to Korea had conceived of religion solely "in terms of dogma and ecclesiasticism" and therefore failed to properly comprehend Korean religious attitudes.[140] He described the average Korean of that time as simultaneously participating in ancestor worship, reciting Confucian classics, sacrificing to animistic spirits, seeking out shamans for healing, and visiting the Buddhist temple for prayer, which demonstrated deep religious sensibilities.[141] Like Paik, Yun asserted that missionaries mistook Korean religious syncretism for indifference.

During the Sino-Japanese War in 1894, Yun searched for as many news reports as he could find in Shanghai. He was deeply concerned for his country and speculated on what the war's outcome would mean for Korea. American missionaries in Korea were ambivalent about the war in Korea. They grieved at the suffering of Korean civilians caught in the crossfire of Japanese and Chinese soldiers, but they also saw the war as an opportunity for increased evangelization to Koreans caught in political turmoil and religious doubt. Missionaries hoped for Japanese victory so that Chinese influence in Korea would diminish. This would lead in turn to Korean disenchantment with Confucianism, a religious import from China. But whereas missionaries viewed the war primarily in religious terms, Yun analyzed the political, social, and religious ramifications of the war on Korea. He also wished for Japan to triumph, but he was more concerned about national reform than religious evangelization. Yun admired how the Japanese government abolished feudalism and embraced modernization in the nineteenth century and recognized that Korea needed to follow suit in order to maintain its independence. In 1869, the Meiji government hired an English engineer to construct a telegraph line from Tokyo to Yokohoma. In 1871, Japan established a postal system, which had evolved by 1890 into a nationwide operation that delivered 225 million pieces of mail and 75 million money orders in over 5,000 post offices.[142] In addition to revamping their communication systems, the Meiji government also modernized their political, economic, and military infrastructures and began pushing Korea to do likewise in 1894. Although Yun agreed with Japan's proposals to Korea, he objected to their coercive approach and preferred "gentle, though resolute pressure" over a heavy hand.[143] Yun shared the same religion as the missionaries in Korea, but he disagreed with their prescriptions for his homeland. Yun also desired a greater number of Korean Protestant converts but believed the most urgent needs in Korea were a well-trained army, a patriotic newspaper, and a new educational system that focused on modern industry.[144] He developed a more detailed ten-point reform plan in his diary, which also included establishing a postal system, streamlining the central government to reduce corruption, and revising the national revenue structure.[145]

As the Sino-Japanese War raged on in Korea, Yun continued teaching at Anglo-Chinese College. Now in his second year of teaching, Yun grew more familiar with missionary operations in Shanghai. Because he was neither a white missionary nor a Chinese student, Yun realized that he had a unique perspective on Anglo-Chinese College. He appreciated the missionary teachers' commitment to teaching religion alongside other academic subjects, but he criticized how the missionaries regarded the Chinese students as inferior human beings. After his experience as a college student in the United States, Yun perceived that the teacher-pupil relationship at Anglo-Chinese College was different because of race. Teachers maintained their authority over students at Vanderbilt and Emory, but Yun also sensed an ethos of mutual respect between the two parties that was missing in Shanghai. Although missionaries and students shared common physical space within the walls of Anglo-Chinese College, Yun found that missionaries had created distinct and unmistakable social boundaries that contradicted their religious teaching. He denigrated teachers who treated Chinese students disrespectfully, writing that some missionaries expressed little esteem for the Chinese and appeared to think that their only duty in China was to teach simplistic lessons about matters like heaven and hell, along with the ridiculous claim "that circus going and smoking are deadly sins."[146] Furthermore, Yun alleged that the missionaries' "long sermons in winning the hearts to Christ" would be far more effective in converting Chinese students if not accompanied by their supercilious paternalism.[147]

As Yun spent more time with the missionaries, he learned of their disagreements with one another. Not unlike any other academic institution in Asia or the United States, teachers at Anglo-Chinese College disparaged one another in private and competed against one another for higher positions at the school. Yun also heard rumors of improper sexual relations among missionaries. He was especially appalled at missionaries who preached to Chinese Protestants that God was using Japan's military triumphs in the Sino-Japanese War to punish China for not accepting Christianity. Yun was astounded at the gall of these missionaries on two levels. They not only attributed Asian events they hardly understood to God's direct invention, but they then propagated their mistaken presumptions to Chinese believers.[148]

Although Allen had not proclaimed these falsities about God's hand in the Sino-Japanese War, Yun was surprised at his mentor's ethnocentric arrogance in other matters, such as Allen's critiques of Asian scholarship and his negative comments about Chinese Protestants. Yun confessed in his diary that he was startled "beyond expression" one day at how Allen, who was not an expert on Japan and could not read Japanese, lambasted Japanese Christian scholar Takahashi Goro's translations of Chinese Protestant literature.[149] Although Allen did not have superior knowledge of Chinese and Japanese scholarship, Yun found that his mentor claimed the right to pronounce these criticisms due to his higher standing as an American missionary. On another occasion, Allen told Yun that "he had never seen a Chinaman with thorough and experimental conviction in Christianity."[150] Yun privately disagreed. Yun felt Allen too easily dismissed Chinese Protestant converts in villages and rural areas who had little interaction with foreign missionaries. These converts were not educated in mission schools like Anglo-Chinese College, but Yun contended that their religious conversion was no less sincere and complete: "But I am sure many of the humble Chinese Christians who can hardly read anything but their colloquial Bibles have as much genuine religion as those who can write autobiographies, evidences of Christianity and even able religious essays."[151] In his criticisms of missionaries, Yun was careful to include praise alongside rebuke. Despite all their shortcomings, Yun commended missionaries for their entrepreneurial efforts in establishing and maintaining churches, hospitals, and schools in foreign countries like China and Korea.

On December 27, 1894, Yun received word that changes in the Korean government created safe conditions for his return. During the Sino-Japanese War, a group of reform-minded Korean progressives had gained influential government positions and now called upon Yun's services.[152] He tendered a letter of resignation to Anglo-Chinese College and prepared to return home. In a conversation with Timothy Richard, a Welsh Baptist missionary in China, Yun explained that his intentions in Korea were two-fold. He wished to collaborate with American missionaries in their production of Protestant literature for Korean commoners and take a position in the government as Minister of Education.[153] Richard, Allen, and other missionaries in Shanghai advised Yun to pursue a high government position rather than mission work because they believed Yun would garner more influence in Korea as a government official. The support of the missionary community in Shanghai encouraged Yun. Two days later, Yun's wife gave birth to their first child, Laura (named after Laura Askew Haygood), in Soochow.

Conclusion

In her work on more recent Korean missionaries in the United States, Rebecca Y. Kim delineates three paradigms for interpreting the changing shape of world Christianity that began at the turn of the twentieth century. The "global Christianity paradigm" connects non-Western Christian expansion to the initiatives of foreign missionaries and indigenous churches that were under the imposition of Western colonialism, whereas the "world Christianity paradigm" emphasizes the emergence of fresh and diverse local religious expressions from non-Western Christians apart from Western control. In addition to these established approaches, Kim importantly introduces what she calls the "American global Christianity paradigm" to capture how some local Christian movements in the Global South continue to be influenced by American neocolonial imperialism, American Protestantism, and "a white dominant racial hierarchy that is embedded in both American imperialism and American Christianity."[154] The evolution of Yun's religious constructions illustrates his participation in the American global Christianity paradigm. He formed his Christian beliefs and practices within a complex web of cultural, political, racial, and social ideologies from Korea and the West.

From 1884 to 1894, Yun both crossed and was confounded by national, racial, and religious boundaries as a Korean exile in China and the United States. In 1887, he converted to Christianity in Shanghai. From 1888 to 1893, he encountered the possibilities and limits that accompanied his Korean Protestant identity in the American South. His hopes for Protestant expansion and political reform in Korea were tempered by racial theories and geopolitical conditions that weighed against his country. In 1894, he married a Chinese Protestant woman, Mo Sien-tsung, and they had their first child. As he lived among the American missionary community in China, he became disenchanted by their ethnocentrism and paternalism. Though he had witnessed more of their faults, Yun wished that the missionaries would remove the boundaries they had erected between themselves and indigenous converts.[155] Although missionaries told him that the boundaries prevented indigenous converts from seeing disharmony within the missionary community, Yun believed that missionaries precluded opportunities for genuine relationships and meaningful interactions to arise between American and Asian Protestants. As long as the racial boundaries remained, there could be no sense of religious partnership and equality between American and Asian Protestants.

Figure 2.2 Yun Ch'iho (bottom row, center) with Emory University Alumni in Korea, 1926 (Stuart A. Rose Manuscript, Archives, and Rare Book Library, Emory University)

After Yun returned home to Korea in 1895, he would continue his quest for political and religious reform alongside both Korean Protestants and American missionaries.[156] But his struggle against Americans would persist in Korea, as he and other Koreans constructed a religious identity that differed from missionary blueprints on the making of Korean Protestantism. At the 1910 World Missionary Conference in Edinburgh, Yun delivered an address that prescribed a reversal of position between missionaries and Korean Protestants. He explained how Koreans deserved the "first place in the work of evangelization" because they better understood the needs and conditions of their own people.[157] Yun called for the missionaries to cede their religious authority to the Korean church leaders: "The Native Church, in short, must fight its own battles, learn its own lessons; feel its own weaknesses, discover its own strength and gather its own trophies."[158] At one level, Yun and other Korean Protestants helped fulfill the ambitions of the first American Protestant missionaries to Korea; at another level, they subverted those ambitions in ways that the missionaries would have found puzzling in the extreme.

Notes

1. Lee Sang-Hoon, "Nomadism and the Discovery of the Nation: The Case of Yun Chiho," in *Critical Readings on Christianity in Korea, Volume 1*, edited by Donald Baker (Leiden and Boston: Brill, 2014), 351, and Kenneth M. Wells, *New God, New Nation: Protestants and Self-Reconstruction Nationalism in Korea, 1896–1937* (Honolulu: University of Hawaii Press, 1990), 48–50.
2. Yun Ch'iho, "Letter on June 5, 1885," in *Letters in Exile: The Life and Times of Yun Ch'iho*, edited by Hyung-Chan Kim (Covington: Rhodes Printing Company, 1980), 78.
3. Ibid., 83. See also Kim, 11.
4. Yun Ch'iho, "Thirty Years Ago," in *Southern Methodism in Korea*, edited by J.S. Ryang (Seoul, Korea: Board of Missions, Korea Annual Conference, Methodist Episcopal Church, South, 1926), 98.
5. During his studies, Yun also took time to read novels such as *Gulliver's Travels, Robinson Crusoe*, and *The Arabian Nights* for enjoyment. John Bunyan's *Pilgrim's Progress*, Walter Scott's *Kenilworth*, and selected works of Ralph Waldo Emerson were among some of his more serious readings. See Kim, 11.
6. During Allen's years at Emory in the 1850s, he had been a religious leader who led revival meetings on campus. As a senior, Allen had gathered his fellow students for prayer meetings around an old log in the woods near the college buildings. Less than two years after his college graduation, Allen had set out for China as a missionary in December 1859. In 1881, he became superintendent of MECS mission work in China. In 1885, he founded Anglo-Chinese College in Shanghai, and served as its president until 1895. See Henry Morton Bullock, *A History of Emory University* (Nashville: Parthenon Press, 1936), 98, and Warren A. Candler, "Young John Allen's Love for 'Dear Emory,'" *Emory Alumnus* (January 1931), 11.
7. In 1885, Yun described America as "that most kind and generous nation." See Yun, in Kim, 78.
8. Kim, 12.
9. For an exploration of how colonial elites like Mahatma Gandhi and Sol Plaatje were shaped by their transnational experiences, see Elleke Boehmer, "Networks

of Resistance," in *The Post-Colonial Studies Reader, 2nd ed.*, edited by Bill Ashcroft, Gareth Griffiths, and Helen Tiffin (London and New York: Routledge, 2006), 113–115, and *Empire, the National, and the Postcolonial, 1890–1920: Resistance in Interaction* (Oxford and New York: Oxford University Press, 2002).

10. "Diary of Yun Ch'iho, December 7, 1889," in Yun Ch'iho Papers, Stuart A. Rose Manuscript, Archives, and Rare Book Library, Emory University, Atlanta, GA. A copy of Yun's diary can be found in his papers. All citations from Yun's diary in this chapter are from this archival collection except for one Korean language entry from March 30, 1889, which is from a published version of the diary from 1973. See *Yun Ch'iho Ilgi, Volume 1* [Diary of Yun Ch'iho, Volume 1] (Seoul, Korea: Kuksa P'yŏnch'an Wiwŏnhoe, 1973), 370.
11. W.E.B. DuBois, *The Souls of Black Folk* (Chicago: A.C. McClurg & Co., 1903), 3.
12. Eric L. Goldstein, *The Price of Whiteness: Jews, Race, and American Identity* (Princeton and Oxford: Princeton University Press, 2006), 51.
13. Yun Ch'iho, "Synopsis of What I Was and What I Am," 1, in Young J. Allen Papers, Stuart A. Rose Manuscript, Archives, and Rare Book Library, Emory University, Atlanta, GA. Yun's conversion narrative was later reprinted in several MECS books, pamphlets, and periodicals. See Warren A. Candler, *T.H. Yun, of Korea and the School at Songdo* (Nashville: Board of Missons of the Methodist Episcopal Church, South, n.d.), 8–10. Although the pamphlet is not dated, it was published shortly after Candler's visit to Korea in 1906.
14. Ibid.
15. Yun Ch'iho, "Synopsis of What I Was and What I Am," 2.
16. Henry G. Appenzeller, "Henry Appenzeller Begins Mission in Korea," in *The Methodist Experience in America: A Sourcebook*, edited by Russell E. Richey, Kenneth E. Rowe, and Jean Miller Schmidt (Nashville: Abindgon Press, 2000), 422–424.
17. Ibid.
18. Paul S. Cha, "Unequal Partners, Contested Relations: Protestant Missionaries and Korean Christians, 1884–1907," *The Journal of Korean Studies* 17:1 (Spring 2012), 10–11.
19. Yun Ch'iho, "Synopsis of What I Was and What I Am," 2.
20. Jennifer C. Snow, *Protestant Missionaries, Asian Immigrants, and Ideologies of Race in America, 1850–1924* (New York: Routledge, 2007), 2–3.
21. Diary of Yun Ch'iho, February 6, 1890.
22. Horace N. Allen, "Diary entry on December 26, 1887," in *Allen Ŭisa ŭi sŏn'gyo, oegyo p'yŏnji* [Horace N. Allen, M.D.'s Missionary and Diplomatic Letters], edited by In-su Kim and Horace Newton Allen, 529–532, and Harrington, *God, Mammon, and the Japanese: Dr. Horace N. Allen and Korean-American Relations, 1884–1905*, 238–239.
23. DuBois, 5.
24. Diary of Yun Ch'iho, December 9, 1889.
25. Diary of Yun Ch'iho, December 14, 1889. An article in the Methodist missionary journal *Heathen Woman's Friend* reported that "most of the Korean people are very poor . . . they do not like to work very well, and they do everything the very hardest way" ("Korean Boys, Birds, Ponies, and People," April 1887, 275).
26. Diary of Yun Ch'iho, January 3, 1890 and January 30, 1890.
27. Diary of Yun Ch'iho, May 4, 1890.
28. Diary of Yun Ch'iho, June 24, 1891.
29. Gary Y. Okihiro, *Margins and Mainstreams: Asians in American History and Culture* (Seattle and London: University of Washington Press, 1994), 44–52.
30. Frederick Douglass, "Our Composite Nationality," in *The Frederick Douglass Papers, Series One: Speeches, Debates, and Interviews, Volume 4: 1864–80*,

edited by John W. Blassingame and John R. McKivigan (New Haven: Yale University Press, 1991), 248.
31. Diary of Yun Ch'iho, June 19, 1892.
32. Diary of Yun Ch'iho, January 5, 1890.
33. Leigh Eric Schmidt, *Restless Souls: The Making of American Spirituality* (San Francisco: HarperSanFrancisco, 2005), 7.
34. Schmidt, 109.
35. Schmidt, 137.
36. Diary of Yun Ch'iho, January 5, 1890.
37. Lillias H. Underwood, *Underwood of Korea*, 109.
38. Leroy Tate Newland, "Tribute to W.D. Reynolds," in Leroy Tate Newland Papers, C. Benton Kline Jr. Special Collections and Archives, John Bulow Campbell Library, Columbia Theological Seminary, Decatur, GA.
39. Diary of Yun Ch'iho, October 23, 1891.
40. Diary of Yun Ch'iho, October 25, 1891.
41. Ibid.
42. Diary of Yun Ch'iho, November 19, 1890.
43. Ibid.
44. Kim, 13.
45. J. Earnest Fisher, "Yun: Statesmen, Scholar," in *Korea Times* (Seoul), August 27, 1972, as cited in Vipan Chandra, *Imperialism, Resistance, and Reform in Late Nineteenth-Century Korea: Enlightenment and the Independence Club* (Berkeley: University of California Press, 1988), 91.
46. Edwin Mims was a student at Vanderbilt University from 1890 to 1893 and later taught as an English professor at the university from 1912 to 1942. In his history of the university, Mims wrote that Yun "made a deep impression on the student body." See Edwin Mims, *History of Vanderbilt University* (Nashville: Vanderbilt University, 1946), 179. Yun's diary entries illustrate his ambivalence toward other students. He appreciated several of his classmates but the racism he experienced from other students wounded him in deep and lasting ways.
47. Wayne Patterson, *The Ilse: First-Generation Korean Immigrants to Hawai'i, 1903–1973* (Honolulu: University of Hawaii Press, 2000), 1. Yun would later visit Hawaii in 1905 to investigate the labor conditions of Korean immigrants on the sugar plantations for the Korean government. See Patterson, 4–5.
48. Kim, 4.
49. Diary of Yun Ch'iho, March 25, 1891. A reader of Yun's diary knows it was a cold and rainy day on March 25, 1891, because he began every entry with a brief description of the weather.
50. Diary of Yun Ch'iho, November 28, 1891.
51. Diary of Yun Ch'iho, March 15, 1892.
52. Henry Yu, "Mixing Bodies and Cultures: The Meaning of America's Fascination with Sex between 'Orientals' and 'Whites,'" in *Sex, Love, and Race: Crossing Boundaries in North American History*, edited by Martha Rhodes (New York and London: New York University Press, 1999), 446.
53. Yu, 449.
54. Diary of Yun Ch'iho, November 5, 1892.
55. Ibid.
56. Diary of Yun Ch'iho, May 2, 1893.
57. Diary of Yun Ch'iho, January 16, 1891.
58. DuBois, 126.
59. Diary of Yun Ch'iho, May 10, 1891.
60. Diary of Yun Ch'iho, April 10, 1891.
61. Diary of Yun Ch'iho, May 2, 1891.
62. Diary of Yun Ch'iho, January 7, 1893.

63. Diary of Yun Ch'iho, March 11, 1891.
64. Diary of Yun Ch'iho, May 21, 1892 and June 24, 1892.
65. Diary of Yun Ch'iho, March 14, 1891.
66. Yun, "Letter on June 5, 1885," in Kim, 77.
67. Chandra, 93.
68. Diary of Yun Ch'iho, February 2, 1891.
69. "Letter to Allen on January 24, 1891," in Kim, *Letters in Exile: The Life and Times of Yun Ch'iho*, 101.
70. Yun, "Synopsis of What I Was and What I Am," 2.
71. Diary of Yun Ch'iho, December 12, 1893.
72. Choe Byeong-Heon, *Seongsan Myeong Gyeong (The Clear Mirror of Sacred Mountain): Korean Christian Classics Series, Volume 4* (Seoul, Korea: KIATS Press, 2010), 125.
73. Choe, 162–164.
74. Gil Seon-Ju, *Han'guk Kidokkyo chidoja kangdan sŏlgyo [Korean Christian Leader Pulpit Sermons]* (Seoul, Korea: KIATS Press, 2008), 38–41. Gil was baptized at Jangdaehyeon Church, founded by Samuel A. Moffett, in 1897, and became the church's pastor in 1907, serving there for twenty years. See Jae-Buhm Hwang, "Rev. Kil Son-Ju's Theology Emphasizing Spiritual Endeavor, Revivalism and Biblical Inerrnacy: Commemorating the Centenary of the Great Revival of 1907 in P'yŏngyang," in *Critical Readings on Christianity in Korea, Volume 1*, 337, and In Soo Kim, *Protestants and the Formation of Modern Korean Nationalism, 1885–1920: A Study of the Contributions of Horace G. Underwood and Sun Chu Kil* (New York: Peter Lang, 1996), 111–112.
75. Wells, 52–53.
76. Yun Ch'iho, "March 30, 1889," in *Yun Ch'iho Ilgi, Volume 1* [Diary of Yun Ch'iho, Volume 1], 370.
77. Diary of Yun Ch'iho, November 6, 1892. Lee Sang-Hoon argues that Yun's criticism of Confucianism did not mean he completely abandoned his Confucian worldview, particularly because of Yun's own adherence to filial piety toward his father. Yun's respect for his father was genuine and reflects in part his Confucian upbringing, but it does not detract from his embrace of Christianity over Confucianism for national reform. See Lee Sang-Hoon, 353–354.
78. Diary of Yun Ch'iho, December 23, 1889.
79. Diary of Yun Ch'iho, October 14, 1892.
80. Stephen Jay Gould, *The Mismeasure of Man, Revised and Expanded* (New York and London: W.W Norton & Co., 1996), 143.
81. Ibid.
82. Herbert Spencer, *The Principles of Sociology, 3rd ed.* (New York: D. Appleton and Company, 1895), 89–90, as cited in Gould, 146.
83. Josiah Strong, *Expansion under New-World Conditions* (New York: Baker and Taylor, 1900), 290–291.
84. Diary of Yun Ch'iho, October 14, 1892.
85. Diary of Yun Ch'iho, January 1, 1893.
86. Ibid.
87. Diary of Yun Ch'iho, June 7, 1891 and April 8, 1893.
88. Diary of Yun Ch'iho, September 10, 1890.
89. Diary of Yun Ch'iho, November 27, 1890.
90. "Letter from Yun Ch'iho to Young John Allen, March 16, 1893," in Kim, 110.
91. Diary of Yun Ch'iho, December 25, 1891.
92. "Letter from Yun Ch'iho to Young John Allen, April 8, 1889," in Kim, 87.
93. Diary of Yun Ch'iho, February 17, 1892.
94. Henry H. Em, *The Great Enterprise: Sovereignty and Historiography in Modern Korea* (Durham and London: Duke University Press, 2013), 63.

95. Catherine A. Brekus, "Writing as a Protestant Practice: Devotional Diaries in Early New England," in *Practicing Protestants: Histories of Christian Life in America, 1630–1965*, edited by Laurie F. Maffly-Kipp, Leigh E. Schmidt, and Mark Valeri (Baltimore: The Johns Hopkins University Press, 2006), 19.
96. Diary of Yun Ch'iho, January 8, 1892.
97. Diary of Yun Ch'iho, January 10, 1892, January 16, 1892, January 31, 1892, February 7, 1892, and February 17, 1892.
98. Diary of Yun Ch'iho, September 13, 1892.
99. Diary of Yun Ch'iho, December 30, 1892.
100. See Wells, 50–53, and Chandra, 90–94.
101. Josiah Strong, *Our Country, Its Possible Future and Its Present Crisis* (New York: The Baker & Taylor Co., 1885), 209–227.
102. Josiah Strong, *The New Era or the Coming Kingdom* (New York: The Baker & Taylor Co., 1893), 354.
103. Diary of Yun Ch'iho, April 15, 1893.
104. Ibid.
105. Martin E. Marty, *Modern American Religion, Volume 1: The Irony of It All, 1893–1919* (Chicago and London: The University of Chicago Press, 1986), 17.
106. Richard Hughes Seager, *The World's Parliament of Religions: The East/West Encounter, Chicago, 1893* (Bloomington and Indianapolis: Indiana University Press, 1995), 104.
107. Marty, 20.
108. Diary of Yun Ch'iho, September 24, 1893.
109. George S. Goodspeed, "Introduction," *The World's Parliament of Religions: Its Christian Spirit, Historic Greatness and Manifold Results. A Brief Summary of Testimonies Gathered from Many Lands, Indicating what the World Has Said of This Memorable Congress of the Creeds, of Its Organizer and Chairman, John Henry Barrows, and of the Official Literature of the Parliament*, edited by George S. Goodspeed (Chicago: Hill and Shuman, 1895), 5, as cited in Eric J. Ziolkowski (ed.), *A Museum of Faiths: Histories and Legacies of the 1893 World's Parliament of Religions* (Atlanta: Scholars Press, 1993), 2.
110. Marty, 22.
111. Ibid.
112. Diary of Yun Ch'iho, September 24, 1893.
113. Ibid.
114. *Chicago Daily Tribune*, September 23, 1893.
115. Kinzo Riuge M. Hirai, "The Real Position of Japan Toward Christianity," in *The World's Parliament of Religions: an illustrated and popular story of the World's First Parliament of Religions, held in Chicago in connection with the Columbian Exposition of 1893, Volume I*, edited by John Henry Barrows (Chicago: The Parliament Publishing Company, 1893), 448.
116. Seager, 75.
117. Diary of Yun Ch'iho, September 26, 1893.
118. Ibid.
119. Hirai, 449.
120. Diary of Yun Ch'iho, September 25, 1893.
121. Diary of Yun Ch'iho, January 23, 1894 and January 24, 1894.
122. Diary of Yun Ch'iho, February 2, 1894.
123. Laura Askew Haygood, "Letter to Mollie Stevens, February 15, 1894," in *Life and Letters of Laura Askew Haygood*, edited by Oswald Eugene Brown and Anna Muse Brown (Nashville: Publishing House of the M.E. Church, South, 1904), 320.
124. Ibid.
125. Diary of Yun Ch'iho, February 12, 1894.
126. Diary of Yun Ch'iho, February 22, 1894.

127. Ibid.
128. Diary of Yun Ch'iho, March 21, 1894.
129. Diary of Yun Ch'iho, April 20, 1894.
130. Dana L. Robert, *American Women in Mission: A Social History of Their Thought and Practice, 1792–1992* (Mercer, GA: Mercer University Press, 1996), 412.
131. Diary of Yun Ch'iho, December 1, 1893.
132. Ibid.
133. G.T. Candlin, "The Bearing of Religious Unity upon the Work of Missions," *The Chinese Recorder* (December 1893), 563.
134. Candlin, 562.
135. Diary of Yun Ch'iho, December 17, 1893.
136. Ibid.
137. Ibid.
138. George Heber Jones, "The Religious Development of Korea," *The Gospel in All Lands* (September 1891), 417.
139. Diary of Yun Ch'iho, June 9, 1894.
140. Paik, 19.
141. Paik, 26–27.
142. James L. McClain, *Japan, a Modern History* (New York and London: W.W. Norton & Co., 2002), 211.
143. Diary of Yun Ch'iho, August 7, 1894.
144. Diary of Yun Ch'iho, August 24, 1894.
145. Diary of Yun Ch'iho, September 28, 1894.
146. Diary of Yun Ch'iho, September 9, 1894.
147. Ibid.
148. Diary of Yun Ch'iho, November 14, 1894.
149. Diary of Yun Ch'iho, November 24, 1894.
150. Diary of Yun Ch'iho, November 27, 1894.
151. Ibid.
152. Kim, 20.
153. Diary of Yun Ch'iho, December 27, 1894.
154. Rebecca Y. Kim, *The Spirit Moves West: Korean Missionaries in America*, 9.
155. Diary of Yun Ch'iho, September 29, 1894.
156. Yun worked as a governmental official until 1905 and then worked primarily as a religious educator. Yun initially resisted Japanese imperial rule in Korea, but he eventually accepted Korea's colonization and became a vocal supporter of the imperial government in the last several years of his life before his death in December 1945. Yun's collaboration with the Japanese was at first gradual and then coerced under intense pressure from imperialists who targeted him for his elite standing, but he received great scorn for his actions from the Korean public after Korea's liberation in August 1945. Yun's religious convictions from the late nineteenth century nonetheless illumine significant insights on Korean Protestantism, American Protestant foreign missions, and world Christian studies that should not be disregarded because of his later political activities. For critical studies on Yun Ch'iho's complicated legacy in South Korea, see Koen De Ceuster, *From Modernization to Collaboration: The Dilemma of Korean Cultural Nationalism: The Case of Yun Ch'iho, 1865–1945* (Leuven, 1994), and Mark Caprio, "Loyal Patriot? Traitorous Collaborator? The Yun Ch'iho Diaries and the Question of National Loyalty," *Journal of Colonialism & Colonial History* 7:3(2006), https://muse.jhu.edu, accessed on November 19, 2015.
157. Yun Ch'iho, "The Place of the Native Church in the Work of Evangelization," *The Korea Mission Field* (February 1911), 49.
158. Yun, 50.

Bibliography

Archives and Manuscript Collections

Kline, C. Benton, Jr. *Special Collections and Archives*. Decatur, GA: John Bulow Campbell Library, Columbia Theological Seminary.

Rose, Stuart A. *Manuscript, Archives, and Rare Book Library*. Atlanta, GA: Emory University.

Books and Journal Articles

Blassingame, John W. and John R. McKivigan, eds. *The Frederick Douglass Papers, Series One: Speeches, Debates, and Interviews, Volume 4: 1864–80*. New Haven: Yale University Press, 1991.

Boehmer, Elleke. *Empire, the National, and the Postcolonial, 1890–1920: Resistance in Interaction*. Oxford and New York: Oxford University Press, 2002.

Boehmer, Elleke. "Networks of Resistance." In *The Post-Colonial Studies Reader, 2nd ed.*, edited by Bill Ashcroft, Gareth Griffiths, and Helen Tiffin. London and New York: Routledge, 2006.

Brekus, Catherine A. "Writing as a Protestant Practice: Devotional Diaries in Early New England." In *Practicing Protestants: Histories of Christian Life in America, 1630–1965*, edited by Laurie F. Maffly-Kipp, Leigh E. Schmidt, and Mark Valeri. Baltimore: The Johns Hopkins University Press, 2006.

Brown, Oswald Eugene and Anna Muse Brown, eds. *Life and Letters of Laura Askew Haygood*. Nashville: Publishing House of the M.E. Church, South, 1904.

Bullock, Henry Morton. *A History of Emory University*. Nashville: Parthenon Press, 1936.

Candler, Warren A. *T.H. Yun, of Korea, and the School of Songdo*. Nashville: Board of Missions of the Methodist Episcopal Church, South, n.d.

Caprio, Mark. "Loyal Patriot? Traitorous Collaborator? The Yun Ch'iho Diaries and the Question of National Loyalty." *Journal of Colonialism & Colonial History* 7:3 (2006): https://muse.jhu.edu.

Cha, Paul S. "Unequal Partners, Contested Relations: Protestant Missionaries and Korean Christians, 1884–1907." *The Journal of Korean Studies* 17:1 (Spring 2012): 5–37.

Chandra, Vipan. *Imperialism, Resistance, and Reform in Late Nineteenth-Century Korea: Enlightenment and the Independence Club*. Berkeley: University of California Press, 1988.

Choe, Byeong-Heon. *Seongsan Myeong Gyeong (The Clear Mirror of Sacred Mountain): Korean Christian Classics Series, Volume 4*. Seoul, Korea: KIATS Press, 2008.

De Ceuster, Koen. *From Modernization to Collaboration: The Dilemma of Korean Cultural Nationalism: The Case of Yun Ch'iho, 1865–1945*. Leuven, 1994.

DuBois, W.E.B. *The Souls of Black Folk*. Chicago: A.C. McClurg & Co., 1903.

Em, Henry H. *The Great Enterprise: Sovereignty and Historiography in Modern Korea*. Durham and London: Duke University Press, 2013.

Gil, Seon-Ju. *Han'guk Kidokkyo chidoja kangdan sŏlgyo* [Korean Christian Leader Pulpit Sermons]. Seoul, Korea: KIATS Press, 2008.

Goldstein, Eric L. *The Price of Whiteness: Jews, Race, and American Identity*. Princeton and Oxford: Princeton University Press, 2006.

Gould, Stephen Jay. *The Mismeasure of Man, Revised and Expanded*. New York and London: W.W. Norton & Co., 1996.

Harrington, Fred Harvey. *God, Mammon, and the Japanese: Dr. Horace N. Allen and Korean-American relations, 1884–1905*. Madison: The University of Wisconsin Press, 1944.

Hirai, Kinzo Riuge M. "The Real Position of Japan Toward Christianity." In *The World's Parliament of Religions: An Illustrated and Popular Story of the World's First Parliament of Religions, Held in Chicago in Connection with the Columbian Exposition of 1893, Volume I*, edited by John Henry Barrows. Chicago: The Parliament Publishing Company, 1893.

Hwang, Jae-Buhm. "Rev. Kil Son-Ju's Theology Emphasizing Spiritual Endeavor, Revivalism and Biblical Inerrnacy: Commemorating the Centenary of the Great Revival of 1907 in P'yŏngyang." In *Critical Readings on Christianity in Korea, Volume 1*, edited by Donald Baker. Leiden and Boston: Brill, 2014.

Kim, Hyung-Chan. *Letters in Exile: The Life and Times of Yun Ch'iho*. Covington, GA: Rhoades Printing Company, 1980.

Kim, In Soo. *Protestants and the Formation of Modern Korean Nationalism, 1885–1920: A Study of the Contributions of Horace G. Underwood and Sun Chu Kil*. New York: Peter Lang, 1996.

Kim, In-su and Horace Newton Allen. *Allen Ŭisa ŭi sŏn'gyo, oegyo p'yŏnji* [Horace N. Allen, M.D.'s Missionary and Diplomatic Letters]. Seoul, Korea: K'umnan Ch'ulp'ansa, 2007.

Kim, Rebecca Y. *The Spirit Moves West: Korean Missionaries in America*. Oxford and New York: Oxford University Press, 2015.

Lee, Sang-Hoon. "Nomadism and the Discovery of the Nation: The Case of Yun Chiho." In *Critical Readings on Christianity in Korea, Volume 1*, edited by Donald Baker. Leiden and Boston: Brill, 2014.

Marty, Martin E. *Modern American Religion, Volume 1: The Irony of It All, 1893–1919*. Chicago and London: The University of Chicago Press, 1986.

McClain, James L. *Japan, a Modern History*. New York and London: W.W. Norton & Co., 2002.

Mims, Edwin. *History of Vanderbilt University*. Nashville: Vanderbilt University, 1946.

Okihiro, Gary Y. *Margins and Mainstreams: Asians in American History and Culture*. Seattle and London: University of Washington Press, 1994.

Paik, George L. *History of Protestant Mission in Korea, 1832–1910, 4th ed*. Seoul, Korea: Yonsei University Press, 1987.

Patterson, Wayne. *The Ilse: First-Generation Korean Immigrants to Hawai'i, 1903–1973*. Honolulu: University of Hawaii Press, 2000.

Richey, Russell E., Kenneth E. Rowe, and Jean Miller Schmidt, eds. *The Methodist Experience in America, Volume 2: A Sourcebook*. Nashville: Abingdon Press, 2000.

Robert, Dana L. *American Women in Mission: A Social History of Their Thought and Practice, 1792–1992*. Macon, GA: Mercer University Press, 1996.

Schmidt, Leigh Eric. *Restless Souls: The Making of American Spirituality*. San Francisco: HarperSanFrancisco, 2005.

Seager, Richard Hughes. *The World's Parliament of Religions: The East/West Encounter, Chicago, 1893*. Bloomington and Indianapolis: Indiana University Press, 1995.

Snow, Jennifer C. *Protestant Missionaries, Asian Immigrants, and Ideologies of Race in America, 1850–1924*. New York: Routledge, 2007.

Strong, Josiah. *Expansion under New-World Conditions*. New York: Baker and Taylor, 1900.

Strong, Josiah. *The New Era: Or, the Coming Kingdom*. New York: The Baker & Taylor Co., 1893.

Strong, Josiah. *Our Country, Its Possible Future and Its Present Crisis*. New York: The Baker & Taylor Co., 1885.

Underwood, Lillias H. *Underwood of Korea: Being an Intimate Record of the Life and Work of the Rev. H.G. Underwood, D.D., LL.D., for Thirty One Years a Missionary of the Presbyterian Board in Korea*. New York: Fleming H. Revell, 1918.

Wells, Kenneth M. *New God, New Nation: Protestants and Self-Reconstruction Nationalism in Korea, 1896–1937*. Honolulu: University of Hawaii Press, 1990.

Yu, Henry. "Mixing Bodies and Cultures: The Meaning of America's Fascination with Sex between 'Orientals' and 'Whites.'" In *Sex, Love, and Race: Crossing Boundaries in North American History*, edited by Martha Rhodes. New York and London: New York University Press, 1999.

Yun, Ch'iho. "Thirty Years Ago." In *Southern Methodism in Korea*, edited by J.S. Ryang. Seoul, Korea: Board of Missions, Korea Annual Conference, Methodist Episcopal Church, South, 1926.

Yun, Ch'iho. *Yun Ch'iho Ilgi, Volume 1* [Diary of Yun Ch'iho, Volume 1]. Seoul, Korea: Kuksa P'yŏnch'an Wiwŏnhoe, 1973.

Ziolkowski, Eric J., ed. *A Museum of Faiths: Histories and Legacies of the 1893 World's Parliament of Religions*. Atlanta: Scholars Press, 1993.

Newspapers and Periodicals

Chicago Daily Tribune
The Chinese Recorder
Emory Alumnus
The Gospel in All Lands
Heathen Woman's Friend
The Korea Mission Field

3 Which Christ to Follow?

The Emergence of Transnational Discord

Introduction

In 1885, a desperate Korean mother reluctantly turned to an American missionary physician to cure her ailing nine-year-old son. From her village in the southern outskirts of Seoul, she viewed the missionaries in the heart of the city with suspicion. The devout Buddhist noblewoman believed the foreigners threatened traditional Korean norms. But now her son had contracted smallpox and suffered from blinding pain in his eyes. After trying every possible remedy to no avail, she had her son treated by the strange new doctor. The doctor examined the boy and prescribed medicine that restored him to full health in three days. After his recovery, the boy presented a straw bundle of ten eggs to the doctor as a token of gratitude. The doctor politely refused, telling the boy to keep the eggs and feed his own family.[1] The boy, Syngman Rhee, grew up to become a political and religious leader among Koreans in Hawaii and the United States for nearly forty years before his election as the Republic of Korea's first president in 1948. This was the first of Rhee's many relationships with American missionaries. They were happier when he was a young boy than when he later matured to become Korea's political leader. American missionaries and Korean Protestants transmitted the religion among Koreans at home and abroad, but their religious ideas clashed as much they converged during the Japanese occupation, and Rhee, as much as anyone, exemplified the sometimes subtle, sometimes overt conflict.

In 1909, American Presbyterian missionaries celebrated twenty-five years of mission work in Korea. They met in Pyongyang to reminisce over fond memories, discuss their work, and plan for the future. As the first missionary in Korea, Horace Newton Allen delivered introductory remarks. He described how the failed coup d'état in 1884 opened a door for missionaries. In their attempt to overthrow the conservative Korean government, progressive revolutionaries assassinated several rival officials and gravely injured the queen's nephew, Prince Min Yeong-ik. During three months of intensive care, Allen successfully treated the prince's severed arteries and sword wounds. The Korean royal family lavished expensive gifts on Allen in appreciation of his medical work. More importantly, Allen used his favorable standing with the Korean royals to establish a modern hospital and pave the way for additional American missionaries. He resigned from mission work in 1893, rose in 1897 to the highest position in the U.S. diplomatic corps, and served as the U.S. Minister until 1905. Allen noted to his Presbyterian colleagues in Pyongyang that "poor old Korea has sunk in public esteem" and surmised that he was more respected in the United States for his work as a missionary despite serving as America's leading diplomat in Korea for eight years.[2] Although the Western world regarded Korea as a lowly nation, he said, missionary advances in medicine, education, and evangelization over twenty-five years had "made Korea the banner country for missions" and the Protestant mission was the only remaining cause of Western interest in Korea.[3] In the same year, another missionary summarized the Western view: "Politically she is nil, but in the missionary circle she is a first-rate power."[4]

In 1905, the United States closed the legation in Korea in recognition of the Japanese Protectorate, which was established after Japan's victory in the Russo-Japanese War. The United States was the first Western nation to acknowledge both Korea's independence in 1882 and Japanese rule in 1905. President Theodore Roosevelt supported Japan's takeover and believed that Japanese conquest would curb Russian power in Asia and benefit Koreans with civilizing reforms.[5] U.S. magazines, such as *North American Review, The Outlook*, and *World's Work*, also contrasted the modernizing Japanese to primitive Koreans.[6] In 1905, an American correspondent in East Asia compared the two nations: "The first thing that strikes a traveler in going from Japan to Korea is the extraordinary contrast between the cleanness, good order, industry, and general prosperity of one country, and the filthiness, demoralization, laziness, and general rack and ruin of the other."[7]

When American missionaries had arrived in 1884, they imagined that Korea was a religious *tabula rasa* for their making. In the first decade of the twentieth century American missionaries exulted in the Protestant expansion that was transforming the religious landscape. Between 1904 and 1909, the number of Korean Protestants rose from 31,905 to 161,468.[8] After a wave of revivals in 1907, missionaries became more convinced that they could achieve their religious ambitions. They also acknowledged Korea's political misfortune, which culminated in Japan's outright annexation in 1910. In order to remain in the country, the missionaries maintained a position of political neutrality to appease the new Japanese rulers. They increasingly saw the Korean mission field as a laboratory with the right conditions to create a purified Christianity unencumbered by the denominational strife and theological liberalism that marked American Protestantism.

Yet Rhee's religious activism in the United States, which intensified but complicated his relationship with missionaries, demonstrates how Korean Protestants reinterpreted the religion according to their cultural context, their colonial experience, and Western influence. Postcolonial scholar Sara Suleri argues that the telling of colonial stories requires "a more naked relation to the ambivalence represented by the greater mobility of disempowerment" and the recognition that some colonial elites' politics and writings were profoundly shaped by their transnational experiences.[9] Elleke Boehmer identifies how transnational connections between colonial powers and the peoples they ruled over created subversive networks of communication and exchange for anti-colonial resistance.[10] Korean Protestants and American missionaries created a web of cross-colonial connections and transnational infrastructures during the age of Japanese imperialism that simultaneously facilitated and hampered the aspirations of both parties. As Korean Protestants fused their religious persuasions and political interests to resist the Japanese, missionaries instructed Koreans to focus on religious expansion instead of colonial resistance. The missionary blueprint for an idealized Korean Christianity was restricted to church planting, not nation building. Trying to propagate this purified form of Christianity, missionaries warned the churches against political entanglements. But Korean Protestants like Rhee constructed religious practices and theological beliefs set in opposition to missionary intentions.

Rhee's Conversion to Christianity: Beholding the Spirit of God and the Spirit of National Independence

Ten years after Rhee's initial encounter with a missionary, he enrolled at a Methodist mission school, Pai Chai Academy, to learn English. Although a Christian doctor had cured him of smallpox, Rhee and his family continued to practice Buddhism and Confucianism. His mother taught him the Chinese language so that he could read and memorize Confucian teachings from the *Analects* and regularly sent him to the Buddhist temple to offer prayers and sacrifices. After the Sino-Japanese War, Rhee found foreign affairs enthralling and used the mission school to acquire knowledge of Western culture and politics. But he resisted Christianity and viewed conversion as a betrayal of his Korean identity. Rhee agreed to submit to missionary instruction at Pai Chai Academy but told a classmate: "Let them change the order of heaven and earth, but I never shall give up my mother's religion."[11] Over the next four years, Rhee mastered English at the mission school and worked as a Korean language tutor for newly arriving missionaries. But his heart guided him more toward Western literature and politics than toward religion classes. He tolerated them but leapt at the opportunity to read American magazines like *McClure's* and *The Outlook*.[12] His insights into the United States, Western colonialism in Asia, and Japan's modernization fired his imagination about Korean society and politics.

As a reformer against the royal Korean government Rhee suffered imprisonment in 1899 for sedition. Before his arrest, he sought protection from Korean authorities in the Methodist mission compound, and during his imprisonment, missionaries unsuccessfully sought his release. They asked Horace Allen, who had a powerful post in the U.S. legation, to appeal on Rhee's behalf because of his value as a translator for American medical work. But the interventions failed and Rhee languished in prison, bound by manacles on his hands and feet. In the midst of his anguish, he dimly remembered sermons from Pai Chai Academy and cried out, "O God, save my country, and save my soul."[13] He then felt peace and converted to Christianity. Soon after, he began evangelizing to fellow inmates and prison guards. He eventually received release from the shackles and could read letters, books, and magazines sent by missionaries. In 1903, George Heber Jones encouraged him to remain faithful in prison and optimistic about his release: "I hope and pray that the Emperor will grant you a full pardon and you will come out to help us in making Korea a Christian land."[14] Rhee read the Bible and other Western literature and taught Bible classes, established a library of more than five hundred books within the prison, started an English-Korean dictionary project, and wrote a book fittingly entitled *The Spirit of Independence*.[15]

Rhee's book contended that Korea must open her doors to the West in order to learn modern technology and adopt Western methods. He divided the world into three groups of peoples: barbarian, semibarbarian, and civilized. Koreans were encamped within the second group and needed to learn from civilized nations like the United States in order to exploit their natural resources and maintain their independence. Inspired by the American Revolutionary and Civil Wars, Rhee depicted an America that had once been unenlightened but had risen to power by embracing democracy, modern industry, international trade, and equal rights. He found in the Revolutionary War a host of Americans "with blood boiling fervor" who risked their lives for national independence: "The farmers came forward with hoes and sickles, while even women and children took clubs with them and if one fell the person behind came forward to fight."[16] He saw the Civil War as a crusade "for the sake of the rights of black persons"—a crusade that demonstrated the depths of America's morality.[17] Rhee implored his people to discard their old ways and look to the example of the United States, "a civilized world that is like a paradise across the seas."[18] From his prison cell, Rhee's romanticized America reflected his reading and the stories he had heard from missionaries. After several years, America looked to him less and less like paradise.

Though Rhee prescribed for Korea large doses of American republicanism and democracy, the impetus for change was Christianity, with its compassionate God who opened the way to salvation and civilization for all peoples through Jesus Christ. Although Christianity was no Western religion—Jesus lived and taught in the East—the Easterners rejected his teachings whereas Westerners, who accepted them, built a high civilization drawing on Christian wisdom to manage wisely the natural resources that God had given to every nation. But only conversion to Christianity elevated the nations beyond the unenlightened state that prevented their cultivation of nature to national ends. Christianity brought economic prosperity, equal rights, and democracy. In contrast to traditional Korean class distinctions, the "heavenly principles" of Christianity celebrated the commonality of "the so-called noble and highborn person" and "the weak and humble person," teaching that every human being is the child of one God.[19] Koreans needed to relinquish their mistaken notions of Christianity as a foreign religion or an example of Western learning *(Seohak)* and instead embrace its teachings for individual redemption and national development: "We must adopt this religion as the basis for everything and work for the benefit of others rather than for ourselves. We must do our best in supporting the nation with one mind to achieve the same level of civilization as that of Great Britain and the United States."[20] There is no reason to doubt the sincerity of Rhee's religious convictions, but one would not be amiss to see him as a convert who, above all, believed in the nation-building power of Christian faith and had an interest in converted individuals because he had a passion for building a new Korea. In one sense, the missionaries would have agreed with his hopes for a Christian Korea. But his blending of Christianity and Korean patriotism would have made some of them uneasy.

In 1904, the government freed Rhee from prison after a political realignment during the Russo-Japanese War. After the United States decided to close the American legation and honor the Japanese Protectorate over Korea, the Korean government sent Rhee promptly to America to seek out U.S. officials in Washington and ask for American support of Korean independence at peace talks to end the Russo-Japanese War. Rhee had come to the United States with endorsement letters from Methodist and Presbyterian missionaries, who encouraged him to present the letters to their friends. They vouched for Rhee's conversion and asked friends to support his studies. Presbyterian missionary James S. Gale affirmed that Rhee was "a gentleman born a scholar and a Christian whom God has used" and urged his friends to help the Korean "find many good friends among his white brethren in the free land of America" and aid his academic endeavors so that he might return "to do a great work for his people."[21] Before leaving Korea, Rhee had approached Gale for advice and asked for baptism. Gale encouraged study in the United States, but refused baptism because Rhee had attended a Methodist mission school, which meant that "the Methodists had a rightful claim to him."[22] Rhee found this puzzling and saw little difference between Methodists and Presbyterians. Rhee was baptized in 1905 at a Presbyterian church in Washington, but he joined Methodist churches in Boston and Korea before accepting in 1913 a position with the Korean Methodist Mission in Hawaii. Largely indifferent to denominational labels, he would ally himself with any group of Christians committed to freeing Koreans from Japanese rule.

From 1905 to 1910, Rhee earned three academic degrees: a BA from George Washington University (1907), an MA from Harvard University (1908), and a PhD from Princeton University (1910). The pastor who baptized him also introduced him to Charles Needham, the president of George Washington University, who awarded Rhee a scholarship with the understanding that Rhee would work as a pastor in his homeland. But Rhee became more and more interested in resisting Japanese colonialism than in studying theology. In 1907, Rhee protested when Methodist bishop and *The Christian Advocate* editor A.B. Leonard returned from Asia marveling at Japanese reforms in Korea and praying that Japan might rule Korea forever. Rhee wrote to Leonard, criticizing his indifference to Japanese imperialism and insisting that Koreans wanted to govern their own affairs. The *Asbury Park Press* printed Rhee's letter, but Leonard ignored it.[23] After his graduation from George Washington University, Methodist missionaries wanted Rhee to return to Korea as a preacher. But Rhee believed he could best serve his country by learning more about politics, and he enrolled at Harvard to take courses in American history, international law, European colonialism, and diplomacy.

During his studies at George Washington and Harvard, Rhee earned extra money by delivering speeches about Korea, especially at Y.M.C.A. events in cities throughout the East Coast. He illustrated his talks with eighty colored slides that accentuated the progress of missionaries, Korean initiatives to improve society, and Korean desire for independence.[24] His eloquence made him popular, but his Y.M.C.A. sponsors urged him to refrain from talking about politics. In 1908, Y.M.C.A. general secretary C.C. Michener invited Rhee to speak at an annual national convention in Pittsburgh but instructed Rhee to talk only about Korea's Christian progress: "I think it would not be wise for you to talk on the treatment which Korea has received at the hands of Japan. I do not believe it would be worthwhile to spend much time on the political situation. The religious needs are the ones which should be emphasized at this gathering."[25] Americans wanted stability and trading partners in Asia; political agitators worried them. Hidden beneath the indifference to Korean desires one could sense the old condescension of the Americans toward Korean culture and promise.

Although Rhee acquiesced to Michener, he traveled to Denver later in the year to chair an international conference of thirty-six Koreans from Russia, China, England, Hawaii, and the United States. They met for five days in July at Grace Methodist Church to organize politically and discuss national independence. Rhee delivered the opening address on "Korea's Glorious Past," followed by Korean and American speakers who spoke about "Relations Between Korea and Japan," "Things Oriental," "America in the East," "Politics and Good Citizenship," "National Greatness," and the "Awakening of Korea."[26] Rhee's closing address encouraged the delegates to remain hopeful. Although American newspapers reported that Japan was too strong for Korea to resist, Rhee proclaimed, in effect, that Korea could be too persistent for Japan to retain its colonial ambitions there.[27]

After the conference, Rhee left Denver for New York City to enroll at Union Theological Seminary, where he wished to earn a doctorate, but not in religion or theology. In New York, Rhee visited the Presbyterian foreign missions home office and encountered Ernest F. Hall, a former missionary to Korea. Hall insisted that Rhee pursue his doctorate at Princeton instead of Union. Hall immediately made arrangements for Rhee to meet with the deans of Princeton Theological Seminary and the Princeton Graduate School, Charles Erdman and Andrew F. West. He soon entered the graduate program of the University's Political Science Department; he lived in the Seminary dorms.[28] Just as missionaries supported Rhee in Korea, they opened doors for his educational ambitions in the United States.

At Princeton, Rhee studied international law and politics and became in 1910 the first Korean to earn an American doctorate. His dissertation, *Neutrality as Influenced by the United States*, did not cover Korean-American relations, but it alluded to the Korean situation when it examined policies and practices of neutrality from the Roman Empire to the nineteenth century. Rhee argued that the principle of neutral jurisdiction emerged in the eighteenth century during the Revolutionary War; previously, European maritime war codes mainly protected the cargo of neutral ships from seizure. But without strict regulations, different European nations administered their own policies; the Dutch, for example, introduced the liberal principle of *free ship, free goods* to avoid belligerent searches on the high seas whereas the French condemned neutral vessels that carried enemy goods. The U.S. Declaration of Independence shifted attention to the protection of free commerce and private property in wartime: "From the early days of its history the United States had earnestly endeavored to restrict the list of contraband articles to the narrowest possible limit, in opposition to the English tendency of expanding it."[29] This American precedent, he thought, influenced European nations to expand freedom for neutral commerce. Rhee did not mention the conflict between Korea and Japan, but an alert reader might have seen its shadow when he contended that the formation of the United States not only marked "a new era on the laws of neutrality" but also inspired other European colonies in the Western hemisphere, especially those under Spain and Portugal, to seek independence through military and diplomatic means.[30] Like the United States, these colonies revolted against their colonial rulers and demanded that neutral nations recognize their political existence.[31] Nothing could have better described his hopes for Korea, even though a casual reader of the dissertation might never have seen the connections.

The Missionary Blueprint for Korean Christianity and the Realpolitik of Japanese Rule: A Steadfast Commitment to Evangelization

Rhee, along with other Korean Protestants at home and abroad, combined faith and politics to protest Japanese imperialism. American missionaries sympathized with these Korean convictions, but their greatest determination was that imperial Japanese rule would not derail evangelization. Though Korea had lost national independence, missionaries believed that Protestantism would become the national religion. In 1906, one Methodist missionary,

A.W. Wasson, wrote that the most significant fact in Korean affairs was not the political conditions, but rather "the almost unparalleled opportunity which this country presents for effective missionary work."[32] Wasson reported that Koreans were dismayed over the fragile state of their government and that some Korean officials were "despairing of their country even unto death," but that the Koreans' "unusual hospitality" toward the gospel and responsiveness to missionary efforts reflected "a truer indication of the future of the country" than its political subordination.[33] Missionaries acknowledged, with some indifference, Korea's diminishing geopolitical position, but they emphasized that Protestant expansion was the solution for a nation now subjected to Japanese imperialism.

One year after Roosevelt closed the American legation in Seoul, he had the word "Korea" deleted from the U.S. government's Record of Foreign Relations and placed all Korean files under the heading "Japan."[34] Although Korea ceased to exist in U.S. government records, American missionary magazines increased their articles on the country after 1906. *The Missionary Review of the World*, a leading pan-denominational periodical edited by A.T. Pierson, devoted fifteen articles to Korea that year. In 1907, there were twenty-five articles on Korea; in 1908, thirty-eight; in 1909, thirty-four; and in 1910, forty-six, over triple the number in 1906.[35] Missionaries in Korea and such American Protestant leaders as Pierson and William T. Ellis, a journalist with *The Philadelphia Press*, exuberantly praised the quantity and quality of Korean converts, whom they alleged to be devoted to Bible study, prayer, and financial giving, respectful of missionaries, and orthodox. Underwood believed that American and Korean Protestants together might be able to win the entire nation for Christ.[36] In 1907, Susan Wilson traveled to Korea with her husband, MECS bishop Alpheus W. Wilson. She marveled at the number of Protestants in Songdo and praised their enthusiastic Christian worship and their respect for missionaries.[37]

John Nevius, an American Presbyterian missionary in China, had drawn the blueprint for a purely spiritual Protestantism in the mission field. In 1869 he had formulated an evangelistic strategy based on Henry Venn and Rufus Anderson's principles of self-supporting, self-governing, and self-propagating indigenous churches. Nevius stressed that the primary missionary task was to evangelize and "not to teach mechanics or civil engineering, or foreign languages or sciences; not to Christianize heathen nations by civilizing them, as some plainly assert; but to Christianize them, and leave them to develop their own form of civilization."[38] Nevius also criticized the use of foreign funds to plant indigenous churches and instead endorsed the principle of self-support as the means to growth within indigenous communities. Underwood was impressed with Nevius's work and invited him to Seoul in 1890. After Nevius's visit, Underwood and his missionary colleagues adopted Nevius's methods.[39] They settled on four guiding principles: First, Korean Protestants were to "abide in the calling wherein he was found," meaning that no convert was to be removed from their neighborhood or paid by missionaries. Each convert was to remain at home to evangelize friends and family members without missionary finances. Second, missionaries should develop indigenous churches with simple operations that Korean Protestants could readily understand and manage. Third, Korean churches could appoint and pay evangelists among their most qualified members as long as the pay came strictly from Korean giving. Fourth, missionaries must let converts erect church buildings in accordance with Korean architectural styles and financial resources.[40]

Despite their nod toward indigenous autonomy, missionaries governed every sphere of Korean Protestant practice. During his furlough in 1892, Appenzeller told Methodist congregations in New York and Pennsylvania that missionaries in Korea preached only the most basic Protestant doctrines to Koreans.[41] In 1901, he recalled his first sermon in the Korean language on Christmas Day in 1887, in which he taught the simple promise of salvation through the name of Jesus from Matthew 1:21; he claimed that he and others enjoyed success because they never deviated from that biblical verse.[42] Koreans were purchasing more and more Methodist literature from the missionaries, as well as historical and scientific works from the mission's "general bookstore," but Appenzeller judged that Koreans were not ready for advanced theological instruction on topics like higher criticism.[43] Even after witnessing remarkable Protestant expansion over seventeen years, Appenzeller insisted that missionaries preached only elementary doctrines—"the old gospel"—to their converts.[44]

In their educational work, missionaries debated whether or not to teach English in their schools. In 1898, Gifford wrote that Presbyterian mission schools had decided to teach strictly in Chinese and Korean.[45] Missionaries observed that Koreans were most interested in the mission schools in order to acquire Western education and learn English. Although some American teachers wished to teach English in order to civilize Koreans, others feared that English classes would detract from religious education. The missionaries' blueprint for a purified Christianity required that Koreans be interested in mission schools more for religion than English. In 1888, Scranton wrote that the Methodist mission school for girls in Korea was not training their eleven enrolled students to become more like Americans but rather to become better Koreans. He declared that the missionaries were not cultivating the Koreans over in their own image—"after our foreign ways of living, dress, and surroundings"—but took "pleasure in making Koreans better Koreans only." He summarized, "We want Korea to be proud of Korean things, and more, that it is a perfect Korea through Christ and His teachings."[46] In 1887, Appenzeller founded Pai Chai Academy after teaching English to students eager to learn the language.[47] At the time, the government prohibited evangelism, and Appenzeller taught English as a means to remain in the country. The king supported Appenzeller's school and provided the name, Pai Chai Academy, which meant "Hall for Rearing Men."[48] In 1903, missionary administrators at Pai Chai Academy removed English courses from the curriculum to accentuate their commitment to Christianity. One missionary teacher noted that the school's restriction appeared "absurd to the man who stands outside and looks on," but he maintained that "many of the missionaries have the feeling that instruction in English is not only a waste of time but positively injurious to the Koreans."[49] Inchoate Korean minds might adopt Western ways over Christian ones. After implementing their new policy, missionaries reported a decline in the number of students. They were also surprised that some students organized a strike against the school for changing the curriculum.[50] But the principal chafed at student demands and insisted that the school was for religious education.[51]

In 1906, after the Japanese began operating schools in Korea, Scranton confessed that the elimination of English was a mistake. The students needed to learn English because they lacked adequate textbooks in Korean and because English would promote modern civilization. With increasing Japanese encroachment into Korean affairs, which included schools that taught exclusively in Japanese, Scranton believed that it was time for Koreans to learn English so that they might be led "out of ignorance to abreast with the rest of the world and out from every form of bondage into freedom and equality with the rest of humanity."[52] He defended his position by referring to Methodism's founder, John Wesley, who, Scranton claimed, had "said that our people are not more holy because they are not more knowing."[53] Although Scranton had reversed his position of nearly twenty years, he remained arbiter of what was best for Korean Protestants. He and other missionaries would make the correct adjustments to their experiment.

Missionaries also passed a resolution in 1905 for a "simultaneous revival movement" that would commence during the Korean New Year *(Seolnal)*, which was a three-day holiday that started on the first day of the lunar calendar.[54] They wanted a nationwide revival because of the political conditions. Just as the Japanese began imposing their will, the missionaries' highly publicized revival campaign served their own interests. It reached unconverted Koreans while also preventing churches from becoming overtly political organizations.[55] Before the Russo-Japanese War, Presbyterians had set upon 1907 as the date for the first Korean Presbytery—a date coinciding with the planned graduation ceremonies for the first class of young ministers at the theological seminary in Pyongyang.[56] The Presbytery would include one Korean elder from each organized church and have more Korean than missionary voting members. The missionary William Newton Blair noted that the Presbytery's founding marked a truly independent Church in which Koreans would evangelize their own people. In accord with Nevius's blueprint, Blair insisted that after the creation of the Presbytery Koreans would control their churches.[57]

But missionaries worried that the churches would become hubs of nationalism. They did not fail to notice widespread Korean resistance to Japanese rule after the Protectorate Treaty. Blair observed: "In a day, what centuries of misrule of the part of her own rulers had failed to do, Japanese occupancy accomplished: patriotism was born in Korea. A wave of intense national feeling swept over the land."[58] Shouts of "Korea for the Koreans" and "It is better to die than to be slaves" could be heard throughout the country, and some Koreans in the mountains were waging guerilla warfare against the Japanese.[59] Nationalists looked for support in the Protestant churches because the members were educated persons in a well-developed organization.[60] Missionaries, however, demanded a policy of political non-interference. Although Blair insisted that missionaries desired a Korean church for Koreans, he still wanted the churches to preserve "spiritual purity" by dissuading Koreans from joining churches for political purposes and avoiding the mistakes of the fourth century, when Constantine converted to Christianity and made it the state religion of the Roman Empire: "Had she departed even a little from the strict principle of non-interference in politics . . . we might have again witnessed the cross of Constantine leading a great army. I believe Korea, like the Roman Empire, would have adopted Christianity in a day, and I believe, too, we would have had another Roman Church."[61]

The missionaries stated that the revival campaign was to be "a spiritual work within the church"—a sign of religion's preeminence over politics.[62] They were to preach on topics that "teach the *heart* rather than the *head*" to ensure that Koreans would experience the assurance of salvation.[63] After the revivals in 1906, missionaries reported a wave of converts in several different parts of the country, but they did not achieve the wider national impact for which they had hoped.[64] Later that year, Presbyterian missionaries in Seoul and Pyongyang welcomed Howard Agnew Johnston, the minister of Madison Avenue Presbyterian Church in New York City and the special representative of the denomination's mission in Asia. Johnston shared stories of religious revivals that recently occurred in India and Wales, stirring anew hopes for similar events in Korea.[65] But after months of coordinated prayer campaigns, missionaries despaired in the meager results. Revival in Korea did not come close to the revivals reported in India and Wales.

In January 1907, the revival came. As they gathered for worship in Pyongyang, the two Presbyterian missionaries who led the meeting, Blair and Graham Lee, called for the Korean Protestants to pray aloud and confess their sins to one another. With the public confession, Lee observed that "immediately the Spirit of God seemed to descend on that audience."[66] For the next several days, numerous Koreans, including some of the most prominent members of the church, confessed their sins in worship services marked by weeping, shouting, and falling to the floor. Koreans confessed of stealing, adultery, and resentment, not only against one another but also against the missionaries. Blair was stunned when one Korean elder confessed: "I have been guilty of fighting against God. An elder in the church, I have been guilty of hating not only Kang You-moon, but Pang Mok-sa."[67] Blair explained that Kang You-moon was another Korean church member and Pang Mok-sa was Blair's Korean name. The elder resented the missionary for treating him disrespectfully. "I never had a greater surprise in my life," Blair remembered.

"To think that this man, my associate in the Men's Association[,] had been hating me without my knowing it."[68]

The events in Pyongyang initiated a surge of religious revivals. The reports elicited an initial skepticism from a few of the missionaries, who frowned on the spectacle of loud prayer and uncontrollable weeping, which "seemed like such a perversion of the proper decorum to be observed in church."[69] But after witnessing communal audible prayer *(tongseonggido)* firsthand, one of the skeptics, Henry M. Bruen from Daegu, concluded that it did not subvert the principle of orderly worship. He explained how the practice—which persists in Korean Protestant worship today—did not mean that that worshippers competed to lead the congregation in a "formal audible prayer in public service," but consisted of exercises in which each person prayed "for himself but audibly because of the intense earnestness which made it impossible to keep quiet."[70] As the praying services spread through the country, the missionaries saw them as the result of the work of the Holy Spirit.

By February 1907, churches in most of the major cities, such as Seoul, Songdo, and Daegu, had hosted revivals that produced results like those in Pyongyang. By June 1907, every Protestant mission station recorded news of revivalistic fervor in the churches.[71] Missionaries across the nation celebrated the revivals as a step toward a purified Protestantism. They saw the revivals as producing "genuine" Korean converts who believed in the Bible, prayed earnestly, and refrained from using the gospel to advance political agendas against Japanese occupation.[72] As one Methodist put it, the praying Christians were "not satisfied by mere intellectual belief, but press for evidences of a real spiritual experience."[73] A Presbyterian, seeing the revival in the seminary in Pyongyang, felt reassurance that the first ordained Presbyterian ministers in the nation would be "Holy Spirit filled men," able to testify to the experience of divine grace.[74] This was what the missionaries had always wanted from Korean ministers: gospel simplicity and experimental piety rather than theological complexity. In 1908, *The Missionary Review of the World* described the first seven ordained Korean Presbyterian ministers as honest and pious men who did not dabble in theological intricacies but rather preached the simple gospel message with "power," "force," and "directness."[75]

As reports of the Korean Protestant revivals spread throughout East Asia, Chinese Protestants and Western missionaries in China went to Pyongyang to learn more. They returned home convinced that the Korean movement was the work of the Holy Spirit and started their revivals in 1908, which became known as the Manchurian Revival. Chinese Protestants and Methodist missionaries in the town of Xinghua conducted a series of revival meetings in which thousands wept loudly and confessed their sins publicly.[76] Early Korean Protestantism grew in part because of the proliferation of Chinese Protestant texts in Korea from 1880 to 1900. Because educated Koreans could read Chinese fluently, foreign missionaries widely distributed popular Chinese Protestant texts as part of their evangelistic strategy. In addition to the Chinese Bible, more than forty Chinese Protestant books and tracts were distributed among educated Koreans by 1900.[77] After 1907, religious currents from the Korean revivals led to growth in Chinese Protestantism. One Canadian Presbyterian missionary, Jonathan Goforth, incorporated stories from the Korean revivals in his sermons and led worship services involving participants who engaged in "simultaneous prayer and open confessions of sins mixed with anguished cries for mercy."[78]

Japanese imperial officials and some Westerners in Japan were less sanguine about the Korean revivals. In 1907, George Trumball Ladd, a professor of psychology at Yale University, traveled to Korea with Japanese Resident-General Ito Hirobumi, and published his account as *In Korea with Marquis Ito*.[79] He supported the Japanese occupation of Korea and contrasted the primitive and effete Korean race to the more enlightened and vigorous Japanese.[80] Unlike Japan, Korea stubbornly maintained an isolationist foreign policy and aggression toward foreigners into the nineteenth century. Ladd recalled Korean persecution of French Catholic missionaries and the killing of three Americans when their merchant schooner landed off the banks of the Taedong River near Pyongyang in 1866 as evidence of their provincial thinking.[81] He also refuted laudatory American Protestant mission reports about Korea by charging that the majority of Korean converts failed to comprehend even the most basic conceptions of God and Christian ethics. The so-called revivals revealed lurid confessions of lying, avarice, sexual impurity, and malice toward others, which demonstrated that Korean commoners, with their low intellectual and moral ideals, could not grasp "the genuine spirit and true practice of the religion of Christ" without at least three generations of missionary instruction.[82] In 1908, after two Koreans in California murdered Durham White Stevens, an American adviser to the Korean government who supported Japanese imperial interests, Ladd wrote in the *New York Times* that the Koreans were a "bloody race" with a long history of resorting to crude assassinations instead of civil discourse with political enemies.[83]

Although American Protestants labored to refute popular Western notions of the lowly Korean race, they shared some of the same racial opinions. In his 1901 report on the Presbyterian mission in Korea, Brown inferred that one of the causes for Protestant growth in Korea was because Koreans were "undoubtedly a weaker race than the Japanese and Chinese," which made it easier for missionaries to make an impression on them.[84] In 1909, Brown detailed the distinctions between Japan, China, and Korea in a printed report meant for private circulation.[85] The Japanese moved as one unit "in politics, in war, in commerce, and in the activities of their daily lives," and the defining characteristic of the Japanese was solidarity. The Chinese were, because of the "conspicuous absence of centralization, an individualistic race who engaged in continued popular uprisings against both Chinese ruling authorities and foreign inhabitants." Then came Korea: "The key idea of Korea is not so easily stated in one word. We might call it subjectivity. The people are less virile, less ambitious, less independent in spirit."[86] The Korean temperament was more emotional than the Japanese or Chinese, which made it "comparatively easy to reach [the Korean] heart and to arouse [Korean] sympathies." This tendency toward sentimentality was "one reason why Christianity has made more rapid progress in Korea than in either China or Japan."[87]

In 1919, Brown published *The Mastery of the Far East: The Story of Korea's Transformation and Japan's Rise to Supremacy*, in which he again attributed the greater success of the Protestant mission in Korea to racial characteristics: "Korean temperament is quite distinct from that of China and Japan. Less stolid and materialistic than the Chinese, less alert and martial than the Japanese, the Korean is more susceptible and trustful than either."[88] These weaker racial characteristics made the country a more fertile mission field than Japan because Korean converts did not deviate from missionary instruction: "The Japanese Christian subjects the teachings of the missionaries to his own independent scrutiny. The Korean Christian takes them without question. The former is a theological progressive; the latter a theological conservative."[89] Brown compared Koreans to African Americans. Just as white American Protestants long marveled at the seemingly innate religiosity of African Americans, Brown celebrated the intrinsic religious virtues of Koreans, which endowed them with special gifts for preaching and prayer.[90] Yet, like African Americans, Koreans lacked the practical wisdom for autonomous rule. Until 1907, Presbyterian missionaries described Korean Protestant congregations as "groups" and not "churches" because they felt that Korean converts were not ready to assume the mantle of a full-fledged ecclesial organization.[91] In 1909, Brown described missionaries in Korea as parents who cared for children.[92] Although missionaries spoke publicly about self-governing indigenous churches, they remained privately hesitant, Brown wrote in 1919, about turning over ecclesial affairs to Koreans.

Brown surveyed the geopolitical situation in Korea after the Protectorate Treaty and compared the strained relations between the Japanese and Koreans to those of whites and blacks in America. Although Japan claimed that their benevolent rule would promote Korean interests, Brown wrote that it was "the type of kindness which characterizes a Georgia gentleman toward a Negro . . . the Georgian may be a friend and benefactor of the negro, but he does not consider himself on the latter's level."[93] Brown did not disagree with Japanese assessments: Koreans were an inferior race in need of foreign guidance. Although he sympathized with Korean calls for independence, Brown believed that missionaries should cooperate with Japanese authorities. American Protestants could provide religious supervision; Japanese imperialists could implement modernizing reforms.

The missionaries in Korea did not disdain such a call for cooperation, but they found it more difficult to overlook Japanese misrule. In 1905, Scranton wrote his mission board in New York. He told his supervisors that the Japanese wantonly destroyed Korean property and threatened Koreans with physical harm: "As foreigners living in Korea . . . we are all nearly pro-Japanese to the extent of wishing well for Japan in Korea, if she will do well by Korea. We are Korean sympathizers first and look at Korea from the local standpoint."[94] In 1906, Mattie Wilcox Noble complained in her diary of how Japanese soldiers seized homes and the most valuable tracts of land for military purposes without fairly compensating the owners. Japanese soldiers also tried to confiscate mission property until the missionaries threatened to go to higher Japanese imperial officers. Noble observed that "the poor Koreans suffer thus all the time" with no one to defend their cause.[95]

Critical of some aspects of Japanese imperialism, the missionaries also disparaged Korean nationalism. In fact, missionaries had little praise for Korea apart from its hospitality to Protestant expansion. In their eyes—as one of them wrote—Korea had made no important contribution to Asia over the nation's three-thousand-year history. Japan seemed to be modernizing Asia through her commercial strength and China contributed a rich tradition of Oriental scholarship, with philosophers such as Confucius and Mencius, but Korea was "the slave child" of Asia with little impact on the region's growth.[96] Only missionary success would give the nation a place in world history; it would give the one true religion, Protestant Christianity, to all of Asia: "Poor, despised, oppressed Korea, what is to be her part in the great East that is to be? Not commerce, not learning, but infinitely greater than these, she is to be God's messenger bringing the true light of Christianity in the midnight darkness of the Eastern situation."[97] In 1910, Homer Hulbert wrote that Korea was a country without a national ideal—an underlying principle defining and guiding a nation's progress. Though critical of Japanese atrocities, he had little respect for Korean civilization. It had little ability in politics, war, or commerce; it was "no longer politically independent," "never developed the military spirit," and did not cultivate the land as resourcefully as either China or Japan.[98] Hulbert concluded that Korea's national ideal must be established by her religious spirit. The Koreans were at least capable of "adopting genuine Christianity."[99]

While they criticized Japanese brutality, the missionaries remained politically neutral for the sake of their religious work. When one missionary inserted criticism of Japan in his annual report, the denomination publicly rebuked him for expressing an unauthorized political opinion.[100] In his 1909 report, Brown observed that "Japan is in Korea to stay, and we cannot aid the Koreans by cursing their rulers."[101] The great Protestant experiment must not be sacrificed, especially after the religious revivals in 1907. Westerners had come too far in their creation of a purified Protestantism to lose it all by supporting Korean independence. Secretly many professed sympathy for Koreans, but most missionaries did not believe resistance against Japan stood any chance of success. Instead, missionaries accepted the realpolitik of Japanese rule and endeavored to preserve their religious gains. Lillias Underwood believed that Korean political conditions after 1905 enhanced the importance of the religious progress, partly because it served as a rebuke to Protestant liberals in North America. Underwood declared that God was "intending to use one of the weakest and most despised peoples to illustrate what the gospel pure and simple can do to evangelize a whole nation."[102] Success would vindicate the "old time religion," a conservative theological system that held to the inerrancy of Scripture and Christian doctrines like Jesus Christ's bodily resurrection, against "Higher Critics" and "liberal New Theologians."[103] The MEC Woman's Foreign Missionary Society declared that the Korean mission field demonstrated the power of "the straight, plain, old gospel, enforced by the Holy Spirit."[104]

Missionaries did not consider the Japanese annexation as a threat to their holy experiment. Instead, annexation provided another opportunity for mission-directed purification. But despite their best efforts, patriotic agitators still sought church membership for political reasons. Some joined churches to petition missionaries for American assistance. In 1910, missionaries believed that annexation had eradicated misguided hopes that Protestants could convince America to intervene. *The Missionary Review of the World* wrote that every Western nation accepted Japan's annexation and that this should end "the days of ceaseless intrigue and hopes of foreign intervention and claims for extra-territorial privileges" in Korean churches.[105] Indeed, annexation could assist the great Protestant experiment. If Korean Protestantism—unfettered from politics—continued to grow, the churches would exemplify more and more the ideal model of Christianity.

Missionaries also understood that Western Protestant esteem for Korea entailed high acclaim for both the converts and the missionaries.[106] In 1908, Yale professor Harlan P. Beach studied the American missionary enterprise throughout the world and ascertained that Korea had eclipsed Uganda to become the most productive foreign mission field.[107] In 1909, prominent American politicians lauded the missionaries for their extraordinary work. Democratic Party leader William Jennings Bryan praised them for making Korea into "one of the most important mission fields."[108] Former Republican senator and vice president Charles Warren Fairbanks admired them for their having transformed Koreans from the status of an oppressed people who "suffered the evils of misgovernment from time immemorial" into pious Christians.[109] The same year, Horace Underwood disclosed in a letter that California oilman and fundamentalist champion Lyman Stewart provided "the largest gift we have yet received" by donating $78,000 to support the Presbyterian mission.[110] One MECS missionary in 1910 compared the slow progress of their denominational mission efforts in Japan to prodigious results in Korea. He reported "a net gain of 33 per cent" in converts over the past year and vibrant churches springing up from every mission station; surely the mission provided substantive evidence in support of traditional Methodist approaches to evangelism over Social Gospel teachings: "I never felt the power of the gospel more in all my life than in this distressed land. Have we not here a new apologetic? When fools begin to talk of our holy religion as a spent force, lo! It breaks out with the energy of a

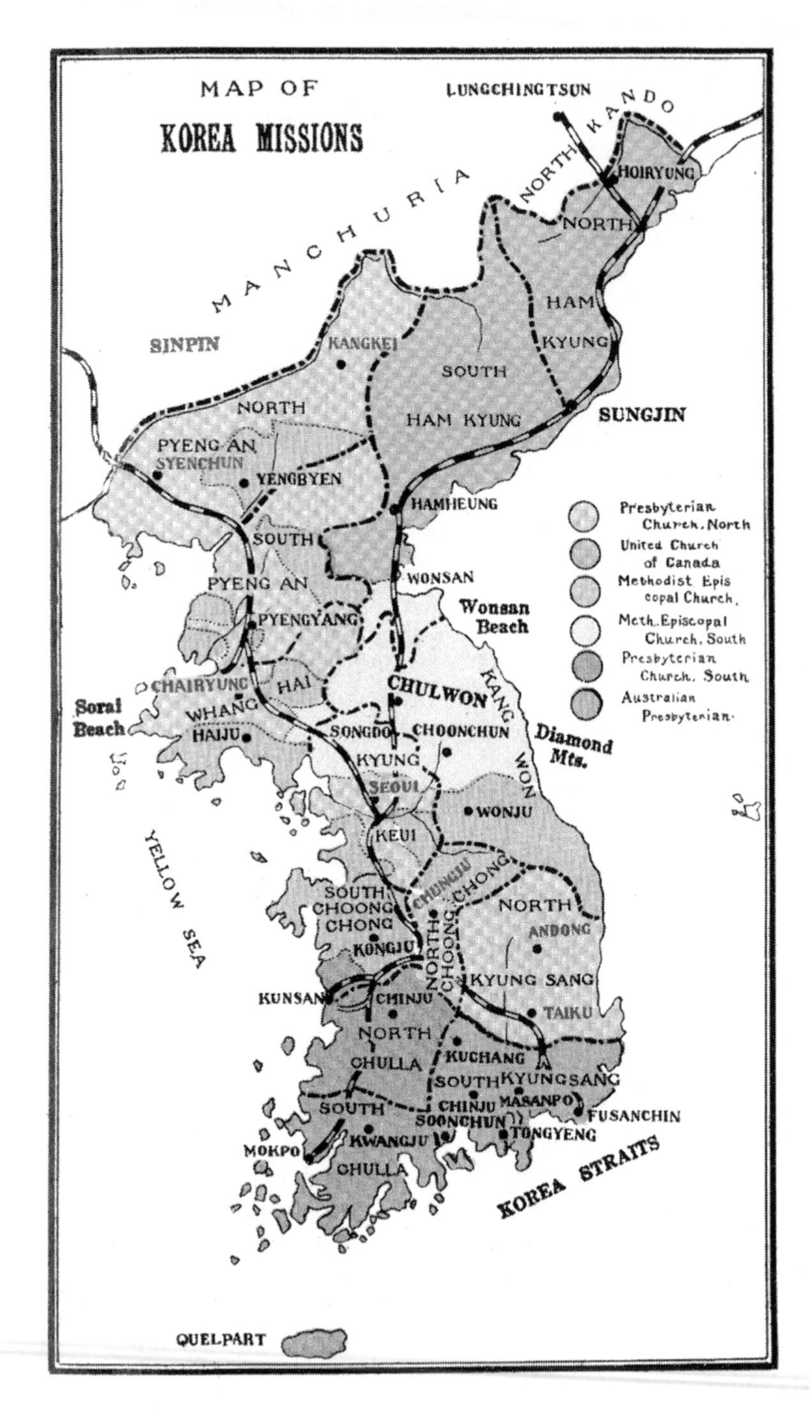

Figure 3.1 Presbyterian Church in the U.S.A. Map of Korea Missions, 1910 (Presbyterian Historical Society, Philadelphia, PA)

volcano."[111] American missionaries had produced a religious antidote to theological liberalism in a nation the rest of the world overlooked as small and inconsequential.

Promoting Korean Liberation and Protesting Missionary Indifference in the West

Missionaries therefore urged Korean Christians to stay out of politics; Rhee thought that an apolitical Christianity would be a diminished form of the faith. After leaving Princeton, he accepted a post with the Y.M.C.A. in Korea. He wrote first to Horace Underwood to inquire about opportunities in the Presbyterian mission. Rhee shared Underwood's vision of "true Christian education" in Korea and wished to teach, preach, and translate religious literature.[112] But Rhee also offered to teach classes in international law, modern European history, the U.S. Constitution, and Western philosophy; he wanted to teach students about modern-state building. Missionaries like Samuel A. Moffett protested when Underwood inserted secular news in Korean Protestant newspapers, but Rhee admired Underwood's practice. He believed that Protestant expansion organically nurtured modernization: "Koreans must be taught to know what Christianity would give us in the present life as well as in our life to come, and that all the blessings of Western civilization are based upon the Cross of Jesus Christ."[113] And modernization would produce liberation—it would teach Koreans democratic self-rule and economic development. The Japanese would have nothing to do with such a vision. Imperial officials thwarted his every move. After two years of intense Japanese surveillance and suppression, Rhee set out to promote Korean liberation by becoming a political activist and religious educator in the United States.

In America, Rhee's aims were two-fold: to persuade Americans and to organize an independence movement among Koreans in the United States. Rhee appealed to Korea's modernization and Christianization to rally American audiences. In 1912, Rhee began an interview with *The Washington Post* by declaring that "the old-time 'Hermit Kingdom' is no more . . . Within the space of three years Korea has been transformed from a slow-going country, where tradition reigned, into a live, bustling center of industrialism."[114] With newly developed trolley lines, city lights, mills, factories, and department stores, Seoul could "hardly be told nowadays from Cincinnati, except for the complexion of its residents."[115] And this was a country in which Christians had attracted over three hundred thousand adherents in fewer than thirty years of mission work. Koreans, he reiterated in numerous speeches, were following America's example. Just as American missionaries preached the gospel in remote lands, Korean Protestants traveled to China, Japan, Manchuria, and Siberia to do likewise. The success of the first Korean missionary, Yi Gi-bung, who began ministering in Jeju Province, an island sixty miles south of the Korean mainland, in 1907, encouraged Korean Presbyterians to send missionaries to neighboring countries.[116] Rhee asserted that Korea and the United States were kindred peoples, related by Christian ties that transcended distance, language, and cultural tradition: "What Judea has done in a religious way for the Occident will be done by Korea for the Orient, and this work, moreover, will be accomplished within the next 100 years."[117]

But in the next several years, Rhee grew increasingly frustrated with missionaries for their indifference—sometimes even hostility—to his religious-based nationalism. In 1913, he arrived in Honolulu to work as principal for a Methodist mission school for Korean boys. Founded in 1906, the Compound School offered primary education through the eighth grade in English and Korean. But prior to Rhee's arrival, Korean Methodists in Honolulu had protested when John Wadman, superintendent of the Hawaii Mission of the Methodist Episcopal Church, accepted contributions from the Japanese consul in Hawaii. The Koreans had previously resisted the Japanese consul general's offer and so they regarded Wadman's acceptance of money on their behalf as traitorous. Wadman should return the money; he should even resign. Wadman's reaction was to hire Rhee to work at the school and broker peace between the missionaries and Koreans.[118] Yet Rhee clashed with the missionaries. He charged that the Mission discriminated against Korean girls, and he insisted that the school admit them to classes. The school resisted, then acquiesced.[119] The conflict was an early milestone in Rhee's once uncritical view of America. He wanted a democratic Korea; in Hawaii he found a discriminatory American institution. This was not what he had anticipated.

Despite the school's concession, Rhee resigned and formed the Korean Christian Institute in Honolulu. The new superintendent, William Fry, opposed Rhee's demands that his school be financially and academically independent. He demanded the submission of detailed budgets and objected to classes in which teachers brought up Korean nationalism. Like missionaries in Korea, Fry called for abstinence from politics. But Rhee would not surrender: religion and politics belonged together. And since the school adhered to the missionary principles of self-support and self-propagation, it should also be self-governing. Korean money supported both the Korean Methodist Church and the Compound School; Koreans—meaning Rhee—should be able to teach what Korean children needed to learn.[120] In a letter to one of his graduates bound for college in Oregon, Rhee challenged him to become an advocate for "our great Cause" of Korean liberation.[121] Good Christians studied hard and worked for national independence. Somehow his beloved Americans failed to understand the second part of the equation, despite their history.

Missionaries in Korea implored Rhee to be more cautious in his public statements about missions and politics. In 1915, George S. McCune rebuked Rhee for printing the Presbyterian missionary's private criticism of Japanese imperialism. Japanese officials in Korea had previously accused McCune of conspiring with Korean dissidents. In 1912, imperial police searched the missionary's home during their investigation of a Korean plot to assassinate Governor-General Terauchi Masatake, the highest-ranking Japanese ruler.[122] The police also interrogated other missionaries and several hundred Koreans. Although they had scant evidence of an assassination ploy, the Japanese indicted 123 Koreans for their supposed criminal activity. Of the 123 suspects, 84 were Christian. Yun Ch'iho, who was then working as the vice president of the Y.M.C.A. in Seoul, was charged as the mastermind of the conspiracy. Despite an unjust trial that drew criticism from American, Korean, and Japanese observers, Yun and 104 other Korean men were judged guilty of treason.[123] Charles W. Eliot, former president of Harvard, witnessed the trial and went to Tokyo to share his misgivings over the unfair judicial process with the Japanese emperor. Eliot also assured Arthur Judson Brown that "no American would believe on any Korean evidence that a single American missionary was in the slightest degree concerned with the alleged conspiracy."[124]

But Rhee's revelation again raised Japanese suspicions and McCune required a retraction from Rhee of any statements he had attributed to the missionary. Mission work would do more than political posturing to help a people who, both men agreed, remained "poor and helpless and hopeless." What they needed was revival, not doomed revolutions. McCune reminded Rhee that five recent revivals in Pyongyang produced nearly two thousand new believers: "I want this work to go on and I do not want anything to come between me and God in bringing Korea to Christ." All of Rhee's talk about independence and atrocities could bring revival to a halt. If the Japanese forced the missionaries from Korea, conversions would dwindle. He pled with Rhee: "Of course I can go back to U.S.A. and work for God and be more peaceful too. But God needs us here."[125] In the same year another missionary reported how revivals in Seoul had provided "great comfort and strength to the Koreans who were discouraged over the loss of their country" and hoped Korean believers would continue to "see that God has a greater mission for them than a mere political one."[126] But the missionaries did not know precisely what to do with Koreans—like Rhee—who had their own ideas about the aims of Christianity. Missionaries envisioned a strong indigenous church with Bible-believing Korean converts. They did not want Koreans to convert to Christianity for political reasons. A few Koreans—and Rhee was an archetypal example—could not understand the need to separate the offices. Rhee's vision for Korean Christianity did not align with the missionaries' religious aspirations.

Rhee's Cross-Colonial Appeals and Disagreements over the March First Movement

In 1917 and 1918, at the end of World War I, Woodrow Wilson's calls for international justice and self-determination encouraged Rhee and other Koreans. Wilson's 1918 Fourteen Points speech championed "a free, open-minded, and absolutely impartial adjustment of all colonial claims" based upon national aspirations for autonomous rule.[127] Inspired Koreans believed the time was ripe for revolt. In January 1919, Korean exiles in Shanghai sent John Kiusic S. Kimm to France to head an unofficial Korean delegation at the Paris Peace Conference, in which diplomats from over thirty countries set the terms for the defeated Central Powers.[128] One month later, six hundred Korean students in Tokyo demanded Korean independence. In Korea, thirty-three representatives planned to sign a declaration of independence and stage a non-violent demonstration in Seoul on March 1. At the event, Koreans took to the streets, waving Korean flags and shouting: "Long live Korean independence *(Mansei)*!" News of the protest ignited similar events throughout the country—a protest movement soon known as the March First Movement. More than two million Koreans appeared at more than 1,500 gatherings.[129] Japanese authorities, initially surprised, suppressed the movement with brutal military force, arresting nearly 20,000 demonstrators, injuring thousands more, and burning houses, churches, and schools. In one village near Suwon, Japanese forces burned alive Korean protesters inside a church. The movement confirmed Japanese suspicions about Korean Christians: they were dangerous. Fifteen of the thirty-three signers were Protestant, and so were the majority of those who were arrested, including 244 church leaders (54 ministers, 127 Bible teachers, and 63 elders).[130]

The U.S. State Department denied Rhee a passport to attend the Paris Peace Conference, explaining that his status as a Japanese subject required a passport from the Japanese embassy. In Paris, the Conference denied the Korean delegation's request to address the group on the grounds that Korea lacked recognition as nation. Kimm nonetheless wrote France's prime minister, George Clemenceau, and Woodrow Wilson, asking them to read aloud a petition "for liberation from Japan and for the reconstitution of Korea as an independent state."[131] He reminded Wilson (but not the "realist" Clemenceau) of Japan's hostility against Korean Christians: "Is not the gravest indictment of Japan's work in Korea to be read in the fact that Christianity is seriously regarded as a force hostile to the success of the Japanese system of government in the country?"[132] Rhee also sent letters to leaders at the Paris Conference emphasizing Japanese restrictions upon Korean Christians and appealing for international action to free Korea.[133]

In addition, Rhee turned to American Protestants with missionary ties to Korea. He informed John R. Mott and Arthur Judson Brown that he was mobilizing Koreans in America to support their countrymen in the wake of the Japanese suppression. He reminded them that Christians had suffered arrest and torture in the crackdown. Rhee explained the situation to Mott: "In the name of humanity and for the protection of all the Christians from cruel treatment and barbarous torture, we the Koreans abroad should do something."[134] To Brown he praised the missionaries in Korea who had been "insulted and maltreated by the Japanese on account of their sympathy and love for the Korean people."[135] He also did not fail to mention that Koreans in the United States would "stand by the American missionaries and do everything in their power to help the cause of Christianity and freedom in Korea."[136] Rhee was pulling American Protestants step by step deeper into the crisis, and he was using Christianity—a Korean Christianity—to persuade them to do more.

In his eyes, they did not do enough. Herbert Welch, MEC bishop for the Japan and Korea Missions, argued with him about an appropriate response to the March First Movement, and Welch refused Rhee's pleas for open political support from him. Welch insisted on distinguishing "very clearly between the political question, that is the question of national independence or of government reform, and the other questions which relate to justice and humane treatment."[137] He decried Japanese violence against Korean Christians, but he stayed away from questions about imperial rule: missionaries had "no neutrality on brutality" and refused to remain silent on "questions of violence and cruelty." But Welch remained silent about Korean political interests.[138] He made it clear that in his eyes, mission schools and Korean churches were more important than politics: "To make Korea intelligent and to make Korea Christian means even more than to make Korea fundamentally free."[139] Rhee replied that Korean liberation was more than a political movement inspired by Wilsonian democracy; it was a religious cause grounded in Christian teachings. "What I and my countrymen expect the Foreign Mission Board to take up in regard to the Korean situation is not that it should take up the political side of it," Rhee retorted, "but that it should uphold courageously the elements of Justice, Righteousness, Truth, and Humanity, for these are the things for which Christianity stands."[140] The American Protestant mission to Korea underwent a reversal. Americans had once preached to Koreans in Korea; now a Korean was preaching to Americans in America, and he was implying that they had shortcomings. The breach widened another inch.

Rhee appreciated Welch's religious labors, and he said so, but he would not let the bishop off the hook when it came to geopolitics. The March First Movement plainly revealed that Koreans deplored overlords from Japan. Missionaries saw the chaos and understood Korean desires more acutely than American politicians at home, but they did not speak out. To Rhee this apolitical stance was parochial, making it appear that missionaries cared more about preserving their small stations than about Korean independence and national dignity. He preached again to Welch: "America, as well as the world at large, knows very little about Korea. What we want is that the truth of Korea be known, because in truth we can rely with our cause."[141] But the missionaries, to Rhee's consternation, remained quiet. John Fairman Preston's letter to his father on March 17, 1919 confided that their superiors instructed them to remain quiet on political matters. Preston, who had written endorsement letters for Rhee on his first trip to the United States, told his father that Koreans felt "discriminated against and treated as half civilized"; they also openly resented the Japanese. But Preston said that he was "very careful to express no opinions on political matters and carefully avoid mixing up in politics, as has been enjoined upon us both by our Consul and by [the Presbyterian Church in the U.S. foreign missions home office in] Nashville." But a public announcement by Preston would not have bolstered Rhee's cause: "The cry for independence is, of course, ill-timed and impracticable. Like a child crying for a wasp, one wonders what the Koreans would do with it if they had it!" [142] It was hard for the Americans not to be patronizing to the Koreans; it was becoming even harder for the Koreans to accept being patronized, even by people who wanted to be their friends.

Preston was not the only missionary skeptical of the independence movement. Both Welch and Brown publicly stated that a number of missionaries doubted that Koreans could govern their own affairs without Japanese control. Welch reported that "some of the missionaries who are long-standing and devoted friends of Korea are not convinced that independence would be a genuine blessing at this time."[143] Brown cautioned relatives and friends of Presbyterian missionaries to learn more about Korea before condemning the Japanese, noting that two Japanese groups, one civil and the other military, disagreed over imperial policy. The civil party felt outrage at the violence, but the military wanted to deter rebellion with swift and overwhelming force. Brown felt sympathetic toward Koreans, but he saw their protests as misguided and unwise.[144]

Brown's letter angered Rhee, who sent a copy to Welch with a letter underscoring his dissent. He charged that Brown had betrayed his professed political neutrality by demarcating Japanese political factions: "Is it a more important question to find out which party is more directly responsible for the atrocities and which party is not, while wanton brutalities continue, than to find out how to stop these atrocities?"[145] Rhee felt that Brown had pro-Japanese political sentiments that led him to defend Japanese rule and criticize the March First Movement. If missionaries wanted to tell Korean Protestants to stay out of politics, they ought to follow their own advice: "For the sake of Christian missions in Korea . . . the authorities of the mission boards who feel that they must not advocate the cause of Korean independence, because it is a political question, must not condemn that cause, because it is the same political question."[146] The Americans, in short, were guilty of hypocrisy, though Rhee was too polite, or perhaps shrewd, to use the word.

Brown managed to offend Rhee at every turn. Rhee disliked it when he used the term "Chosen" instead of Korea. In 1910, Japan had renamed Korea as "Chosen" and designated their presence there as a "Governor-Generalship," which amounted to an announcement of full colonization.[147] Koreans despised the Japanese names, and the missionaries knew it. One sympathetic missionary in 1920 criticized the term "Chosen" because it insulted Koreans and tacitly supported Japanese efforts to eradicate their cultural identity and historical memory: "It is of greatest importance that we do our part for the preserving of the idea of Korea as a separate and distinct mission field, with individual problems and needs, and this can best be done by the use of Korean descriptive at all times."[148] Rhee was tempted to mobilize Korean opposition to the missionaries: "If Dr. Brown thinks that the Japanese military forces alone can injure the influence of the American missionaries, he is mistaken. The Korean people in Korea can injure it even more effectively than the Japanese, if they know that the American mission boards are against their national movement."[149]

The Korean Protestant nationalists felt no hesitation in using Christian language to describe their cause. Hugh Heung-wo Cynn, a Korean Methodist pastor in the United States, compared the independence movement to the death and resurrection of Christ. Like Jesus at Golgotha, Korea was crucified by the Annexation Treaty in 1910. But Korea had risen from the grave with the March First Movement.[150] From his pulpit in Korea, Gil Seon-ju reflected upon the unfavorable result of the Paris Peace Conference for Korean independence and implored his colonized parishioners to continue seeking the messianic promise Jesus fulfilled on the cross by praying for "the curtain of peace to open upon the stage of righteousness," as written in Psalm 85:10.[151] The majority of American missionaries and possibly the majority of Korean Protestants saw the world, Christianity, and Korea differently. Could Christ call on a people to seek national independence? Or did he merely call upon them to save their souls? The Americans—at least most of them—thought they were following the Christ who preached and healed without interfering with Rome. The Koreans—at least many of them—thought that they followed the Christ who refused to grovel before Pontius Pilate.

Transnational Movements and Tensions among Korean Protestant Migrants in Hawaii and the United States

Rhee argued, debated, and exhorted, but he also organized. He traveled throughout the United States to organize an independent movement among Koreans, using Korean American churches to raise funds and garner support for liberation. But Rhee could be an authoritarian, and some Korean Americans balked at his imperious tactics. Proclaiming the virtues of democracy, he demanded absolute control and treated co-ethnic allies as potential rivals. In Hawaii, Rhee required unquestioned obedience from his followers and cast aside anyone who broached questions about his directives.[152] After the March First uprising, Koreans established three different provisional governments in Manchuria, Shanghai, and Seoul. Two of the three, in Shanghai and Seoul, elected Rhee as Chief of Executive of their cabinets, whereupon he opened an office in Washington to represent the provisional government as its president. Cabinet members in Shanghai objected to Rhee's self-designation without their approval: he had, they said, violated their constitution. But Rhee refused to relent, and he told them that he used the title of president when he communicated with other nations so that he could gain recognition for the provisional government. An alteration in the title would disclose the internal conflicts. The cabinet yielded and revised their constitution to name him president, but his strong-arm tactics led to his political demise. After years of irritation with his dictatorial ways, the cabinet passed a non-confidence resolution against him in 1922 and impeached him in 1925.[153]

Rhee's relationship with Philip Jaisohn illumines his fractured relationships with even his closest allies. Like Rhee, Jaisohn was a nobleman and progressive reformer in Korea before migrating to North America. In 1884, Jaisohn participated in the abortive coup d'état against his government and had to flee to Japan, where he taught Korean to American missionaries. After three months in Japan, Jaisohn came to the United States to obtain a Western education. Upon landing in San Francisco, he worked at menial jobs while attending English classes at a local Y.M.C.A. During this time, Jaisohn converted to Christianity and attended a Presbyterian church. He admired the teachings of Jesus that displayed God's compassion for humanity and the imperative for Christians to help the weak and powerless.[154]

When Rhee arrived to the United States in 1904, he turned to Jaisohn for guidance. By that time, Jaisohn had earned a medical degree from George Washington University Medical School, married Muriel Armstrong, the daughter of U.S. military major George Armstrong, and had become a naturalized American citizen. Even before meeting in the United States, the two men had befriended one another in Korea when Jaisohn returned home to work as a government adviser from 1896 to 1898. In Korea, Jaisohn founded the nation's first modern newspaper in Korean script instead of Chinese characters. Rhee worked with him for social and political reform before conservative government leaders expelled Jaisohn for pushing a modernizing agenda.

When the two reunited, they again became close friends and allies. During his years in North America, Rhee exchanged more letters with Jaisohn than with anybody else: sixty-two exchanges over thirty years.[155] Both men saw Korean liberation as a religious cause inspired by Christian principles.[156] Like Rhee, Jaisohn believed that Christianity paved the path for Korean modernization. In 1897, Jaisohn's newspaper, *The Independent*, identified Korean Protestants as the "most wide-awake people" in the country because of their moral regeneration and rapid absorption of "the Western idea of enterprise in their daily life," which inclined them to adopt Western technologies.[157]

The two had ambivalent attitudes toward the missionaries. In Korea, Jaisohn and his American wife, Muriel, spent many hours socializing with them. In 1896, Eugene Bell wrote to his parents about befriending the Jaisohns in Seoul, describing Muriel as "young looking and quite pretty" and Philip as "universally popular" among Koreans and missionaries. In their conversations, Jaisohn "had come to the conclusion that the only hope of the country was through missionaries."[158] But after Japanese conquest, Jaisohn was irate at missionaries who refused to support Korean liberation. He bristled at missionary friends who counseled him to patiently trust that God knew the trials of the Korean people: "God," he said, "is too slow."[159] Missionaries praised such Japanese-led improvements as telephone poles and clean streets; Jaisohn asked them how they would feel if robbers painted the fence posts and decorated the front porches of their stolen homes.[160] In 1913, Rhee and Jaisohn thought about starting an English-language newspaper devoted to Korean political issues because the missionaries reported only on religious matters.[161] Yet when Jaisohn made diplomatic overtures to powerful Americans, he touted Korea's Christian progress. In 1920, he shared with Rhee a copy of his letter to President Warren G. Harding, informing the president that Japan suppressed Christianity, hampered evangelism, and violated the freedom to worship. He reminded Harding that Korea was both "the one Christian nation in the Orient" and "the one country of the Orient that is not receiving the full active support of Christian nations."[162]

Jaisohn advised the Korean provisional government in America on foreign affairs. As president, Rhee established the Korean Commission in Washington by executive order in September 1919 as a means for lobbying the U.S. Congress for support and for raising funds. During the fall, the Commission had some victories. On three occasions, congressional members spoke in the Senate and the House of Representatives to sympathize with Korean aspirations for liberty and criticize Japan's violation of Korean human rights.[163] But the Commission's fund-raising campaign bogged down in controversy. Without consulting the cabinet, Rhee issued $250,000 of bonds in the name of the provisional government. The bonds, paying an interest of 6 percent, were redeemable within one year after the United States recognized the provisional government. Without support from other Korean leaders abroad, the bond sale faltered. Koreans in North America, who gave generously to the provisional government, did not purchase the bonds and disliked Rhee's disingenuous method of tying bond redemption to the unlikely odds of U.S. recognition of the provisional government.[164]

Rhee's financial opportunism and disregard for democratic government upset Jaisohn, who in 1920 called upon Rhee to cooperate with other leaders and admonished him for creating friction among Korean patriots in the United States, Hawaii, and Asia. One letter commended Rhee for his efforts to free Korea but also asked Rhee to be tolerant to those who opposed his views and engage dissenting parties without undue anger. Rhee should debate with "decency and politeness" and refrain from underhanded actions when he lost a majority vote: "Therefore, even if the majority sentiment is against [you], you must take that majority sentiment like a man and cooperate with them to the best of your ability. Personal pride and private interest should not enter into your consideration at this time."[165] Authoritarian leadership would lead to failure. But Rhee continued to create the kind of discord that culminated in the government's vote of no confidence in 1922. Another of Rhee's partners, Ahn Chang-ho, tried to broker a compromise between Rhee and his opponents in the provisional government. Like Jaisohn and Rhee, Ahn was a Protestant and a political exile in the United States. But Ahn failed in his negotiating attempts and soon thereafter distanced himself from Rhee to form his own Korean independence group.[166]

Despite his impeachment from political office, Rhee retained Korean supporters in Hawaii and the United States. In 1922, Rhee resumed his educational and religious work with the Korean Christian Church in Hawaii. His educational aims differed from those of the mission schools. In Korea, missionaries taught academic subjects but bore down on religion. Rhee's school also taught religion, alongside daily Bible studies, but he pressed students to pursue academic training in such fields as economics, engineering, and medicine. He was thinking ahead, planning for the cultivation of people who would lead an independent Korea. In Hawaii, Methodist schools tried to Americanize young Korean people, educating for assimilation by training Hawaii-born Asian children in American ways.[167] Rhee followed the public school curriculum so that his students could matriculate into the local public high school, but he added classes in the Korean language, Korean history, and Sino-Korean classics *(hanmun)*.[168] Rhee wanted his students to succeed in American higher education, but not at the expense of losing their Korean roots.

Other immigrant Koreans had similar concerns about vocational diversity and cultural retention. In the *Korean Student Bulletin*, students encouraged industrial and technical training. Contributors to the magazine came mainly from the ranks of international Korean students with study visas and from American-born Korean students. In 1926, a student named Y.H. Choy addressed international students and advocated "vocational education" over the humanities. Too many students, he said, chose to study theology and psychology instead of farming and manufacturing. Korea needed economic independence; this meant that it needed "vocationally trained men, [because] there is a comparative small percent of our students who are studying in vocationally trained lines."[169] Some other international students agreed with him, noting the bleak prospects for obtaining government, academic, and ecclesial positions. The imperial government favored either the Japanese in Korea or Koreans educated in Japan. Korean graduates from the United States usually found work in Christian colleges, but only three—Union Christian College, Ewha College for Women, and Chosen Christian College—existed, and they could offer employment only to a small fraction of applicants.[170] Students with theology degrees also returned home to discover a scarcity of ministerial positions. In 1934, a student named John Chung complained that some fundamentalist churches in Korea would never hire him because they believed that an American education would have corrupted his theological orthodoxy: "When I think of such things, they say I have too much education! Besides, one evangelist in Korea told me that the real enemy of Korea is none but the education of the Korean people. To a Fundamentalist, the welfare of a church and Christian theology is preferable to the welfare of a people."[171] Despite Chung's educational accomplishments at a mission college in Korea and State Teachers' College in Tennessee, he lamented his future job prospects: "Suppose I go home next summer, what do you think I can do in Korea? Preaching? Teaching? Or what? As far as I know I may be a coolie who carries a jiggie, or a farmer who eats snails and jellyfish with chopsticks."[172] Not every Korean student in the United States was bitter; probably every Korean student in the United States was realistic about the challenges that awaited at home.

International students wrote about vocational obstacles; American-born Korean students wrote about their uneasy entrapment between two cultures. In 1930, Martha Choy wrote about the "confessions of an American-born Korean" and described the generational tensions she and others like her encountered as second-generation Korean Americans.[173] Unlike their parents, the first generation of Koreans in the West, American-born Koreans embraced assimilation, adopted Western ways, and befriended Americans of all races. Their parents accused them of betrayal and rebuked them for abandoning their Korean heritage. Choy felt confounded by what she called a "veritable enigma" in Hawaii, with parents who disapproved of her life choices because they were "dogmatically conservative in their Orientalism" and "suspiciously skeptical of the whole program of 'Americanization.' "[174] Choy resented that her parents sent her to a Korean-language school and a Korean church for the sake of cultural retention, portraying the institutions as hollow instruments for "the propagation of dogmas and prejudices."[175]

Choy also described tensions between American-born Korean and international students. As a child growing up in Hawaii, she heard fanciful stories about Korea and yearned to visit. When she arrived in college, she was eager to meet Korean students: "All in all, a Korean student, who in the pursuit of such learning had crossed such distances, was a marvel to me; he could not help but be a hero in my eye."[176] But the Korean-born students Choy encountered belittled her as an American-born Korean. Choy accused them of holding to a "strange paternalism" that classified her as less Korean because of her American birth. Choy came to distrust the Korean students: "An American-born Korean . . . finds [the Korean international student] sluggish, somewhat uncouth, stubborn in his provincialism, and all in all, quite impossible. He does much lip-service and raving regarding independence, economic regeneration, speaks disparagingly of American materialism. Little wonder then that the other regards this stranger-countryman with bewilderment."[177]

Other American-born students, less antagonistic to their parents and to their Korean-born counterparts, still had to wrestle with their identities. In 1935, Anne Kim wrote that the greatest struggle facing American-born Koreans like herself was the feeling of not entirely belonging in either Korea or America. Kim went to high school in New York City and earned a scholarship to Mount Holyoke College. She wrote an essay entitled "Whither American-Born Korean," in which she observed that American-born Koreans could not count on recognition either as Americans or as Koreans. White Americans classified them as second-class citizens on account of their race whereas native-born co-ethnics regarded them as less authentic Koreans because of their assimilation. Kim was still hopeful that American-born Koreans could overcome the ambiguity by embracing their Korean identity and accepting their role as bridge-builders for native-born Koreans in unfamiliar surroundings. She wanted both groups of Koreans to "understand each other so that we may give and receive help."[178] Kim encouraged American-born Koreans to "learn all things Korean, particularly the language, classics, customs, and ideals" and native-born Koreans to be tolerant of American-born Koreans who did not share their knowledge of Korean culture or their passion for Korean independence.[179] The goal should be mutual understanding.

Other first-generation Koreans were not as optimistic about the next generation. Some in Hawaii doubted that their children would be able to maintain Korean institutions like schools and churches because they lacked both language skills and piety.[180] Young Kang, editor in Honolulu of *The American-Korean*, said that second-generation Koreans did not speak Korean fluently, cared more about American events than Korean politics, did not participate in larger Korean social gatherings, and were lax about church attendance.[181] In 1937, ethnographer Bernice B.H. Kim studied Koreans in Hawaii for four years and identified Korean politics as one significant reason for familial strife. The first generation supported the independence movement; their children remained lukewarm. Parents harangued children for being indifferent about their homeland and children accused parents of being more concerned about Korean politics than about finding a rewarding position in their new country.[182]

Rhee knew about these generational tensions in Hawaii. Although he supported American-born Korean students in their academic hopes, he denounced their attempts to disconnect from their Korean heritage and the independence movement: "You are Americans by birth, but you are Koreans by blood. Someday you will be builders of new Korea. Mingle yourselves with Korean boys and girls. Study hard the Korean language and Korean history if you truly love your fatherland. Do not marry foreigners."[183] He was touching a sensitive nerve. As a small minority group, second-generation Koreans dated and married non-Koreans, taking Chinese, Filipino, and Japanese spouses. In 1933, there were 2,033 Koreans, 6,668 Chinese, 4,686 Filipino, and 44,774 Japanese students enrolled in Hawaiian schools.[184] Margaret K. Pai recounted her experiences growing up in Hawaii and recalled the fierce opposition to a young Korean woman's marriage to a Japanese man in 1937. The bride's aunt, a church leader, refused to endorse the interracial marriage, and her church disapproved the use of their chapel. Pai wrote that she and her friends had no objections to interracial dating but agreed not to have romantic liaisons with non-Koreans because of first-generation hostility.[185] Rhee, on the other hand, railed against interracial marriage in

Korean Pacific Magazine, a magazine he founded shortly after his arrival to Hawaii in 1913.[186] Yet he disobeyed his own directive when he married Francesca Donner, an Austrian woman, in 1934. They met during his travels in Europe in the early 1930s and soon became romantically involved.[187] In 1934, Donner left her Vienna home to marry Rhee in the United States. They wed in New York City in a bilingual ceremony with vows delivered in Korean and English.[188] When Rhee returned to Hawaii with his Austrian wife, he shocked his supporters, who criticized both his hypocrisy and his foreign wife.[189]

Rhee remained active in the Korean Christian Church in Hawaii. After leaving from the Methodist mission to form his own school, Rhee and eighty of his supporters also began in 1916 to worship separately from the Korean Methodist Church. They formed their own church in Honolulu in 1918, which led to the formation of several related churches in Hawaii and Los Angeles, which united as the Korean Christian Church. Although Rhee never served as a pastor, he wielded his influence to shape the denomination's polity, organizational structure, and church architecture. He told Bernice Kim that his driving vision for the denomination was independence from the Methodists so that his church members could say: "This is really our church which rests upon our land."[190] During the construction of the Korean Christian Church in the Liliha Street neighborhood of Honolulu in 1935, Rhee instructed the architect to consult Korean art books and adopt Korean architectural styles.[191] He gave instructions for the interior plan of the church, requesting two pulpits on the stage, one for public Bible reading and the other for the sermon, and he wanted the choir seating to be arranged so that the singers would face the preacher during the sermon.[192] In 1938, the church was officially dedicated with a brightly colored and elaborate gateway to the main sanctuary that replicated an ancient palace entrance in Seoul.[193] It was both a sacred place of worship and a national symbol evoking the rich culture and history of Korea.

As Rhee's denomination was growing, Korean Methodists were also flourishing in Hawaii. Arriving in 1903, they had been among the first Koreans in Hawaii, partly because George Heber Jones helped recruit Koreans from his church in Incheon to migrate. American recruiters for the Hawaiian sugar planters were initially unsuccessful in attracting Koreans until Jones convinced some of his parishioners about the pleasant weather, financial benefits, and evangelistic opportunities. Fifty-eight of the first 102 Korean immigrants to Hawaii were Methodists. They organized their Methodist Episcopal Church in the midst of prayer meetings in the steerage of the ship that brought them.[194] By 1906, they had thirty mission stations, ten evangelists, and four teachers for nearly two thousand Methodists (out of approximately seven thousand Koreans).[195] Even after the forming of the Korean Christian Church in 1918, Korean Methodists kept pace with the new denomination. Inexact estimates suggest that the two churches had equal membership numbers. In the Wahiawa community in 1937, the

Korean Christian Church had 210 members, the Korean Methodist Episcopal Church, 150.[196] In 1947, both churches in Honolulu had about a thousand members each; they were the two largest Korean congregations in Hawaii.[197]

Like the Korean Christian Church, Korean Methodists also combined politics and religion. One prominent Methodist minister in Hawaii, Soon Hyun, joined the independence movement before accepting, in 1923, the pastorate of the Korean Methodist Episcopal Church in Honolulu. Hyun also participated from 1896 to 1898 in Jaisohn's progressive reform movement. In 1899, Hyun studied in Japan and learned something about Western approaches to chemistry, geography, history, and physics. Bible study and church attendance led in 1901 to his conversion. He was persuaded by Christ's promise of eternal life and his call to action on behalf of the poor and oppressed. He believed that Jesus inspired national liberation and resistance against Japanese imperialism. When asked why he had chosen Christianity, Hyun answered, "Because I believed Jesus was more militant than Buddha."[198] After returning home in 1902 from Japan, Hyun accepted a position as an overseer and translator for American recruiters for the Hawaiian sugar cane planters. From 1903 to 1907, he and his wife lived in Hawaii, where they worked on the sugar cane plantations and joined the Methodist Episcopal Church. Because of Hyun's religious faith, leadership skills, and bilingual abilities, the Methodist Mission appointed him as a preacher on the island of Kauai. He then received a call to serve a Methodist church in Korea but fled to Shanghai in 1919 as a political exile. In 1920, the provisional government appointed Hyun as head of the Korean Commission and Minister Plenipotentiary to the United States.[199] Rhee confirmed Hyun's appointment in a cablegram, but in 1921 he ousted him, probably because they disagreed on one issue or another.[200]

Hyun returned to Hawaii and resumed religious duties at the Korean Methodist Episcopal Church in Honolulu, serving both first- and second-generation Koreans. After three years in Honolulu, the denomination transferred Hyun in 1926 to the island of Kauai, where he served as an itinerant minister who traveled to seventeen sugar plantation camps and little towns. At each station, Hyun performed worship services, shared news about the independence movement, and collected donations to support the provisional government's political operations.[201] In careful handwriting, he listed his monthly itinerary schedule and reported on the numbers of parishioners and Koreans at each of his seventeen visits. His largest station consisted of 40 parishioners out of 65 Koreans and his smallest one consisted of 2 parishioners out of 12 Koreans. At one station, he had no parishioners from the 12 Koreans who lived there. In total, Hyun ministered to 221 of the 322 Koreans on the island.[202]

One of Hyun's children, Peter, left Hawaii in 1929 to enroll at DePauw University in Greencastle, Indiana, with the hopes of becoming a Methodist minister like his father.[203] He soon lost interest in theology and developed a passion for theater arts. At DePauw he met with frustrating racial discrimination, and on campus he had no close companions except for his professors. He resented classmates who leered at him, called him an "Oriental," and assumed that his family was in the laundry business. When venturing into Indianapolis, he recalled the "surreptitious stares of people around me; stares of curiosity, stares of scorn, even of hate."[204] Although Peter Hyun was born in Hawaii and spoke English fluently, he never felt at home in the United States. He achieved some success as an actor and theater director but felt that racial prejudice held him back.[205]

Like Rhee and so many other Koreans, Peter Hyun also felt disappointment at the broken promises of American politicians and missionaries. He accused the U.S. government of first reneging on the Korean-American Treaty of 1882 and then turning a blind eye to Korea after the March First uprising, despite its origins in the idealism of Woodrow Wilson. Missionaries struck him as simply indifferent toward Korean Protestant resistance to Japanese imperialism: "Was it a mistake for millions of Koreans to have embraced the religion preached by the American missionaries? Was it foolish to have believed in the new faith and to have placed so much trust in its homeland America—'The Land of Freedom'?"[206] He finally adopted a strategy of humor to counter the ignorance of white prejudices: Did Koreans appear odd to white Americans, who laughed at their accented English and their appearance? "You think the Koreans speak funny English? You should hear the American missionaries speaking Korean . . . You think Orientals with slanted eyes are funny looking? Ask a Korean farmer to tell you how the American missionaries look: Watery eyes, yellow hair, long nose!"[207] Beneath the humor was an enduring resentment of the missionaries and of white ignorance.

Conclusion

In their survey of world Christianity, Sebastian Kim and Kirsteen Kim contend that "Christianity is a world religion because it is present across the globe in countless local expressions which are linked by criss-crossing networks."[208] Because of the polycentric and transnational flows in world Christianity, they argue that Western and non-Western Christian manifestations are inextricably linked to one another through global Christian organizations and intercontinental immigration. Rhee's religious journey—with his genuine appreciation for and deep frustration with American forms of Christianity—illustrates the cross-cultural patterns and cross-colonial tensions that ran throughout relations between white American Protestants and Koreans. White Americans found it hard to move beyond their great experiment for a Korean Eden, a Christian nation redeemed by Christ and by the sacrifices of the missionary. That was the vision that initially drew the passion of the young Syngman Rhee. Without recognizing its darker side, he shared the missionaries' hope for a Christian Korea, formed in the image of a Christian America and marked by views of Christianity that permeated conservative—and often liberal—Protestantism. It was a soul-saving vision with a humanitarian dimension, but it had no place for meddling with political matters like Japanese imperialism, whether in the United States or in Korea. It was also a vision marred by prejudice, often unconscious, on the part of missionaries who loved Korea but distrusted the abilities of Koreans to build their own church and nation. At the end of his life, Rhee still admired America and he still practiced his own form of Christianity, but his admiration had been chastened. The tensions that had marked the inception of the American Protestant mission to Korea had never entirely disappeared, even as late as 1965.

In 1945, a seventy-year-old Rhee returned home after Japanese surrender in the Second World War. His wife, Francesca, remained in Washington, as Rhee entered into the chaos and uncertainty of a divided Korea under American and Soviet control. During Rhee's first weeks in Korea, his wife wrote letters giving him political information and encouraging his piety: "Sometimes my heart is heavy and I pray to the good Lord to help you and guide you. It is this belief that makes me go on and keeps me from getting desperate."[209] Several months later, the couple reunited in Korea. As the leader of the Republic of Korea, Rhee continued during his twelve-year presidency from 1948 to 1960 to collect as many enemies as followers, and his autocratic and self-interested governance led again to his removal from office. After massive groups of protesters charged Rhee with election fraud and abuse of power, he had to resign in 1960 and died as an exile in Hawaii five years later. In his last years, Rhee grew weary of the political tensions in churches and stopped attending worship services. After years of fighting others to advance his vision of Christianity, Rhee's religious journey ended peacefully in solitary communion with God.

Rhee's legacy in the United States and Korea is mixed. Some criticize still his corrupt and totalitarian methods; others commend him as a political and religious leader who preached about Korean liberation and Christian redemption.[210] On August 19, 1985, a statue of Syngman Rhee was dedicated on the grounds of the Korean Christian Church of Honolulu on the fortieth anniversary of the liberation of Korea. Rhee holds an open Bible in his left hand and raises his right hand heavenward, and a plaque identifies him as the father of the Republic of Korea and the founder of the Korean Christian Church.[211]

The missionaries probably never saw themselves as prejudiced, and all of them felt that they were involved in a great sacrificial endeavor that would prepare Koreans to live in a great culture and abide with Christ eternally in the Christian heaven. When Koreans like Philip Jaisohn and Soon Hyun came to the United States, however, they also found white Americans who saw nothing wrong with being prejudiced against anyone who was different, and the shock of that recognition intensified in some Koreans the desire for a distinctively Korean form of Christianity, free from such instances of

Figure 3.2 Statue of Syngman Rhee, Korean Christian Church, Honolulu (Michael E. Macmillan)

discrimination. Rhee's life, with its authoritarian and corrupt underside, demonstrated that Koreans, too, could never fit the mold of the paragon of Christian virtue, and Korean disputes, arguments, internal divisions, and prejudices also chipped away at the idyllic vision that had inspired the first American missionaries. In the United States, the growing chasm between younger and older generations of Korean Americans on religious and cultural identities demonstrate that Koreans engaged in diverse and differing Christian expressions that belied the missionaries' simplistic representations. But above all, the life of Syngman Rhee reminds us that the Koreans did not remain content to fit into molds prepared for them by idealistic but sometimes overweening white American Protestants.

Despite the accomplishments of Syngman Rhee, there was something tragic about his life. He aimed high and hubris helped bring him down. Despite the accomplishments of the Protestant mission to Korea, it too had a tragic dimension. The missionaries aimed high, but with their limitations as people ensconced in their own culture and unable to see beyond it, they too had to experience a kind of fall as they saw Koreans take their message, alter its cultural dressing, reject some (but not all) of its American features, and move toward a Christian expansion that would cause some Americans, by the late twentieth century, to see the Korean churches as models to imitate.

The story was largely one of American and Korean men. In an age when women usually assumed secondary positions in both societies, they too suffered from a certain condescension, a tendency to have to suffer patronizing attitudes, and a sad recognition of cultural boundaries that held them in their place. But that was hardly the whole story of women in the Korean and American transnational Protestant narrative. Women have already made their appearance, but not to the extent that does justice to the history. Korean women would challenge missionaries with contrasting perspectives on the independence movement but also on matters of womanhood, domesticity, and education. Like Syngman Rhee, women in both Korea and the United States would recognize, with the Koreans usually in advance of the Americans, that Korean Christianity must have its own face.

Notes

1. Robert Tarbell Oliver, *Syngman Rhee: The Man Behind the Myth* (New York: Dodd, Mead, 1954), 10–12.
2. Horace N. Allen, "Greetings," in *Quatro Centennial, Papers Read before the Korea Mission of the Presbyterian Church in the U.S.A. at the Annual Meeting in Pyeng Yang, August 27, 1909* (Seoul, Korea: 1909), 2.
3. Ibid., 12.
4. James S. Gale, *Korea in Transition* (New York: Young People's Missionary Movement of the United States and Canada, 1909), xiii.
5. James Bradley, *The Imperial Cruise: A Secret History of Empire and War* (New York, Boston, and London: Little, Brown and Company, 2009), 208–209.

6. Alexis Dudden, *Japan's Colonization of Korea: Discourse and Power* (Honolulu: University of Hawaii Press, 2005), 84.
7. George Kennan, "Korea: A Degenerative State," *The Outlook* (October 7, 1905), 307.
8. Gale, 258–259.
9. Sara Suleri, *The Rhetoric of English India* (Chicago and London: The University of Chicago Press, 1992), 2.
10. Elleke Boehmer, *Empire, the National, and the Postcolonial, 1890–1920: Resistance in Interaction*, 12–23.
11. Oliver, 14.
12. Oliver, 21.
13. Margaret Ernestine Burton, *Comrades in Service* (New York: Missionary Education Movement of the United States and Canada, 1915), 171.
14. George Heber Jones, "Letter to Syngman Rhee, March 26, 1903, in *The Syngman Rhee English Correspondence, Volume* 2, edited with an introduction by Young Ick Lew in collaboration with Yeong Sub Oh, Steve G. Jenks, and Andrew D. Calhoun (Seoul, Korea: Institute for Modern Korean Studies, Yonsei University, 2009), 1.
15. Syngman Rhee, *Tongnip chŏngsin* [The Spirit of Independence] (Seoul, Korea: Tongsŏ Munhwasa, 2010), 11–16. See also Han-Kyo Kim's introduction in Syngman Rhee and Han-Kyo Kim, *The Spirit of Independence: A Primer of Korean Modernization and Reform* (Honolulu: University of Hawaii Press, 2001), 1–21.
16. Rhee, *Tongnip chŏngsin*, 77.
17. Ibid., 86.
18. Ibid., 60.
19. Ibid., 61.
20. Ibid., 275.
21. James S. Gale, "Letter to Christian Friends in Washington D.C. on November 2, 1904," in *The Syngman Rhee Correspondence, Volume* 4, 7.
22. Oliver, 95.
23. Syngman Rhee, *Japan Inside Out: The Challenge of Today, 2nd ed.* (New York: Fleming H. Revell, 1941), 180–181.
24. "Korean Will Tell of Korea," *The Washington Post*, June 5, 1907, and "Will Lecture at the Y.M.C.A.: J.A. Dummett to Describe Mountain Climbing in West," *The Washington Post*, June 10, 1907. See also Oliver, 99–100.
25. C.C. Michener, "Letter to Syngman Rhee on March 2, 1908," in *The Syngman Rhee Correspondence, Volume* 2, 24.
26. "Koreans Meet in Denver: Discuss Measures of Making Their Country Independent," *Colorado Spring Gazette*, July 13, 1908, and "Hope to Get independence: Koreans From All Over World to Meet in Denver Today," *The Idaho Daily Statesman*, July 13, 1908. One of the American speakers was Methodist bishop and co-founder of Iliff School of Theology Henry W. Warren.
27. Oliver, 108–109.
28. Oliver, 109–110.
29. Syngman Rhee, *Neutrality as Influenced by the United States: A Dissertation Presented to the Faculty of Princeton University in Candidacy for the Degree of Philosophy* (Princeton: Princeton University Press, 1912), 109.
30. Rhee, 104–105.
31. Rhee, 105.
32. A.W. Wasson, "The Land of Opportunity," *The Korea Mission Field* (February 1906), 68.
33. Ibid.

34. Bradley, 313–314.
35. "Index," *The Missionary Review of the World* (December 1906), 969, "Index," *The Missionary Review of the World* (December 1907), 969–970, "Index," *The Missionary Review of the World* (December 1908), 969, "Index," *The Missionary Review of the World* (December 1909), 970, and "Index," *The Missionary Review of the World* (December 1910), 970.
36. Horace G. Underwood, "The Growth of the Church in Korea," *The Missionary Review of the World* (February 1908), 101.
37. "Letters from Susan Wilson to Nina Wilson, June 24, July 1, and July 4, 1907," in Alpheus W. Wilson Papers, Stuart A. Rose Manuscript, Archives, and Rare Book Library, Emory University, Atlanta, GA.
38. John Livingstone Nevius, *China and the Chinese: A General Description of the Country and Its Inhabitants; Its Civilization and Form of Government; Its Religious and Social Institutions; Its Intercourse with Other Nations, and Its Present Condition and Prospects* (New York: Harper & Brothers, 1869), 336.
39. Horace G. Underwood, *The Call of Korea: Political-Social-Religious* (New York: Fleming H. Revell Company, 1908), 109, and Sung-Deuk Oak, "Presbyterian Mission Methods and Policies in Korea," in *Korean Church, God's Mission, Global Christianity*, 40–41.
40. Underwood, 109–110.
41. Appenzeller, "Report of the Spies," in *The Appenzellers: How They Preached and Guided Korea into Modernization, Volume 1*, 29. He preached this sermon to Methodist Episcopal Church congregations in New York and Pennsylvania on September 25, October 2, November 20, and December 11, 1892.
42. Appenzeller, "Korea: The Field, Our Work, and Opportunity, Philadelphia Preacher's Meeting, 21 January 1901," in *The Appenzellers, Volume 1*, 70–85.
43. Ibid., 83.
44. Ibid., 79.
45. Daniel L. Gifford, *Every-Day Life in Korea: A Collection of Studies and Stories* (Chicago: Fleming H. Revell, 1898), 188.
46. "Notes from Korea," *The Gospel in All Lands* (August 1888), 373.
47. Henry G. Appenzeller, "Henry Appenzeller Begins Mission in Korea," in *The Methodist Experience in America: A Sourcebook*, 422–424.
48. Paik, 128–129.
49. C. G. Hounshell, "C. G. Hounshell's Report," in *Minutes of the Seventh Annual Meeting of the Korean Mission of the Methodist Episcopal Church, South, 1903* (Seoul, Korea: Methodist Publishing House, 1903), 23.
50. Paik, 310.
51. Ibid.
52. W. B. Scranton, *Minutes of the Annual Meeting of the Korean Mission of the Methodist Episcopal Church, South* (June 1906), 32.
53. Ibid.
54. "The Time Opportune," *The Korea Mission Field* (December 1905), 29–30.
55. Ibid.
56. William Newton Blair, *The Korea Pentecost and other Experiences on the Mission Field* (New York: The Board of Foreign Missions of the Presbyterian Church in the U.S.A, 1910), 38.
57. Ibid.
58. Blair, 39.
59. Ibid.
60. Lee, *Born Again: Evangelicalism in Korea*, 16–17.
61. Blair, 39.
62. "A Call to a Special Effort," *The Korea Mission Field* (December 1905), 30.
63. Ibid. Italics in original.

64. Lee, 18.
65. Graham Lee, "How the Spirit Came to Pyeng Yang," *The Korea Mission Field* (March 1907), 33.
66. Lee, 34.
67. Blair, 46.
68. Ibid.
69. Henry M. Bruen, "Letter to Arthur J. Brown in March 1907," in *40 Years in Korea*, edited by Clara Hedberg Bruen, 131–132. Clara Hedberg Bruen compiled Henry M. Bruen's writings from Korea into a self-published book, *40 Years in Korea*. There are thirteen copies of her book in U.S. libraries. I discovered the book at John Bulow Campbell Library, Columbia Theological Seminary, Decatur, GA.
70. Ibid.
71. Timothy S. Lee, *Born Again: Evangelicalism in Korea*, 22.
72. W.G. Cram, "A Genuine Change," *The Korea Mission Field* (April 1907), 67–68.
73. J.L. Gerdine, "The Colporters' Share," *The Korea Mission Field* (April 1907), 72.
74. W.L. Swallen, "God's Work of Grace in Pyeng Yang Classes," *The Korea Mission Field* (April 1907), 80.
75. James S. Gale, "The First Presbytery in Korea," *The Missionary Review of the World* (January 1908), 42–44.
76. Lian Xi, *Redeemed by Fire: The Rise of Popular Christianity in Modern China*, 87–89.
77. Sung-Deuk Oak, "Chinese Protestant Literature and Early Korean Protestantism," in *Christianity in Korea*, edited by Robert E. Buswell Jr. and Timothy S. Lee (Honolulu: University of Hawaii Press, 2006), 72–77.
78. Lian, 89.
79. George Trumbull Ladd, *In Korea with Marquis Ito* (New York: C. Scribner's Sons, 1908). As Japanese Resident-General, Ito Hirobumi ruled over Korea as the highest-ranking Japanese official.
80. Ladd, 162.
81. Ladd, 194 and 401.
82. Ladd, 391–393.
83. George Trumbull Ladd, "Koreans A Bloody Race," *New York Times*, March 26, 1908.
84. Arthur Judson Brown, *Report of a Visitation of the Korea Mission of the Board of Foreign Missions of the Presbyterian Church in the U.S.A* (New York: The Board, 1902), 7.
85. Arthur Judson Brown, *Report on a Second Visit to China, Japan, and Korea, 1909, with a Discussion of Some Problems of Mission Work* (New York: The Board of Foreign Missions of the Presbyterian Church in the U.S.A., 1909). On the cover page, the words "PRINTED BUT NOT PUBLISHED FOR PRIVATE CIRCULATION ONLY" are included.
86. Ibid., 12–14.
87. Ibid., 15.
88. Arthur Judson Brown, *The Mastery of the Far East: The Story of Korea's Transformation and Japan's Rise to Supremacy* (New York: C. Scribner's Sons, 1919), 539.
89. Ibid., 539–540.
90. For a historical analysis of white American interpretations of African American religiosity, see Curtis J. Evans, *The Burden of Black Religion* (Oxford and New York: Oxford University Press, 2008).
91. Norman C. Whittemore, "The Growth of a Korean 'Group' or Congregation," *Woman's Work for Woman* (November 1905), 257–258.

92. Brown, *Report on a Second Visit to China, Japan, and Korea, 1909, with a Discussion of Some Problems of Mission Work*, 94.
93. Brown, *The Mastery of the Far East*, 584.
94. W.B. Scranton, "Letter to Stephen Olin Benton on May 15, 1905," in *Letters of William B. Scranton*, 355.
95. Mattie Wilcox Noble, "Diary entries on April 30, 1906, and August 6, 1906," *The Journals of Mattie Wilcox Noble, 1892–1934*, 151–152.
96. J.Z. Moore, "The Vision and the Task," *The Korea Mission Field* (April 1906), 108.
97. Ibid.
98. Homer B. Hulbert, "The Needs of a National Ideal for Korea," *The Korea Mission Field* (January 1910), 23.
99. Hulbert, 24.
100. Homer B. Hulbert, "Japanese and Missionaries in Korea," *The Missionary Review of the World* (March 1908), 205.
101. Brown, *Report on a Second Visit*, 78.
102. Lillias H. Underwood, *Fifteen Years among the Top-Knots or Life in Korea, 2nd ed.*, 333.
103. Ibid.
104. Jennie Fowler-Willing and Mrs. George Heber Jones, *The Lure of Korea*, 38.
105. "Annexation and Missions in Korea," *The Missionary Review of the World* (December 1910), 952.
106. "The Example of Korea Missionaries," *The Missionary Review of the World* (May 1910), 380–381.
107. Harlan P. Beach, "Korea Outdoing Uganda," *The Missionary Review of the World* (May 1908), 391.
108. William Jennings Bryan, "Korea, One of the Most Important Fields," in *Competent Witnesses on Korea as a Mission Field* (New York: Board of Foreign Missions of the Methodist Episcopal Church, 1909), 5.
109. Charles Warren Fairbanks, "Korea's Redemption," in *Competent Witnesses on Korea as a Mission Field*, 7.
110. Horace G. Underwood, "Letter to Dwight H. Day on February 15, 1909," in *Ŏndŏudŭ Moksa ŭi sŏn'gyo p'yŏnji: 1885–1916* [Rev. Underwood's Missionary Letters], edited by Kim and Underwood, 1085–1086.
111. "Letter from E.E.H. to Warren A. Candler, September 30, 1910," in Warren A. Candler Papers, Stuart A. Rose Manuscript, Archives, and Rare Book Library, Emory University, Atlanta, GA.
112. Syngman Rhee, "Letter to H.G. Underwood on April 19, 1910," in *The Syngman Rhee Correspondence, Volume 1*, 1.
113. Ibid.
114. "Chats of Visitors to the Capital," *The Washington Post*, November 18, 1912.
115. Ibid.
116. Yi Mahn-yol, "The Life and Faith of Yi Gi-Pung," translated by John S. Park, *Missionary and Martyr: The Life and Faith of Rev. Yi Gi-Pung, 1868–1942*, edited by Yi Sa-Rye (Seoul, Korea: KIATS Press, 2008), 37–42.
117. "Korea Christianizing the East," *The Washington Post*, December 2, 1912.
118. Yong-ho Ch'oe, "Syngman Rhee in Hawaii: His Activities in the Early Years 1913–1915," in *From the Land of Hibiscus: Koreans in Hawai'i*, edited by Yong-ho Ch'oe (Honolulu: University of Hawaii Press, 2007), 59–61, and David K. Yoo, *Contentious Spirits: Religion in Korean American History, 1910–1945* (Stanford: Stanford University Press, 2010), 66–68.
119. Koreans in Hawaii, as well as newspapers in Hawaii and the United States, praised Rhee's plan. See "Korean School to Admit Girls to its Classes: Institution

Broadens its Original Scope Under Representations Made by Dr. Syngman Rhee," *Christian Science Monitor*, November 15, 1913.

120. Kingsley K. Lyu, "Korean Nationalist Activities in Hawaii and the Continental United States, 1900–1945, Part I: 1900–1919," *Amerasia* 4:1 (1977), 78. Lyu (1904–1976) was a pastor in charge of Methodist churches on the island of Kauai, Hawaii, and editor of the Honolulu-based *Korean Pacific Weekly* from 1944 to 1946. Many of his sources were from personal interviews with Koreans who lived in Hawaii during the early twentieth century.
121. Syngman Rhee, "Letter to Chisung Pil on December 2, 1919," in *The Syngman Rhee Correspondence, Volume 1*, 179.
122. Japanese investigators were suspicious of McCune's influence among Korean Christians. After learning that McCune preached a sermon on the biblical narrative of David and Goliath, the investigators charged that McCune was instructing Korean Christians to confront the Japanese just as the Israelite David defeated his larger Philistine oppressor. See Alexis Dudden, *Japan's Colonization of Korea* (Honolulu: University of Hawaii Press, 2005), 120–123, Hyung-Chan Kim, *Letters in Exile: The Life and Times of Yun Ch'iho* (Covington: Rhodes Printing Company, 1980), 56–57, and Chung-Shin Park, *Protestantism and Politics in Korea* (Seattle and London: University of Washington Press, 2003), 64–65.
123. During two retrials, 99 of the 105 defendants were acquitted of any wrongdoing. The other 6 defendants, including Yun Ch'iho, served prison sentences of five to six years despite producing strong evidence of their innocence. Several Japanese lawyers denounced the legality of the trials and surmised that the imperial government wanted to imprison the Koreans on account of their Christian beliefs. The criminal proceedings were known as the "Korean Conspiracy Case" and "105 Persons Incident." See Kenneth M. Wells, *New God, New Nation: Protestants and Self-Reconstruction Nationalism in Korea, 1896–1936* (Honolulu: University of Hawaii Press, 1990), 74–78.
124. Arthur Judson Brown, *The Korean Conspiracy Case* (New York: Board of Foreign Missions, Presbyterian Church in the United States of America, 1912), 15. Brown quoted a portion of Charles W. Eliot's letter to him from September 4, 1912.
125. George McCune, "Letter to Syngman Rhee on January 12, 1915," in *The Syngman Rhee Correspondence, Volume 2*, 107.
126. E.M. Cable, "Letter on February 3, 1915," in George Heber Jones Papers, Missionary Research Library Collection, Burke Theological Library, Columbia University, New York, NY.
127. Frank Prentiss Baldwin, Jr., *March First Movement: Korean Challenge and Japanese Response*, PhD diss., Columbia University, 1969, 18.
128. Ki-baek Lee, *A New History of Korea*, 340–341. The Korean delegation had no official status because Korea was not recognized internationally as an independent nation after Japanese annexation in 1910.
129. Lee, 344.
130. Baldwin, 120–123, and Lee, 344.
131. John Kiusic Kimm, "Letter to le President de Conseil Clemenceau on May 12, 1919," and "Letter to President Woodrow Wilson on May 12, 1919," in United Presbyterian Church in the U.S.A. Commission on Ecumenical Mission and Relations, Korea Mission, RG140, Presbyterian Historical Society, Philadelphia, PA.
132. John Kiusic Kimm, "Letter to President Woodrow Wilson on May 12, 1919," in United Presbyterian Church in the U.S.A. Commission on Ecumenical Mission and Relations, Korea Mission, RG140, Presbyterian Historical Society, Philadelphia, PA.

133. "Wilson is Urged to Free Korea," in *The Atlanta Constitution*, March 17, 1919, and Syngman Rhee and Henry Chung, "Letter to Paris Peace Conference on February 25, 1919," in *The Syngman Rhee Correspondence, Volume 1*, 66–70.
134. Syngman Rhee, "Letter to John R. Mott on March 14, 1919," in *The Syngman Rhee Correspondence, Volume 1*, 79.
135. Syngman Rhee, "Letter to Arthur J. Brown on March 19, 1919," in *The Syngman Rhee Correspondence, Volume 1*, 82.
136. Ibid.
137. Herbert Welch, "Letter to Syngman Rhee on July 1, 1919," in *The Syngman Rhee Correspondence, Volume 1*, 240.
138. Herbert Welch, "The Korean Independence Movement of 1919," *The Christian Advocate*, July 31, 1919, 972.
139. Herbert Welch, "The Korean Independence Movement of 1919," *The Christian Advocate*, August 14, 1919, 1039.
140. Syngman Rhee, "Letter to Herbert Welch on July 5, 1919," in *The Syngman Rhee Correspondence, Volume 1*, 153.
141. Ibid., 154.
142. John Fairman Preston, "Letter to His Father on March 17, 1919," in John Fairman Preston Papers, RG441, Presbyterian Historical Society, Philadelphia, PA. Preston was one of several missionaries who wrote endorsement letters for Rhee in 1904. See "Letter to R.D. Wilson on November 5, 1904" and "Letter to Eleanor Watkins on November 5, 1904," *The Syngman Rhee Correspondence, Volume 4*, 39–42.
143. Herbert Welch, "The Korean Independence Movement of 1919," *The Christian Advocate*, August 14, 1919, 1038.
144. Arthur Judson Brown, "Letter to the Relatives and Friends of the Chosen Missionaries, June 30, 1919," in United Presbyterian Church in the U.S.A. Commission on Ecumenical Mission and Relations, Korea Mission, RG140, Presbyterian Historical Society, Philadelphia, PA.
145. Syngman Rhee, "Letter to Herbert Welch on July 28, 1919," in *The Syngman Rhee Correspondence, Volume 1*, 169.
146. Ibid.
147. Dudden, 119.
148. G. Bonwick, "Korean Place Names," *The Korea Bookman* (December 1921), 33.
149. Rhee, 169.
150. Hugh Heung-Wo Cynn, *The Rebirth of Korea: The Reawakening of Its People, Its Causes and Its Outlook* (New York and Cincinnati: Abingdon Press, 1920), 15, and Yoo, 89–91.
151. Gil, Seon-Ju, *Han'guk Kidokkyo chidoja kangdan sŏlgyo* [Korean Christian Leader Pulpit Sermons] (Seoul, Korea: KIATS Press, 2008), 187.
152. Lyu, 84–85.
153. Choy, 156–165.
154. Channing Liem, *Philip Jaisohn* (Elkins Park, PA: Philip Jaisohn Memorial Foundation, 1984), 103, and Hyung-Chan Kim, "Philip Jaisohn (Seo, Jae-P'il)," in *Distinguished Asian Americans: A Biographical Dictionary*, edited by Hyung-Chan Kim, et al. (Westport, CT: Greenwood Press, 1999), 141–142. Like Rhee, Jaisohn was not concerned about denominational allegiances. He attended a Presbyterian church in San Francisco in 1886, partnered with the Methodist Episcopal Church Mission during his years in Korea from 1896 to 1898, and was buried in Pennsylvania with an Episcopalian funeral service in 1951.
155. Young Ick Lew, "Introduction," in *The Syngman Rhee Correspondence, Volume 1*, 8–26.
156. Although Yun Ch'iho had worked with Rhee and Jaisohn in the past, he did not share their political views. After his release from prison in 1915, Yun

maintained that Koreans should accept Japanese rule and direct all of their energies toward social, economic, and educational improvements. Yun resisted overtures to join the independence movement because he believed that Koreans would only achieve independence through gradual internal developments and peaceable relations with the Japanese. In 1917, Yun advised Rhee to be more cautious about his public criticism of the Japanese and expressed to Rhee that his most valuable contributions to Korea were found in his educational work among young Koreans in the United States. See Yun Ch'iho, "Letter to Syngman Rhee on January 16, 1917," in *The Syngman Rhee Correspondence, Volume* 2, 120–124.

157. "Editorial Notes," *The Independent* (February 9, 1897), 2.
158. Eugene Bell, "Letter to His Parents on October 23, 1896," in Eugene Bell and Lottie Bell Papers, RG435, Presbyterian Historical Society, Philadelphia, PA.
159. Liem, 224.
160. Philip Jaisohn, "Dr. Philip Jaisohn's Address, July 1919," in *My Days in Korea and Other Essays*, edited by Sun-pyo Hong (Seoul, Korea: Yonsei University Press, 1999), 179–182.
161. Philip Jaisohn, "Letter to Syngman Rhee on March 20, 1913," in *The Syngman Rhee Correspondence, Volume* 2, 68–71, and Syngman Rhee, "Letter to Philip Jaisohn on June 24, 1913," in *The Syngman Rhee Correspondence, Volume 1*, 5–9.
162. Philip Jaisohn, "Letter to President-elect Warren G. Harding on November 15, 1920," in *The Syngman Rhee Correspondence, Volume* 5, 465.
163. On September 19, Senator Selden P. Spencer (Missouri) read a statement submitted by the Korean Commission. On October 9, Senator James D. Phelan (California) introduced a resolution expressing the U.S. government's sympathy for Korea. On October 25, Representative William F. Mason (Illinois) delivered a similar speech in the House of Representatives. See Choy, 157.
164. Choy, 156–159, and Lyu, 57–58.
165. Philip Jaisohn, "Letter to Syngman Rhee on September 22, 1920," in *The Syngman Rhee Correspondence, Volume* 2, 527.
166. Wells, 102.
167. Ch'oe, 65.
168. Ch'oe, 70.
169. Y.H. Choy, "What Vocational Education Is and Why We Are Needing It," *Korean Student Bulletin* 4:4 (October 1926), 3.
170. "Unemployment Question at Home," *Korean Student Bulletin* 6:2 (April 1928), 1, 4.
171. John Chung, "A Korean Student's Life in America," *Korean Student Bulletin* 12:2 (April-May 1934), 6.
172. Ibid.
173. Martha Choy, "Confessions of an American-born Korean," *Korean Student Bulletin* 8:2 (May 1930), 6.
174. Ibid.
175. Ibid.
176. Ibid.
177. Ibid.
178. Anne Kim, "Whither American-born Korean," *Korean Student Bulletin* 13:2 (March–April 1935), 6.
179. Ibid.
180. Duke Cho Choy, "Can Youth Improve and Maintain Korean Institutions in Hawaii," *Korean Student Bulletin* 15:2 (December 1936–January 1937), 6–7.
181. Young Kang, "Our Second Generation is a Problem," *Korean Student Bulletin* 8:2 (May 1930), 1, 5.
182. Bernice B.H. Kim, *The Koreans in Hawaii*, Master's thesis, University of Hawaii, June 1937, 194–195.

183. Lyu, 79.
184. Kim, 190.
185. Margaret K. Pai, *The Dreams of Two Yi-min* (Honolulu: University of Hawaii Press, 1989), 121–122.
186. Lyu, 79.
187. "Vienna-born Wife of Rhee Korea Puzzle: Is She Housewife or Real Political Power, Seoul Asks," *Los Angeles Times*, July 19, 1953.
188. Oliver, 163–164. Like many Korean noblemen, Rhee's parents arranged his marriage to a Korean woman when he was a young man. He was married sometime in 1896 or 1897 (date uncertain) and had a son. After Rhee's prison sentence, his wife's whereabouts became unknown. His son was sent to America when Rhee was studying at George Washington University but died from illness in 1908 (See Oliver, 52–53).
189. Lyu, "Korean Nationalist Activities in Hawaii and the Continental United States, 1900–1945, Part II: 1919–1945," 75.
190. Kim, 144. Kim interviewed Rhee in Honolulu on July 22, 1935.
191. Syngman Rhee, "Letter to Y.T. Char, April 5, 1935," in *The Syngman Rhee Correspondence, Volume 1*, 515.
192. Rhee, 517.
193. Yoo, 58.
194. Wayne Patterson, *The Korean Frontier in America: Immigration to Hawaii, 1896–1910* (Honolulu: University of Hawaii Press, 1988), 47–50.
195. Kim, 139.
196. Kim, 177.
197. Yoo, 53.
198. Peter Hyun, *Mansei!: The Making of a Korean American* (Honolulu: University of Hawaii Press, 1986), 92.
199. Ibid., 158–159.
200. "Cablegram from Syngman Rhee to Soon Hyun on April 4, 1921," in The Reverend Soon Hyun Collected Works, Korean American Digital Archive, University of Southern California Digital Library, Los Angeles, LA.
201. Peter Hyun, *In the New World: The Making of a Korean American* (Honolulu: University of Hawaii Press, 1995), 37.
202. "Map of Kauai: Showing Churches, Preaching Stations, and Visiting Camps, no date" in The Reverend Soon Hyun Collected Works, Korean American Digital Archive, University of Southern California Digital Library, Los Angeles, LA.
203. Hyun, *In the New World: The Making of a Korean American* (Honolulu: University of Hawaii Press, 1995), 46–47.
204. Hyun, 75.
205. Hyun, 138–158.
206. Hyun, *Mansei!: The Making of a Korean American*, 163–164.
207. Hyun, *In the New World: The Making of a Korean American*, 278.
208. Sebastian Kim and Kirsteen Kim, *Christianity as a World Religion* (London and New York: Continuum, 2008), 210.
209. Francesca Rhee, "Letter to Syngman Rhee on November 2, 1945," in *The Syngman Rhee Correspondence, Volume 3*, 420.
210. In a recent biography of Syngman Rhee, Young Ick Lew argues for a "reassessment of Rhee's legacy" that acknowledges his significant contributions to Korean independence from Japanese imperial rule and early South Korean nation-building alongside his well-documented leadership "deficiencies," which include his stubbornness, mistrust of others, and authoritarianism. See Young Ick Lew, *The Making of the First Korean President: Syngman Rhee's Quest for Independence, 1875–1948* (Honolulu: University of Hawaii Press, 2014), 293.

211. "Statue of Syngman Rhee," Agnes Rho Chun Collection, Center for Korean Studies Digital Archive, University of Hawaii, Manoa, http://cksdigital.manoa.hawaii.edu/photo/items/show/352, accessed on November 21, 2015.

Bibliography

Archives and Manuscript Collections

Center for Korean Studies Digital Archive. University of Hawaii, Manoa.

Korean American Digital Archive. Los Angeles, CA: University of Southern California Digital Library.

Missionary Research Library Collection. New York, NY: Columbia University, Burke Theological Library.

Presbyterian Historical Society. Philadelphia, PA.

Rose, Stuart A. *Manuscript, Archives, and Rare Book Library*. Atlanta, GA: Emory University.

Books and Journal Articles

Allen, Horace N. "Greetings." In *Quatro Centennial, Papers Read before the Korea Mission of the Presbyterian Church in the U.S.A. at the Annual Meeting in Pyeng Yang, August 27, 1909*. Seoul, Korea, 1909.

The Appenzellers: How They Preached and Guided Korea into Modernization, Volumes 1–2. Daejeon, Korea: Pai Chai University Press, 2010.

Baldwin, Jr., Frank Prentiss. *March First Movement: Korean Challenge and Japanese Response*. PhD diss., Columbia University, 1969.

Blair, William Newton. *The Korea Pentecost: And Other Experience on the Mission Field*. New York: The Board of Foreign Missions of the Presbyterian Church in the U.S.A., 1910.

Boehmer, Elleke. *Empire, the National, and the Postcolonial, 1890–1920: Resistance in Interaction*. Oxford and New York: Oxford University Press, 2002.

Bradley, James. *The Imperial Cruise: A Secret History of Empire and War*. New York: Little, Brown and Co., 2009.

Brown, Arthur J. *The Korean Conspiracy Case*. New York: Board of Foreign Missions, Presbyterian Church in the United States of America, 1912.

Brown, Arthur J. *The Mastery of the Far East: The Story of Korea's Transformation and Japan's Rise to Supremacy*. New York: C. Scribner's Sons, 1919.

Brown, Arthur J. *Report on a Second Visit to China, Japan, and Korea, 1909, with a Discussion of Some Problems of Mission Work*. New York: The Board of Foreign Missions of the Presbyterian Church in the U.S.A., 1909.

Brown, Arthur J. *Report of a Visitation of the Korea Mission of the Board of Foreign Missions of the Presbyterian Church in the U.S.A.* New York: The Board, 1902.

Bruen, Clara Hedberg. *40 Years in Korea*.

Bryan, William Jennings. "Korea, One of the Most Important Fields." In *Competent Witnesses on Korea as a Mission Field*. New York: Board of Foreign Missions of the Methodist Episcopal Church, 1909.

Burton, Margaret Ernestine. *Comrades in Service*. New York: Missionary Education Movement of the United States and Canada, 1915.

Ch'oe, Yong-ho. "Syngman Rhee in Hawaii: His Activities in the Early Years 1913–1915." In *From the Land of Hibiscus: Koreans in Hawai'i*, edited by Yong-ho Ch'oe. Honolulu: University of Hawaii Press, 2007.

Choy, Bong Youn. *Koreans in America*. Chicago: Nelson-Hall, 1979.

Cynn, Hugh Hyeng-wo. *The Rebirth of Korea: The Reawakening of the People, Its Causes, and Its Outlook*. New York and Cincinnati: Abingdon Press, 1920.

Dudden, Alexis. *Japan's Colonization of Korea: Discourse and Power*. Honolulu: University of Hawaii Press, 2005.

Evans, Curtis J. *The Burden of Black Religion*. Oxford and New York: Oxford University Press, 2008.

Fairbanks, Charles Warren. "Korea's Redemption." In *Competent Witnesses on Korea as a Mission Field*. New York: Board of Foreign Missions of the Methodist Episcopal Church, 1909.

Fowler-Willing, Jennie and Mrs. George Heber Jones. *The Lure of Korea*. Boston: Methodist Episcopal Church Woman's Foreign Missionary Society Publishing Office, 1910.

Gale, James Scarth. *Korea in Transition*. New York: Young People's Mission Movement of the United States and Canada, 1909.

Gifford, Daniel L. *Every-Day Life in Korea: A Collection of Studies and Stories*. Chicago: Fleming H. Revell, 1898.

Gil, Seon-Ju. *Han'guk Kidokkyo chidoja kangdan sŏlgyo* [Korean Christian Leader Pulpit Sermons]. Seoul, Korea: KIATS Press, 2008.

Hyun, Peter. *In the New World: The Making of a Korean American*. Honolulu: University of Hawaii Press, 1995.

Hyun, Peter. *Mansei!: The Making of a Korean American*. Honolulu: University of Hawaii Press, 1986.

Jaisohn, Philip and Sun-pyo Hong. *My Days in Korea and Other Essays*. Seoul, Korea: Yonsei University Press, 1999.

Kim, Bernice B.H. *The Koreans in Hawaii*. Master's thesis, University of Hawaii, June 1937.

Kim, Hyung-Chan. *Letters in Exile: The Life and Times of Yun Ch'iho*. Covington, GA: Rhoades Printing Company, 1980.

Kim, Hyung-Chan. "Philip Jaisohn (Seo, Jae-P'il)." In *Distinguished Asian Americans: A Biographical Dictionary*, edited by Hyung-Chan Kim, et al. Westport, CT: Greenwood Press, 1999.

Kim, In-su and Horace Grant Underwood. *Ŏndŏudŭ Moksa ŭi sŏn'gyo p'yŏnji: 1885–1916* [Rev. Underwood's Missionary Letters]. Seoul, Korea: Changnohoe Sinhak Taehakkyo Ch'ulp'anbu, 2002.

Kim, Sebastian and Kirsteen Kim. *Christianity as a World Religion*. London and New York: Continuum, 2008.

Ladd, George Trumbull. *In Korea with Marquis Ito*. New York: C. Scribner's Sons, 1908.

Lee, Ki-baek. *A New History of Korea*. Translated by Edward Wagner with Edward J. Schulz. Cambridge and London: Harvard University Press, 1984.

Lee, Timothy S. *Born Again: Evangelicalism in Korea*. Honolulu: University of Hawaii Press, 2010.

Lew, Young Ick. *The Making of the First Korean President: Syngman Rhee's Quest for Independence, 1875–1948*. Honolulu: University of Hawaii Press, 2014.

Lew, Young Ick, Yeong Sub Oh, Steve G. Jenks, and Andrew D. Calhoun, eds. *The Syngman Rhee English Correspondence, Volumes 1–10*. Seoul, Korea: Institute for Modern Korean Studies, Yonsei University, 2009.

Lian, Xi. *Redeemed by Fire: The Rise of Popular Christianity in Modern China*. New Haven and London: Yale University Press, 2010.

Liem, Channing. *Philip Jaisohn*. Elkins Park, PA: Philip Jaisohn Memorial Foundation, 1984.

Lyu, Kingsley K. "Korean Nationalist Activities in Hawaii and the Continental United States, 1900–1945, Part I: 1900–1919." *Amerasia* 4:1 (1977): 23–90.

Lyu, Kingsley K. "Korean Nationalist Activities in Hawaii and the Continental United States, 1900–1945, Part II: 1919–1945." *Amerasia* 4:2 (1977): 53–100.

Nevius, John Livingstone. *China and the Chinese: A General Description of the Country and Its Inhabitants; Its Civilization and Form of Government; Its Religious and Social Institutions; Its Intercourse with Other Nations, and Its Present Condition and Prospects*. New York: Harper & Brothers, 1869.

Noble, Mattie Wilcox. *The Journals of Mattie Wilcox Noble, 1892–1934*. Seoul, Korea: Han'guk Kidokkyo Yŏksa Yŏn'guso, 1993.

Oak, Sung-Deuk. "Chinese Protestant Literature and Early Korean Protestantism." In *Christianity in Korea*, edited by Robert E. Buswell Jr. and Timothy S. Lee. Honolulu: University of Hawaii Press, 2006.

Oak, Sung-Deuk. "Presbyterian Mission Methods and Policies in Korea." In *Korean Church, God's Mission, Global Christianity*, edited by Wonsuk Ma and Kyo Seong Ahn. Eugene, OR: Wipf & Stock, 2015.

Oliver, Robert Tarbell. *Syngman Rhee, the Man Behind the Myth*. New York: Dodd, Mead, 1954.

Pai, Margaret K. *The Dreams of Two Yi-min*. Honolulu: University of Hawaii Press, 1989.

Paik, George L. *History of Protestant Mission in Korea, 1832–1910, 4th ed*. Seoul, Korea: Yonsei University Press, 1987.

Park, Chung-Shin. *Protestantism and Politics in Korea*. Seattle and London: University of Washington Press, 2003.

Patterson, Wayne. *The Korean Frontier in America: Immigration to Hawaii, 1896–1910*. Honolulu: University of Hawaii Press, 1988.

Rhee, Syngman. *Japan Inside Out: The Challenge of Today, 2nd ed*. New York: Revell, 1941.

Rhee, Syngman. *Neutrality as Influenced by the United States: A Dissertation Presented to the Faculty of Princeton University in Candidacy for the Degree of Philosophy*. Princeton: Princeton University Press, 1912.

Rhee, Syngman. *Tongnip chŏngsin* [The Spirit of Independence]. Seoul, Korea: Tongsŏ Munhwasa, 2010.

Rhee, Syngman and Han-Kyo Kim. *The Spirit of Independence: A Primer of Korean Modernization and Reform*. Honolulu: University of Hawaii Press, 2001.

Richey, Russell E., Kenneth E. Rowe, and Jean Miller Schmidt, eds. *The Methodist Experience in America, Volume 2: A Sourcebook*. Nashville: Abingdon Press, 2000.

Scranton, William B. *Letters of William B. Scranton*. Korea: William Scranton Foundation, 2010.

Suleri, Sara. *The Rhetoric of English India*. Chicago and London: The University of Chicago Press, 1992.

Underwood, Horace G. *The Call of Korea: Political-Social-Religious*. New York: Fleming H. Revell, 1908.

Underwood, Lillias H. *Fifteen Years among the Top-Knots, 2nd ed*. Boston: American Tract Society, 1908.

Wells, Kenneth M. *New God, New Nation: Protestants and Self-Reconstruction Nationalism in Korea, 1896–1937*. Honolulu: University of Hawaii Press, 1990.

Yi, Sa-Rye. *Missionary and Martyr: The Life and Faith of Rev. Yi Gi-Pung, 1868–1942*. Translated by John S. Park. Seoul, Korea: KIATS Press, 2008.

Yoo, David K. *Contentious Spirits: Religion in Korean American History, 1910–1945*. Stanford: Stanford University Press, 2010.

Newspapers and Periodicals

The Atlanta Constitution
The Christian Advocate
Christian Science Monitor
Colorado Spring Gazette
The Idaho Daily Statesman
The Independent
The Korea Bookman
The Korea Mission Field
Korean Student Bulletin
Los Angeles Times
Minutes of the Annual Meeting of the Korean Mission of the Methodist Episcopal Church, South
The Missionary Review of the World
New York Times
The Outlook
The Washington Post
Woman's Work for Woman

4 Contestation and Cooperation in the Making of the Indigenous Christian Woman

Introduction

On June 19, 1934, the American Methodist mission celebrated their fiftieth anniversary in Seoul. Although the semi-centennial event heralded the partnership between American and Korean Methodists, the two groups were looking in different directions. Missionaries gazed backward into the past. They cherished the early years, when they had first introduced the gospel to a timid but teachable people who knew little about Christianity, modern technology, or the West. Koreans, in contrast, looked forward to the promising future of an autonomous Church. Bishop J.S. Ryang, the first Korean general superintendent, began the commemoration by stating that Korean Methodism was no longer a foreign mission field but a fully independent indigenous church.[1] Four years earlier, Korean Methodists formed their own denomination, separate from American Methodists. Of the one hundred delegates at their first General Conference in 1930, eighty-four were Koreans and sixteen were missionaries.[2] Another Korean speaker, Helen Kim, a widely recognized college professor, proclaimed that Christ had inspired her countrywomen to rise up as "leaders of movements and carriers of public burdens" in and outside the church.[3] The inclination of the missionaries, however, was to reminisce about the early years. The physician Annie Ellers Bunker recalled her first adventures in the primitive nation when she and her fellow pioneers overcame hostility from Koreans, who saw them as "foreign devils," in order to heal sick patients in the new modern hospital.[4]

A keen observer would have noticed that this difference between American and Korean perspectives at the semi-centennial event—Americans glorifying the past, Koreans anticipating the future—represented not simply a coincidental difference but a hint of wider conflict between two groups over the direction of the Korean Church. Missionaries distrusted at least some Korean initiatives and longed for the days of uncontested authority. Koreans spoke glowingly of the missionaries but welcomed a change in leadership. The disagreements mostly simmered, but they occasionally reached the boiling point, and no conflict was hotter than the debate over Christian womanhood. As Korean Protestant women chose their own paths in the twentieth century, they clashed with female missionaries about nearly everything, from education, political activism, and religious beliefs to vocational choices and dress.

The First Impression: The Missionary Making of the Korean Christian Woman

When missionaries arrived in the late nineteenth century, they felt appalled by the lowly status and degraded conditions of Korean women. During his first excursion through the nation's interior, one missionary thought it ludicrous that the women would "run away for dear life" as he approached them.[5] The strict customs of gender separation and the seclusion of women from the public sphere surprised and worried the missionaries. Huldah A. Haenig described young Korean women as "conspicuous by their absence" in public places.[6] She could not quite grasp the curious practice of keeping "the Korean maiden . . . closely sheltered in the privacy of home" until she was twelve.[7] *The Gospel in All Lands* noted in 1889 that only men occupied the streets; women remained secluded in the inner chambers of their homes: "You see a hundred men to one woman in the throngs on its streets, and Korean women are never seen by other men than their husbands and brothers."[8]

These restrictions upon women did not exist in Korea until the reign of the Joseon dynasty beginning in the late fourteenth century. Prior to the Joseon dynasty (1392–1910), women freely mingled with men in the streets, participated in seasonal outings, frequented Buddhist temples, and bathed nude in rivers and streams.[9] But neo-Confucian scholars of the early Joseon dynasty imposed reforms that curtailed women's public activity in order to divide the sexes according to a "natural" order in which women were subordinate to men and were encased in the fixed social categories of chaste maiden, diligent wife, and devoted mother. By confining women to their homes and restricting their access to Buddhist temples and shaman houses, neo-Confucianists sought to protect the virginity of women and diminish their religious authority among ordinary Koreans.[10] These regulations led to what became known as the *inside-outside rule*—"it meant that women should not see or talk with men who were not family members and should stay in the inner chambers."[11] Unlike upper-class women, lower- and middling-class women enjoyed more time in public because of their work in the fields and marketplace.[12]

But the missionaries were not pleased by what they saw from common women. They were aghast at the lack of hygiene and clothing among some women in the streets and villages. In 1901, one missionary complained in her diary, after encountering an elderly Korean woman, that "this old woman wore simply a dress skirt over her lower undergarments, but above her waist was bare. She looked as if water had never touched her skin. She was simply scurvy, the dirt scaling off here and there, and her hair was filled with nits."[13]

Missionaries lamented the uncouth appearance of young Korean girls and objected to the garments of nursing mothers that exposed their breasts. One older female missionary in Seoul, outraged by these revealing outfits, took to the streets to reprimand the women for their impropriety, making what one of her colleagues described as "energetic though futile attempts to pull their skirts and jackets together across the objectionable gap."[14]

Missionaries attributed such improprieties to disadvantages imposed on Korean women from an early age. Even in the upper classes, boys alone received a formal education. Equally or more disturbing were the compulsory marriages of young girls. Although the government in 1894 set the legal age of marriage at twenty for men and sixteen for women, girls as young as twelve commonly underwent arranged marriages with older men.[15] As one female missionary wrote: "The Korean woman received no welcome at birth, no love in life, and has no hope in death."[16] Their condition evoked pity from the missionaries and prompted indictments of the society. Henry Appenzeller described Korean gender relations as such: "Education is for man, stupidity is for woman." He concluded that Korean women were "secluded, subjected, degraded, [and] enslaved" with slim odds for progress because they lacked "literary advantages as a child" and possessed "shadowy legal rights as a woman."[17] He later preached that the unfair treatment of Korean women demonstrated the inferiority of Confucianism and Buddhism to Christianity: "Confucius never spoke a kind word for woman . . . Buddha had 48 wishes—one was, may I never become woman. Jesus is the only oriental who has a good word for woman."[18]

In 1909, Annie Baird wrote *Daybreak in Korea* after spending nearly two decades in Korea. Her fictive tale is told from the perspective of a twelve-year-old Korean girl, Pobai. But Baird explained in her preface that her book was a reliable source to learn about "facts and incidents such as come daily under the observation of missionaries in Korea."[19] Her work emerged as one of the leading textbooks to train prospective missionaries to Korea. In mission study classrooms across the United States, students had to read *Daybreak in Korea* in order to learn about Korean women. In one classroom exercise, female students would "impersonate the life of a Korean girl" as depicted by the book.[20] The depictions were bleak and pathetic, for Baird presented her protagonist, Pobai, as a sweet and innocent girl trapped in a village beset by filth, poverty, debauchery, and corruption:

> She was nearly twelve years old, with round cheeks that glowed red under the olive skin, and a heavy braid of glossy black hair hanging down her back. Only perfect cleanliness was lacking to make her a very wholesome girl to look upon but Pobai was almost always rather dirty. She would have liked to be clean, but so much of her time and strength went into helping her mother keep the men of the family immaculately clad, that she hardly ever had time to think of herself.[21]

The reader follows Pobai on a daily walk through her village as she encounters gambling men, a shrieking woman with torn clothes fleeing from her drunken husband, prostitutes combing their hair and adorning their bodies with oil and perfume, the wretched stench of a festering corpse, and demon-possessed brothers wearing old straw shoes and filthy rags.[22] Pobai later has to marry a cruel and abusive Korean man, but eventually she overcomes the tribulations after meeting American missionaries, who teach her the gospel and lead her to Christian conversion.

Missionaries believed that they alone could save poor and helpless Koreans, especially the women. Though they criticized the harsh conditions of Korean women, female missionaries found that Korea's strict gender separation gave them some freedom to practice ministry apart from men. Across Asia, American women gladly assumed leadership in education, evangelism, and public health, a leadership that far exceeded the limits placed on them at home.[23] In 1909, Presbyterian missionary Margaret Best celebrated her female colleagues in Seoul for service beyond the capacities of their male counterparts: "They gathered the street children into Sabbath Schools and through them gained access to the inner quarters of the high walled houses that shut in women from the outside world."[24] With this greater access came demands from the American women for more autonomy and equality in decision-making.[25] In 1912, Lillias Underwood protested against a resolution adopted by her Presbyterian mission that threatened to restrict equal voting rights for married female missionaries. She pointed out that the women worked no less hard than their spouses to meet "the awful need of Korean womanhood in the utter barrenness of her social, intellectual, and spiritual existence."[26]

They might have sometimes worked harder. In their Bible training classes, they pursued rigorous group study from morning to evening. "The method usually pursued is to teach the lesson verse by verse, chapter by chapter, book by book," explained one instructor, "to make it so familiar that it becomes part of their life."[27] Because of low literacy rates among Korean women, missionaries employed older female converts, known as Bible Women *(jeondo buin)*, to assist them.[28] Because most Korean Protestants came from the middling classes, missionaries understood that a Bible Woman occupied an enviable position that promised income and prestige. At first, missionaries recruited any female convert who could read. As the Bible classes expanded and trained more converts, the missionaries raised their hiring standards. In about twenty years, one Presbyterian Bible class for women in Pyongyang had expanded by 1909 to ninety-three classes with 3,202 students.[29] In order to cultivate virtuous women, female missionaries wanted to produce Korean assistants who would manifest not only the image of God but also the image of the missionaries. They preferred widows, who had no familial household responsibilities, and women whom they had educated and trained for mission.[30]

The missionaries of course wanted their converts to be faithful, but they also wanted them to be physically clean. Cleanliness would improve public health, and clean bodies would evidence godliness.[31] But ideals of Western hygiene sometimes bumped up against cultural traditions. In 1906, M.J. Edmunds told of the difficulties in training Korean nurses. They worked hard to learn but they "came from the crude native environment" and knew nothing about Western instruments, rubber appliances, thermometers, and even ordinary medicines.[32] But as female converts adopted Western hygienic norms, missionaries considered their cleaner and healthier bodies as markers of evangelistic success. In 1916, as one missionary put it, both the piety and the physical appearance of the women at her Pyongyang mission station radiated light in comparison to the darkness and decay enveloping the rest of the country: "It was a hot day and a sultry room with two or three hundred women sitting on the floor and a baby to about every fourth woman . . . The women were all in their clean linen skirts and white head covering. Christianity has done so much to make the women of Korea clean, on the outside as well as within."[33] The pious minds and clean bodies of once ignorant and degraded Korean Protestant women confirmed the transformative power of the Christian gospel and validated the distinctive achievements of women in the missions.

Korean marital customs, however, posed a threat, both to the spiritual welfare of female converts and to the religious authority of missionary women. Because Korean women did not choose their spouses, they could not select a Protestant partner. Often converts wed husbands who forbade them to attend church or enroll in the mission school. After losing numerous students to these marriages, missionaries adopted a resolution in 1900 to discourage their students from marriage before eighteen, and to press the matter with parents.[34] At the same time, they endorsed Western notions of courtship as morally superior to arranged marriages. They claimed that arranged marriages too often led to spousal abuse. In 1911, J. Robert Moose argued that American courtships—which led to marriages based on mutual love—were closer to biblical teaching than Korean marital customs: "The wife is selected by the relatives of the husband without his having anything to do with the matter. Of course under these circumstances there can be no courtship, and in most cases little or no love. If a Korean man loved his wife, he would be ashamed to acknowledge it."[35]

The missionaries instructed their students to adopt modified American courtship patterns. They understood that Korean women could not mingle with men in social settings, so they acquiesced in Korean gender relations by placing curtains in the middle of their churches to separate men and women during worship.[36] Although young Koreans could not court one another, missionaries encouraged Protestant parents to select their children's spouses from within their churches. They also promoted letter-writing as "a new style of courtship" between arranged couples so that future spouses could come to know one another and share religious convictions.[37] Even if missionaries could not replicate American-style courtships, they could do something to improve relationships among young Korean men and women. Some of the missionaries even took the initiative and arranged Protestant marriages by having Korean preachers and Bible Women intercede as matchmakers:

> Of course the young man had not been courting her a la American—her village would have been scandalized if he had—even if he had known how; besides, the young lady would have been dreadfully embarrassed ever to have been confronted by him. But neither had the match been made through a go-between, for a better day is dawning in the land of Morning Calm. The circuit preachers and the Bible Women had conveyed the messages back and forth while the parents had talked it over with the young people who had consented. Their ages were respectively 18 and 17, but would probably have been 8 and 7 years, prior to Christian influence. The young gentleman was studying in Seoul and the young lady in an advanced mission school.[38]

A year later, another missionary observed that young converts were "beginning to choose their own helpmeets." This was a "tremendous break with the past" that evinced gratifying progress in the mission.[39] Female missionaries thought that these changes would increase the odds that their students would marry Protestant men. The result would be women converts with sound minds, clean bodies, and converted husbands.

Some Western practices, however, struck the missionaries as threatening. How much Western education was appropriate for Korean women? Should they teach English and other Western subjects? The questions produced disagreement. Methodist Mary Scranton, who established the first girls' school, *Ewha Haktang*, said that it would not Westernize Korean girls. Presbyterians also distinguished Westernizing and evangelizing in their schools. "In all meetings for women and in the home life of the girls' school," wrote Margaret Best, "the effort was made to keep surrounding and atmosphere Korean and not introduce disturbing, distracting, and useless foreign elements."[40] Others countered that Western subjects like arithmetic and science did not distract from the mission. In 1914, one Ewha teacher, Lulu Frey, argued that her students could learn from a diverse curriculum, both Western and Korean, without losing their orthodox faith. Frey acknowledged that both sides in the educational debate had some valid arguments, but concluded that students should be afforded the same quality education as their teachers, regardless of race. "In coveting for the Korean women lives of rich service," Frey asked, "dare we offer them any less preparation than we considered necessary for ourselves?"[41] Grace Harmon McGary advocated the teaching of advanced topics like psychology and sociology, insisting that Christian education for women in Korea should be no different from education in the United States: "I defend higher education for Korean women from much the same standpoint as for American women, for what difference ought color and country to make in the privileges of creatures all alike in God's image!"[42] Annie Baird agreed that racial discrimination was an evil, but she wondered if the absence of algebra made much difference. Did students—or missionaries, for that matter—need to learn "Differential Calculus" and "Spherical Geometry"? She wrote: "One would like to know just as a matter of information how many women missionaries on the field ever studied these subjects, and of those who did, how many shudder at the recollection."[43]

They may have disagreed about Western education but they found no reason for debate about the superiority of traditional Korean dress. Korean women during the Joseon period wore long skirts *(chima)* and blouses *(jeogori)* in a triangular silhouette that de-emphasized the upper torso and covered the arms and legs. Upper-class women chose brightly colored dresses made with silk, gauze, satin, and damask. Lower-class women typically wore white dresses made of cotton, ramic, and hemp. Traditional male clothes consisted of long, flowing pants and shirts made of white woven hemp and a black cylindrical hat made of horsehair and bamboo *(gat)*.[44] Although the first mission school for boys in 1897 discarded Korean dress for European military garb, school uniforms for girls followed Korean styles.[45] The missionaries were pleased; while Western women wore tight-fitting gowns and short skirts—provocative clothing that drew indelicate glances—Korean traditional dress conveyed a modesty that exemplified an image of Christian womanhood.[46] A Korean woman once gently but insistently told Baird that the placket of her shirtwaist sleeve exposed her forearms and that the gap required immediate attention. In other words, Korean women could teach Americans a thing or two about propriety. Best said that the Americans had learned "that as true a Christian heart could beat beneath the dainty silk gown of the Korean lady or the homely cotton garment of her lowlier sister as beneath the strangely fashioned dress of the Westerner."[47] But the missionaries had to accept another failure: Some Korean Protestant women in the twentieth century defied mission school regulations and adopted Western dress, especially after Japanese colonization. They not only defied regulations about dress; they also had their own ideas about proper beliefs and practices.

On Second Thought: Korean Protestant Women Make Their Own Choices

During the Joseon dynasty, most Koreans had little to no hope of obtaining a formal education. Even upper-class women received only informal training in the basics of domesticity.[48] The few literate women studied textbooks about their household duties as wives and mothers. One popular manual, the *Naehun* (Instructions for Women), consisted of seven chapters that covered a woman's manner of speech, her conduct, filial piety, matrimony, marital relations, motherhood, family relations, and thrift.[49] Neo-Confucian scholars saw learned women as threats to patriarchal gender boundaries. Yi Ik (1681–1763) declared that "reading and learning are the domains of men. For a woman it is enough if she knows the Confucian virtues of diligence, frugality, and chastity. If a woman disobeys these virtues, she will bring disgrace to the family."[50] Even the sharpest Korean detractors of the missionaries conceded that women like Mary Scranton advanced female education. In 1918, Yun Ch'iho explained that "indeed, if the Christian missionaries had accomplished nothing else in Korea, the introduction of female education alone deserves our lasting gratitude. Up to a few years ago girls' schools were not even thought of outside the Christian church."[51] The first generation of female professionals in the early twentieth century was not uniformly Christian, but most had studied at mission schools. One of them, Hwang Sin-dok, observed in 1933 that "almost all women over thirty who were educated and had worked in society had been exposed to Christianity, even if it was only minor contact."[52]

But as educated Korean women sought to rise in the public sphere, they discovered repeated resistance: from Japanese imperialists, Korean neo-Confucians, and American Protestants. After the Japanese colonized Korea in 1910, they founded their own government schools to train their subjects in modern and Japanese ways. Over time they also set restrictions on instruction in religion and in the Korean language for all schools. The first Japanese Governor-General declared that the new purpose of education was "to cultivate such character as befitting the imperial subject through moral development and dissemination of the national [Japanese] language."[53] Both missionaries and Koreans felt the burden of the new ordinances. Annie Baird's zoology textbook failed to earn the imprimatur of the Vice-Minister of Education because she wrote it in Korean.[54] In 1916, the director of the Internal Affairs Department reminded Hugh Heong-wo Cynn, a Korean Methodist teacher, about the ordinances. This official gave Cynn's students permission for religious meetings outside the school building and after school hours, but he forbade religious instruction in the classroom: "I will call your attention to the Instruction of the Governor-General, issued on March 24, 1915, which says, 'In such schools no religious teaching is permitted to be included in their curricula nor religious ceremonies can be allowed to be performed.' "[55]

Missionaries and Koreans shared grievances about imperial educational restrictions, but they disagreed about the purpose of mission schools. Many Korean women enrolled in them primarily to learn English and Western subjects. With the opening of Korea to foreign nations, Korean women saw the possibility of breaking free from neo-Confucian norms, and they saw the schools as a means to this end. As Korea modernized, these women embraced new opportunities to work outside the home in education, medicine, art, literature, and social work. Though they were zealous Christians, their leap into the public sphere troubled their American tutors. Even as Korea changed before their very eyes, women missionaries still strove to raise virtuous wives and mothers. As late as fifty years into the mission work, Margaret Best boasted in 1934 that her school promoted domesticity "so that our graduates may be fitted to fill placers of responsibility and usefulness in their own homes."[56] But instead of following the missionaries' script, the Korean women appealed to Jesus as they forged their own path forward. A number of them—including women of influence—remained single, cut their hair, dressed like Westerners, entered the workforce, joined the Korean independence movement, and spoke out against Japanese soldiers, Korean males, or female missionaries who stood in their way.

Helen Kim was a Korean woman who embraced Christianity to become a pioneer in her own right. Born in 1899 into a poor family of subsistence farmers in Incheon, she eventually graduated from a mission school and received a scholarship to study in America because of her academic promise and her piety. Kim earned a BA from Ohio Wesleyan College (1924) and an MA from Boston University (1925) and then returned to Korea to work as a teacher at Ewha College. In 1930, she traveled again to America to study at Columbia Teachers College, becoming in 1931 the first Korean woman to earn an American doctorate. In 1939, she became the first Korean president of Ewha. Kim's relationship with missionaries was complex. She numbered some among her dearest friends, but she was often at odds with them.

As a young girl, Kim gravitated toward the mission school's offerings in literature, geology, astronomy, and geometry. As she and her older sisters studied at Ewha, their middling class family admired the missionaries for reforming Korea's patriarchal and elitist society by teaching common women. Kim wrote of how Ewha's first college graduation in 1914 ushered in a new era of hope and promise for Korean women. As she watched the three college graduates in their caps and gowns, she shed "tears of joy for the accomplishments of girls so long neglected and looked down upon" in her society.[57]

Initially, at least, she had little enthusiasm for missionary religious instruction. She attended church with her family and later at Ewha, but she realized at fourteen years of age that her faith was "a nominal acceptance of a set of frozen dogmas [that] was expressed in a routine of lifeless exercises."[58] Hearing a preacher ask a congregation to confess their sins, Kim at first resisted because she felt that she had no reason to confess. But as she deliberated on the Christian doctrine of repentance, first during the church service and then into the night, Kim concluded that she "had to get at the reality of religion or else give up altogether the meaningless and therefore hypocritical observances of religious practices."[59] She prayed desperately, asking for a revelation of God's existence and of Christ's redemptive work. Her prayer resulted in the illumination that her sins were "pride, self-will, and hatred for the Japanese."[60] Kim fell to the floor and repented. Sensing that God forgave her, she had a vision in which God removed from her three bags (symbolizing her three chief sins) and directed her toward a large moat filled by a mass of entrapped Korean women with outstretched hands. Kim interpreted the vision as a divine call to help women in her country and beyond.[61]

Like the missionaries, Kim placed her hope in education but not in mere domestic and industrial training. She wanted to push beyond a curriculum formed by the notion that domesticity was the sole option for women. Some of the missionaries moved in the opposite direction. In 1918, Alice Appenzeller, a second-generation missionary and instructor at Ewha, praised graduates for cultivating Christian homes, "quietly and sweetly spreading the leaven of the Master's spirit wherever they go."[62] Charlotte Bell Linton concurred six years later that the great accomplishment of the schools was the training of women as mothers who would ensure a "proper sort of godly atmosphere at home."[63]

Kim, who never married, preferred that educated Korean women seek leadership positions in the church and the political order and that they constantly pursue gender equality. In the journal *Sin yŏja* (New Woman), she excoriated Korean men who desired pure and upright wives without first improving themselves. She depicted Christian men—at least some of them—as charlatans who displayed outward expressions of piety but mainly attended church to gaze at women.[64] Kim would not be confined to the home, and she wanted other educated women to help change Korean society by claiming equality in the work of reform. Men and women possessed the same rights and responsibilities to advise and criticize one another in a mutual process that would ultimately uplift their nation.[65]

Educated Korean women like Kim distinguished themselves by fierce rhetoric and Western dress. By the 1920s, many urban intellectual men had adopted Western dress. Although traditional garments were markers of ethnic identity in the face of Japanese imperialism, the men eventually turned away from tradition. Clothing assumed a different meaning as traditional dress began to suggest primitiveness while Western dress represented progress.[66] Educated Korean women were quicker than men to take up the Western style because it was less cumbersome and more practical, but their openness to change engendered more controversy than the male transition.

Korean newspapers derided them for wearing shorter skirts that exposed their calves and knees. These "new women" were vain, materialistic, and overtly sexual. In 1928, the newspaper *Chosŏn ilbo* printed cartoons depicting the "new woman" with an obsession for expensive Western clothing and jewelry.[67] But having changed their clothes, the women also changed their hairstyle to short bobbed hair, a turn that distressed male intellectuals, who claimed that bobbed hair confused gender norms and promoted sexual permissiveness.[68] Kim had to defend her bobbed hair: It was attractive, was easy to clean, and facilitated the cause of women's liberation because it removed a physical distinction between the sexes.[69]

The American women allied themselves with the Korean male intellectuals. They scolded their students for giving up their modest dress and insisted that traditional garments pleased Christ more than suggestive Western skirts. But at least some Korean Protestant women believed that Christ had freed them from traditional clothing, which they associated with gender inequality and subservience. Louise Yim explained that she and her classmates wanted to escape the "yards and yards of linen cloth, which covered our bodies from head to foot and made us look like piles of dry goods."[70] Yim felt dismay when her missionary instructor insisted that "the mission is here to improve your morals, not to change customs!"[71] Yim led a boycott of classes and worship services. The students gained the right to dress as they pleased.[72]

The sartorial disagreements symbolized a break between two groups of women over the future direction of the Korean Church. Female missionaries saw themselves as pioneers whose success derived from teaching conservative theological doctrines like biblical inerrancy and complementarian gender roles. They viewed Western dress as a portent of modernity in their mission field. Even as they celebrated the Korean Church's increasing autonomy in the 1920s and 1930s, they feared that modernity would erode the pure and orthodox faith of Korean Protestants. Gathered in 1934 for the fiftieth anniversary of Presbyterian missions, the Americans advanced ambivalent and cautious opinions. Gordon Holdcroft's "forward look" had as its shadow side worries whether the Koreans, without help, could withstand theological modernism and the "material allurements of present day civilization."[73] Missionaries had once battled against the seclusion of women from the public sphere, but when young Korean women in Western dress began to assert equal rights and to take positions in schools, factories, and department stores, missionaries worried that modernity was a snare. Eva Pieters put it this way:

> Even the short hair, the permanent wave, the rouge, the lipstick, the short skirt, and the French heeled slippers have found ready entrance into the hearts of the Korean young ladies. These radical changes in the social life of the Korean young woman—changes that have been rather imposed from without than resulting from gradual development—have brought with them new needs as well as new dangers, of which we, as missionaries, have been keenly aware. How to help these girls to acquire the right outlook upon the world, to develop their mental and moral stamina, to satisfy the craving for social life, to guard against their seeking quick means of gratifying their natural desire for self-adornment[?] These and similar problems have been keenly felt by our women workers.[74]

Pieters could not see that Korean Protestant women themselves sought some of these changes. Women like Helen Kim and Louise Yim were not succumbing to societal pressures; Western dress was for them a symbol of a religiously motivated push for gender equality.

Korean Protestant women forged their own identities. They also sought an indigenous identity for the Korean Church. While grateful to the missionaries, they were ready to lead. In 1923, Pilley Kim Choi observed that educated Korean women were doctors, teachers, school principals, bank clerks, industrialists, and journalists. They no longer required nannies: "Ten years ago women's work in the church was of necessity largely in the hands of the women missionaries . . . Now most of such church business is in Korean women's hands."[75] To the missionaries, such assertions threatened the survival of the Church in Korea. They viewed themselves as indispensable.

Emerging Tensions between Korean Protestant and American Missionary Women

The relationship between two instructors at Ewha College, Alice Appenzeller and Helen Kim, embodied the cross-cultural tensions between Korean Protestant and American missionary women. Appenzeller was the eldest child of the first Methodist missionaries; she had returned to the place of her birth to continue her parents' work. Kim was a mission school graduate who had earned a doctorate in the United States. But behind closed doors the two wrangled over who was best qualified to set the school's agenda and vision. Kim pushed for a women's medical department and a merger with the neighboring men's school, Chosen Christian College, but the conservative Appenzeller argued that the school was already overextended. In 1939, Appenzeller nominated Kim to succeed her as school president only after the Japanese forced all missionary instructors to resign.[76] Appenzeller struggled to accept this reversal of authority. Over the next several years, Appenzeller questioned Kim's decision-making at Ewha in letters to her friends.[77]

When missionaries kept harping on domesticity, some Korean women began to associate Christianity with patriarchy and gender discrimination. The missionaries recalled that they had freed the women from neo-Confucian shackles, but Korean women replied that they had no interest in a cultural imprisonment grounded on a religious message. In 1930 Kim Kangch'un scathingly asserted that both "Western Christianity and Eastern Confucianism" held women back.[78] Even the Christian Scriptures, she said, treated women as subordinate: "First, man came from God, while woman came from man. It was easily inferred that man is the most powerful being after God, and while God rules the universe, man rules woman. Indeed, Paul insisted upon this interpretation."[79] Any serious reader of the Bible would conclude that according to Christian teaching women were created to serve men. To Kim, Korean Protestant women fleeing from oppressive Confucian doctrines were exchanging one set of shackles for another.

A closer look into Helen's Kim family reveals a household that flouted missionary expectations. Prior to their conversion, Kim's parents followed Confucian teachings, especially ancestral worship. On the anniversary of the birth or death of each ancestor, they held elaborate ceremonies in which the table overflowed with the finest foods, candles, and incense to honor the ancestor. Dressed in new mourning clothes, Kim's father read from his scroll a newly written message to the spirit of the ancestor as the other male family members stood behind him before they all bowed three times in unison. Even after her own conversion, Kim defended these ceremonial practices as something other than idolatry or paganism; they signified a moral remembrance of their ancestors and manifested a vibrant cultural heritage. Unlike her missionary friends, who had little good to say about Confucianism, Kim prized the ethical values conveyed by her Confucian upbringing.[80]

Kim's parents held on to some Confucian ways after they became Protestants. Missionaries prohibited ancestral worship, but Kim's father thought it unethical to forsake his ancestors in order to become a Christian. In an act of religious hybridity, the Confucian ancestral dates remained on Kim's family calendar, but with Christian memorial services in place of former veneration practices. In 1959, a Korean scholar, David Chung, wrote his dissertation at Yale University on religious syncretism in Korean society, highlighting the complex cross-cultural processes that formed early Korean Protestantism. Chung argued that both American missionary teachings emphasizing fundamentalist interpretations of the Bible and traditional Korean religious elements created "numerous labyrinthine channels" for Korean Protestants to combine different practices and beliefs from multiple sources on their own terms.[81] Kim likewise saw how her mother embraced Christianity but "never quite made the complete transfer from the conception of many spirits to monotheism."[82] She attended church regularly, expressed her love for Christ daily, and testified to her friends and neighbors, but she always had Confucian sensibilities, which were visible when she comforted a grieving Kim after the unexpected death of two of her siblings:

> These two tragedies in my family made me think seriously for the first time about life and death. Mother was very brave and told me not to grieve. When I asked her "What is death?" her answer was, "when Confucius was asked the same question he said, 'Man does not know what life is, how can he know what death is?' " Then she added, "God knows best and they are in his hands. We need only believe and wait for the day we meet them again in heaven."[83]

Kim's account of her mother's blending of Christianity and Confucianism hardly corresponded to missionary ambitions, but Kim attributed to her mother a faith fully as strong as "the faith of those well versed in theology."[84] She implied that the missionaries were wrong; converts like Kim's mother did not have to abandon all of their older beliefs and practices.

The sharpest conflict was about politics and the Korean independence movement during Japanese imperial reign from 1910 to 1945. While sympathetic to Korea's geopolitical plight, female missionaries wanted in their mission schools no rebels and political activists. The goal was a sacred home life in which wives and mothers would win souls to Christ. But some Korean Protestant women believed that their faith required them to fight for national independence. Louise Yim did not want to become a housewife; she would be, in her fondest dreams, a Joan of Arc leading an army against imperialists.[85] Imprisoned for her actions in the independence movement, Induk Pahk claimed that her Bible reading strengthened her political will:

"Stirred by what I read I wanted God to use me just as He used Paul, and kneeling in that lonely cell I dedicated myself to His service."[86]

Helen Kim also believed—it was a lifelong passion—that Christ had beckoned her to support Korean independence.[87] The emergence of Korean feminism was connected to the cause of national liberation. After Japan established their protectorship over Korea in 1905, the first organized women's movement mobilized to raise funds to pay the Korean debt to Japan with the hope repayment would nullify the Japanese occupation.[88] As a teacher at Ewha College in the 1920s, Kim formed the "Ewha evangelistic band" with six other women and they barnstormed around the nation hosting revival meetings. They sang hymns, preached, and testified, but they also called for resistance to Japanese imperialism and highlighted the liberating principles of Christianity: "Our talks had individual and social appeal, usually ending with a highly patriotic note, for the ideals of human dignity and social justice are so linked with Christian teaching and practice that they are inseparable."[89] Kim's dissertation, *Rural Education for the Regeneration of Korea*, criticized the Japanese for forcing Korean students to learn their language. She challenged a 1922 ordinance that described Japanese language instruction as "indispensable for daily life" by noting that subjects like public health, economics, and science were far more important for the majority of Korean students who did not even speak Japanese outside of school.[90] Between 1920 and 1930, the percentage of Koreans conversant in Japanese increased from 2.12 to 8.27 percent, but as the figures illustrate, few Koreans spoke Japanese even after two decades of imperial rule.[91]

In 1928, Kim delivered a speech at the International Missionary Council meeting in Jerusalem. The Christian gospel, she said, had empowered Korean women to take the lead in church and society. "I think Christ would pity us women," Kim remarked, "if we still are timid and hesitate about bearing witness to Him in all walks of life, not only in domestic life, but also in the industrial, commercial, political, and international life of humanity."[92] Kim interrupted a session on international affairs to speak out against comments from Japan's delegation. *New York Times* reporter Howard A. Bridgman described how she "claimed the platform and in sweet but vigorous tones set forth Korea's objection to being under the domination of Japan."[93] She refuted Japanese denials of racial discrimination by pointing out that few Koreans served in the imperial government and police force.[94]

The massive uprising against imperial rule during the March First Movement in 1919 surprised the missionaries, who had underestimated the intensity of Korean resistance, particularly among their female students. As Koreans gathered in Seoul to protest, the teachers at Ewha stopped students from participating.[95] In Songdo, one hundred students defied their principal, Ellasue Wagner, and marched toward the city gates, with hymn books in one hand and Bibles in the other, to pledge solidarity with their compatriots.[96]

The missionaries wanted to be politically neutral, but they acted, as they saw it, to protect their students from Japanese retaliation. The brutal tactics of the imperial police force, who struck female protesters with their batons, horrified the teachers. When policemen came to arrest students, missionaries pressed for humane treatment. At Ewha, Lulu Frey asked that her students not be bound with rope en route to prison.[97] As they learned about abusive interrogations in female prisons, missionaries spoke out against the Japanese. After their students were released, missionaries collected their testimonials to report to mission boards at home, revealing to the world that the Japanese stripped, starved, beat, and tortured women prisoners. One Ewha student told of being forced to kneel alongside others, who had to hold chairs over their heads, remove their clothes, and endure verbal and physical assaults.[98] The Federal Council of Churches in the United States published her account along with others.[99]

After the March First Movement, Korean women in the United States joined in their nation's push for liberation. At the Student Volunteer Movement (SVM) for Foreign Missions convention in Des Moines, Iowa in 1920, one young Korean lobbied for American support by arguing that instead of sending missionaries Americans should help the country resist Japan: "Korea needs you because Korea is looking to America as a savior of other peoples . . . You have developed as a free people, intellectually, physically, and morally, and now is a chance for you to go out and help other people to share these blessings with you."[100] She praised Christ for inspiring young women like her to leave the shelter of their homes and "march down the street fearlessly."[101]

As Korean women continued to address the SVM convention each year, its delegates began to take notice. African American theologian and civil rights leader Howard Thurman recalled an experience when he was a seminary student:

> One afternoon some seven hundred of us had a special group meeting, at which a Korean girl was asked to talk to us about her impression of American education. It was an occasion to be remembered. The Korean student was very personable and somewhat diminutive. She came to the edge of the platform and, with what seemed to be obvious emotional strain, she said, "You have asked me to talk with you about my impression of American education. But there is only one thing that a Korean has any right to talk about, and that is freedom from Japan." For about twenty minutes she made an impassioned plea for the freedom of her people, ending her speech with this sentence: "If you see a little American boy and you ask him what he wants, he says, 'I want a penny to put in my bank or to buy a whistle or a piece of candy.' But if you see a little Korean boy and you ask him what he wants, he says, 'I want freedom from Japan.' "[102]

Thurman then compared Koreans to the outcast Jewish minority in the Roman Empire and "the Negro in American life," arguing that the quintessential question of the disinherited in every age was to discern the right attitude toward the rulers who controlled their lives.[103] Some Korean students in the United States related their anti-colonial struggle to the civil rights movement. After returning home from her studies at Wesleyan College in Macon, Georgia, Induk Pahk taught Negro spirituals to her Methodist church in Seoul.[104] In 1950, Helen Kim told an American interviewer, Laura Boulton, that the political activism of courageous Korean women seeking national liberation had contributed to developing a global moral consciousness in support of autonomous rule for colonized nations.[105]

Female missionaries had mixed feelings about a Korean Christian feminism that fused faith and politics. They reacted to the activism of their students with astonishment. Martha Scott Bruen saw the Koreans in a new light after the March First uprising: They no longer filled "the places of underlings and servants" but revealed a capacity for tenacity, courage, and leadership that had the potential to change "their home and civic life."[106] Bruen still wanted the missionaries—herself included—to mold the Koreans, but unfortunately, from the missionary perspective, the Koreans seemed less pliable than they once had been.

After 1919, the Americans began to show increasing frustration with Korean Protestant women. They complained among themselves about how their once demure and daintily clad Korean girls now acted and looked no different than Western women. Some longed for the days of "Old Korea," when the Korean girls obeyed their instructions and set out to fulfill their religious duties as wives and mothers. In 1948, one retired missionary looked back upon her forty years in Korea. The early years, she said, were good. But then came the "New Korea," with its "hodge-podge" of "half-baked ideas" that led the Korean Church away from the ancient gospel of conservative evangelical Christianity.[107]

The Third Space: Agnes Davis and the Making of a Biracial Christian Marriage in Korea

In 1934, a white American woman named Agnes Davis arrived in Korea to marry David Chuhwang Kim, a Korean whom she met and fell in love with during their time together as classmates at Drew University. Because interracial marriages were uncommon and unlawful in a number of U.S. states, some of Davis's classmates and teachers and some missionaries in Korea attempted to dissuade her.[108] Motivated, however, by religious faith and love for her fiancé, a resolute Davis married him and then lived with her husband's family in a Korean village. Davis was unique in Korea. She occupied what postcolonial theorist Homi Bhabha identified as a "Third Space," in-between the colonizing and the colonized.[109] She was a committed American Protestant, but she was no missionary. She married a Korean and resided within his community, but stood apart as an outsider because of her race. Davis lived in the interstices, caught between two cultures.

Because she experienced both sides of the encounter between missionaries and Korean Protestants, her insights illuminate with special clarity the gap between them.

When Davis and Kim began dating in America, her classmates and teachers objected. Like many Korean students in America, Kim had graduated from a mission school and received a scholarship to study at Drew. The couple met when Davis loaned her class notes to Kim and helped him with English. She fell in love with him, admiring his kind spirit, inquisitive mind, and religious faith. Kim also felt attracted to Davis, but he sought to end their relationship because of what he saw as the hopeless prospect of a Korean marrying a white American. But Davis persisted, and when the Dean of Students admonished her, she replied that God had no interest in preventing interracial marriage. She had nothing but disdain for U.S. anti-miscegenation laws that forbade interracial unions as unnatural and evil corruptions of some divine plan.[110] "If ever such prejudice is to be overcome, and our talk of Christian brotherhood to mean anything, someone has to begin acting as if the people of other races were brothers," Davis told her dean. "I will glory in meeting it with my head held high, and with unruffled faith in the rightness of my stand."[111]

Yet when Davis arrived in Korea, she found that missionaries had the same racial prejudices as white Americans at home. Despite their preachments about the virtues of domesticity, they also displayed more than a small degree of condescension toward Korean wives, whom they saw as subservient to men and paternal families. In 1891, Henry Appenzeller lamented that married Korean women were obliged to serve both their husbands and mothers-in-law. A Korean wife, he observed, could do little but iron, cook, clean, and sew; "her world centers around a smoky kitchen and the needle."[112] Another observer reported that a married Korean woman "belongs almost body and soul to her husband."[113] Forty years after these comments, missionaries still were bewildered that an American woman would become a Korean wife. In 1938, the women's section of the MECS Board of Missions published a pamphlet that lamented the tragic conditions of Korean wives subjected to a vicious chain of submission that culminated in obedience to their mothers-in-law.[114] Missionaries therefore warned Davis about *samjong chido*, the three rules for women in Korean Confucian teaching: When a child, she must submit to her father; in marriage, to her husband; in widowhood, to her eldest son.[115] They also told Davis about unsanitary conditions in rural Korea and warned her about the cruel treatment she would be certain to receive from her tyrannical mother-in-law.[116] Missionaries celebrated Christian romance in Korea and wrote sentimental fictive tales about romances between missionaries or between converts, but they felt some dismay at the thought of Davis and Kim's interracial coupling.[117]

After the wedding, Davis discovered that her mother-in-law was neither to be feared nor pitied. As the two women shared the numerous household chores, Davis learned to appreciate the rhythms of female companionship as women washed and ironed clothes or cooked food. Davis affectionately called her mother-in-law "O-man-ee (the Korean word for mother)," and claimed that the seeming meekness and submission of Korean wives were signs of strength, not degradation.[118] The work was taxing but not symbolic of primitive backwardness. Missionaries failed to understand how Korean women used domestic tasks as social gatherings. Although her mother-in-law never attended a mission school, Davis found in her the Christian values of selflessness, serenity, and patience through her daily living. Davis called her the best teacher she ever had. Korean women, she wrote, were not lost without missionaries. Her mother-in-law, for one, did not require missionary instruction to exemplify the love of Christ in her home and community.

From her village, Davis better understood Korean critiques of missionary lifestyles. In stark contrast to the missionaries, Davis lived in a typical Korean house with three rooms each eight feet square: "The home was built with a framework of small logs, the wall spaces formed by a lattice of rice-straw rope and corn or cane stalks, made wattlelike and plastered inside and out with mud or clay."[119] Although Davis liked some of the missionaries, she grew increasingly aware of their ostentation and luxury in comparison to the simplicity reflected both in the lives of Koreans and the teaching of Jesus. At the same time Davis was adjusting to her outdoor toilet, mud walls, and the persistent odor of manure from nearby farms, Marie Adams, a missionary from China visiting Korea on furlough, was frequenting Western-style hotels, sightseeing in the mountains, and enjoying camaraderie with the "Southern Methodist ladies" in Seoul.[120] And Frank Herron Smith was telling friends that his wife and children missed having Korean servants during their furlough in the United States and wanted to return to Korea because they did not like having to do a "good deal of dish-washing and such work" themselves.[121] Davis had once read E. Stanley Jones's *Christ of the Indian Road* and had desired to imitate Christ's humility. She had wanted to learn both from the missionaries and from immersion into her husband's way of life. She discovered that the missionaries she had admired from afar now seemed materialistic. She learned more about humility from her mother-in-law.[122]

Davis recognized the paradoxical quandary of married female missionaries who criticized Korean women for adopting modern Western norms yet wanted American comforts for their own families. Before marrying Kim, Davis stayed in several missionary homes. She observed how the women worried about household finances, budgeting expenses with frugal vigilance. "Missionaries have to shave corners financially," Davis observed. "They have to pay servant salaries, keep up large houses, and they try to maintain the American standard of living, for the sake of their children, I was told."[123]

Missionaries wanted Korean women to be attentive mothers, but they sent their own children to boarding schools in America or Seoul and Pyongyang. Boarding schools like Pyongyang Foreign School (PYFS) charged less than schools in other countries, but for some missionaries, the expense seemed daunting. In 1921, tuition and housing for four months at PYFS cost $72.50.[124] Parents considered homeschooling, but most determined that boarding school was a worthwhile investment. It also alleviated "the exacting and exhausting duties of teaching one's own children" and eased other "ordinary responsibilities of the wife and mother on the mission field."[125]

Foreign schools in Korea tried to replicate both an American curriculum and way of life for their students. The students sometimes wrote their parents that they missed them, but they also enjoyed their American friends and teachers.[126] In 1931, the PYFS student newspaper, *The Kum and Go*, reported about pep rallies, sports teams, difficult tests, debate meets, and field trips, the ordinary features of a school in the United States.[127] Missionaries' children thrived academically and socially alongside other Americans at these schools, but they knew few Korean peers.

One of them remembered that his rare interactions with Korean children were hostile, with the young boys hurling stones and insults at one another: "We got ourselves into stone throwing fights—something about which our parents would really get upset saying that we were setting back their hard mission work ten years . . . The Korean kids would yell in Korean at us—things like 'Yang Gook Nome a Coe Boodee,' which means 'Foreign Devil with a Big Nose.' "[128] As Davis worked with her husband to start a school and hospital in their village, she saw that Koreans wanted to work and live alongside Americans in genuine partnerships. Missionaries criticized the strict separation of genders, but they maintained racial divisions by building Western homes and founding foreign schools restricted to white children. Davis understood that they had no malicious intentions, but she understood why Koreans felt a burden of discrimination.

Proclaiming that the gospel had united American and Korean women, the missionaries often told their children not to play with Korean children, even those who attended church. They wished to protect their children from diseases and unsound spiritual habits.[129] Davis, like Korean women, took note of this distance between the children. Missionaries taught Korean parents in the classroom how to rear their children, but the Koreans recognized that they implicitly assumed that Korean children were less precious than white American ones. Stacy L. Roberts, Jr., recalled that in his first eighteen years, 1921 to 1939, he had a lively and joyous childhood in Korea, but he also remembered that he was "isolated in a kind of ivory tower." He did not play with Koreans.[130]

From her "Third Space," Davis could also see that Korean Protestants in her village did not practice religion like the Americans. Sensing the ambivalence and ambiguity of the colonial encounter—experiencing, in other words, the way in which postcolonial identity was, as Bhabha would later write, a hybrid of colonial and indigenous cultures—Davis discovered that Korean converts combined traditional beliefs with Christian ones.[131] She was at first surprised that so many turned to shamanistic tradition when they or their family members became ill. They prayed to the Christian God for healing but also asked local shamans to drive out the evil spirits causing the physical ailments. In her memoir, Ch'oe Cha-sil, one of the founding pastors of Yoido Full Gospel Church, recounted how Koreans in rural villages regularly turned to both shamans and Christian leaders throughout the colonial period and as late as the 1960s.[132] Like the missionaries, Davis disapproved of this religious syncretism. Whereas Helen Kim defended her mother's religious blending, Davis felt disappointed that so many converts in her village held on to a shamanism that filled them with "unreasonable" fears incompatible with the Christian faith.[133] The missionaries had responded to syncretism among Korean Protestants with increased biblical instruction. Davis preferred modern medicine. It would relieve suffering and replace shamanistic belief at the same time.[134]

"Would I Do It Again?" An older Davis, who titled a chapter of her book with this question, was not so sure. Though she loved her husband deeply, she recalled the prejudice she—and he—had to endure.[135] Though he had passed his ordination exams and demonstrated the highest level of ministerial competence, the Korean Methodist bishops refused to ordain Kim, for he had an American wife. Koreans had their own prejudices about interracial marriage. His religious superiors believed that Kim would be too distracted by his foreign wife's adjustment to Korea and that his lowly pastor's salary would not meet her extravagant needs.[136] Kim worked as a farmer, school teacher, and translator for the U.S. military during the Korean War.

In an evaluation of her husband's life, Davis wondered whether his "contribution to world Christianity" would have been greater if he had not married her.[137] But her commitment to her husband and Korea never wavered. During the hard years of the Korean War and its aftermath, Davis moved away from her husband to live in America. In 1961, she returned and the couple reunited on their farm in Susaek. After her husband's death, Davis taught English Bible classes in their Korean home until she died in 1986 at the age of eighty-five.[138]

Conclusion: The Agency of Korean Protestant Women and Their Tangled Relationships with American Missionaries in the (Re)Making of Indigenous Christian Womanhood

In 1958, Methodist missionary Sadie Maude Moore delivered an address at Ewha Womans University to congratulate Helen Kim for her groundbreaking work of educating and emancipating Korean women. Born on separate shores one month apart from each other, the two became close friends through their work in higher education. Moore arrived to Korea in 1924 and later taught at the Methodist Theological Seminary in Seoul and served as the English secretary for the Ewha Board of Trustees. She began her address by apologizing for her poor Korean language skills and speaking like a kindergartener despite her advanced age. The missionary then praised, in English, Kim's bright mind and vigorous health and, in Korean, her "*ingyeog* (special personality)" and "*haengbog* (good fortune)." She concluded with a story about Kim's strong faith.[139]

Three years later, Kim presented Moore with an honorary doctorate from Ewha, commending her as an exemplary educator who understood that the missionary's duty was "to work behind the scenes and identify with the nationals as cooperative fellow workers, giving friendship and counsel without showing authority or making demands."[140] The remarks hint at progress in relations between American and Korean Protestant women over time as the two groups learned to respect each other. But they do not erase the contentious history. For several decades, American and Korean women disagreed about matters of faith. They clashed over dress and behavior, actions, and dreams for a different life. The missionaries were breaking with their traditions and embracing new opportunities to lead, but they sought to prevent Koreans from making a similar break from a Western and conservative form of Christianity.

In the twentieth century, American Protestant missionaries around the world, including Korea, introduced "partnership" as a model for cooperative transnational religious endeavors. In his study of the relationships between Christians in the Global North and the Global South, Jonathan S. Barnes traces the reasons why the two parties struggled to find "concrete ways to live out mutuality and solidarity": The missionaries' concept of partnership partly resembled the Western colonial formation of "trusteeship," which imperial rulers employed to offer colonies some autonomy while maintaining their own power.[141] The main point to be made about the female missionaries in Korea is the most obvious one: They were Christians. Although they dealt with complicated matters of politics, education, and health care, they were primarily religious actors who believed that they were offering the promise of salvation by preaching the gospel and teaching God's word. This overriding evangelical intention meant that the missionaries had clear objectives but also narrow perspectives that led them to envision Korean women, no matter their age or ability, as daughters who required maternal protection in order to be faithful Christians. Although the missionaries publically proclaimed the ideals of equality and mutuality in their relations with Koreans—and many American women internally understood and sincerely sought these ideals—they could not move away from seeing themselves as trustees responsible for the development of Korean Protestant women.

One historian has argued that Western female missionaries in China at the turn of the twentieth century were most effective as agents of cultural transfer rather than evangelization, muting their religious influence.[142] Another historian has argued against the connection between American Protestant foreign missions and religious imperialism by pointing out that Americans were "almost always lousy at converting large numbers of non-Westerners."[143] However, in one of the few nations where they experienced success, American female missionaries could be identified as religious imperialists, in the sense that they endeavored to impress their Protestant vision of indigenous

Christian womanhood upon Koreans. In his study of the American Protestant foreign missionary enterprise, Arthur Schlesinger, Jr. determined political, sociological, and economic understandings of imperialism were not useful tools to analyze missionary ambitions and activities. He therefore proposed that "a cultural interpretation of imperialism" more accurately illumined the "purposeful aggression" of missionaries in their propagation of Christian ideas and systems in other countries.[144] Several scholars have identified American mission work for Korean women as a form of cultural colonialism.[145] In the absence of political power, which belonged firmly in the hands of the Japanese, American missionaries nonetheless had significant influence in shaping and directing Korean converts. But a closer look at American female missionaries in Korea demonstrates their main interest was to advance their religious beliefs, not Western cultural values.

Ryan Dunch observes that few discussions of cultural imperialism precisely define it but finds an "implicit definition along the following lines: certain cultural products (for example, socially-accepted beliefs, ideologies, entertainment commodities) have attained a position of dominance in a foreign culture through a process of coercive imposition, usually through their ties to political or economic power."[146] Applications of cultural imperialism inadequately convey the desires and designs of female missionaries in Korea. For these female missionaries, they wielded power in religious institutions distinct from the regnant political and economic orders. Because their main focus was Christianity, their engagement with Korean women—the multifarious impositions, inspirations, and tensions—is best understood with a religious interpretation of imperialism.

The missionaries' Protestant religious enthusiasm even led them to protect their converts from American culture. Some of the American women banished English from their school curriculums and forbade their students to wear Western clothing because they feared that the currents of modernity would sweep away the piety of Korean women. They desired to help "Koreans become better Koreans only."[147] But the underlying assumption was not hard to miss—Korean converts would lose their religious zeal if they absorbed Western ideas. In her work on Korean Bible Women, Christine Sungjin Chang contends the female missionaries' ideology of Christian womanhood "hindered female advance in Korean society" and created "real tension at times" between the two groups.[148]

Young-Iob Chung finds that American missionaries played a vital role in the modernization of Korea through their educational initiatives. Although the missionaries endeavored to emphasize Christianity in their pedagogy, the schools became "hotbeds of revolution and Westernization."[149] Missionaries were surprised when Koreans integrated Western ideas into their Christian beliefs and practices. The missionaries dressed and talked like Koreans to present Christianity as a Korean religion. But Korean Protestants adopted some American cultural, political, and economic ideas to fulfill their religious ambitions.

In their minds, the missionaries had constructed a beautiful template for Korean women to follow, but Koreans like Helen Kim had their own ideas about what it meant to be Christian women in their changing country. Attention to Korean Protestant women on their own terms—as "historical subjects" instead of "missiological objects"—recognizes their agency and creativity in remaking the religion with their own rituals and theologies.[150] Female missionaries determined that Western influences could corrupt the Korean Church, but Korean women decided for themselves how to combine certain Western elements like clothing and secular education with their cultural context.

But it is too simplistic to characterize the missionaries as agents of intolerance who cared only about advancing their religious agenda. They lamented the suffering of Koreans at the hands of foreign rulers and defended the rights of imprisoned Korean women. They established the first modern schools and hospitals in Korea and helped Koreans who desired to study in the United States.[151] The women's Bible institutes provided Korean Protestant women new opportunities to enter into the public sphere and biblical teaching became one of the first professional forms of female leadership in Korea.[152] Over time, a number of missionaries became self-critical about their own racism and spoke out against prevailing American preconceptions about Korean backwardness. They heard Korean criticisms, and some accepted them. In 1917 Kate Cooper asked her colleagues to consider how their condescending attitudes dishonored the ministry of Christ and distanced them from the people they had come to serve.[153]

The fractured relationships were part of a larger fissure between American missionaries and Korean Protestants in the age of Japanese imperialism. Koreans, men and women alike, were profoundly discouraged by the missionaries' political neutrality and paternalistic insistence that they knew what was best in Korean matters. They also resented how the missionaries created their own racially discriminatory community with superior houses and segregated schools. But as Koreans began to lead their own churches and schools, missionaries felt disappointment at Korean theological and political positions.

Like American Protestants, Koreans fell into doctrinal controversies between fundamentalist and modernist camps, debating rancorously about Moses's authorship of the Book of Genesis at the Presbyterian General Assembly in 1934. Conservative missionaries felt dismay when they met progressive Korean pastors. And the missionaries also felt a sense of trepidation when some Korean church leaders became interested in the possibilities of a socialist economic order. As much as the missionaries publicly declared their desires for autonomous Korean leadership, they still wanted to hold on to the keys to the kingdom for as long as they could.

In 1940, the missionaries finally ceded their claim to the Korean Church. They succumbed to geopolitical forces beyond their control. During the Second World War, all but a few missionaries followed the recommendation of the U.S. State Department that they leave the country. In 1945, Korea finally attained independence from Japan. But it then divided into two nations. Five years later, the United States would go to war in the Korean peninsula. Now the foreigners in Korea were predominantly soldiers, not missionaries. Koreans, whether at home or abroad, now came to know a diverse array of American Protestants who were not connected to mission work. New bonds would form, new challenges would arise, but some of the tensions between the first missionaries and the first converts, who had to learn to live together in a strange and fragmented set of relationships, would persist.

Notes

1. J.S. Ryang, "Chairman's Opening Address," in *Within the Gate: Addresses Delivered at the Semi-Centennial of the Methodist Church of Korea*, edited by Charles A. Sauer (Seoul, Korea: Y.M.C.A. Press, 1934), 1.
2. Charles August Sauer, *Methodists in Korea, 1930–1960* (Seoul, Korea: The Christian Literature Society, 1973), 27.
3. Helen Kim, "Methodism and the Development of Korean Womanhood," in *Within the Gate*, 82.
4. Annie Ellers Bunker, "Personal Recollections of Early Days," in *Within the Gate*, 63.
5. Henry Appenzeller, "Diary entry on April 22, 1887," in Henry Gerhard Appenzeller Papers, Missionary Research Library Collection, Burke Theological Library, Columbia University, New York, NY.
6. Huldah A. Haenig, "From West Gate to East Gate," *Woman's Missionary Friend* (January 1911), 11.
7. Ibid.
8. Frank Carpenter, "The Koreans at Home," *The Gospel in All Lands* (October 1889), 439.
9. Hyaeweol Choi, *Gender and Mission Encounters in Korea: New Women, Old Ways*, 47.
10. Theodore Jun Yoo, *The Politics of Gender in Colonial Korea: Education, Labor, and Health, 1910–1945*, 23.
11. Choi, 48.
12. Yoo, 23.
13. Mattie Wilcox Noble, "Diary entry on October 1, 1901," *The Journals of Mattie Wilcox Noble, 1892–1934*, 101.
14. Annie Baird, *Inside Views of Mission Life* (Philadelphia: Westminster Press, 1913), 19.
15. Choi, 77.
16. Lulu E. Frey, "The Bible Woman," *The Korea Mission Field* (March 1907), 42.
17. Appenzeller, "Notes on Women," in Henry Gerhard Appenzeller Papers, Missionary Research Library Collection, Burke Theological Library, Columbia University, New York, NY.
18. Appenzeller, "Help Those Women," in *The Appenzellers: How They Preached and Guided Korea into Modernization, Volume 1*, 357.
19. Annie Baird, *Daybreak in Korea: A Tale of Transformation in the Far East* (New York: Fleming H. Revell, 1909), 5.
20. *Suggestions to Leaders of Classes: Korea in Transition* (New York: Missionary Education Movement of the United States and Canada, n.d.), 23.
21. Baird, 12.
22. Baird, 12–17.

23. Ian R. Tyrrell, *Reforming the World: The Creation of America's Moral Empire*, 34–35.
24. Margaret Best, "Development of Work among Women," in *Quatro Centennial, Papers Read before the Korea Mission of the Presbyterian Church in the U.S.A. at the Annual Meeting in Pyeng Yang, August 27, 1909* (Seoul, Korea: 1909), 45–46.
25. Choi, 26–29.
26. Lillias Underwood, "Shall Married Women Have a Vote on Mission Matters," *The Korea Mission Field* (November 1912), 345–346. In the Presbyterian mission, single female and all male missionaries had full voting rights after passing the first-year Korean language test, but married female missionaries needed to pass the more rigorous third-year language test to vote. The mission was concerned that married women would simply duplicate their spouses' votes to create unfair majorities. See Choi, 27.
27. Best, 51.
28. In 1899, one female missionary in Pyongyang estimated that one in forty Korean women at her dispensary could read. See Choi, 66.
29. Of the ninety-three classes, seven were taught by missionaries and eighty-six were taught by Bible Women. See Best, 52.
30. Choi, 65–66.
31. Carol C. Chin also argues that American female missionaries in China at the turn of the twentieth century came "from a stratum of American society that placed a high value on cleanliness and godliness and at a time when Progressive reformers were focusing attention on public sanitation." See Carol C. Chin, "Beneficent Imperialists: American Women Missionaries in China at the Turn of the Twentieth Century," *Diplomatic History* 27 (June 2003), 334.
32. M.J. Edmunds, "Training Native Nurses," *The Korea Mission Field* (June 1906), 154.
33. Belle S. Luckett, "With the Missionaries' Children," *Woman's Work for Woman* (February 1916), 29.
34. Choi, 78.
35. J. Robert Moose, *Village Life in Korea* (Nashville and Dallas: Publishing House of the M.E. Church, South, Smith & Lamar, 1911), 235.
36. H.T. Owens, "Korea, the 'Permit' Nation," *The Missionary Survey* (December 1919), 728.
37. J.S. Gale, "A New Style of Courtship," *The Korea Mission Field* (April 1906), 119–120.
38. Cordelia Erwin, "Transition, a Korean Christian Wedding," *The Korea Mission Field* (April 1918), 73.
39. Owens, 728.
40. Best, 47.
41. Lulu E. Frey, "Higher Education for Korean Girls," *The Korea Mission Field* (October 1914), 308.
42. Grace Harmon McGary, "Higher Education for Women in Korea," *The Korea Mission Field* (August 1916), 214.
43. Annie L.A. Baird, "Higher Education of Women in Korea," *The Korea Mission Field* (April 1912), 115.
44. Hyung Gu Lynn, "Fashioning Modernity: Changing Meanings of Clothing in Colonial Korea," *Journal of International and Area Studies* 11:3 (2004), 77.
45. Huntley, *Caring, Growing, Changing: A History of the Protestant Mission in Korea*, 86.
46. Baird, *Inside Views of Mission Life*, 19.
47. Best, 47.
48. Yoo, 38.
49. Yoo, 39.

50. Yung-Chung Kim (ed.), *Women of Korea: A History of Ancient Times to 1945* (Seoul, Korea: Ewha Womans University Press, 1976), 154.
51. Yun Ch'iho, "The Sort of Education Korean Girls Need," *The Missionary Voice* (April 1918), 114.
52. Choi, 39.
53. Han-Kyo Kim, "The Japanese Colonial Administration in Korea: An Overview," in *Korea under Japanese Rule*, edited by Andrew C. Nahm (Western Michigan University: The Center for Korean Studies Institute of International and Area Studies, 1973), 50.
54. M. Tawara, "Letter to Annie Baird on August 10, 1909," in Annie Laurie Adams Baird Papers, RG172, Presbyterian Historical Society, Philadelphia, PA.
55. K. Usami, "Letter to H.H. Cynn on August 29, 1916," in General Commission on Archives and History, The United Methodist Church, Drew University, Madison, NJ.
56. Margaret Best, "Fifty Years of Women's Work," in *The Fiftieth Anniversary Celebration of the Korean Mission of the Presbyterian Church in the U.S.A., June 30–July 3, 1934* (Seoul, Korea: 1934), 89.
57. Helen Kim, *Grace Sufficient: The Story of Helen Kim* (Nashville: Upper Room, 1964), 31.
58. Ibid., 29.
59. Ibid.
60. Ibid.
61. Ibid., 30.
62. Alice Appenzeller, "Higher Education for Women," *The Korea Mission Field* (October 1918), 213.
63. Charlotte Bell Linton, "Letter to Family on October 31, 1924," in Presbyterian Church in the U.S. Korea Mission Records, RG444, Presbyterian Historical Society, Philadelphia, PA.
64. Helen Kim, "Namsŏng ŭi pansŏng ŭl ch'ok ham (Urging men to critically reflect on themselves)," *Sin yŏja* 4 (June 1920), in *New Women in Colonial Korea: A Sourcebook*, compiled and translated with an introduction by Hyaeweol Choi (London and New York: Routledge, 2013), 33.
65. Choi, 34.
66. Lynn, 79–87.
67. "Kkore p'i nŭn kongjak (Peacock with its tail feathers on display)," and "Mo-dŏn kkŏl ŭi changsin undong (Modern Girls' race for accessories)," *Chosŏn ilbo*, February 9, 1928 and February 5, 1928, in Choi, 83 and 85.
68. Yoo, 74–76.
69. Kim, "Nam yeo toron: Yŏja tanbal i ka hanga pul hanga (Is short hair good or bad?)," *Pyŏlgŏn'gon* 18 (January 1929), 128–133. See also Choi, 158–163.
70. Louise Yim, *My Forty-Year Fight for Korea* (New York: A.A. Wyn, 1951), 68.
71. Ibid.
72. Yim, 70. According to Yim, this protest occurred at a mission school during October 1915.
73. J. Gordon Holdcroft, "The Forward Look," in *The Fiftieth Anniversary Celebration of the Korean Mission of the Presbyterian Church in the U.S.A., June 30–July 3, 1934*, 208.
74. Eva Pieters, "Undated Report by Eva," *The Pieters in Korea*, 133. The report comes from the Pieters family's personal memory book (Pieters Family Archives, Presbyterian Historical Society, Philadelphia, PA).
75. Pil Ley Choi, "The Development of Korean Women during the Past Ten Years," *The Korea Mission Field* (November 1923), 223.
76. Donald N. Clark, *Living Dangerously in Korea: The Western Experience, 1900–1950*, 184.

77. Alice Appenzeller, "Letter to Moneta Saher on February 24, 1948," in Marion Lane Conrow Papers, General Commission on Archives and History, The United Methodist Church, Drew University, Madison, NJ.
78. Kangch'un Kim, "Yŏnae kaejoron (A thesis on the reform of romance)," in *Han'guk kŭndae yŏsŏng ŭi ilsang munhwa* [Everyday culture of Korean modern women, Volume 1], edited by Yi Hwa-hyŏng (Seoul, Korea: Kukhak Charyowŏn, 2004), 204. See also Hyaeweol Choi, *New Women in Colonial Korea*, 112–116.
79. Ibid.
80. Kim, *Grace Sufficient*, 7–8.
81. David Chung, *Religious Syncretism in Korean Society*, PhD diss., Yale University, 1959, 123. Chung's dissertation supervisor was H. Richard Niebuhr; he also acknowledged Roland Bainton, James M. Gustafson, Norvin Hein, and Kenneth S. Latourette as professors who guided him during his graduate studies at Yale University.
82. Kim, 12.
83. Kim, 34–35.
84. Kim, 12.
85. Yim, 34.
86. Induk Pahk, *September Monkey* (New York: Harper & Brothers, 1954), 65.
87. In the last years of the Japanese occupation (1941–1945), Kim collaborated with Japanese imperialists in order to keep the doors open at Ewha College. As the school's president, she read speeches at Ewha in support of Japanese war efforts during World War II. In her autobiography, Kim explained that Japanese government officials had composed the speeches and that her students knew that she did not mean what she said: "They were all good speeches from the Japanese standpoint, but I knew all the time that the girls were understanding my unspoken words." See Kim, 98.
88. Elaine H. Kim and Chungmoo Choi, "Introduction," in *Dangerous Women: Gender and Korean Nationalism*, edited by Elaine H. Kim and Chungmoo Choi (New York and London: Routledge, 1998), 2.
89. Helen Kim, *Grace Sufficient*, 59.
90. Helen Kim, *Rural Education for the Regeneration of Korea* (New York: Kim, 1931), 32–34.
91. Wonmo Dong, "Assimilation and Social Mobilization in Korea," in *Korea Under Japanese Rule*, 158–159.
92. "Miss H.K. Kim spoke on behalf of women in Korea," in *The Jerusalem Meeting of the International Missionary Council, March 24–April 8, 1928: The Christian Life and Message in Relation to Non-Christian Systems of Thought and Life, Volume 1* (New York City and London: International Missionary Council, 1928), 304.
93. Howard A. Bridgman, "As Missionaries View Their Growing World: At the Recent Jerusalem Conference Delegates From Many Countries Exchanged Views on Nationalism, Child Labor and Other Problems," *New York Times*, May 6, 1928. Helen Kim's picture accompanies Bridgman's article, with the caption, "A Delegate at Jerusalem: Miss Helen Kim, Dean of the Women's College at Seoul, Korea."
94. Ibid.
95. Mattie Wilcox Noble, "Diary entry on March 1, 1919," *The Journals of Mattie Wilcox Noble, 1892–1934*, 275.
96. Walter R. Lambuth, "A Korean Joan of Arc," in Walter R. Lambuth Papers, General Commission on Archives and History, The United Methodist Church, Drew University, Madison, NJ.
97. Pahk, 59.

98. "The Experience of a Korean Girl Under Arrest by the Japanese Police," in Esther and Jeanette Hulbert Papers, General Commission on Archives and History, The United Methodist Church, Drew University, Madison, NJ.
99. See *The Korean Situation: Authentic Accounts of the Recent Events by Eyewitnesses* (New York: The Committee on Relations with the Orient of the Federal Council of the Churches of Christ in America, 1919).
100. "Korea Needs You," in *North American Students and World Advance: Addresses Delivered at the Eighth International Convention of the Student Volunteer Movement for Foreign Missions, Des Moines, Iowa, December 31, 1919 to January 4, 1920*, edited by Burton St. John (New York: Student Volunteer Movement for Foreign Missions, 1920), 335.
101. Ibid.
102. Howard Thurman, *A Strange Freedom: The Best of Howard Thurman on Religious Experience and Public Life*, edited by Walter Earl Fluker and Catherine Tumber (Boston: Beacon Press, 1998), 138–139.
103. Thurman, 139.
104. Pahk, 169.
105. "Interview of Helen Kim by Laura Boulton, September 22, 1950," in Archives of Traditional Music, Indiana University, Bloomington, IN.
106. Martha Scott Bruen, "Personal Report, 1918–1919," in *40 Years in Korea*, edited by Clara Hedberg Bruen, 262.
107. Ellasue Wagner, "Personal letter on May 24, 1948," in Ellasue Wagner Collection, General Commission on Archives and History, The United Methodist Church, Drew University, Madison, NJ.
108. In 1934, most U.S. states had anti-miscegenation laws that banned interracial marriage. For example, Virginia passed the Racial Integrity Act of 1924, which criminalized marriage between white and non-white persons. In 1948, the California Supreme Court in *Perez v. Sharp* ruled that the state's anti-miscegenation law violated the Fourteenth Amendment of the Federal Constitution, becoming the first state court to declare its anti-miscegenation law as unconstitutional. It was not until 1967, when the U.S. Supreme Court in *Loving v. Virginia* ruled that Virginia's anti-miscegenation law was unconstitutional, that all U.S. states repealed anti-miscegenation laws. See Fay Botham, *Almighty God Created the Races: Christianity, Interracial Marriage, and American Law* (Chapel Hill: University of North Carolina Press, 2009), 1–5.
109. Homi Bhabha, *The Location of Culture* (New York: Routledge, 1994), 36–39.
110. Botham, 5.
111. Agnes Davis Kim, *I Married a Korean* (New York: The John Day Company, 1953), 10.
112. H.G. Appenzeller, "Woman's Work in Korea," *The Gospel in All Lands* (September 1891), 424.
113. Frank Carpenter, "The Koreans at Home," *The Gospel in All Lands* (October 1889), 439.
114. Elizabeth Watson, *Bringing Korea to Christ* (Nashville: Methodist Episcopal Church, South, 1938), 3.
115. Kim, 30.
116. Kim, 31.
117. James S. Gale's *The Vanguard: A Tale of Korea* (New York: Fleming H. Revell, 1904) and Lois Hawks Swinehart's *Jane of the Orient* (New York: Fleming H. Revell, 1924) are examples of fictive tales about romances between single missionaries in Korea. William Newton Blair's *Chansung's Confession* (Topeka, KS: H.M. Ives and Sons, 1959) and W. Arthur Noble's *Ewa: A Tale of Korea* (New York: Eaton & Mains, 1906) are examples of romances between Korean Protestants. Ellasue Wagner wrote an unpublished book, *The Concubine*, which presents a cautionary tale about how an American woman who "hates religion

and despises missionaries" struggles to adjust to Korean life after marrying an aristocratic Korean man (See "The Concubine Book Proposal," in Ellasue Wagner Collection, General Commission on Archives and History, The United Methodist Church, Drew University, Madison, NJ).
118. Kim, 229.
119. Kim, 58.
120. Marie Adams, "A Vacation in Korea," *Woman's Missionary Friend* (November 1939), 303.
121. Frank Herron Smith, "Letter on January 20, 1922," in Korea General Collection, Missionary Research Library Collection, Burke Theological Library, Columbia University, New York, NY.
122. Kim, 12–13, 55–66, 222–233.
123. Kim, 42.
124. "Pyongyang Foreign School Bill for Bruce F. Hunt, March 29, 1921," in Hunt Family Papers, Montgomery Library Archives, Westminster Theological Seminary, Philadelphia, PA.
125. J. Fairman Preston, "The Problem of the Primary Education of Missionaries' Children," *The Korea Mission Field* (March 1919), 51.
126. Bruce F. Hunt, "Letter to Parents on February 7, 1913 and January 18, 1918," in Hunt Family Papers, Montgomery Library Archives, Westminster Theological Seminary, Philadelphia, PA.
127. "Boys Entertain on Halloween," "Hurrah for the New Gym," "Pupils Begin School Routine," "School Spirit," and "P.Y.F.S Diary," *The Kum and Go* (November 1931), 1–4. The newsletter also reported that the school had 101 students and 14 teachers. One-fifth of the enrolled students were children of missionaries in China. In the 1930s, Ruth Graham, whose parents were missionaries in China, was enrolled at PYFS.
128. Stacy L. Roberts, Jr., My Memoirs, Presbyterian Historical Society, Philadelphia, PA.
129. Mary Ames Sharrocks, "The Influence of the Missionary's Home," *The Korea Mission Field* (April 1916), 99–102.
130. Roberts, *My Memoirs*.
131. Bhabha, 19–39.
132. Ch'oe Cha-sil, *Na nŭn hallelluya ajumma yŏtta* [Hallelujah Lady] (Seoul, Korea: Seoul Malssŭmsa, 1999), 190–196.
133. Kim, 104–105.
134. Kim, 102–110, 144–146.
135. Kim, 222.
136. Kim, 35–38.
137. Kim, 222.
138. Donald N. Clark, "Mothers, Daughters, Biblewomen, and Sisters: An Account of 'Women's Work' in the Korea Mission Field," in *Christianity in Korea*, edited by Robert E. Buswell Jr., and Timothy S. Lee (Honolulu: University of Hawaii Press, 2006), 189.
139. Sadie Maude Moore, "Congratulations, Dr. Kim, Ewha University, May 9, 1958," in Sadie Maude Moore Papers, 1928–1982, Archives and Manuscripts Department, Pitts Theology Library, Emory University, Atlanta, GA.
140. Helen Kim, "Tribute to Sadie Maude Moore, 1961," in Sadie Maude Moore Papers, 1928–1982, Archives and Manuscripts Department, Pitts Theology Library, Emory University, Atlanta, GA.
141. Jonathan S. Barnes, *Power and Partnership: A History of the Protestant Mission Movement* (Eugene, OR: Pickwick, 2013), 3–4.
142. Chin, 327–352.
143. Jay Riley Case, *An Unpredictable Gospel: American Evangelicals and World Christianity, 1812–1910* (Oxford and New York: Oxford University Press, 2012), 7.

144. Arthur Schlesinger, Jr., "The Missionary Enterprise and Theories of Imperialism," in *The Missionary Enterprise in China and America*, edited by John K. Fairbank (Cambridge: Harvard University Press, 1974), 363–373.
145. See Yoo, 10–12, and Yunseong Kim, "Protestant Missions as Cultural Imperialists in Early Modern Korea: Hegemony and its Discontents," *Korea Journal* 39:4 (1999), 205–233.
146. Dunch, 302.
147. "Notes from Korea," *The Gospel in All Lands* (August 1888), 373.
148. Christine Sunjin Chang, "Hidden but Real: The Vital Contribution of Biblewomen to the Rapid Growth of Korean Protestantism, 1892–1945," in *World Christianity: Critical Concepts in Religious Studies, Volume 2*, edited by Elizabeth Koepping (London and New York: Routledge, 2011), 240.
149. Young-Iob Chung, *Korea under Siege, 1876–1945: Capital Formation and Economic Transformation*, 45.
150. Kwok Pui-lan argues for an approach that treats indigenous Christian women as "historical subjects" instead of "missiological objects" to better understand their conversions to Christianity in their own contexts. See Kwok Pui-lan, "Chinese Women and Protestant Christianity at the Turn of the Twentieth Century," in *Christianity in China: From the Eighteenth Century to the Present*, edited by Daniel H. Bays (Stanford, CA: Stanford University Press, 1996), 194–208. Hyaeweol Choi endorses Kwok's approach in her work on modern Korean Protestant women. See Choi, *Gender and Mission Encounters in Korea: New Women, Old Ways*, 17–18.
151. Yunjae Park, "Between Mission and Medicine: The Early History of Severance Hospital," in *Encountering Modernity: Christianity in East Asia and Asian America*, edited by Albert L. Park and David K. Yoo (Honolulu: University of Hawaii Press, 2014), 140–161.
152. Lee-Ellen Strawn, "Protestant Bible Education for Women: First Steps in Professional Education for Modern Korean Women," *Journal of Korean Religions* 4:1 (April 2013), 99–121.
153. Kate Cooper, "The Peculiar Temptations of Missionaries," *The Korea Mission Field* (April 1917), 103–104.

Bibliography

Archives and Manuscript Collections

Archives and Manuscripts Department. Atlanta, GA: Emory University, Pitts Theology Library.

Archives of Traditional Music. Bloomington, IN: Indiana University.

General Commission on Archives and History. Madison, NJ: The United Methodist Church, Drew University.

Missionary Research Library Collection. New York, NY: Columbia University, Burke Theological Library.

Montgomery Library Archives. Philadelphia, PA: Westminster Theological Seminary.

Presbyterian Historical Society. Philadelphia, PA.

Books and Journal Articles

The Appenzellers: How They Preached and Guided Korea into Modernization, Volumes 1–2. Daejeon, Korea: Pai Chai University Press, 2010.

Baird, Annie L.A. *Daybreak in Korea: A Tale of Transformation in the Far East*. New York: Fleming H. Revell, 1909.

Baird, Annie L.A. *Inside Views of Mission Life*. Philadelphia: Westminster Press, 1913.

Barnes, Jonathan S. *Power and Partnership: A History of the Protestant Mission Movement*. Eugene, OR: Pickwick, 2013.

Best, Margaret. "Development of Work among Women." In *Quatro Centennial, Papers Read before the Korea Mission of the Presbyterian Church in the U.S.A. at the Annual Meeting in Pyeng Yang, August 27, 1909*. Seoul, Korea, 1909.

Best, Margaret. "Fifty Years of Women's Work." In *The Fiftieth Anniversary Celebration of the Korean Mission of the Presbyterian Church in the U.S.A., June 30–July 3, 1934*. Seoul, Korea, 1934.

Bhabha, Homi. *The Location of Culture*. New York: Routledge, 1994.

Blair, William Newton. *Chansung's Confession*. Topeka, KS: H.M. Ives and Sons, 1959.

Botham, Fay. *Almighty God Created the Races: Christianity, Interracial Marriage, and American Law*. Chapel Hill: The University of North Carolina Press, 2009.

Bruen, Clara Hedberg. *40 Years in Korea*.

Case, Jay Riley. *An Unpredictable Gospel: American Evangelicals and World Christianity, 1812–1910*. Oxford and New York: Oxford University Press, 2012.

Chang, Christine Sunjin. "Hidden but Real: The Vital Contribution of Biblewomen to the Rapid Growth of Korean Protestantism, 1892–1945." In *World Christianity: Critical Concepts in Religious Studies, Volume 2*, edited by Elizabeth Koepping. London and New York: Routledge, 2011.

Chin, Carol C. "Beneficent Imperialists: American Women Missionaries in China at the Turn of the Twentieth Century." *Diplomatic History* 27:3 (June 2003): 327–352.

Choi, Hyaeweol. *Gender and Mission Encounters in Korea: New Women, Old Ways*. Berkeley: University of California Press, 2009.

Choi, Hyaeweol, ed. *New Women in Colonial Korea: A Sourcebook*. London and New York: Routledge, 2013.

Clark, Donald N. *Living Dangerously in Korea: The Western Experience, 1900–1950*. Norwalk, CT: EastBridge, 2003.

Clark, Donald N. "Mothers, Daughters, Biblewomen, and Sisters: An Account of 'Women's Work' in the Korea Mission Field." In *Christianity in Korea*, edited by Robert E. Buswell Jr. and Timothy S. Lee. Honolulu: University of Hawaii Press, 2006.

Ch'oe, Cha-sil. *Na nŭn hallelluya ajumma yŏtta* [Hallelujah Lady]. Seoul, Korea: Seoul Malssŭmsa, 1999.

Chung, David. *Religious Syncretism in Korean Society*. PhD diss., Yale University, 1959.

Chung, Young-Iob. *Korea under Siege, 1876–1945: Capital Formation and Economic Transformation*. Oxford and New York: Oxford University Press, 2006.

Dong, Wonmo. "Assimilation and Social Mobilization in Korea." In *Korea under Japanese Rule*, edited by Andrew C. Nahm. Western Michigan University: The Center for Korean Studies Institute of International and Area Studies, 1973.

Dunch, Ryan. "Beyond Cultural Imperialism: Cultural Theory, Christian Missions, and Global Modernity." *History and Theory* 41:3 (October 2002): 301–325.

Fluker, Walter Earl and Catherine Tumber, eds. *A Strange Freedom: The Best of Howard Thurman on Religious Experience and Public Life*. Boston: Beacon Press, 1998.

Gale, James Scarth. *The Vanguard: A Tale of Korea*. Chicago and New York: Fleming H. Revell, 1904.
Holdcroft, J. Gordon. "The Forward Look." In *The Fiftieth Anniversary Celebration of the Korean Mission of the Presbyterian Church in the U.S.A., June 30–July 3, 1934*. Seoul, Korea, 1934.
Huntley, Martha. *Caring, Growing, Changing: A History of the Protestant Mission in Korea*. New York: Friendship Press, 1984.
International Missionary Council. *The Jerusalem Meeting of the International Missionary Council, March 24-April 8, 1928: The Christian Life and Message in Relation to Non-Christian Systems of Thought and Life, Volume 1*. New York City and London: International Missionary Council, 1928.
Kim, Agnes Davis. *I Married a Korean*. New York: John Day, 1953.
Kim, Elaine H. and Chungmoo Choi. "Introduction." In *Dangerous Women: Gender and Korean Nationalism*, edited by Elaine H. Kim and Chungmoo Choi. New York and London: Routledge, 1998.
Kim, Han-Kyo. "The Japanese Colonial Administration in Korea: An Overview." In *Korea under Japanese Rule*, edited by Andrew C. Nahm. Western Michigan University: The Center for Korean Studies Institute of International and Area Studies, 1973.
Kim, Helen. *Grace Sufficient: The Story of Helen Kim by Herself*. Nashville: The Upper Room, 1964.
Kim, Helen. "Methodism and the Development of Korean Womanhood." In *Within the Gate: Addresses Delivered at the Semi-Centennial of the Methodist Church of Korea*, edited by Charles A. Sauer. Seoul, Korea: Y.M.C.A. Press, 1934.
Kim, Helen. *Rural Education for the Regeneration of Korea*. New York: Kim, 1931.
Kim, Yung-Chung, ed. *Women of Korea: A History of Ancient Times to 1945*. Seoul, Korea: Ewha Womans University Press, 1976.
Kim, Yunseong. "Protestant Missions as Cultural Imperialists in Early Modern Korea: Hegemony and its Discontents." *Korea Journal* 39:4 (1999): 205–233.
The Korean Situation: Authentic Accounts of the Recent Events by Eyewitnesses. New York: The Committee on Relations with the Orient of the Federal Council of the Churches of Christ in America, 1919.
Kwok Pui-lan. "Chinese Women and Protestant Christianity at the Turn of the Twentieth Century." In *Christianity in China: From the Eighteenth Century to the Present*, edited by Daniel H. Bays. Stanford, CA: Stanford University Press, 1996.
Lynn, Hyung Gu. "Fashioning Modernity: Changing Meanings of Clothing in Colonial Korea." *Journal of International and Area Studies* 11:3 (2004): 75–93.
Methodist Episcopal Church Woman's Foreign Missionary Society. *Fifty Years of Light*. Seoul, Korea: The Society, 1938.
Moose, J. Robert. *Village Life in Korea*. Nashville: Publishing House of the M.E. Church, South, Smith & Lamar, 1911.
Noble, Mattie Wilcox. *The Journals of Mattie Wilcox Noble, 1892–1934*. Seoul, Korea: Han'guk Kidokkyo Yŏksa Yŏn'guso, 1993.
Noble, W. Arthur. *Ewa: A Tale of Korea*. New York: Eaton & Mains, 1906.
Pahk, Induk. *September Monkey*. New York: Harper & Brothers, 1954.
Park, Yunjae. "Between Mission and Medicine: The Early History of Severance Hospital." In *Encountering Modernity: Christianity in East Asia and Asian America*, edited by Albert L. Park and David K. Yoo. Honolulu: University of Hawaii Press, 2014.

Ryang, J. S. "Chairman's Opening Address." In *Within the Gate: Addresses Delivered at the Semi-Centennial of the Methodist Church of Korea*, edited by Charles A. Sauer. Seoul, Korea: Y.M.C.A. Press, 1934.

Schlesinger, Jr., Arthur. "The Missionary Enterprise and Theories of Imperialism." In *The Missionary Enterprise in China and America*, edited by John K. Fairbank. Cambridge: Harvard University Press, 1974.

St. John, Burton, ed. *North American Students and World Advance; Addresses Delivered at the Eighth International Convention of the Student Volunteer Movement for Foreign Missions, Des Moines, Iowa, December 31,1919, to January 4, 1920.* New York: Student Volunteer Movement for Foreign Missions, 1920.

Strawn, Lee-Ellen. "Protestant Bible Education for Women: First Steps in Professional Education for Modern Korean Women." *Journal of Korean Religions* 4:1 (April 2013): 99–121.

Suggestions to Leaders of Classes: Korea in Transition. New York: Missionary Education Movement of the United States and Canada, n.d.

Swinehart, Lois Hawks. *Jane of the Orient*. New York: Fleming H. Revell, 1924.

Tyrrell, Ian R. *Reforming the World: The Creation of America's Moral Empire.* Princeton: Princeton University Press, 2010.

Watson, Elizabeth. *Bringing Korea to Christ*. Nashville: Methodist Episcopal Church, South, 1938.

Yi, Hwa-hyŏng, ed. *Han'guk kŭndae yŏsŏng ŭi ilsang munhwa* [Everyday culture of Korean modern women, Volume 1]. Seoul, Korea: Kukhak Charyowŏn, 2004.

Yim, Louise. *My Forty-Year Fight for Korea*. New York: A.A. Wyn, 1951.

Yoo, Theodore Jun. *The Politics of Gender in Colonial Korea: Education, Labor, and Health, 1910–1945*. Berkeley: University of California Press, 2008.

Newspapers and Periodicals

The Gospel in All Lands
The Korea Mission Field
The Kum and Go
The Missionary Survey
The Missionary Voice
New York Times
Pyŏlgŏn'gon
Woman's Missionary Friend
Woman's Work for Woman

5 New Transnational Christian Partnerships and Shifting Power Dynamics in World Christianity during and after the Korean War

The Emergence of Korean Protestant Influence in the United States

Introduction

In 1960, the Presbyterian Church in the U.S. held its one hundredth General Assembly in Jacksonville, Florida. A Korean minister, Duk Hwan La, traveled to the gathering as a representative of the Presbyterian Church in his homeland. He thanked the Americans for their mission work in Korea. As commissioners from the U.S. southern states celebrated denominational growth, La asked them to also remember the historic relationship between American and Korean Presbyterians. He prayed that the two groups would continue to "bind together the strong ties of friendship" in the future.[1] The choice of words was telling. La's emphasis on friendship signaled an era in which the Americans and Koreans built partnerships marked by respect and reciprocity.

In the late nineteenth century, the first American missionaries arrived eager to evangelize Koreans and establish churches, hospitals, and schools. But encountering a culture and history entirely different from their own, missionaries found it hard to regard Koreans as their equals. The traditional clothing, mud-walled huts, and wooden rickshaws appeared primitive to their Western eyes. One missionary confessed that it was impossible for him and other Americans not to feel superior to Koreans because of the cultural and technological differences between the two peoples.[2]

But as Koreans began converting to Protestantism, American missionaries soon treasured Korea as one of their most promising foreign mission fields. Nearly a century before U.S. president George W. Bush identified North Korea together with Iraq and Iran as a tripartite "axis of evil,"[3] American missionaries lauded Pyongyang, the present-day capital of North Korea, as a wellspring of Christianity. They lauded not simply the "multiplicity of converts," but even more the "supreme faith and apostolic fervor of the believers," who served as an "inspiration to the entire Christian world."[4] After visiting the country in 1907, John R. Mott predicted that Korea would be the first nation in the non-Christian world to become a Christian nation. "I know of no mission field," Mott declared, "where larger or more substantial results have been secured, in proportion to the expenditure, than in Korea."[5]

Although Korean Protestants cultivated strong relationships with some American missionaries, Americans largely perceived the Korean Church as their foreign mission project rather than an equal partner in world Christianity. During the years of Japanese colonialism from 1910 to 1945, Koreans resented the missionaries' political neutrality, and Americans viewed the Korean independence movement as futile. They wanted Koreans to direct their energies toward religious expansion instead of colonial resistance.

As Koreans entered into a new stage of its national history after liberation in 1945, Korean Protestantism also began its emergence as a leading force in East Asian and world Christianities. During and after the Korean War, American Protestants looked at the Korean peninsula as a pivotal battlefield in the geopolitical clash between Communism and Christianity. The evolving relationships between Korean and American Protestants—from prominent ministers and missionaries to more common housewives and female students—illumine the origins of new Christian transnational partnerships and the shifting power dynamics in world Christianity as Koreans became religious allies and mentors to Americans. Koreans and Americans formed intimate friendships and institutional partnerships, and the Americans began to admit something that would have been hard for the first generation of missionaries to acknowledge: Despite a disturbing tendency toward conflict, Korean Christianity sometimes seemed more lively and compelling than the forms that prevailed in the United States. As Koreans began to see themselves as equal partners in ministry and more influential within their culture than American Protestants were in their own culture, some sought to reverse their relationships with Americans. They increasingly felt that their forms of faith were superior to American forms and considered it their mission to revive what they saw as an American Church in decline.

From Mission Field to Battlefield: New Global Threats and a New World Christian Presence

At the onset of the Korean War in 1950, the American public knew little about Korea except that their soldiers were fighting there against evil Communist forces. The American media followed a precedent familiar in the history of Western rhetoric during warfare: They depicted Western soldiers as "'professional,' 'confident,' 'loyal,' 'resolute,' and 'brave,'" in contrast to enemies who were "'brainwashed,' 'desperate,' 'blindly obedient,' 'ruthless,' and 'fanatical.'"[6] So Hanson W. Baldwin, the military editor of the *New York Times*, depicted the North Koreans as an "army of barbarians" and all Koreans as "simple, primitive, and barbaric peoples" who needed to be instructed that U.S. forces, not the Communists, were their friends on the battlefield.[7]

Letters written during the war sometimes captured the mood of hostility: Koreans were "bastards" and "the world's worst bunch of cutthroats."[8] American soldiers found the country drab and desolate, surrounded by hostile Communists in China and the Soviet Union and cursed by bad roads and frigid winters.[9] One of them found Korea "strange and unworldly, as if I had been dropped on another planet." Another had a more graphic response: "Look at this shit hole. Why are we over here fighting for this?"[10] Letters from soldiers expressed pity for beggars and orphans, who pestered them for candy and cigarettes, and they complained about Korean barbers and cooks who stole from soldiers in the camps. "Trust and honesty were not apparent morals in Korea," wrote one soldier. "The desperate, displaced people took what they could, robbing, stealing, commandeering anything in order to survive."[11] Soldiers typically referred to all Koreans as "gooks," a term that probably came from American usage in the Philippines and then the Pacific War. In Korea, it represented the namelessness of both North Korean enemies and South Korean allies.[12] As Secretary of State Dean Acheson recalled: "If the best damn minds in the world had set out to find us the worst possible location to fight this damnable war politically and militarily, the unanimous choice would be Korea."[13]

In contrast, at least some American missionaries, who had cultivated friendships with Koreans for decades, insisted that Koreans were a dignified people ensnared in a war not of their own making. They criticized their government for agreeing to the division of Korea and then mishandling the occupation. In 1945, the U.S. government wanted to establish its presence in South Korea quickly, so it selected General John R. Hodge to lead the occupation because his forces were nearby in Japan. Hodge, an effective officer on the battlefield, had little knowledge of Korea and little skill in governing. Initially, U.S. authorities ordered South Koreans to obey the Japanese Governor-General and his seventy thousand Japanese officials, but Korean protests led to a gradual removal of the Japanese from the country. Fearful of Communist infiltration, American generals and diplomats distrusted local Korean gatherings. They lacked translators and interpreters and struggled to understand the competition for power among South Korean leaders.[14]

While American officials complained about the Koreans' inability to govern themselves, Methodist missionary Thoburn T. Brumbaugh argued that Koreans could become a "rampart in the advance of Christian democracy" if the United States gave them more effective help.[15] He noted that hundreds of thousands of Korean Protestants had worked with American missionaries to sustain their churches against Japanese suppression.[16] Presbyterian missionary William Newton Blair wrote that Korean believers had withstood "the fires of continued suffering and loss" and proven that they were up to the task of democratic self-rule.[17]Another Presbyterian complained privately that American officials were not supporting Korean political and economic initiatives. Instead, they treated Koreans as "a doormat on which everybody rubs their feet" and gave them few opportunities to lead.[18]

Missionaries challenged Western perceptions of Korean ineptitude by recalling how Korean Protestants resisted Japanese mandates. Beginning in 1935, the Japanese forced Koreans to bow before Shinto shrines and pledge loyalty to the emperor. The Japanese insisted that this was merely a civic act, but a number of missionaries and Koreans refused, on religious grounds, to participate. In 1936, the Vatican agreed that the ceremony was civic, as did the Korean Methodist Church, and Presbyterian missionary Horace H. Underwood maintained that it was no more religious than American rituals at the Lincoln Memorial or the Tomb of the Unknown Soldier.[19] But most of Underwood's Presbyterian colleagues disagreed. The northern and southern missions closed their schools rather than acquiesce in compulsory Shinto ceremonies. After imperial officials coerced the Korean Presbyterian Church in 1938 to accept the policy, recalcitrant Koreans either went to prison or fled to Manchuria.[20] Some Americans also suffered. In 1941, imperial authorities jailed two Presbyterian missionaries for removing Shinto shrines from their Korean servants' homes.[21] But the resistance ultimately drew favorable attention from American Protestants. A writer in *The Christian Century* surmised that "the long years" of suffering under "the cruel power of the Japanese army" had deepened the faith of Korean Protestants; he lifted them up as spiritual exemplars for the world Christian community in the global struggle against Communism.[22]

Underwood further criticized American perceptions of Koreans as primitive and barbaric, explaining that they possessed a quiet pride that Americans misunderstood as passivity. He recognized all too well that "like men all over the world, the Korean has faults. He can be cruel, he can be selfish, he can become insanely angry, he is too prone to be cliquish and to split union movements wide open with schism and divisions."[23] A year before the war, young Korean Communists had murdered Underwood's wife, Ethel, after they broke into the Underwood home to attack her guest, Mo Yunsuk, a poet who worked with the United Nations.[24] But Underwood still described Koreans as "sincere and zealous in [their] Christian faith," and fully able to rebuild their nation.[25]

Kyung-Chik Han: Mighty Pastor in Korea and Noble Example for the West

One of Underwood's Korean friends was renowned Presbyterian minister Kyung-Chik Han. Han was born in Pyongyang in 1902 and first met Presbyterian missionaries there as a child. He attended a mission school and worked as a secretary and translator for several missionaries. While accompanying one missionary couple, William and Annie Baird, on a vacation to Sorae Beach in 1923, Han, who was studying to become a chemist, had a religious experience in which he prayed in tears as he heard God's voice beckoning him to preach the gospel.[26] William Baird arranged for Han to study in Kansas at the College of Emporia. After graduating, Han attended Princeton Theological Seminary from 1926 to 1929 before returning to work as an instructor, pastor, and orphanage director in northern Korea. In 1945, he fled from the north and founded Young Nak Presbyterian Church in Seoul. By 1971, the church had twelve thousand members and was the largest Presbyterian congregation in the world.[27]

As his church grew, U.S. chaplains, evangelists, missionaries, soldiers, and statesmen made it a point to visit. In the 1950s, Han welcomed John Foster Dulles, Billy Graham, E. Stanley Jones, Bob Pierce, and two Chiefs of Chaplains of the U.S. Army to speak from his pulpit.[28] *The Christian Century* editor Harold E. Fey visited Han's church in 1951 and marveled at the spiritual vibrancy of the worship with the "close participation by all sorts and conditions of men and women in each phase of the service."[29] The following December, Billy Graham joined with Han to host revival meetings at Han's church.[30] Han also befriended Bob Pierce, served as his translator during one of Pierce's evangelistic tours, worked with him in providing relief to widows and orphans, and helped him organize the first World Vision humanitarian programs.[31] These leading American Protestants looked to Han as an exemplary pastor. Their admiration was an early sign of the evolving relationships between the two groups. Korean church leaders like Han saw themselves as equal partners with Americans in transnational ministries. And some Americans increasingly looked to Korean Christianity as a source to revitalize their own institutions and congregations at home.

During the war, Pierce published a book on "The Untold Korea Story." He explained that neither the religious nor the secular press had told Americans about the wonder of Korean Protestantism. Pierce described the passion Koreans exhibited in worship services from dawn to dusk. He depicted Presbyterians at Han's church praying aloud, weeping and shouting, and he said that he had never seen anything like it in the United States except among Pentecostals. Pierce also viewed Koreans more favorably than the Japanese Christians he had visited, who were "shot through with modernism and higher criticism."[32] In contrast, the Koreans he had met held fast to conservative theological beliefs. Pierce had found in the Korean Church a modern-day example of Christian expansion that confirmed the potency and relevance of his own evangelicalism.

Pierce called Han a "Korean saint," praising his preaching, piety, and humanitarian work among war refugees. Han's daily pastoral activities, which occupied as many as eighteen hours a day, would, Pierce thought, topple any American clergyperson.[33] And because he had met so many others like Han, Pierce wrote that complacent American Christians had much to learn from Koreans. In 1959, he pointed to his religious experiences with Korean Protestants as one of the reasons why "Korea is so close to the hearts of all the World Vision people."[34] In 1975, Han paid tribute to Pierce as an honored guest speaker at the twenty-fifth anniversary of World Vision in Los Angeles. Han treasured his friendship with Pierce and considered him "a true servant of Jesus Christ who loved his neighbors as himself," wherever they might live.[35]

Both U.S. mainliners and evangelicals admired Han not only for his religious successes but also for his anti-Communism. Reinhold Niebuhr's *Christianity and Crisis* and its liberal editorial board, which included the ethicist Liston Pope and the dean of Union Seminary in New York, Henry Sloane

Coffin, had advocated the use of U.S. military force in Korea to thwart Communism.[36] In *The Christian Century*, Fey argued that Korea presented "ultimate issues" in the "life-and-death struggle" between "Christ and communism."[37] On the evangelical side, Billy Graham and Bob Pierce also supported resistance to Communism in Korea. Pierce's observation echoed many others: "It took G.I. blood to inform most Americans—including a good many evangelical Christians—that the peninsular nation of Korea is one of great significance in the confused pattern of present-day world history."[38]

As a stalwart in the Christian struggle against Communism, Han became an inspiration to Americans. Before he fled to Seoul in 1945, he had opposed Communism in northern Korea. Because he had suffered persecution and witnessed atrocities against Christians, Americans viewed him as an authority on the ideological battle. In 1961, Carl F. Henry published an interview in which Han detailed how he and another pastor escaped imprisonment by walking over mountain paths for fifty miles through the night to cross the thirty-eighth parallel into South Korea. But Han also told Henry—and Henry's readers in *Christianity Today*—how North Korean forces occupying Seoul had seized five hundred Christian leaders and massacred them in North Korean prisons.[39] Henry asked Han what lesson the world Christian community needed to learn. Han gave the answer that Henry expected: "Well, we must tell to all Christians who are living in the free world that as long as Communists remain in power in any country, Christian activities will almost be impossible. That doesn't mean you can't have Christian faith."[40] Han held literal views of the second coming of Christ, and he encouraged believers, especially in Communist countries, to "fight the good fight of faith and give everything we have for the cause of Christ," bolstered by the confidence that Jesus could return at any time.[41]

In 1966, Billy Graham introduced Han as a speaker at the World Congress on Evangelism in Berlin. Evangelicals viewed the meeting, which was sponsored by *Christianity Today* and the Billy Graham Evangelistic Association, as a successor of the 1910 World Missionary Conference in Edinburgh and a showplace for the growth of evangelicalism in Africa, Asia, and Latin America. Twelve hundred participants, including three hundred Roman Catholic and Jewish observers, met to discuss how Christians across the globe could work together in world mission.[42] Han spoke on the same day as John R.W. Stott of All Souls Church in England and Harold John Ockenga of Park Street Church in the United States, two celebrities of the Western evangelical world.[43] He talked there about Christian growth in Korea as a continuation of earlier European and American movements. And he gratified evangelicals by telling them how important they had been to Koreans. They had overcome impossible obstacles to teach the gospel to his people. Now the Koreans were creating churches admired throughout the Christian world. The Christians at the Congress needed a "worldwide missionary vision and strategy" to contest the threat of Communism—a fount of "atheism, materialism, and totalitarianism"—and resist the forces of secularism throughout every continent.[44] The implication was that the example of Korean Christians could provide a model.

At his church in Seoul, Han preached on these themes. He claimed that the same Holy Spirit that appeared at the Pentecost event recorded in Acts 2 also appeared in the 1907 revivals, using them to expand the church. It was no coincidence, he added, that in the days before the revival "missionaries at that time, both Presbyterian and Methodist, frequently and ecumenically gathered to pray for God's grace to bless Korea."[45] He also told his Korean congregation that the Korean Church understood Jesus's instruction on persecution in the Beatitudes because of their struggle against Japanese imperialism and Communism:

> In fact, I know that there are those among us, during the Japanese occupation and afterwards under the Communist regime, who were not only insulted, persecuted, and falsely accused of being evil, but also as Jesus says here those who literally lost their houses, lost their hometown, lost their parents, brothers, sisters, wives, and even their land. Furthermore, among you are those severely tormented in prison and those who survived a narrow escape from a gunshot. Jesus says to all who suffer and are persecuted for the sake of their faith, "Rejoice and be glad, because great is your reward in heaven, for in the same way they persecuted the prophets who were before you (Matthew 5:12)."[46]

Such experiences, he explained elsewhere, were a sign of "God's providence to entrust the mission of preaching the gospel of Christ to all the one billion peoples in East Asia through us Korean people."[47] Han appreciated his American friends, but he insisted that now Koreans needed to create their own methods of expanding the mission.

The end of the Korean War found some American missionaries ambivalent about themselves and baffled not only by the successes but also the demands and divisions of the Korean churches. They praised Korean Protestants but worried about what seemed to be a sudden proclivity toward schism, generated by theological disputes, ecumenism, and issues of church discipline. After the liberation, Korean Protestants had to make decisions about church leaders who had complied with the imperial law and participated in Shinto ceremonies. The issue hit the Presbyterians especially hard, and in 1952 hard-line Presbyterian resisters formed their own denomination rather than worship with compromisers.[48] Presbyterians divided again after conservatives complained that participation in the World Council of Churches (WCC) sullied the church with liberalism.[49] The Americans found the discord unsettling. The churches were growing beyond all expectation, but at the same time they were unable to speak with a united voice. One experienced missionary, Samuel Hugh Moffett, said that Koreans were dishonoring the name of Christ with their acrimony and disunity: "Where else, in the world, for example, is there a Jesus Presbyterian Church and a Christ

Presbyterian Church, and neither in fellowship with the other? Is Jesus Christ divided?"[50]

American foreign missionaries throughout the world grappled over questions about their influence with the emergence of indigenous Christian leadership after the Second World War. One historian connects these missionary discussions to broader public discourse about American foreign policy. Just as Americans supported the rights of people abroad to make their own decisions while maintaining that they knew what was best for the rest of the world, missionaries also held a paradoxical understanding of their own work.[51] Missionaries in South Korea welcomed the autonomy of Korean Protestants, but they also wanted to retain power in the institutions they had founded. In 1956, Korean Presbyterians demanded oversight over where American missionaries were sent in South Korea as part of their pursuit for full autonomy. The northern Presbyterian mission agreed to consult with Koreans about mission strategies but refused to cede their control over the decision-making process. The southern Presbyterian mission was unwilling to budge on their stance that consultations with Korean members were unnecessary.[52]

In his work on Western missionaries throughout the Global South, Scott W. Sunquist argues that their public "rhetoric of 'fully independent' churches and 'full partnership' among them" did not match their private thinking in the 1950s and the 1960s.[53] In reality, many missionaries questioned whether indigenous leaders could govern over churches, hospitals, schools, and other complex institutions by themselves. The correspondence between two southern Presbyterian missionaries in 1957 unveils the reasons for their refusal to grant Koreans more control. Both missionaries endorsed the impulse to empower indigenous churches to make their own decisions, but they expressed doubts over whether their Korean partners could be trusted on two matters: managing financial budgets that included large American contributions and navigating ecumenical relations with the more liberal parties in the world Christian community.[54] One of them confessed that their mission was not "infallible" and may have been too slow in recognizing the "judgment and ability" of Korean Protestant leaders. But he nonetheless believed Americans should continue to supervise the Korean churches because the missionaries were like the "wise parent" guiding a child through "later adolescent experiences." He expressed deep affection for the Korean Church and asked if their situation was akin to the "growing pains" every family encounters—even parents and children in the most stable and devoted family systems—as teenagers mature into adults.[55]

These missionaries continued to see themselves as parental figures despite repeated calls from both Korean Protestants and the American mission boards to embrace new models of equal partnership. After the Second World War, northern Presbyterians began self-identifying as "fraternal workers" instead of as "missionaries" to signal their intentions to minister alongside Christian nationals as mutual allies.[56] But even as late as 1964, southern

Presbyterians balked at the change to "fraternal worker" and insisted that the term "missionary" best described their soul-saving vocation in Korea.[57]

A more public disagreement illustrating the escalating tensions between American missionaries and Korean leaders occurred at Yonsei University in 1960. Methodist missionary Charles A. Sauer chaired the board of directors of the prestigious institution when the board dismissed two South Korean faculty members and selected Horace G. Underwood, a descendant of one of the school's founders, to serve as acting president. Students and faculty alike resented the decisions. At violent demonstrations, some students demanded that the missionaries go back to America—waving signs that read "Take Your Dictatorship to Your Country, Underwood" and other placards that conveyed similar sentiments.[58] The unrest produced a confrontation with the police after students attempted to raid the homes of Sauer and Underwood.[59]

In 1961, Moffett addressed the future of mission work in postwar Korea. He acknowledged the missionaries had to adapt to a new situation. They needed to be aware of the tangled history of Western missions and colonialism in order to divorce themselves from "political imperialism, dollar diplomacy, cultural aggression and ecclesiastical paternalism."[60] But he bristled at the notion that the Koreans no longer required missionaries. Because the Koreans were a "younger church," the missionaries still provided invaluable counsel as more experienced Christians who had overcome many of the obstacles that the Koreans would face. Instead of feeling "crippled with a guilt complex" about their "foreignness" and "incomplete indigenization," missionaries were to use their American identities—just as Paul used his Roman citizenship—to be both prophet and partner, instructing with authority while cooperating with respect.[61]

Han and Moffett were close friends, but the two men had slightly different assessments of what was happening and what should happen in the Korean Church. Moffett accepted the need for indigenous leadership, but he wanted Americans to retain authority as mentors. Moffett especially wanted Americans to instruct Koreans about methods that had worked in America. Han, however, wanted Koreans to learn from American mistakes. Missionaries like Moffett were obsessed with what they saw as a disturbing Korean inclination toward division, yet they failed to acknowledge the same schismatic impulse was no less true about Protestantism in the United States. As a student at Princeton Seminary, Han had seen the faculty divide between fundamentalists and modernists. The experience predisposed Han to favor ecumenical cooperation. Like other conservatives, he worried about liberalism in the WCC, but he endorsed Korean Presbyterian membership as a means to participate in its global Christian community.

In a letter to American Presbyterians in 1956, Han explained the reasons behind the divisions within Korean Presbyterianism and the recent departures of the fundamentalist "Koryu" *(Goryeo)* group and the more liberal "Chosun" *(Joseon)* group from the larger Church. But Han also made clear that he was not asking for help. These challenges comprised "an internal problem" for Han and his Korean colleagues to resolve. Han's motivation for writing was to simply provide a "clear summary" of the Korean situation to prevent "any misunderstanding or twisting of the facts" among "our sister churches abroad."[62] Han's tone was gracious yet assertive—his letter expressed appropriate appreciation for his American partners but ultimately conveyed the message that Korean Presbyterians would discover their own solutions apart from the missionaries.

Han's combination of ecumenism and evangelicalism won endorsements from mainline and evangelical Protestants in the United States, but also demonstrated the ways in which both groups continued to project their agendas upon Korean Protestants. Mainline Protestants blamed the mission boards for the fighting among Koreans, complaining that they continued to send denominational missionaries who competed for converts and refused to cooperate with each other.[63] *The Christian Century* challenged the missionaries to "follow the example of the Koreans and work together on plans that have as their goal the best interests of the Kingdom in Korea rather than the best interests of any particular denomination."[64] Conversely, evangelicals suggested that Americans could learn from the daybreak prayer meetings at churches like Han's throughout South Korea. One evangelical missionary used the Korean example to rebuke lukewarm American Protestants and especially women: "While the American Church is giving up its mid-week prayer meeting, the Korean Church takes up pre-dawn prayer . . . it is amazing to witness the uninhibited public prayer of these believing women in open meetings. They put far to shame their supposedly advanced and emancipated sisters of the west."[65] Korean successes, he added, vindicated the traditional missionary methods of proselytism and biblical instruction above newer approaches that emphasized cultural exchange and social work.[66]

Evangelical missionaries had long insisted the steady growth of the Korean Church provided substantive evidence in support of their methods. In 1905, Samuel Austin Moffett counseled new Presbyterian missionaries to resist the temptation of prioritizing the ample physical needs of the persons they encounter over evangelism. He underscored the primary and most important work of Christian mission was spiritual conversion and not social uplift: "We are not commissioned to introduce Western civilization, but Scriptural Christianity. Another vital distinction to be made is that *education is not regeneration*."[67] At an event in 1934 celebrating fifty years of Presbyterian mission in Korea, Moffett and his colleagues were particularly attentive to the release of the Laymen's Report on U.S. foreign missions two years prior, in which a fifteen-member commission led by Harvard professor William Ernest Hocking proposed more collaborative approaches to Christian witness that emphasized interreligious dialogue and philanthropic aspects such as medical and educational endeavors over direct evangelism.[68] Instead of "rethinking missions," the title of the Laymen's Report, Presbyterian missionaries in Korea sharply criticized the report's findings in 1933 as contradictory to their experience on the mission field and charged that following the report's recommendations would lead to widespread mayhem and confusion in the Korean churches. Of the 84 missionaries who voted on the Laymen's Report, 82 rejected its conclusions.[69] In his address at the fiftieth anniversary celebration of the Korea mission, Moffett unequivocally maintained the "unique and preeminent place given to instruction in the Scriptures as the very word of God has been the outstanding factor through these fifty years in the evangelization of Korea."[70]

Missionaries in Korea further responded to Hocking's report with analysis of their increasing numbers of converts in comparison to much lesser gains in China and Japan. *Re-Thinking Missions* found the lack of mission success in the two countries, citing significant indigenous resistance to Christianity among non-Christians and pervasive in-fighting over theological controversies among Christians, as evidence of the need for new and alternative approaches.[71] Statistics from the Presbyterian Church in the U.S.A. revealed the significantly higher rates of growth in Korea over Japan. In 1895, there were 57 missionaries and 11,126 communicants in Japan compared to 28 missionaries and 236 communicants in Korea.[72] Forty years later, there were 63 missionaries and 54,006 communicants in Japan compared to 141 missionaries and 108,392 communicants in Korea.[73] Charles Allen Clark argued that Christianity expanded more rapidly in Korea than in China or Japan because the missionaries unwaveringly adhered to Nevius's principles: "missionary personal evangelism with wide itineration" and the creation of self-propagating, self-governing, and self-supporting indigenous churches.[74] Clark explained how the American mission in China rejected Nevius's ideas in favor of recommendations akin to Hocking's "liberal" proposals. In contrast, missionaries in Korea succeeded precisely because they adopted Nevius's principles and upheld "the conservative type of theology."[75] According to Clark, the solution to the problems in foreign mission fields in China and Japan was in Korea—more specifically the Presbyterian mission there—and not in Hocking's report.

Two decades after the Laymen's Report, the two competing American factions now had conflicting explanations of Korean Christian expansion and the emergence of large churches like Young Nak Presbyterian Church under Han's leadership. In 1958, *The Christian Century* explained that "the reasons for the proportionately large growth of Protestantism are elusive" but warned against attributing it simply to noble American missionaries. The mainline journal pointed instead to the combination of evangelism and ecumenism in most of the Korean churches.[76] The evangelical *Christianity Today*, by contrast, emphasized how "the names of Allen, Underwood, Appenzeller, Moffett and Baird" had become "an inseparable part of the history of modern Korea."[77] Revising history, the editors claimed that the missionaries helped plan the Korean independence movement and March 1919 demonstrations, conveniently forgetting that the political events had caught the Americans by surprise and that some missionaries had prevented their Korean students from participating.[78] The moral of the story, for

Christianity Today, was that liberal critics of evangelical foreign missions were wrong: "In a day when some critics are morbidly proclaiming the demise of foreign missions it is refreshing to have this further confirmation of the power of the Gospel in changing men's lives and elevating the standing of human society."[79]

L. Nelson Bell, Billy Graham's father-in-law, later asserted that "there is no church in the world more conservative in theology than the Korean Presbyterian Church" and that Presbyterian missionaries likewise "have for generations been as one in their allegiance to the historic evangelical faith."[80] In 1961, John Coventry Smith, secretary of the United Presbyterian Church in the U.S.A. Commission on Ecumenical Mission and Relations, argued that the unique concentration of theologically conservative missionaries in Korea had simultaneously contributed to the growth and the divisiveness of Korean Presbyterians. He criticized mission policies like strict adherence to inerrantist understandings of the Bible "that sought to protect national leaders from new ideas" because they left the Korean Church unprepared "to meet the criticisms of the more liberal Christian faith" that were a part of global ecumenical conversations.[81]

Han's American friends used him to support their positions on economics, ecumenism, evangelism, and theology. They often overlooked the nuances of his anti-Communism, forgetting that he not only criticized Communism but also insisted that the gospel transcended every human economic order, including capitalism. Christians were to criticize every social order, and Korean believers had a duty to "criticize and struggle with the defects and shortcomings of capitalism" in order to remake their society according to the biblical principles of justice and mercy.[82] This did not mean, however, that the Marxists had it right. Although Christianity, like socialism, stood in favor of the "laborers and farmers rather than the bourgeoisie class," Marxists wrongly sought social revolution solely through changes in the means of production.[83] They reduced the dignity of human beings by stressing only their social location and mistakenly saw religion as an opiate that "dulls the painful reality of the worker."[84]

A Methodist Minister's Wife Befriends Two South Korean Women in North Georgia

On September 30, 1948, Etta Pursely Barton, a Methodist minister's wife, met two female Korean students, Chungil (Gail) Choo and Chinsook (Sue) Kwon, at the Georgia State College for Women in Milledgeville. Barton was a fifty-year-old woman teaching Sunday School to young adults, and she invited college women to her church. She and her husband, J. Hamby Barton, had lived in the town since his appointment to Milledgeville's First Methodist Church in 1945. Choo and Kwon were among the first Korean students to come to the United States after the liberation. Dressed in traditional clothing, a long, colorful skirt and short jacket, the two Korean women were reticent and apprehensive. Barton asked them if they were Christians; they told her that they were followers of Confucius. Barton welcomed them to her church, and the three women began a friendship encompassing over forty years. Barton did not hesitate to say that she learned more about the world from her two friends than she ever taught them.

In the United States, Choo and Kwon converted to Methodism, graduated from the college, and completed graduate studies in Tennessee before returning to South Korea in the last months of the war. Choo then taught in the College of Education at Seoul National University and Kwon worked in public health as a nutritionist. In 1950, two years after meeting the two Korean women, Barton began a foundation that provided financial aid for foreign students in the United States. Barton's friendship with Choo and Kwon influenced her actions; it also propelled her work against anti-Asian racism in the American South and expanded her religious vision. Barton explained that she did not go to Korea, but that Korea had come to her in the form of the two students: "They have broadened our horizon and deepened our faith so we give thanks to God for sending Korea to us."[85]

When the two students arrived in 1948, the registrar's office asked Barton to meet them. Barton had become a maternal figure to many of the students, who referred to her as "Ma Barton."[86] Choo and Kwon were among the two hundred students sent to the United States by the South Korean government to study and receive training as prospective leaders. Unlike many earlier students from Korea, Choo and Kwon did not come from mission schools. Choo's closest interaction with an American had occurred when she ran away from an U.S. soldier in Korea who whistled at her, but she was overjoyed to be selected to study in the West.[87]

Though they were not Christian, Choo and Kwon frequently went to Barton's church. Barton taught there about international relations and global justice from books like Stringfellow Barr's *Let's Join the Human Race* (1950), advancing Barr's notions of cross-cultural partnerships and global neighbors.[88] Barton's religious persuasions reflected currents within mid-twentieth-century American Methodism as it evolved into a "responsible world political organization promoting peace with justice."[89] She took the two Koreans to Methodist student conferences throughout Georgia not only to expose Choo and Kwon to Christian students but also to introduce American students to a wider world. She invited the two Koreans to spend time with her family for Christmas, along with two Chinese students and five Korean students from other colleges in Georgia.[90]

Nine months after Choo and Kwon visited Barton's church, they converted to Christianity. When she was baptized, Choo spoke publicly of her conversion: "I came to America wanting to learn only two things, your scientific achievements and your economic success. But I have learned that you have something much more valuable to give. That is your Christian philosophy of life."[91] Sixteen years after her conversion, Choo described the Bartons as "true Christians" who were "devoted to their religion and to the belief in [the] brotherhood of all mankind." It impressed her that they opened their home to foreign students every Christmas, and she credited them with enlarging her vision of the world in "a quiet loving way, and not in a preaching way."[92]

Choo's account unveiled a difference from the experience of some of the earlier Korean students in the United States. After studying in mission schools, those students had embraced Christianity as a religion of hope and liberation but some ended up deploring the racism of Americans and eventually the paternalism of the missionaries. The *Korean Student Bulletin* decried missionary literature that featured intrepid white Americans saving uncouth Koreans. One student insisted that missionary literature contributed to racism in the West: "We wonder who will solve the vexing problem of our racial prejudice which our present day missionaries pour into the formative minds of young Americans through tales such as this."[93] In contrast, Choo and Kwon experienced the Bartons as parental figures—their "American parents"—who related to them without paternalism.

When the two Korean women received scholarship aid to study at the University of Tennessee but lacked the funds for board and books, Barton appealed to several foundations, had no success, and decided to raise the money herself. She established the *Student Educational Foundation* to solicit tax deductible funds, which first aided Choo and Kwon, and then she devoted her life to supporting foreign students in the United States. She

Figure 5.1 Gail Choo, Etta Pursely Barton, and Sue Kwon, no date (Stuart A. Rose Manuscript, Archives, and Rare Book Library, Emory University)

Figure 5.2 Etta Pursely Barton, Gail Choo, Sue Kwon, and J. Hamby Barton at Georgia State College for Women, 1950 (Stuart A. Rose Manuscript, Archives, and Rare Book Library, Emory University)

wanted the foundation to aid students who wanted to return to their home countries. Renamed in 1982 as the *Barton Education Trust*, the organization stressed "mutual trust and understanding" between the nations through support of "worthy students" who become "our ambassadors, spreading our philosophy of peace and goodwill around the world."[94] By 1989, three years before Barton's death, her foundation had helped fifty-four students from fourteen nations.[95]

Increasing Korean Protestant Influence within the Deepening of Transnational Friendships

During the Korean War, Barton exchanged letters with Choo, Kwon, and Choo's fiancé, Bom Mo Chung, who was studying psychology at Louisiana State University and the University of Chicago. From Tennessee, Kwon wrote letters expressing her religious faith in the face of sorrow and worry about her family's safety in Seoul. After hearing the news of the attack on Seoul, Kwon attended church with Choo in Knoxville: "We were almost overcome with grief and knew not what to do. But, kneeling at the altar of the church in prayer, we received strength and comfort. We then were able to get up and go on with our studies with the hope and faith that a better day would dawn for our people."[96] In reply, Barton told Choo and Kwon how her relationship with them formed her view of the Korean War. She did not see the Korean people as shadowy enemies or hapless victims but as intelligent human beings and faithful Christians. "Wherever we go people are asking about you and wishing you a good year in school," Barton shared. "Then lots of folk are seeing the liberation of Seoul as a more personal matter since they know you and are interested in the welfare of your people. You have made a worthwhile contribution toward world brotherhood as you have walked the ways of America."[97] In a six-month period in 1950, Barton and Choo exchanged forty-six letters.[98]

Choo and her fiancé returned to South Korea several months before the Armistice Agreement ended the Korean War in July of 1953. The war claimed the lives of 33,000 Americans, 415,000 South Koreans, and 1.5 million North Koreans and Chinese.[99] Staggering Korean civilian death tolls resulted from relentless aerial bombing campaigns.[100] Choo and Chung wed in 1953 and began working as college teachers in Seoul. Choo gave birth to a daughter the following year. Choo told Barton that she wept constantly over the plight of her country.[101] Chung described the destruction in Seoul to the Bartons as a "ghost-city with vast area[s] of brick-skeleton" but maintained his resolute faith in God, who "created man so that he keeps on hoping and hoping persistently in the future even in such a circumstance."[102]

In 1957, Barton delivered an address to a local woman's organization in Georgia entitled "The Shrunken Globe," in which she challenged her audience to seek cross-cultural Christian partnerships. She shared the history of her foundation, which emerged from her friendships with Choo and Kwon, and she urged her listeners to befriend the thousands of foreign students who were entering American colleges and universities: "You and I may not have the opportunity to promote world changing legislations, or introducing wide sweeping reforms, but we all have the everyday opportunity of learning about our neighbors, seeking to understand them, and building friendship with them."[103] In the *Wesleyan Christian Advocate*, Barton recounted an unfortunate incident in which one of her Korean friends in Augusta experienced racial discrimination and denounced how Americans had "created a form of hysteria" that labeled anything foreign or unfamiliar as Communism.[104] In the 1950s, two newspapers, *The Atlanta Journal* and *Rome News-Tribune*, published stories about Barton's remarkable transnational friendships with South Koreans.[105]

Choo, however, carried neither bitterness nor distrust from her experience in the United States. She recalled her friendship with the Bartons: "Never before in our lives, had we been offered by anybody who was not related closely to us by blood, color, race, or otherwise the kind of generosity that the Bartons showed us that day."[106] To Choo, the Bartons embodied Wesleyan teachings that combined personal piety and social witness.[107] After returning to Korea she found that her Methodism helped her not only expand her vision of God's redemptive activity in the world but also remain open to the insights of other religious traditions, such as Buddhism, that had attracted her interest as a young girl.

In 1965, Choo wrote a memoir and sent Barton a copy. In it, Choo articulated her Christian faith but also explained her newly discovered appreciation for Korean traditions and popular beliefs. Her first child, Etta Jean Kyung, contracted polio as an infant in 1955. After doctors had told Choo that there was nothing they could do to cure her daughter, she turned to traditional Korean medicine and went to an elderly Korean women who cured diseases by cauterization. Choo acknowledged that Westerners in Korea dismissed traditional Korean medical practices as primitive and ineffective remedies. American missionary literature described how traditional Korean medical practices were widely popular among the uneducated and unconverted masses, which was evidence for their folly and unbelief. In 1959, one missionary published a fictive tale of Korean life that pitted the wisdom and compassion of missionary doctors over the ignorant and avaricious ways of Korean healers.[108] Choo did not deny the methods were primitive, but she contended they represented the wisdom and survival instincts of the Korean people, who for thousands of years not only struggled against disease but also persevered against oppression from larger geopolitical forces.[109]

In addition to traditional Korean medical practices, Choo also examined traditional Korean religious beliefs. She wrestled with whether she had committed a sin when she poured boiling water to kill a baby snake that had crawled into her kitchen. When she was a child, Choo remembered that her mother did not kill snakes because she believed that dead persons' spirits inhabited the creatures. She meditated and wondered if the baby snake possessed a dead person's spirit, as her mother believed, or was the disguised image of evil, in accordance with Western religious thought. She concluded that both Korean and Western interpretations together were true. Although aware that American Protestants likely criticized her mother's "naïve way of practicing religion," Choo believed her sinful act of murdering an innocent snake contributed to her child's sickness.[110] Ultimately, Choo believed that experience was the highest authority. "No religious creed could have possibly taught me this much about life and God's fairness in forgiving the error and punishing the sin," Choo determined. "If I make enough atonement in my daily life for my past sins beginning right this moment, perhaps God may forgive me and cure my daughter afresh so that she and I may together serve His Will on Earth."[111]

Although Choo's blending of traditional Korean religious traditions and Christianity deviated from the Wesleyan emphasis on the free grace of God, Barton praised Choo's memoir and sought, without success, a U.S. publisher for the manuscript. Choo wrote much too favorably of Buddhism, traditional Korean religions, Korean traditional medicine, and folk beliefs about the natural world, all of which would have troubled most Protestant lay readers in the middle of the twentieth century. Korea was an example of Protestant missionary success, but the Americans were never able to remake the Koreans in their own image. Koreans were never of one mind about Christian thought and practice, but as more and more of them became Christian, they found their own ways of combining their faith and their culture.

Barton continued to support Korean students in the United States through her foundation and exchanged letters with Choo's daughter as she completed undergraduate studies in South Korea and graduate studies at the University of Illinois. She visited South Korea twice, in 1969 and 1980, and stayed with Choo and Kwon. During her first visit in 1969, at the age of seventy-two, Barton attended Methodist and Presbyterian churches in South Korea and addressed four thousand female Korean college students at the chapel of Ewha Womans University, an educational institution founded by American Methodist missionaries in 1886.[112] In 1980, Barton not only visited Protestant churches but also went to a Won Buddhist temple with Choo. Barton observed how the priest's teachings shared some similarities with the Golden Rule.[113] A year earlier, Barton, a month shy of her eighty-second birthday, identified her time in Milledgeville from 1948 to 1950 as the most rewarding years of her ministry. It was there she acquired the title "Ma Barton," through her mentoring relationships with college students, most notably Choo and Kwon.[114]

Conclusion: The Birth Pangs and Growing Pains of the "Reverse Mission" from Korea to the United States

In 2000, Billy Graham wrote a eulogy for Han the day after his death at the age of ninety-seven. Graham recalled praying with Han at his church in the frigid mornings at daybreak during his initial visit to Korea. "In Dr. Han's presence," Graham recalled, "I felt my own inadequacy and often prayed that I could be more like him."[115] In 1992, Graham sought Han's advice when presented with the opportunity to visit North Korea. Although the trip was controversial in America and South Korea, Han privately urged Graham to go with the hope that Graham's visit would make even a small dent in the many barricades that isolated North Korea from the rest of the world. Graham's admiration for Han was unbounded: "[Han's] love, humility, and boldness combined to make him one of the greatest men of God in the twentieth century."[116] Han felt an equally intense fondness for Graham and for many of the missionaries. He expressed deep appreciation for the Presbyterian missionaries who had counseled him when he decided to pursue ministry.[117] He also cherished Graham and Bob Pierce for their support of his ministry and their efforts to rebuild his country after the war. And no doubt he felt some degree of pleasure when Graham, probably the best-known American evangelist in the world, sought his advice and counsel.[118]

Han began his career working as a lowly assistant in the Protestant mission. As his ministry flourished, he became a respected adviser to Americans who admired his religious success. Han's rising stature across churches in Korea and the United States represented the larger shift in world Christianity as the numbers of adherents and churches in the Global South exceeded those in the Global North. Paul Kollman observes the emergence of world Christianity as a field of study marks a "turn" similar to other "turns" in the academy over recent decades, such as the postmodern, postcolonial, or feminist turns.[119]

The growth of Korean Protestantism was part of this "world-Christian turn" as South Korea became a leading force in global missions just as Han had envisioned in the years following the Korean War. By 2005, the odds were likely that a Protestant foreign missionary was either American or Korean. With 13,000 long-term missionaries in every corner of the world, South Korea ranked second only to the United States in the number of mission workers, and there were predictions that the country could soon be the world's leader in the foreign mission enterprise.[120] Koreans had once been America's finest converts, but now they had emerged as America's greatest competitors in global missions.

Beginning in the 1980s, American clergy also frequently visited South Korea to learn from Korean pastors. *Christianity Today* observed in 1987 that "the phenomenal growth of the church in South Korea has made it the darling of countless church-growth consultants, and a supreme model for aspiring mega-visioned pastors here in the U.S."[121] The journal sent writers to interview such pastors as Kyung-Chik Han and Yonggi Cho, who had founded the world's largest church with five hundred thousand members.[122] The writers came back with stories about the prayer practices of Korean Protestants, the high respect they showed to church leaders, the commitment of the laity, a confrontational style of evangelism and church leadership, and an intense belief in supernatural occurrences.

The early missionaries would have been astonished and gratified at the intensity of Korean worship. Churches held daily daybreak services at 4:30 in the morning and a weekly all-night prayer meeting, usually on Fridays, which lasted from 10:00 in the evening until 4:00 the next morning. A Korean survey of one hundred pastors revealed that all of them engaged in daybreak prayer, with 80 percent continuing to pray for an hour after the corporate worship. Half the pastors participated in overnight prayer once a week.[123] And the pastors expected the laity, especially deacons and elders, to attend these prayer services. They also instructed them to give at least a tithe, a tenth of their income, to the churches. But the laity were willing to do even more. After giving tithes and other offerings, many also supported building projects. And they organized weekly small group meetings of ten to twelve parishioners for Bible study and prayer. Even the darker side of Korean churches—a tendency to split apart after aggressive confrontations—led to church growth: both factions became as large as or larger than "the sum total of the united body before division."[124]

In 1985, seven African American clergy from Los Angeles visited the country and studied the prayer practices and the leadership style of Korean pastors.[125] They were among a significant number of Americans who made a similar pilgrimage and who found much to admire in Korean churches. American observers wrote back home that Korean pastors seemed not to worry much about being liked, and that they placed high demands on the laity: "Every convert is immediately put to work at spiritual tasks, not just painting the basement. Each learns that to be a Christian is to be a minister."[126] At least some, perhaps most, American Protestants no longer went to Korea to convert unbelievers. They wanted to learn secrets of revival and church growth.

Korean immigrant churches, moreover, conducted what was in effect a mission to the United States. Between 1965 and 1989, the number of Korean American churches increased from fewer than 30 to 2,000, with more than 600 churches in Southern California, 400 in New York City, 140 in Chicago, and 120 in the area of Washington, D.C. and Baltimore.[127] By the end of the 1980s, Young Nak Presbyterian Church in Los Angeles, carrying the name and following the principles of Han's church in Seoul, ranked fourth among the fastest-growing American churches, with more than 4,000 weekly congregants. The church constructed a nine-million-dollar worship and study complex. The immigrants changed some large denominations, especially the Methodists and Presbyterians, who had once taken the lead in the Korean mission. Between the mid-1970s and the late 1990s, Korean American congregations in the United Methodist Church increased from fewer than twenty to more than 280.[128] A Methodist official in Southern California praised Korean Americans for "revitalizing the denomination."[129] In the Presbyterian Church (U.S.A.), the largest Presbyterian denomination,

Koreans were the fastest-growing ethnic group. By the end of the 1990s they numbered 50,000 members organized into 320 congregations.[130]

Korean American pastors insisted that their conservative theology should be the model for American churches. They believed that mainline denominations were declining because they did not follow Korean examples of evangelism and piety. One such pastor named Samuel Kim observed: "On the whole, American Presbyterians lack that explicit evangelism—the idea of spreading the gospel. That's why they have not experienced any growth."[131] On social issues, too, the Koreans insisted on conservative teachings. Although the Presbyterian Church (U.S.A.) General Assembly was almost evenly divided on an amendment in 1997 banning gays from church ministry, Koreans almost unanimously voted against allowing gay clergy.[132] In 2001, thirty-seven thousand Korean American Presbyterians united behind a letter demanding a ban on same-sex ceremonies in order to prevent the denomination's "demise."[133] It was now the Koreans, not the American missionaries, who were offering instruction, trying to persuade the American churches to look and act a little more like the churches in Korea.

The evolution of the transnational relationships between American and Korean Protestants reveals how an understanding of world Christianity that simply details demographic changes and the rise of missionary initiatives from the Global South to re-evangelize the West—with the accompanying rhetoric of "reverse mission" to describe this phenomenon—overlooks the complicated histories of cooperation and contestation behind cross-cultural networks between Christians from the Global South and the Global North.[134] Mark R. Gornik contends scholarly analysis that stops at citing world Christian population figures inadequately captures a "nuanced story of changes, connections, convergences, and differences."[135] The rise of autonomous Korean Christian expressions and the decline of the American Protestant mission were interconnected movements. Koreans and Americans both experienced the birth pangs and growing pains of these shifting dynamics in the mid-twentieth century.

Many new transnational Christian programs and partnerships between Korean and American Protestants began during the Korean War, such as the founding of the World Vision organization, but American missionaries also struggled to adapt to new roles that called for them to work together with Koreans as equal partners. For his part, Han was of two minds about the missionaries. He liked them and he wanted them to stay; but he also wanted them to recognize that they could no longer dominate Korean Protestant institutions.[136] As Han and other Korean pastors emerged as influential leaders on the world Christian stage in the second half of the twentieth century, one of the obstacles to their leadership at home and abroad was American missionaries reluctant to relinquish their power. American Protestants looked to Korean ministries like Han's as models to revitalize their own churches at home, but they were not prepared for Korean initiatives that diminished and ultimately challenged their own ministry and mission.

In the last decade, Western Christians in the academy and the church have turned their gaze toward the Global South, as evinced by the growing number of journals and book series with the words "world Christianity" or "global Christianity" affixed to their titles and the increasing partnerships that American congregations have established with "sister churches" in Africa, Asia, and Latin America.[137] But even as the West looks southward, Sathianathan Clarke criticizes approaches to world Christianity that analyze non-Western developments through the lens of "what is lost or needs to be found in the West."[138] Americans in the mid-twentieth century rightly recognized Han's ministry, but their interpretations often glossed over the complexities of the Korean pastor's engagement with intricate social, political, and theological developments in his particular cultural context. Despite their lavish praise for Han, Americans oversimplified his life and ministry. They continued to filter their interpretations of Korean Christianity through the normative lens of their own religious sensibilities. Han's American admirers chose conflicting traits to valorize. Some praised his ecumenism, some his theological conservatism. All praised his anti-Communism, but most overlooked his criticisms of capitalism. Han became the object of American affection in part because Americans could project their values through the Korean pastor and use Han's example to advance their agendas at home.

On a smaller scale, the change in Barton's relationships with her Korean friends also illustrates the shifting dynamics in world Christianity. As they grew older, Barton became the one eager to learn what the Korean women had to teach about the wider world. Although Barton introduced Choo to Christianity when she was a young woman, the two women became friends who reciprocally enriched one another. Barton embraced Choo's memoir, in which Choo synthesized indigenous Korean religions and Methodism to formulate her theological convictions.

In their work on world Methodism, Kenneth Cracknell and Susan J. White observe how negative missionary attitudes toward indigenous values and customs were internalized within new indigenous converts themselves throughout Africa, Asia, and the Pacific, which created a cross-cultural Methodist rejection of indigenous cultures. But they also note that theologians from these places are now looking at "the resources that Methodist theology provides for a new missionary theology."[139] The authors point to Korean theologians who present a new vision of a "global and humane faith with its promises of appreciation and celebration of the best of Korean spirituality."[140] Oscar Garcia-Johnson likewise calls for the remaking of "theology in a global context" that affirms the "complex cultural existences" of persons in Africa, Asia, and Latin America and ultimately delinks "Christian knowledge from the epistemic captivity of Western modernity and coloniality."[141] Yet Choo's religious persuasions, which stretch if not cross the bounds of Methodist orthodoxy, illustrate the complexity of efforts to indigenize Protestant theology across different cultures. Choo's memoir may not be reflective of orthodox Korean Protestant thought in 1965, but her beliefs nonetheless illumine Dana L. Robert's contention that one of the "knottiest problems" in understanding world Christianity is "the tension between a worldwide community of people who call themselves Christians" and a myriad of local adherents "for whom Christianity represents a particular culture's grappling with the nature of divine reality."[142]

The story of the American mission to Korea is a narrative of reversal, though the term carries multiple meanings. One reversal of expectation came when the Americans found that Koreans could steadfastly hold to beliefs and practices that they had learned from generations of cultural transmission. Korea was no *tabula rasa*, and the Americans could not realize the Christian utopia that they had envisioned. In this sense, reversal meant failure, at least in the eyes of the missionaries themselves. From the beginning, Koreans evidenced ample suspicion of paternalism. They could be incisively critical of what they saw as the luxurious homes, extravagant diets, and elegant clothing of some of the missionaries, and eventually they could also be suspicious of too much American control over their institutions and their forms of Christian faith. The Koreans wanted to reverse positions with the Americans, to seize control. This was not the reversal of failure, though it did bring with it a measure of psychic suffering on the part of at least some of the missionaries. It was more like what one might call, from the vantage of some of the missionaries, a disappointing reversal, and from the perspective of most Korean Protestants, a satisfying reversal. By the late twentieth century, however, almost all American missionaries in the ecumenical traditions, and probably most in conservative evangelical missions, not only accepted but also encouraged this transition. The reversal of position, they saw, resulted in a powerful Christian presence.

Notes

1. See La Duk Hwan Papers, Presbyterian Historical Society, Philadelphia, PA.
2. Homer B. Hulbert, *Echoes of the Orient: A Memoir of the Far East* (Seoul, Korea: Tosŏ ch'ulp'an Sŏnin, 2000), 147.
3. See President George W. Bush's, State of the Union Address, January 29, 2002, http://georgewbush-whitehouse.archives.gov/news/releases/2002/01/20020129–11.html, accessed on November 8, 2015.
4. George T.B. Davis, *Korea for Christ: The Story of the Great Crusade to win one million souls from Heathenism to Christianity* (London: Christian Workers' Depot, 1910), 6.
5. John R. Mott, *The Korea Mission Field* (May 1908), 67.
6. R.S. Sugirtharajah, "Postcolonialism: Hermeneutical Journey through a Contentious Discourse," in *Exploring Postcolonial Biblical Criticism*, edited by R.S. Sugirtharajah (Chichester, UK: Wiley-Blackwell, 2012), 23. See also Edward W. Said, *Orientalism* (New York: Pantheon Books, 1978).
7. *New York Times*, July 14, 1950, and August 21, 1950. See also Bruce Cumings, *The Korean War: A History* (New York: The Modern Library, 2010).
8. "Letter from Roderick McKay Montgomery to Helen Pindar Montgomery on August 9, 1950," in Pindar Family Papers, 1800–1979, Stuart A. Rose Manuscript, Archives, and Rare Book Library, Emory University, Atlanta, GA.

9. David Halberstam, *The Coldest Winter: America and the Korean War* (New York: Hyperion, 2007), 1.
10. Richard B. Holmsten, *Ready to Fire: Memoir of an American Artilleryman in the Korean War* (Jefferson, NC: McFarland & Company, 2003), 42–44.
11. Holmsten, 54.
12. Cumings, 80.
13. Halberstam, 1.
14. Michael J. Seth, *A Concise History of Modern Korea: From the Late Nineteenth Century to the Present* (Lanham, MD: Rowman & Littlefield Publishers, 2010), 88–89.
15. T.T. Brumbaugh, "Behind America's Shield of Steel," *The Christian Century*, June 30, 1948, 643.
16. Ibid.
17. William Newton Blair, *Gold in Korea, 3rd ed.* (Topeka, KS: H.M. Ives and Sons, 1957), 3.
18. "Letter from Bruce F. Hunt to his parents on September 25, 1947," in Hunt Family Papers, Montgomery Library Archives, Westminster Theological Seminary, Philadelphia, PA.
19. "Religion: Respectful Salute!," *TIME*, May 2, 1938.
20. Timothy S. Lee, *Born Again: Evangelicalism in Korea*, 54–60.
21. "Religion: Persecution," *TIME*, May 26, 1941.
22. Winburn T. Thomas, "Christian Survival in Korea," *The Christian Century*, November 10, 1948, 1203.
23. Horace H. Underwood, *Tragedy and Faith in Korea* (New York: Friendship Press, 1951), 17.
24. "Religion: Missionary's Reward," *TIME*, March 28, 1949, and Donald N. Clark, *Living Dangerously in Korea: The Western Experience, 1900–1950*, 355.
25. Underwood, 17. When the war began, Underwood left New York, where he was receiving medical treatment for a heart condition, to help repair the damage at the Christian college in Seoul. In 1951, the sixty-year-old missionary died from the physical rigors of fleeing the city after Chinese forces entered into the conflict. His sons buried him next to their mother, Ethel, after U.N. forces recaptured Seoul. See Clark, 400.
26. Kyung-Chik Han, "My Gratitude," in *Kyung-Chik Han Collection (hereafter KCHC), Volume 1*, edited by Eun-seop Kim (Seoul, Korea: Kyung-Chik Han Foundation, 2010), 102–103.
27. Chul-Shin Lee, "Rev. Kyung-Chik Han's Life and Thought," in *KCHC, Volume 9*, 24, and Timothy S. Lee, 65.
28. Harold Voelkel, *Open Door to Korea* (Grand Rapids, MI: Zondervan Publishing House, 1958), 59.
29. Harold E. Fey, "A Great Church in Seoul," *The Christian Century*, December 26, 1951, 1506.
30. Billy Graham, *Just as I Am: The Autobiography of Billy Graham* (HarperSan Francisco and Zondervan, 1997), 197, and Seungjun Lee, "Rev. Kyung-Chik Han and the Korean War," in *KCHC, Volume 9*, 216.
31. Lee, 215–216.
32. Bob Pierce and Ken Anderson, *The Untold Korea Story* (Grand Rapids, MI: Zondervan Publishing House), 16.
33. Ibid., 45–49.
34. Richard Gehman, *Let My Heart be Broken* (New York, Toronto, and London: McGraw-Hill Company, 1960), 74.
35. Kyung-Chik Han, "My Gratitude," in *KCHC, Volume 1*, 305.
36. Clarence Kilde, "The Gospel for a Day of Dilemma," *Christianity and Crisis*, October 15, 1951, 132.

37. Harold E. Fey, "Korea Must Live!," *The Christian Century*, February 20, 1952, 216.
38. Pierce, 5.
39. Carl F. Henry and Kyung-chik Han, "The Communist Terror: Plight of the Korean Christians," *Christianity Today*, September 25, 1961, 35. See also Timothy S. Lee, 60–69, and Sebastian C.H. Kim and Kirsteen Kim, *A History of Korean Christianity*, 172–174.
40. Henry and Han, 36.
41. Ibid.
42. Scott W. Sunquist, *Understanding Christian Mission: Participation in Suffering and Glory* (Grand Rapids, MI: Baker Academic, 2013), 161.
43. See Billy Graham, Center Archives from the 1966 World Congress on Evangelism, http://www2.wheaton.edu/bgc/archives/docs/Berlin66/audio.htm, accessed on November 7, 2015.
44. Kyung-Chik Han, "By My Spirit," *Christianity Today*, November 11, 1966, 28.
45. Kyung-Chik Han, "Gyohoe buheungui bigyeol [Secret of Church Revival], June 5, 1960," in *Han Kyŏng-jik Moksa sŏlgyo chŏnjip, Volume 3* [Pastor Kyung-Chik Han's Sermon Collection, Volume 3], edited by Han Kyong-jik (Seoul, Korea: Taehan Kidokkyo Sŏhoe, 1971), 448.
46. Kyung-Chik Han, "Uilo pipbak badneun jawa geu bok [The Persecuted for Righteousness and its Blessings], February 21, 1960," in *Han Kyŏng-jik Moksa sŏlgyo chŏnjip, Volume 10* [Pastor Kyung-Chik Han's Sermon Collection, Volume 10], edited by Han Kyong-jik (Seoul, Korea: Taehan Kidokkyo Sŏhoe, 1971), 237.
47. Kyung-Chik Han, "Geuriseudoui jisangmyeonglyeong [The Great Commission of Christ], January 31, 1954," in *Han Kyŏng-jik Moksa sŏlgyo chŏnjip, Volume 1* [Pastor Kyung-Chik Han's Sermon Collection, Volume 1], edited by Han Kyong-jik (Seoul, Korea: Taehan Kidokkyo Sŏhoe, 1971), 266–267. See also Hyae-jeong Yi, "Kyung-Chik Han's Christian Ideology of Founding a Nation: In Light of His Understanding of the Gospels," in *KCHC, Volume 9*, 167–196.
48. Lee, 59.
49. Seongkook Kim, "The Symbolic Leadership of Rev. Kyung-Chik Han, the 'Eternal Puritan,'" in *KCHC, Volume 9*, 503–522.
50. Samuel Hugh Moffett, *The Christians in Korea* (New York: Friendship Press, 1962), 25.
51. Sarah E. Ruble, *The Gospel of Freedom and Power: Protestant Missionaries in American Culture after World War II* (Chapel Hill: The University of North Carolina Press, 2012), 2–3.
52. "Letter from Edward Adams to John Coventry Smith, December 5, 1956," in Presbyterian Church in the U.S.A. Korea Mission Records, RG197, Presbyterian Historical Society, Philadelphia, PA.
53. Sunquist, 135 and 156–159.
54. "Letter from J.N. Talmage to J. Curtis Crane, June 6, 1957," in Presbyterian Church in the U.S. Korea Mission Records, RG444, Presbyterian Historical Society, Philadelphia, PA.
55. "Letter from J. Curtis Crane to J.N. Talmage, May 30, 1957," in Presbyterian Church in the U.S. Korea Mission Records, RG444, Presbyterian Historical Society, Philadelphia, PA.
56. John Coventry Smith, *From Colonialism to World Community: The Church's Pilgrimage* (Philadelphia: Geneva Press, 1982), 166–167.
57. "Letter from Samuel Hugh Moffett to Henry Little, February 6, 1964," in Presbyterian Church in the U.S.A. Korea Mission Records, RG 197, Presbyterian Historical Society, Philadelphia, PA.
58. "Letter from Samuel Hugh Moffett to Henry Little, November 19, 1960," in Presbyterian Church in the U.S.A. Korea Mission Records, RG 197, Presbyterian Historical Society, Philadelphia, PA.

59. *Twelfth Annual Report of the General Council to the General Assembly, Presbyterian Church in the United States, Dallas, Texas, April 27, 1961*, 107. See also Gregg Brazinsky, *Nation Building in South Korea: Koreans, Americans, and the Making of a Democracy*, 204–209.
60. Samuel Hugh Moffett, "Prophet and Partner: The Missionary's Future, February 13, 1961," in Charles A. Sauer Papers, General Commission on Archives and History, The United Methodist Church, Drew University, Madison, NJ.
61. Ibid. In 1964, two other American missionaries, James A. Scherer, Dean of the School of Missions at Chicago Lutheran Seminary, and Ralph E. Dodge, the first Methodist Bishop of the Africa Central Conference, published books on themes similar to Moffett's address. Despite their respective titles, *Missionary, Go Home!* and *The Unpopular Missionary*, Scherer and Dodge also blended criticism of past missionaries' cultural imperialism with affirmation for the future of the mission movement through cooperative work with indigenous church leaders. See James A. Scherer, *Missionary, Go Home!: A Reappraisal of the Christian World Mission* (Englewood Cliffs, NJ: Prentice-Hall, 1964), Ralph E. Dodge, *The Unpopular Missionary* (Westwood, NJ: Fleming H. Revell, 1964), and Ruble, 66–67.
62. "Letter from Kyung-Chik Han and Kwang Kook Ahn to Friends in Christ, February 7, 1956," in Presbyterian Church in the U.S.A. Korea Mission Records, RG197, Presbyterian Historical Society, Philadelphia, PA.
63. "Save Korean Missions!," *The Christian Century*, October 25, 1950, 1255–1257, and "Korea's Effect–Plus and Minus," *The Christian Century*, November 15, 1950, 1351–1353.
64. "Christians Show Martyrs' Spirit," *The Christian Century*, February 21, 1951, 229.
65. Arch Campbell, *The Christ of the Korean Heart* (Columbus, OH: Falco Publishers, 1954), 79–80.
66. Campbell, 180. See William R. Hutchison's treatment of William Ernest Hocking's 1932 book, *Re-Thinking Missions: A Laymen's Inquiry after One Hundred Years*, and "The Ecumenical-Evangelical Standoff" in the years after the Second World War for more about the contentious foreign mission debates between mainline and evangelical Protestants in *Errand to the World: American Protestant Thought and Foreign Missions* (Chicago and London: The University of Chicago Press, 1987), 158–183.
67. Samuel Austin Moffett, "Prerequisites and Principles of Evangelization," in *Counsel to New Missionaries from Older Missionaries of the Presbyterian Church* (New York: Board of Foreign Missions of the Presbyterian Church in the U.S.A., 1905), 67. Italics in original.
68. William Ernest Hocking, et al., *Re-Thinking Missions: A Laymen's Inquiry after One Hundred Years* (New York and London: Harper and Brothers, 1932), 325–326.
69. Harvie M. Conn, "Studies in the Theology of the Korean Presbyterian Church: An Historical Outline, Part II," *The Westminster Theological Journal* 29:2 (May 1967), 142–143.
70. Moffett, "Fifty Years of Missionary Life and Service," in *The Fiftieth Anniversary Celebration of the Korean Mission of the Presbyterian Church in the U.S.A., June 30–July 3, 1934* (Seoul, 1934), 40.
71. Hocking, 49–50 and 84–87. In the Report's Index, China has sixty-two related topics spanning numerous pages and Japan has forty-eight related topics spanning almost as many pages. In compassion, Korea has two topics on three pages.
72. *The Fifty-Eighth Annual Report of the Board of Foreign Missions of the Presbyterian Church in the United States of America* (New York: Mission House, 1895), 118–139.
73. *The Ninety-Eighth Annual Report of the Board of Foreign Missions of the Presbyterian Church in the United States of America* (New York: Presbyterian Building, 1935), 140.

74. Charles Allen Clark, *The Nevius Plan for Mission Work in Korea* (Seoul, Korea: Christian Literature Society, 1937), 42.
75. Clark, 275.
76. "Korea Moves Toward a New Faith," *The Christian Century*, November 12, 1958, 1294.
77. "The Gospel, the Power that Changed Korea," *Christianity Today*, November 23, 1959, 21.
78. Frank Baldwin, "Missionaries and the March First Movement: Can Moral Men be Neutral?," in *Korea under Japanese Rule*, edited by Andrew C. Nahm (Western Michigan University, The Center for Korean Studies Institute of International and Area Studies, 1973), 198–199.
79. "The Gospel, the Power that Changed Korea," *Christianity Today*, November 23, 1959, 22.
80. L. Nelson Bell, "Hopes Rise for Korean Reconciliation," *Christianity Today*, January 18, 1960, 28.
81. John Coventry Smith, "Policy Lessons from Korea," *International Review of Mission* 50:199 (July 1961), 323.
82. Kyung-Chik Han, "Gidokgyowa gongsanjuui [Christianity and Communism], 1947," in *Han Kyŏng-jik Moksa sŏlgyo chŏnjip, Volume 1* [Pastor Kyung-Chik Han's Sermon Collection, Volume 1], edited by Han Kyong-jik (Seoul, Korea: Taehan Kidokkyo Sŏhoe, 1971), 140.
83. Han, 143.
84. Ibid.
85. Etta Pursely Barton, "Korea Came to Me," in Etta Pursely Barton Papers, Stuart A. Rose Manuscript, Archives, and Rare Book Library, Emory University, Atlanta, GA.
86. Etta Pursely Barton, *The Phone Rang: A Story of Long Life and Happiness* (Columbus, GA: Brentwood Christian Communications, 1984), 54–61.
87. Chungil Choo Chung, "The Wisdom of Water," 26, in Etta Pursely Barton Papers. After her marriage to Bom Mo Chung, Choo changed her last name to "Chung." I refer to Chungil Choo Chung by her maiden name, "Choo," in order to maintain consistency and to avoid confusion with references to Bom Mo Chung.
88. Barton, 108–109.
89. Russell E. Richey, Kenneth E. Rowe, and Jean Miller Schmidt, *The Methodist Experience in America, Volume 1: A History* (Nashville: Abingdon Press, 2010), 377. In their history of the Methodist experience in the United States, Russell E. Richey, Kenneth E. Rowe, and Jean Miller Schmidt delineate three distinct phases (Pietist, nurturing, and advocating) in the development of American Methodism.
90. Barton, 64.
91. Ibid., 68.
92. Chung, 41.
93. "Book Review: Sarangie, A Child of Chosen: A Tale of Korea," *Korean Student Bulletin* 4:4 (October 1926), 7.
94. "Statement of Purpose," in Etta Pursely Barton Papers.
95. Etta Pursley Barton, *The Phone Still Rings: Sequel to "The Phone Rang"* (Columbus, GA: Brentwood Christian Press, 1989), 5.
96. Barton, 77.
97. "Letter from Etta Pursely Barton to Gail Choo and Sue Kwon on September 24, 1950," in Etta Pursely Barton Papers.
98. Choo wrote Barton on June 14, 23, and 27, July 3, 8, 19, and 31, August 4, 7, 14, 18, and 23, September 17, 19, 23, and 27, October 1, 8, 13, 20, 25, and 31, November 3, 6, 8, 14, 17, 19, and 27, and December 4, 9, and 14 in 1950. Barton wrote Choo on June 14 and 17, September 16, 24, and 28, October 2, 6, 13, and 31, November 7 and 29, and December 1, 6, and 8 in 1950. See Etta Pursely Barton Papers.

99. Halberstam, 4.
100. Jodi Kim, *Ends of Empire: Asian American Critique and the Cold War* (Minneapolis and London: University of Minnesota Press, 2010), 148–149.
101. "Letter from Gail Chung to Etta Pursely Barton on January 8, 1953," in Etta Pursely Barton Papers.
102. "Letters from Bom Mo Chung to Etta Purlsey Barton on August 29, 1953," in Etta Pursley Barton Papers.
103. "The Shrunken Globe: Address from October 8, 1957 at Sylvania's Women Club," in Etta Pursely Barton Papers.
104. Mrs. J. Hamby Barton, "Why I am a Methodist," *Wesleyan Christian Advocate*, August 4, 1960, 3.
105. "East, West to Join in Rome Wedding," *The Atlanta Journal*, June 13, 1956, and "Romans Entertain for Koreans in College Park," *Rome News-Tribune*, April 2, 1957.
106. Chung, 31.
107. Harold J. Recinos, "In a Divided World, Methodism Matters," in *The Oxford Handbook of Methodist Studies*, edited by William J. Abraham and James E. Kirby (New York and Oxford: Oxford University Press, 2009), 691.
108. William Newton Blair, *Chansung's Confession*, 51–53.
109. Chung, 56–57.
110. Ibid., 58–59.
111. Ibid., 60.
112. Barton, 299.
113. "Letter from Etta Pursely Barton to her family on August 3, 1980," in Etta Pursely Barton Papers, and Barton, 475–485.
114. Barton, "Letter on September 10, 1979," in Etta Pursely Barton Papers.
115. Billy Graham, "With Every Good Wish and Warm Regards," *KCHC, Volume 3*, 17.
116. Ibid.
117. Blair encouraged Han to study at Princeton Theological Seminary, but Moffett advised Han to remain in Korea because of the liberal theological trends in the United States. See Kyung-chik Han and Byeonghui Kim, "Interview," *KCHC, Volume 1*, 382.
118. Han and Kim, 454–458.
119. Paul Kollman, "Understanding the World-Christian Turn in the History of Christianity and Theology," *Theology Today* 71:2 (July 2014), 166.
120. Rob Moll, "Missions Incredible: South Korea Sends More Missionaries Than Any Country But the U.S. and It Won't be Long Before It's Number One," *Christianity Today*, March 1, 2006, 28–34. By 2014, the number of South Korean missionaries grew to 26,667 missionaries working in 170 countries. See Timothy K. Park, "The Missionary Movement of the Korean Church: A Model for Non-Western Mission," in *Korean Church, God's Mission, Global Christianity*, 24.
121. Harold Smith, "Politics Test the Korean Church," *Christianity Today*, May 15, 1987, 15.
122. "Will Success Spoil the South Korean Church?," *Christianity Today*, November 20, 1987, 32–35. In 2007, Cho's church, Yoido Full Gospel Church, remained the largest church in the world with 830,000 members. See "O Come All Ye Faithful," *The Economist*, November 1, 2007, http://www.economist.com/node/10015239, accessed on November 12, 2014. In 2014, Cho was convicted and sentenced to three years in prison for embezzling church funds. His prison sentence was suspended for five years. See "Founder of World's Largest Megachurch Convicted of Embezzling $12 Million," *Christianity Today*, February 24, 2014, http://www.christianitytoday.com/gleanings/2014/february/founder-of-worlds-largest-megachurch-convicted-cho-yoido.html?paging=off, accessed on November 10, 2015.

123. Harold Smith and Myung-Hyuk Kim, "A Lot of Tired Prayer Warriors," *Christianity Today*, November 20, 1987, 37.
124. Will Success Spoil the South Korean Church?, 35.
125. Jarrette Fellows, Jr., "Pastors Learn Secrets of Nation that Arose from Ashes of War," *Los Angeles Sentinel*, October 24, 1985.
126. Kenneth S. Kantzer, "What Happens When Koreans Pray," *Christianity Today*, August 16, 1993, 13.
127. Dan Moul, "For Koreans in America, Growth and Growing Pains," *Christianity Today*, March 3, 1989, 56.
128. Gustav Niebuhr, "Presbyterians Devise Plan to Diversify Denomination," *New York Times*, May 31, 1998.
129. Ira Rifkin, "Korean Immigrants Flock to Growing Congregations," *Los Angeles Times*, December 15, 1988.
130. Gustav Niebuhr, "Presbyterians Devise Plan to Diversify Denomination," *New York Times*, May 31, 1998 and "PCUSA Koreans: A Growing Influence," *The Christian Century*, November 10, 1999, 1080.
131. "PCUSA Koreans: A Growing Influence," 1080.
132. Ibid.
133. "Koreans Plead for Ban on Same-Sex Unions," *The Christian Century*, January 3–10, 2001, 11.
134. According to Janel Kragt Bakker, Claudia Währisch-Oblau first used the term "reverse mission" in 2000 to delineate the emergence of immigrant churches within the Rhein-Ruhr region of Germany. Afe Adogame describes the "reverse mission process" as one in which indigenous Christian movements in the non-Western world provided the background to the reverse direction of missions as "traditional 'mission fields' [in Africa, Asia, and Latin America] have now become the mission bases of renewed efforts to re-evangelise the fast secularizing societies of Europe and North America" through migration and diaspora to the West. But Adogame and other scholars have also challenged the concept of "reverse mission." For example, Jehu J. Hanciles contends the notion of "reverse mission" obscures the transnational and multidirectional facets of newer migrant-missionary initiatives. See Janel Kragt Bakker, *Sister Churches: American Congregations and Their Partners Abroad* (Oxford and New York: Oxford University Press, 2013), Claudia Währisch-Oblau, "From Reverse Mission to Common Mission . . . We Hope: Immigrant Protestant Churches and the 'Programme for Cooperation Between German and Immigrant Congregations' of the United Evangelical Mission," *International Review of Mission* 89:354 (2000), 467–483, Afe Adogame, "Traversing the United Kingdom of God: The Transnationalisation of the New African Religious Diaspora," in *African Christian Presence in the West: New Immigrant Congregations and Transnational Networks in North America and Europe*, edited by Frieder Ludwig and J. Kwabena Asamoah-Gyadu (Trenton, NJ: Africa World Press, 2011), 70–86, and Jehu J. Hanciles, "The Future of Missiology as a Discipline: A View from the Non-Western World," *Missiology* 42:2 (April 2014), 121–138.
135. Mark R. Gornik, *Word Made Global: Stories of African Christianity in New York City* (Grand Rapids and Cambridge: Wm. B. Eerdmans, 2011), 7.
136. Two examples can be found in Han's letter to American Presbyterian missionaries in 1956 and his reflections on partnering with World Vision in South Korea. As Korean Presbyterians experienced divisions over contrasting positions on matters related to polity and theology, Han appreciated the support of American missionaries but insisted that Koreans would solve their own conflicts. Han likewise welcomed and praised Bob Pierce for his relief work in South Korea, but he also emphasized the innovative and important work his church initiated for widows and orphans prior to and independent of World Vision. See "Letter from Kyung-Chik Han and Kwang Kook Ahn to Friends in

Christ, February 7, 1956," in Presbyterian Church in the U.S.A. Korea Mission Records, RG197, Presbyterian Historical Society, Philadelphia, PA, and Kyung-chik Han and Byeonghui Kim, "Interview," *KCHC, Volume 1*, 445–458. See also Yi, 179.

137. Kollman, 166 and Bakker, 2.
138. Sathianathan Clarke, "World Christianity and Postcolonial Mission: A Path Forward for the Twenty-first Century," *Theology Today* 71:2 (July 2014), 194.
139. Kenneth Cracknell and Susan J. White, *An Introduction to World Methodism* (Cambridge and New York: Cambridge University Press, 2005), 90.
140. Ibid.
141. William A. Dryness and Oscar Garcia-Johnson, *Theology without Borders: An Introduction to Global Conversations* (Grand Rapids, MI: Baker Academic, 2015), 20–21.
142. Dana L. Robert, "Shifting Southward: Global Christianity since 1945," in *Landmark Essays in Mission and World Christianity*, edited by Robert L. Gallagher and Paul Hertig (Maryknoll, NY: Orbis, 2009), 57.

Bibliography

Archives and Manuscript Collections

General Commission on Archives and History. Madison, NJ: The United Methodist Church, Drew University.

Montgomery Library Archives. Philadelphia, PA: Westminster Theological Seminary.

Presbyterian Historical Society. Philadelphia, PA.

Rose, Stuart A. *Manuscript, Archives, and Rare Book Library*. Atlanta, GA: Emory University.

Books and Journal Articles

Abraham, William J. and James E. Kirby, eds. *The Oxford Handbook of Methodist Studies*. New York and Oxford: Oxford University Press, 2009.

Adogame, Afe. "Traversing the United Kingdom of God: The Transnationalisation of the New African Religious Diaspora." In *African Christian Presence in the West: New Immigrant Congregations and Transnational Networks in North America and Europe*, edited by Frieder Ludwig and J. Kwabena Asamoah-Gyadu. Trenton, NJ: Africa World Press, 2011.

Bakker, Janel Kragt. *Sister Churches: American Congregations and Their Partners Abroad*. Oxford and New York: Oxford University Press, 2013.

Baldwin, Frank. "Missionaries and the March First Movement: Can Moral Men Be Neutral?" In *Korea under Japanese Rule*, edited by Andrew C. Nahm. Western Michigan University: The Center for Korean Studies Institute of International and Area Studies, 1973.

Barton, Etta Pursely. *The Phone Rang: A Story of Long Life and Happiness*. Columbus, GA: Brentwood Christian Communications, 1984.

Barton, Etta Pursely. *The Phone Still Rings: Sequel to "The Phone Rang."* Columbus, GA: Brentwood Christian Communications, 1989.

Blair, William Newton. *Chansung's Confession*. Topeka, KS: H.M. Ives and Sons, 1959.

Blair, William Newton. *Gold in Korea*. Topeka, KS: H.M. Ives and Sons, 1947.

Brazinsky, Gregg. *Nation Building in South Korea: Koreans, Americans, and the Making of a Democracy*. Chapel Hill: University of North Carolina Press, 2007.

Campbell, Arch. *The Christ of the Korean Heart*. Columbus, OH: Falco Publishers, 1954.
Clark, Charles Allen. *The Nevius Plan for Mission Work in Korea*. Seoul, Korea: Christian Literature Society, 1937.
Clark, Donald N. *Living Dangerously in Korea: The Western Experience, 1900–1950*. Norwalk, CT: EastBridge, 2003.
Clarke, Sathianathan. "World Christianity and Postcolonial Mission: A Path Forward for the Twenty-First Century." *Theology Today* 71:2 (July 2014): 192–206.
Conn, Harvie M. "Studies in the Theology of the Korean Presbyterian Church: An Historical Outline, Part II." *The Westminster Theological Journal* 29:2 (May 1967): 136–178.
Cracknell, Kenneth and Susan J. White. *An Introduction to World Methodism*. Cambridge and New York: Cambridge University Press, 2005.
Cumings, Bruce. *The Korean War: A History*. New York: Modern Library, 2010.
Davis, George T.B. *Korea for Christ: The Story of the Great Crusade to Win One Million Souls from Heathenism to Christianity*. London: Christian Workers' Depot, 1910.
Dodge, Ralph E. *The Unpopular Missionary*. Westwood, NJ: Fleming H. Revell, 1964.
Dryness, William A. and Oscar Garcia-Johnson. *Theology without Borders: An Introduction to Global Conversations*. Grand Rapids, MI: Baker Academic, 2015.
Gehman, Richard. *Let my Heart Be Broken with the Things That Break the Heart of God*. New York, Toronto, and London: McGraw-Hill Company, 1960.
Gornik, Mark R. *Word Made Global: Stories of African Christianity in New York City*. Grand Rapids and Cambridge: Wm. B. Eerdmans, 2011.
Graham, Billy. *Just as I Am: The Autobiography of Billy Graham*. HarperSanFrancisco and Zondervan, 1997.
Halberstam, David. *The Coldest Winter: America and the Korean War*. New York: Hyperion, 2007.
Hanciles, Jehu J. "The Future of Missiology as a Discipline: A View from the Non-Western World." *Missiology* 42:2 (April 2014): 121–138.
Han, Kyung-Chik. "Geuriseudoui jisangmyeonglyeong [The Great Commission of Christ], January 31, 1954." In *Han Kyŏng-jik Moksa sŏlgyo chŏnjip, Volume 1* [Pastor Kyung-Chik Han's Sermon Collection, Volume 1], edited by Han Kyŏng-jik. Seoul, Korea: Taehan Kidokkyo Sŏhoe, 1971.
Han, Kyung-Chik. "Gidokgyowa gongsanjuui [Christianity and Communism], 1947." In *Han Kyŏng-jik Moksa sŏlgyo chŏnjip, Volume 1* [Pastor Kyung-Chik Han's Sermon Collection, Volume 1], edited by Han Kyŏng-jik. Seoul, Korea: Taehan Kidokkyo Sŏhoe, 1971.
Han, Kyung-Chik. "Gyohoe buheungui bigyeol [Secret of Church Revival], June 5, 1960." In *Han Kyŏng-jik Moksa sŏlgyo chŏnjip, Volume 3* [Pastor Kyung-Chik Han's Sermon Collection, Volume 3], edited by Han Kyŏng-jik. Seoul, Korea: Taehan Kidokkyo Sŏhoe, 1971.
Han, Kyung-Chik. "My Gratitude." In *Kyung-Chik Han Collection, Volume 1*, edited by Eun-Seop Kim. Seoul, Korea: Kyung-Chik Han Foundation, 2010.
Han, Kyung-Chik. "Uilo pipbak badneun jawa geu bok [The Persecuted for Righteousness and its Blessings], February 21, 1960." In *Han Kyŏng-jik Moksa sŏlgyo chŏnjip, Volume 10* [Pastor Kyung-Chik Han's Sermon Collection, Volume 10], edited by Han Kyŏng-jik. Seoul, Korea: Taehan Kidokkyo Sŏhoe, 1971.

Han, Kyung-Chik and Byeonghui Kim. "Interview." In *Kyung-Chik Han Collection, Volume 1*, edited by Eun-seop Kim. Seoul, Korea: Kyung-Chik Han Foundation, 2010.

Hocking, William Ernest, et al. *Re-Thinking Missions: A Laymen's Inquiry after One Hundred Years*. New York and London: Harper and Brothers, 1932.

Holmsten, Richard B. *Ready to Fire: Memoir of an American Artilleryman in the Korean War*. Jefferson, NC: McFarland & Company, 2003.

Hulbert, Homer B. *Echoes of the Orient: A Memoir of the Far East*. Seoul, Korea: Tosŏ ch'ulp'an Sŏnin, 2000.

Hutchison, William R. *Errand to the World: American Protestant Thought and Foreign Missions*. Chicago and London: The University of Chicago Press, 1987.

Kim, Eun-seop, ed. *Kyung-Chik Han Collection, Volumes 1–10*. Seoul, Korea: Kyung-Chik Han Foundation, 2010.

Kim, Jodi. *Ends of Empire: Asian American Critique and the Cold War*. Minneapolis and London: University of Minnesota Press, 2010.

Kim, Sebastian C.H. and Kirsteen Kim. *A History of Korean Christianity*. New York: Cambridge University Press, 2015.

Kim, Seongkook. "The Symbolic Leadership of Rev. Kyung-Chik Han, the 'Eternal Puritan.' " In *Kyung-Chik Han Collection, Volume 9*, edited by Eun-seop Kim. Seoul, Korea: Kyung-Chik Han Foundation, 2010.

Kollman, Paul. "Understanding the World-Christian Turn in the History of Christianity and Theology." *Theology Today* 71:2 (July 2014): 164–177.

Lee, Chul-Shin. "Rev. Kyung-Chik Han's Life and Thought." In *Kyung-Chik Han Collection, Volume 9*, edited by Eun-seop Kim. Seoul, Korea: Kyung-Chik Han Foundation, 2010.

Lee, Seungjun. "Rev. Kyung-Chik Han and the Korean War." In *Kyung-Chik Han Collection, Volume 9*, edited by Eun-seop Kim. Seoul, Korea: Kyung-Chik Han Foundation, 2010.

Lee, Timothy S. *Born Again: Evangelicalism in Korea*. Honolulu: University of Hawaii Press, 2010.

Moffett, Samuel Austin. "Fifty Years of Missionary Life and Service." In *The Fiftieth Anniversary Celebration of the Korean Mission of the Presbyterian Church in the U.S.A., June 30–July 3, 1934*. Seoul, Korea, 1934.

Moffett, Samuel Austin. "Prerequisites and Principles of Evangelization." In *Counsel to New Missionaries from Older Missionaries of the Presbyterian Church*. New York: Board of Foreign Missions of the Presbyterian Church in the U.S.A., 1905.

Moffett, Samuel Hugh. *The Christians of Korea*. New York: Friendship Press, 1962.

Nahm, Andrew C., ed. *Korea under Japanese Rule*. Western Michigan University: The Center for Korean Studies Institute of International and Area Studies, 1973.

The Ninety-Eighth Annual Report of the Board of Foreign Missions of the Presbyterian Church in the United States of America. New York: Presbyterian Building, 1935.

Park, Timothy K. "The Missionary Movement of the Korean Church: A Model for Non-Western Mission." In *Korean Church, God's Mission, Global Christianity*, edited by Wonsuk Ma and Kyo Seong Ahn. Eugene, OR: Wipf & Stock, 2015.

Pierce, Bob and Ken Anderson. *The Untold Korea Story*. Grand Rapids, MI: Zondervan Publishing House, 1951.

Recinos, Harold J. "In a Divided World, Methodism Matters." In *The Oxford Handbook of Methodist Studies*, edited by William J. Abraham and James E. Kirby. New York and Oxford: Oxford University Press, 2009.

Richey, Russell E., Kenneth E. Rowe, and Jean Miller Schmidt. *The Methodist Experience in America, Volume 1: A History*. Nashville: Abingdon Press, 2010.
Robert, Dana L. "Shifting Southward: Global Christianity since 1945." In *Landmark Essays in Mission and World Christianity*, edited by Robert L. Gallagher and Paul Hertig. Maryknoll, NY: Orbis, 2009.
Ruble, Sarah E. *The Gospel of Freedom and Power: Protestant Missionaries in American Culture after World War II*. Chapel Hill: The University of North Carolina Press, 2012.
Said, Edward W. *Orientalism*. New York: Pantheon Books, 1978.
Scherer, James A. *Missionary, Go Home!: A Reappraisal of the Christian World Mission*. Englewood Cliffs, NJ: Prentice-Hall, 1964.
Seth, Michael J. *A Concise History of Modern Korea: From the Late Nineteenth Century to the Present*. Lanham, MD: Rowman & Littlefield Publishers, 2010.
Smith, John Coventry. *From Colonialism to World Community: The Church's Pilgrimage*. Philadelphia: Geneva Press, 1982.
Smith, John Coventry. "Policy Lessons from Korea." *International Review of Mission* 50:199 (July 1961): 320–324.
Sugirtharajah, R. S. "Postcolonialism: Hermeneutical Journey through a Contentious Discourse." In *Exploring Postcolonial Biblical Criticism*, edited by R. S. Sugirtharajah. Chichester, UK: Wiley-Blackwell, 2012.
Sunquist, Scott W. *Understanding Christian Mission: Participation in Suffering and Glory*. Grand Rapids, MI: Baker Academic, 2013.
Twelfth Annual Report of the General Council to the General Assembly. Presbyterian Church in the United States, Dallas, Texas, April 27, 1961.
Underwood, Horace H. *Tragedy and Faith in Korea*. New York: Friendship Press, 1951.
Voelkel, Harold. *Open Door to Korea*. Grand Rapids, MI: Zondervan Publishing House, 1958.
Währisch-Oblau, Claudia. "From Reverse Mission to Common Mission . . . We Hope: Immigrant Protestant Churches and the 'Programme for Cooperation Between German and Immigrant Congregations' of the United Evangelical Mission." *International Review of Mission* 89:354 (2000): 467–483.
Yi, Hyae-jeong. "Kyung-Chik Han's Christian Ideology of Founding a Nation: In Light of His Understanding of the Gospels." In *Kyung-Chik Han Collection, Volume 9*, edited by Eun-seop Kim. Seoul, Korea: Kyung-Chik Han Foundation, 2010.

Newspapers and Periodicals

The Atlanta Journal
The Christian Century
Christianity and Crisis
Christianity Today
The Economist
The Korea Mission Field
Korean Student Bulletin
Los Angeles Sentinel
Los Angeles Times
New York Times
Rome News-Tribune
TIME
Wesleyan Christian Advocate

Conclusion

Contested Legacies

After more than twenty-five years of service as a missionary in South Korea, Samuel Hugh Moffett accepted a faculty position at Princeton Theological Seminary in 1981 and taught there for five years before retiring at seventy years of age. Two obituaries for Moffett, who died in 2015, explained how he "returned to America" in order to teach at Princeton Seminary.[1] For most missionaries, the notion of "returning home" accurately describes the transition from working in a foreign mission field to living in the United States. But as the child of missionaries in Korea, Moffett was born in Pyongyang and educated at the Pyongyang Foreign School. He came to the United States for his undergraduate studies at Wheaton College in 1934. Moffett stayed in the country for a master's degree at Princeton Seminary in 1942 and a PhD in history at Yale University three years later but otherwise lived overseas in Asia. Moffett, like so many other missionaries, considered Korea as his home. In 1916, one retired missionary, Annie Baird, left her home in the United States and returned home to Pyongyang in order to die and be buried there. Several other missionaries, including four generations of the Underwood family, are buried at the Yanghwajin Cemetery in Seoul.[2] One missionary's tombstone is inscribed with what he said on his deathbed: "I would rather be buried in Korea than in Westminster Abbey."[3] Ruby Kendrick, who died of appendicitis in 1908, after only one year in the country, expressed her undying affection for the Korean people on her grave: "If I had a thousand lives to give, Korea should have them all."[4]

The missionaries' love for Korea is incontrovertible, but their legacy is more contested. The contrasting opinions of the "Nevius method" provide one such example. In 1987, Moffett attributed the growth of Korean Protestantism to the Presbyterian missionaries' decision in 1890 to implement the Nevius method—emphasizing "ecclesiastical independence, lay evangelism, and self-reliant financial responsibility"—and adding to it a robust system of Bible studies covering the basic foundations of the Christian faith.[5] But some Korean Protestants disagreed with the efficacy of these principles. In 1931, K.S. Yum sharply criticized Charles Allen Clark's book, in which the missionary argued the Nevius method was the primary reason for Korean church growth, for advancing a "superficial" interpretation that overlooked the political and social movements in the country and oversimplified the ministries of the Korean Presbyterians themselves. In the *Korean Student Bulletin*, Yum charged Clark with grossly misrepresenting Korean believers as "a tabula rasa" and "a blank page" for the Americans to test and enact their strategies.[6]

Another Korean, David Chung, agreed with the missionaries' assessment about the success of their approach but lambasted its effects on Korean Protestantism in 1959. Chung saw the Nevius method as a "weapon" the missionaries used to destroy critical thinking in the Korean Church.[7] Because the missionaries were reluctant to give the "fruit of knowledge to the Korean Adams and Eves lest they should fall," Korean Protestants lagged in their spiritual maturation.[8] The Nevius method was "unduly glorified by some missionaries" for protecting the Korean Church from the dangers of liberalism when in fact they should be ashamed of its results: "The Korean Presbyterian Church today looks like an infantile giant under the mission's too careful protection and overly one-sided diet."[9]

In 2006, Samuel Cheon, a professor of Old Testament at Hannam University in South Korea, praised the missionaries for collaborating with Korean Protestants to produce a reliable translation of the Bible in the Korean language by 1911. But he also held the missionaries responsible for the startling dearth of "academic or systematic biblical interpretation" in Korean Protestantism until the 1920s. He found the missionaries' conservative evangelical approach—manifested in their application of the Nevius method—gave scant attention to developing "intelligent Korean Christians" with "a high caliber theological education."[10]

But Korean Protestants also recognized the missionaries' educational and medical initiatives, which emerged as pivotal developments in the modernization of the country. Matthew Whong, a Korean Presbyterian missionary who worked in Brazil from 1967 to 1979, explained in 2009 that Korean Protestants were "very mission minded" and constructed schools and hospitals in addition to churches across the world because the early American missionaries had instituted a comprehensive pattern of social service and evangelism for Koreans to follow.[11] Horace Newton Allen established the first hospital to implement Western medical practices, Gwanghyewon, in 1885, which later became a medical college that produced the first licensed Korean doctors and nurses, in 1908 and 1910 respectively. Two of the premier universities in South Korea, Yonsei University and Ewha Womans University, began as educational institutions of the American mission.[12] In 1920, 65 missionaries from the Presbyterian Church in the U.S. supervised 343 churches, treated 3,958 Korean patients in hospitals and 34,717 patients in dispensaries, and educated 2,221 Korean boys and 701 girls from several schools.[13] During the rebuilding years following Korea's liberation from Japan and especially after the Korean War, American missionaries contributed millions of U.S. dollars in continuing their work.[14]

But missionaries also disagreed in their assessments of the Nevius method in Korea. In 1973, Methodist missionary Charles A. Sauer opposed the Presbyterians for celebrating the method as the primary reason for their mission's greater number of Korean converts in comparison to the Methodists. He contended Methodist approaches also prioritized evangelism—through the circuit system instead of self-supporting churches—and that their denomination's work lagged behind because of financial differences. The Presbyterians were more successful than the Methodists simply because they outspent them, not because they utilized more effective foreign mission practices.[15] In his 1968 study, *Mission Boards and Indigenous Churches*, American Baptist missionary and historian Fred S. Downs found the Nevius method did not adequately consider the crucial role advanced theological education played in the development of local pastors. Downs also criticized how indigenous churches were constantly required to prove their financial independence under the overbearing supervision of the missionaries, which had created feelings of resentment and mistrust among some indigenous church leaders toward American Protestants.[16]

American missionaries after the Second World War devoted serious attention to their legacy in Korea because they regarded it as a remarkable success story. Although the Protestant mission in Korea began significantly later (and initially received less material support) than other missionary endeavors in foreign nations, the growth and expansion of Korean Protestantism garnered the admiration of the world Christian community. In 1960, American Presbyterian missionaries in Ghana asked Samuel Hugh Moffett to send them "lesson materials and textbooks available from the Korean experience in the [mission] field" and to arrange a visit from a skilled Korean pastor to assist them in their ministry.[17] The relationships between Christians in the Global North and the Global South were changing after 1945, but many American missionaries to Korea steadfastly insisted their adherence to conservative evangelical approaches contributed to the rise of Korean Protestantism. In 1951, Presbyterian missionary Leroy Tate Newland reflected upon their work in the "small, insignificant country" and how their "amazing success" served as a powerful example of gospel proclamation: "She was ignorant, superstitious, given to outburst of unbelievable cruelties, poverty ridden, and governed by one of the most corrupt governments in the Orient, yet this was the job that the all wise Lord of the harvest had made ready for that little band of laborers who left America for Korea."[18] Over fifty years later, in 2008, one historian of American Presbyterian foreign missions affirmed Newland's observation: "Of all of the Presbyterian missionary work in the world, Korea must be the most well-known: the jewel in the Presbyterian crown."[19] Sauer disliked the ways in which the Presbyterians lauded their particular methods, but the Methodist missionary shared in the conviction that church growth in Korea was directly connected to the Americans' commitment to evangelism.[20]

A few missionaries doubted the effectiveness of their evangelical methods and proposed different approaches. In 1928, James Earnest Fisher, who worked as an educator in the mission school that later became Yonsei University, criticized his colleagues for oppressively wielding their religious authority to uphold fundamentalist principles. He cited the grievances of one of his Korean students, who complained that the missionaries treated the Koreans as children and endeavored only "to preserve the child-like faith of the Bible Christians in Korea when now they are confronted with the newest radical criticism."[21] Fisher surmised that the mission gave some credence to accusations linking Christianity with political imperialism and recommended the missionaries abandon their obsession with counting the number of indigenous converts. Koreans should not be seen as objects for conversion or exemplars of success to the world Christian community, but rather they ought to be respected as individuals possessing "intelligence, morality, and general desirable qualities."[22] Fisher asked his colleagues to consult *with* the Koreans to improve the conditions in their country instead of maintaining their supercilious attitude of working *for* the Koreans. In 1968, University of Chicago missiologist Robert Pierce Beaver made similar observations about how the American missionaries' cultural prejudices and religious agendas hampered transnational partnerships: "Too many Christian nationals say that the missionary keeps aloof from them; that he is walled off from them by pride, a sense of superiority, and his self-importance, by a clannishness that limits his social contacts to other missionaries."[23] But Fisher's appeals for reform also support Beaver's argument that no other "large-scale long-continuing enterprise" had a stronger record of self-criticism than Protestant foreign missions.[24]

The American missionaries argued among themselves, as did Korean Protestants, and the contestations could be fierce. Despite their comity agreements and ecumenical councils, missionaries from different denominations competed for converts, organized mutually antagonistic churches, and built denominational schools. Should they be simply evangelists? Or should they correct social ills? The questions evoked passionate disagreements. One American diplomat in Korea complained that the only thing he observed missionaries do was argue with one another.[25] These disputes were sometimes personal and petty, but they were largely about religious matters. The in-fighting was contentious because the missionaries believed that they were responsible for the salvation of Korean souls. Koreans were no less divisive in their own clashes because they too believed that false doctrines and wrong practices had eternal consequences.

My examination of Korean Protestants resists the hagiographic tendency to valorize indigenous converts as heroic figures who maintained their agency in the face of powerful forces like Western colonialism and geopolitical conflict.[26] Like the Americans, Koreans were also human beings with admirable and flawed qualities. They could be courageous, selfless, loyal, and kind, but they could also be timid, self-serving, disloyal, and unkind, and they had their own cultural and racial biases. When David Chuhwang Kim and Agnes Davis married, the reaction illustrated that some Koreans were no less disapproving than some Americans of interracial unions.

Contemporary Challenges

The historical legacy of the Protestant mission in Korea also resonates in the United States today because American Christians venture forth as missionaries more often than they ever did in the past. Although some historians say that the peak of the mission enterprise came in the half-century between 1880 and 1930, more American missionaries, more faith-based humanitarian workers, and more short-term volunteers serve abroad today than at any period in the past.[27] American churches spend nearly four billion dollars annually on overseas ministries. Every year, more than 1.5 million Americans participate in short-term foreign mission trips that last anywhere from one week to several months.[28] And they face some of the same dilemmas that once burdened the missionaries to Korea. Christianity has shifted to the Global South, but the financial power remains among Christians in the North. Americans are more cautious about paternalism, but they still come from a nation with vastly more economic resources and global influence than the nations to which they carry the gospel. Cross-cultural relationships can therefore be fraught with unconscious assumptions and tensions lying beneath the surface of even casual conversations or gestures. But as the missionaries to Korea soon learned, the mission field is a place in which preconceptions soon fall apart.

Although this book focuses upon the evolving transnational relationships between American and Korean Protestants from 1884 to 1965, the emergence of Korean American churches over the last thirty years also demonstrates the ways in which world Christian movements are transforming American Christianity. Many Korean American congregations and denominations trace their origins to the American Protestant mission in Korea. The covenant relationship agreement between the Korean Presbyterian Church in America and the Presbyterian Church (U.S.A.) highlights the "emotional ties" that are "the legacy of their mission history."[29] Since 1965, immigrants from Latin America, Africa, and Asia are simultaneously adding to the number of Christians in the United States and increasing the ethnic and racial diversity within American Christianity.[30] But immigrant groups like Korean American Protestants are also challenging white American Christians to relinquish their status as the standard-bearers of the religion. Despite their minority status in the Presbyterian Church (U.S.A.), a denomination in which 90 percent of the membership is white, Korean American Presbyterian leaders have called upon the denomination to condemn racism and recognize the distinctive gifts they contribute to the wider body of believers.[31] But as Korean American Presbyterianism evolves, its members are adding more and different voices to the conversation and thus advocating manifold positions. In 2010, three second-generation Korean American clergywomen spoke at the Presbyterian Church (U.S.A.) General Assembly and successfully persuaded the denomination to deny an overture for a new non-geographic, Korean-language presbytery on the grounds that men would lead this proposed governing body and likely discriminate against women.[32] The majority of

Korean American Presbyterians continue to defend conservative stances on social and theological issues, but others have recently helped to develop new ministries of reconciliation and social justice.[33]

Because nearly 80 percent of Korean Americans today are Protestant, the Korean immigrant church is undoubtedly the center of Korean American community life.[34] But some Korean American church leaders are looking beyond their ethnic parishes and seek to guide all American Christians to better understandings of the different cultural forms of faith that exist in urban, suburban, and rural neighborhoods all across the country.[35] In the history of the relationships between American and Korean Protestants, this call for change is the unintended result of American initiatives from over a century ago. When Korean church leaders sometimes felt the obligation to instruct Americans on how to administer their churches, American Protestants felt the force of a reversal of authority that evoked a wide spectrum of responses, from wonder and admiration to worry and even anger. These tangled patterns of partnership and frustration within the transnational relationships between Korean and American Protestants illumine the persistence of past cross-cultural struggles and the emergence of new challenges as the shape of world Christianity became more interdependent, multidirectional, and polycentric.

Notes

1. Presbyterian Church (U.S.A.), "A Great Man Died Today: Obituary for Samuel Hugh Moffett," February 10, 2015 (https://www.pcusa.org/news/2015/2/10/great-man-died-today, accessed on November 10, 2015), and Timothy C. Morgan, "Died: Samuel Hugh Moffett, 98, Leading Expert in East Asia Christianity," *Christianity Today*, February 11, 2015 (http://www.christianitytoday.com/gleanings/2015/february/died-samuel-hugh-moffett-98-leading-expert-in-east-asia-chr.html, accessed on November 10, 2015).
2. Elizabeth Underwood, "Contested Heritage: The 'Yanghwajin Controversy' and Korean Protestantism," *Journal of Korean Religions* 4:1 (April 2013), 170.
3. Donald N. Clark, *Living Dangerously in Korea: The Western Experience, 1900–1950*, 405.
4. Katherine H. Lee Ahn, *Awakening the Hermit Kingdom: Pioneer American Women Missionaries in Korea* (Pasadena, CA: William Carey Library, 2009), 234.
5. Samuel Hugh Moffett, "Nevius: Starting on the Right Foot," *Christianity Today*, November 20, 1987, 34.
6. K.S. Yum, "Book Review: The Korean Church and the Nevius Methods," *Korean Student Bulletin* 9:2 (May 1931), 5.
7. David Chung, *Religious Syncretism in Korean Society*, 112.
8. David Chung, *Syncretism: The Religious Context of Christian Beginnings in Korea* (Albany, NY: State University of New York Press, 2001), 76–77. In this revised monograph of Chung's dissertation, he adds "Eves" to the original "Korean Adams" from 1959. See Chung, *Religious Syncretism in Korean Society*, 117.
9. Chung, 119.
10. Samuel Cheon, "Biblical Interpretation in Korea," in *Ways of Being, Ways of Reading: Asian American Biblical Interpretation*, edited by Mary F. Foskett and Jeffrey Kah-Jin Kuan (St. Louis, MO: Chalice Press, 2006), 33.

11. Matthew Whong, *Power of Dream, Love, Mission: My Memoir of 54 Years in the U.S.* (Maitland, FL: Xulon Press, 2009), 129.
12. Rebecca Y. Kim, *The Spirit Moves West: Korean Missionaries in America*, 25.
13. See *Minutes of the Twenty-Ninth Annual Meeting of the Southern Presbyterian Mission in Korea, Kwangju, June 18–20, 1920* (Yokohoma, Japan: Japan Gazette Press, 1920), no page number.
14. In 1947, the Presbyterian Church in the U.S. estimated the total cost to rehabilitate their mission was $1,001,500. See "Minutes of Korea Mission 1946–48, Survey Committee Meetings First Postwar Mission Meeting (April 24–26, 1947) and Ad Interim Committee Meetings Second Postwar Mission Meeting (May 27 to June 4, 1948)," in Presbyterian Church in the U.S. Korea Mission Records, RG444, Presbyterian Historical Society, Philadelphia, PA.
15. Charles A. Sauer, *Methodists in Korea, 1930–1960* (Seoul, Korea: The Christian Literature Society, 1973), 45–46. In Sauer's book, he includes an appendix noting there were 864,262 Presbyterians and 246,927 Methodists in South Korea in 1958. See Sauer, 262–263.
16. Fred S. Downs, "Mission Boards and Indigenous Churches," *Occasional Bulletin* 19:3 (1968), 1–9.
17. "Letter from Henry Little to Samuel Hugh Moffett, October 20, 1960," in Presbyterian Church in the U.S.A. Korea Mission Records, RG197, Presbyterian Historical Society, Philadelphia, PA.
18. Leroy Tate Newland, "Tribute to W.D. Reynolds," in Leroy Tate Newland Papers, C. Benton Kline Jr. Special Collections and Archives, John Bulow Campbell Library, Columbia Theological Seminary, Decatur, GA.
19. Scott W. Sunquist, "East Asia: Destructions, Divisions, and Abundance," in *A History of Presbyterian Missions, 1944–2007*, edited by Scott W. Sunquist and Caroline N. Becker (Louisville, KY: Geneva Press, 2008), 204.
20. Sauer, 46.
21. James Earnest Fisher, *Democracy and Mission Education in Korea* (Seoul, Korea: Yonsei University Press, 1970), 172.
22. Fisher, 181.
23. R. Pierce Beaver, *The Missionary Between the Times* (Garden City, NY: Doubleday, 1968), 49.
24. Beaver, 50.
25. Foulk, 123.
26. Charles E. Farhadian, "Introduction," in *Introducing World Christianity*, edited by Charles E. Farhadian (Malden, MA; Wiley-Blackwell, 2012), 3.
27. Robert Wuthnow, 235, and Robert J. Priest, "Short-Term Missions as a New Paradigm," in *Mission after Christendom: Emergent Themes in Contemporary Mission*, 84–86. Both Wuthnow and Priest challenge assumptions about the waning of the American missionary impulse in the mid- to late twentieth century.
28. Wuthnow, 1, and Priest, 85.
29. *The Constitution of the Presbyterian Church, Part II: Book of Order* 2015–2017 (Louisville, KY: The Office of the General Assembly, Presbyterian Church (U.S.A.), 2015), Appendix C-1.
30. Eighty-five percent of post-1965 immigrants in the United States are non-European and at least two-thirds of these immigrants are Christian. See R. Stephen Warner, "The De-Europeanization of American Christianity," in *A Nation of Religions: The Politics of Pluralism in Multireligious America*, edited by Stephen R. Prothero (Chapel Hill: University of North Carolina Press, 2006), 233–255.
31. Timothy S. Lee, "Korean Americans in the Presbyterian Church (U.S.A.): Fruits and Challenges of Building a Racial-Ethnic Community in an Integrationist Church," *Journal of Presbyterian History* 93:1(2015), 5–23.
32. Theresa Cho, "Room to Speak," *The Christian Century*, November 30, 2010, 13.

33. Syngman Rhee, "Reconciliation: A Vision of Christian Mission," in *Teaching Mission in a Global Context*, edited by Patricia Lloyd-Sidle and Bonnie Sue Lewis (Louisville, KY: Geneva Press, 2001), 69–78.
34. Warner, 237, and David K. Yoo and Ruth H. Chung, "Introduction," in *Religion and Spirituality in Korean America*, edited by David K. Yoo and Ruth H. Chung (Urbana and Chicago: University of Illinois Press, 2008), 2. According to Yoo and Chung, "While figures vary, survey data suggests that 80 percent of Korean Americans are affiliated with Protestant ethnic churches, 11 percent are Roman Catholics, 5 percent are Buddhists, and 4 percent are other or no religion."
35. See Hee An Choi, *A Postcolonial Self: Korean Immigrant Theology and Church* (Albany, NY: State University of New York Press, 2015), 115–156 and Soong-Chan Rah, *The Next Evangelicalism: Freeing the Church from Western Cultural Captivity* (Downers Grove, IL: IVP Books, 2009), 164–179.

Bibliography

Archives and Manuscript Collections

Kline, C. Benton, Jr. *Special Collections and Archives*. Decatur, GA: John Bulow Campbell Library, Columbia Theological Seminary.

Presbyterian Historical Society. Philadelphia, PA.

Books and Journal Articles

Ahn, Katherine H. Lee. *Awakening the Hermit Kingdom: Pioneer American Women Missionaries in Korea*. Pasadena, CA: William Carey Library, 2009.

Beaver, R. Pierce. *The Missionary Between the Times*. Garden City, NY: Doubleday, 1968.

Cheon, Samuel. "Biblical Interpretation in Korea." In *Ways of Being, Ways of Reading: Asian American Biblical Interpretation*, edited by Mary F. Foskett and Jeffrey Kah-Jin Kuan. St. Louis, MO: Chalice Press, 2006.

Choi, Hee An. *A Postcolonial Self: Korean Immigrant Theology and Church*. Albany, NY: State University of New York Press, 2015.

Chung, David. *Religious Syncretism in Korean Society*. PhD diss., Yale University, 1959.

Chung, David. *Syncretism: The Religious Context of Christian Beginnings in Korea*. Albany, NY: State University of New York Press, 2001.

Clark, Donald N. *Living Dangerously in Korea: The Western Experience, 1900–1950*. Norwalk, CT: EastBridge, 2003.

The Constitution of the Presbyterian Church (U.S.A.), Part II: Book of Order 2015–2017. Louisville, KY: The Office of the General Assembly, Presbyterian Church (U.S.A.).

Downs, Fred S. "Mission Boards and Indigenous Churches." *Occasional Bulletin* 19:3 (1968): 1–9.

Farhadian, Charles E. "Introduction." In *Introducing World Christianity*, edited by Charles E. Farhadian. Malden, MA: Wiley-Blackwell, 2012.

Fisher, James Earnest. *Democracy and Mission Education in Korea*. Seoul, Korea: Yonsei University Press, 1970.

Foulk, George Clayton and Samuel B. Hawley. *America's Man in Korea: The Private Letters of George C. Foulk, 1884–1887*. Lanham, MD: Lexington Books, 2006.

Kim, Rebecca Y. *The Spirit Moves West: Korean Missionaries in America*. Oxford and New York: Oxford University Press, 2015.

Lee, Timothy S. "Korean Americans in the Presbyterian Church (U.S.A.): Fruits and Challenges of Building a Racial-Ethnic Community in an Integrationist Church." *Journal of Presbyterian History* 93:1 (2015): 5–23.

Minutes of the Twenty-Ninth Annual Meeting of the Southern Presbyterian Mission in Korea, Kwangju, June 18–20, 1920. Yokohoma, Japan: Japan Gazette Press, 1920.

Priest, Robert J. "Short-Term Missions as a New Paradigm." In *Mission after Christendom: Emergent Themes in Contemporary Mission*, edited by Ogbu U. Kalu, Peter Vethanayamony, and Edmund Kee-Fook Chia. Louisville, KY: Westminster John Knox Press, 2010.

Rah, Soong-Chan. *The Next Evangelicalism: Freeing the Church from Western Cultural Captivity*. Downers Grove, IL: IVP Books, 2009.

Rhee, Syngman. "Reconciliation: A Vision of Christian Mission." In *Teaching Mission in a Global Context*, edited by Patricia Lloyd-Sidle and Bonnie Sue Lewis. Louisville, KY: Geneva Press, 2001.

Sauer, Charles A. *Methodists in Korea, 1930–1960*. Seoul, Korea: The Christian Literature Society, 1973.

Sunquist, Scott W. "East Asia: Destructions, Divisions, and Abundance." In *A History of Presbyterian Missions, 1944–2007*, edited by Scott W. Sunquist and Caroline N. Becker. Louisville, KY: Geneva Press, 2008.

Underwood, Elizabeth. "Contested Heritage: The 'Yanghwajin Controversy' and Korean Protestantism." *Journal of Korean Religions* 4:1 (April 2013): 169–188.

Warner, R. Stephen. "The De-Europeanization of American Christianity." In *A Nation of Religions: The Politics of Pluralism in Multireligious America*, edited by Stephen R. Prothero. Chapel Hill: University of North Carolina Press, 2006.

Whong, Matthew. *Power of Dream, Love, Mission: My Memoir of 54 Years in the U.S.* Maitland, FL: Xulon Press, 2009.

Wuthnow, Robert. *Boundless Faith: The Global Outreach of American Churches*. Berkeley and Los Angeles: University of California Press, 2009.

Yoo, David K. and Ruth H. Chung. "Introduction." In *Religion and Spirituality in Korean America*, edited by David K. Yoo and Ruth H. Chung. Urbana and Chicago: University of Illinois Press, 2008.

Newspapers and Periodicals

The Christian Century
Christianity Today
Korean Student Bulletin

Index